All resources associated with this book can be located in MyCourses.

Basic Computer & Information Literacy

Sixth Custom Edition for St. Petersburg College–Office 2016

Taken from:
Technology in Action: Introductory, 13th Edition
by Alan Evans, Kendall Martin, and Mary Anne Poatsy

Skills for Success with Microsoft® Office 2016
by Chaney Adkins, Catherine Hain, Lisa Hawkins, and Stephanie Murre Wolf

Computers Are Your Future: Introductory, 12th Edition
by Catherine LaBerta

Cover Art: Courtesy of Photodisc/Getty Images.

Taken from:

Technology in Action: Introductory, 13th Edition
by Alan Evans, Kendall Martin, and Mary Anne Poatsy
Copyright © 2016, 2015, 2014 by Pearson Education, Inc.
Publishing as Prentice Hall
Upper Saddle River, New Jersey, 07458

Skills for Success with Microsoft® Office 2016
by Chaney Adkins, Catherine Hain, Lisa Hawkins, and Stephanie Murre Wolf
Copyright © 2017 by Pearson Education, Inc.
Publishing as Prentice Hall
Upper Saddle River, New Jersey, 07458

Computers Are Your Future: Introductory, 12th Edition
by Catherine LaBerta
Copyright © 2012, 2011, 2009, 2008, 2006 by Pearson Education, Inc.
Publishing as Prentice Hall
Upper Saddle River, New Jersey, 07458

This special edition published in cooperation with Pearson Education, Inc.

All trademarks, service marks, registered trademarks, and registered service marks are the property of their respective owners and are used herein for identification purposes only.

Pearson Education, Inc., 330 Hudson Street, New York, New York 10013
A Pearson Education Company
www.pearsoned.com

Printed in the United States of America

6

000200010272077606

JK

ISBN 10: 1-323-58063-8
ISBN 13: 978-1-323-58063-9

Table of Contents

Chapter 1

Learning Outcome **You will be able to describe the devices that make up a computer system.**

Objective *Describe the four main functions of a computer system and how they interact with data and information.*
Objective *Define bits and bytes, and describe how they are measured, used, and processed.*
Objective *List common types of computers, and discuss their main features.*

Objective *Identify the main types of keyboards and touch screens.*
Objective *Describe the main types of mice and pointing devices.*
Objective *Explain how images and sounds are input into computing devices.*

Objective *Name common types of monitors, and identify important aspects of their quality.*
Objective *Describe various types of printers, and explain when you would use them.*
Objective *Discuss options for outputting sound from your computing devices.*

Taken from:
Technology in Action: Introductory, 13th Edition
by Alan Evans, Kendall Martin, and Mary Anne Poatsy
Skills for Success with Microsoft® Office 2016
by Chaney Adkins, Catherine Hain, Lisa Hawkins, and Stephanie Murre Wolf
Computers Are Your Future: Introductory, 12th Edition
by Catherine LaBerta

Chapter 2

Chapter 3

Chapter 4

Chapter 5

Chapter 6

Chapter 7

Securing Your System: Protecting Your Digital Data and Devices

Learning Outcome You will be able to describe hackers, viruses, and other online annoyances and the threats they pose to your digital security.

1 Looking at Computers: Understanding the Parts

Understanding Digital Components

Learning Outcome **You will be able to describe the devices that make up a computer system.**

Understanding Your Computer 3

Objective *Describe the four main functions of a computer system and how they interact with data and information.*

Objective *Define bits and bytes, and describe how they are measured, used, and processed.*

Objective *List common types of computers, and discuss their main features.*

Input Devices 7

Objective *Identify the main types of keyboards and touch screens.*

Objective *Describe the main types of mice and pointing devices.*

Objective *Explain how images and sounds are input into computing devices.*

Output Devices 14

Objective *Name common types of monitors, and identify important aspects of their quality.*

Objective *Describe various types of printers, and explain when you would use them.*

Objective *Discuss options for outputting sound from your computing devices.*

Processing, Storage, and Connectivity

Learning Outcome **You will be able to describe how computers process and store data and how devices connect to a computer system.**

Processing and Memory on the Motherboard 21

Objective *Define motherboard and RAM.*

Objective *Explain the main functions of the CPU.*

Storing Data and Information 23

Objective *List the various types of hard drives.*

Objective *Define cloud storage, and explain how to use it.*

Objective *Describe the various portable and optical storage options.*

Connecting Peripherals to the Computer 26

Objective *List the common types of ports used today.*

Objective *List the options for adding ports to your device.*

Power Controls and Ergonomics 30

Objective *Describe how to manage power consumption on your computing devices.*

Objective *Define ergonomics, and discuss the ideal physical setup for using computing devices.*

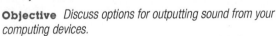

(Edelweiss/Fotolia, Petr Malyshev/Fotolia, Destina/Fotolia, Vizafoto/Fotolia, BillionPhotos/Fotolia, Rukanoga/Fotolia, Sebastian Kaulitzki/Shutterstock)

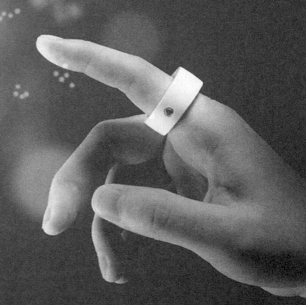

HOW COOL IS THIS?

Now that we are used to the **touch experience** with our devices, where do we go next? How about **no touch**! The Ring ZERO from Logbar Inc. is a wearable device that **senses the movements of the finger** on which it is worn and transmits those gestures to compatible devices (iOS and Android). You can type text, control home appliances, or make payments all by **making gestures with one finger**. The device has preprogrammed gestures, but you can also customize them (or create your own) with the **companion app**. So controlling your devices may soon only require a small wave of your finger! *(Logbar)*

Understanding Digital Components

Learning Outcome **You will be able to describe the devices that make up a computer system.**

You can see why becoming computer literate is important. But where do you start? You've no doubt gleaned some knowledge about computers just from being a member of society. However, even if you have used a computer before, do you really understand how it works, what all its parts are, and what those parts do?

 # understanding your
COMPUTER

Let's start our look at computers by discussing what a computer does and how its functions make it such a useful machine.

Computers Are Data Processing Devices

Objective *Describe the four main functions of a computer system and how they interact with data and information.*

What exactly does a computer do? Strictly defined, a **computer** is a data processing device that performs four major functions:

1. **Input:** It gathers data or allows users to enter data.
2. **Process:** It manipulates, calculates, or organizes that data into information.
3. **Output:** It displays data and information in a form suitable for the user.
4. **Storage:** It saves data and information for later use.

What's the difference between data and information? People often use the terms *data* and *information* interchangeably. Although they may mean the same thing in a simple conversation, the distinction between data and information is an important one.

In computer terms, **data** is a representation of a fact, a figure, or an idea. Data can be a number, a word, a picture, or even a recording of sound. For example, the number 7135553297 and the names Zoe and Richardson are pieces of data. Alone, these pieces of data probably mean little to you. **Information** is data that has been organized or presented in a meaningful fashion. When your computer provides you with a contact listing that indicates that Zoe Richardson can be reached at (713) 555-3297, the data becomes useful—that is, it becomes information.

How do computers interact with data and information? Computers are excellent at **processing** (manipulating, calculating, or organizing) data into information. When you first arrived on campus, you probably were directed to a place where you could get an ID card. You most likely provided a clerk with personal data that was entered into a computer. The clerk then took your picture with a digital camera (collecting more data). All of the data was then processed appropriately so that it could be printed on your ID card. This organized output of data on your ID card is useful information.

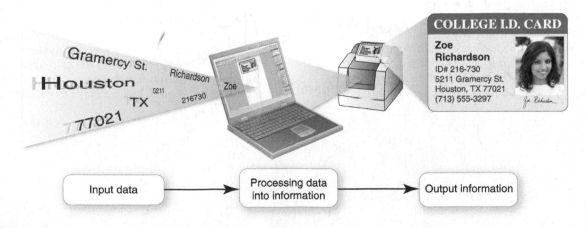

Input data → Processing data into information → Output information

Computers process data into information. *(mocker_bat/Fotolia)*

Bits and Bytes: The Language of Computers

Objective *Define bits and bytes, and describe how they are measured, used, and processed.*

How do computers process data into information? Unlike humans, computers work exclusively with numbers (not words). To process data into information, computers need to work in a language they understand. This language, called **binary language**, consists of just two digits: 0 and 1. Everything a computer does, such as processing data, printing a report, or editing a photo, is broken down into a series of 0s and 1s. Each 0 and 1 is a **binary digit**, or **bit** for short. Eight binary digits (or bits) combine to create one **byte**. In computers, each letter of the alphabet, each number, and each special character (such as @, pronounced "at") consists of a unique combination of eight bits, or a string of eight 0s and 1s. So, for example, in binary language, the letter *K* is represented as 01001011. This is eight bits or one byte.

What else can bits and bytes be used for? Bits and bytes not only are used as the language that tells the computer what to do, they are also used to represent the *quantity* of data and information that the computer inputs and outputs. Word processing files, digital pictures, and even software are represented inside computing devices as a series of bits and bytes. These files and applications can be quite large, containing millions or billions of bytes.

To make it easier to measure the size of such files, we need units of measure larger than a byte. Kilobytes, megabytes, and gigabytes are therefore simply larger amounts of bytes. A **kilobyte (KB)** is approximately 1,000 bytes, a **megabyte (MB)** is about 1 million bytes, and a **gigabyte (GB)** is around 1 billion bytes. Today, personal computers are capable of storing **terabytes (TB)** of data (around 1 trillion bytes), and many business computers can store up to a **petabyte (PB)** (1,000 terabytes) of data. The Google search engine processes more than 1 PB of user-generated data per *hour*!

How does your computer process bits and bytes? Your computer uses hardware and software to process data into information that lets you complete tasks such as writing a letter or playing a game. **Hardware** is any part of the computer you can physically touch. However, a computer needs more than just hardware to work. **Software** is the set of computer programs that enables the hardware to perform different tasks.

There are two broad categories of software: *application software* and *system software*. **Application software** is the set of programs you use on a computer to help you carry out tasks such as writing a research paper. If you've ever typed a document, created a spreadsheet, or edited a digital photo, for example, you've used application software.

System software is the set of programs that enables your computer's hardware devices and application software to work together. The most common type of system software is the **operating system (OS)**—the program that controls how your computer system functions. It manages the hardware, such as the monitor and printer, and provides a means by which users can interact with the computer. Most likely, the computer you own or use at school runs a version of Windows as the system software. However, if you're working on an Apple computer, you're probably running OS X.

Types of Computers

Objective *List common types of computers, and discuss their main features.*

What types of computers are popular for personal use? There are two basic designs of computers: portable and stationary. For portable computers, a number of options exist:

- A **tablet computer**, such as the iPad or Microsoft Surface, is a portable computer integrated into a flat multitouch-sensitive screen. It uses an on-screen virtual keyboard, but you can connect separate keyboards to it via Bluetooth or wires.

- A **laptop** or **notebook computer** is a portable computer that has a keyboard, monitor, and other devices integrated into a single compact case.

- An **ultrabook** is a full-featured but lightweight laptop computer designed to compete with the MacBook Air. Ultrabooks feature low-power processors and solid-state drives and try to reduce their size and weight to extend battery life without sacrificing performance.

- A **2-in-1 PC** is similar to a laptop computer, but the monitor swivels and folds flat. This allows it to function both as a conventional laptop and as a tablet computer using its touchscreen.

- A **Chromebook** is a special breed of laptop that uses the Google Chrome OS and is designed to be connected to the Internet at all times. Documents and apps are stored primarily in the cloud as opposed to on the local hard drive.

A **desktop computer** is intended for use at a single location, so it's stationary. Most desktop computers consist of a separate case or tower (called the **system unit**) that houses the main components of the computer plus peripheral devices. A **peripheral device** is a component, such as a monitor or keyboard, that connects to the computer. An

How Much Is a Byte?

NAME	NUMBER OF BYTES	RELATIVE SIZE
Byte (B)	1 byte	One character of data (8 bits or binary digits)
Kilobyte (KB)	1,024 bytes (2^{10} bytes)	1,024 characters or about 1 page of plain text
Megabyte (MB)	1,048,576 bytes (2^{20} bytes)	About 4 books (200 pages, 240,000 characters)
Gigabyte (GB)	1,073,741,824 bytes (2^{30} bytes)	About 4,500 books or over twice the size of Sir Isaac Newton's library (considered very large for the time)
Terabyte (TB)	1,099,511,627,776 bytes (2^{40} bytes)	About 4.6 million books or about the number of volumes in the Rutgers University Library
Petabyte (PB)	1,125,899,906,842,624 bytes (2^{50} bytes)	About 4.7 billion books, which would fill the Library of Congress (the United States' largest library) 140 times!
Exabyte (EB)	1,152,921,504,606,846,976 bytes (2^{60} bytes)	About 4.8 trillion books, which, if stored as they are in the Library of Congress, would occupy about 11,000 square miles or an area almost the size of the state of Maryland
Zettabyte (ZB)	1,180,591,620,717,411,303,424 bytes (2^{70} bytes)	The library required to house the 4.9 quadrillion books equal to a ZB of data would occupy about 11.3 million square miles or an area about 1 million square miles larger than all of North America

(Ninice64/Fotolia, Georgios Kollidas/Fotolia, Daniel/Fotolia, Flavijus Piliponis/Fotolia)

(a) A 2-in-1 PC has a monitor that swivels (or folds) to become a touch-sensitive input device. (b) An all-in-one computer does not need a separate tower. *(Julie Jacobson/AP Images, best pixels/Shutterstock)*

all-in-one computer, such as the Apple iMac, eliminates the need for a separate tower because these computers house the computer's processor and memory in the monitor. Many all-in-one models also incorporate touch-screen technology.

Are there other types of computers? Although you may never come into direct contact with the following types of computers, they are still very important and do a lot of work behind the scenes of daily life:

- A **mainframe** is a large, expensive computer that supports many users simultaneously. Mainframes are often used in businesses that manage large amounts of data, such as insurance companies, where many people are working at the same time on similar operations, such as claims processing. Mainframes excel at executing many computer programs at the same time.

- A **supercomputer** is a specially designed computer that can perform complex calculations extremely rapidly. Supercomputers are used when complex models requiring intensive mathematical calculations are needed (such as weather forecasting or atomic energy research). Supercomputers are designed to execute a few programs as quickly as possible, whereas mainframes are designed to handle many programs running at the same time but at a slower pace.

- An **embedded computer** is a specially designed computer chip that resides in another device, such as your car or the

electronic thermostat in your home. Embedded computers are self-contained computer devices that have their own programming and that typically don't receive input from you or interact with other systems.

Even your smartphone is a computer. Today's **smartphones** offer many features you probably use day to day, including a wide assortment of apps, media players, high-quality cameras, and web connectivity. And just like your laptop, your smartphone has a CPU, memory, and storage.

Each part of your computer has a specific purpose that coordinates with one of the functions of the computer—input, processing, output, or storage. Additional devices, such as WiFi adapters and routers, help a computer communicate with the Internet and other computers to facilitate the sharing of documents and other resources. Let's begin our exploration of hardware by looking at your computer's input devices. ■

Quadcopters and drones contain embedded computers.
(Kletr/Fotolia)

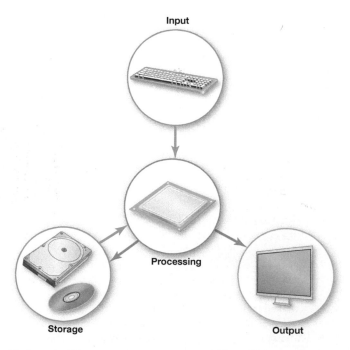

Each part of the computer serves a special function.

 # input
DEVICES

An **input device** lets you enter data (text, images, and sounds) and instructions (user responses and commands) into your computer. Let's look at some of the most popular input devices used today.

Keyboards and Touch Screens

Objective *Identify the main types of keyboards and touch screens.*

What is the most common way to input data and commands? A **keyboard** is an input device you use to enter typed data and commands. However, most computing devices, such as smartphones and tablets, now respond to touch. **Touch screens** are display screens that respond to commands initiated by touching them with your finger or a **stylus**—an input device that looks like a pen and that you use to tap commands or draw on a screen. Touch-screen devices use a virtual keyboard that displays on screen when text input is required. These keyboards show basic keyboard configurations but allow you to switch to numeric, punctuation, and other special keys.

Are all keyboards the same? Whether on-screen touch keyboards or physical keyboards, the most common keyboard layout is a standard **QWERTY keyboard**. This keyboard layout gets its name from the first six letters in the top-left row of alphabetic keys and is the standard English-language keyboard layout. The QWERTY layout was originally designed for typewriters and was meant to slow typists and prevent typewriter keys from jamming. Although the QWERTY layout is considered inefficient because it slows typing speeds, efforts to change to more efficient layouts, such as that of the Dvorak keyboard, have not been met with much public interest.

Virtual keyboards are found on tablets and other touch-screen devices. *(Nathan Alliard/Glow Images)*

The Dvorak keyboard is an alternative keyboard layout that puts the most commonly used letters in the English language on "home keys"—the keys in the middle row of the keyboard. The Dvorak keyboard's design reduces the distance your fingers travel for most keystrokes, increasing typing speed. You can customize the layout of your keyboard using the Windows operating system. *(Windows 10, Microsoft Corporation)*

>*To change your keyboard layout in Windows 10, click* **Settings** *from the Start menu, click* **Time & language,** *then click* **Region & language.** *Select* **Windows display language,** *select* **Options,** *click* **Add a keyboard,** *and then select* **United-States-Dvorak.**

What alternatives are there to an onscreen touch keyboard? Touchscreen keyboards are not always convenient when a great deal of typing is required. Most computing devices can accept physical keyboards as an add-on accessory. Wired keyboards plug into a data port on the computing device. Wireless keyboards send data to the computer using a form of wireless technology that uses *radio frequency (RF)*. A radio transmitter in the keyboard sends out signals that are received either by a receiving device plugged into a port on the device or by a Bluetooth receiving device located in the device. You've probably heard of **Bluetooth technology** if you use a headset or earpiece with your cell phone. Bluetooth is a wireless transmission standard that lets you connect devices such as smartphones, tablets, and laptops to peripheral devices such as keyboards and headsets. Often, wireless keyboards for tablets are integrated with a case to protect your tablet.

Flexible keyboards are a terrific alternative if you want a full-sized keyboard for your laptop or tablet. You can roll one

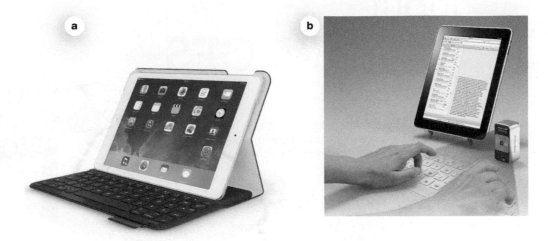

(a) Cases with integrated physical keyboards make tablets more typing-friendly. (b) Virtual keyboard devices project the image of a QWERTY keyboard on any surface. Sensors detect typing motions, and data is transmitted to your device via Bluetooth technology. *(Logitech, Inc.; Splash News/Hammacher Schlemmer/Newscom)*

up, fit it in your backpack, and plug it into a USB port when you need it. Another compact keyboard alternative is a *virtual keyboard*, which is about the size of a matchbox. They project an image of a keyboard onto any flat surface, and sensors detect the motion of your fingers as you "type." Data is transmitted to the device via Bluetooth. These keyboards work with the latest iPhones, iPads, and Android devices.

BITS&BYTES

Distributed Computing: Putting Your Computer to Work While You Sleep

Complex scientific research, such as processing data from radio telescopes, requires vast computing power. Software has been developed to tie individual computing devices (including tablets and smartphones) into a grid to enable them to work together. This is known as **distributed** or **grid computing**. This effectively creates a cheap supercomputer that many not-for-profit research organizations use to research problems that will benefit the greater good—and your computer can help. Visit theSkyNet (**theskynet.org**) and download its software. Once installed, it allows your device to process astronomical data during the many times when your CPU is idle (or at least not working to its full potential). With theSkyNet, your computing device can help astronomers explore the heavens.

Help astronomers process data by having your computer join theSkyNet. *(James Thew/Fotolia)*

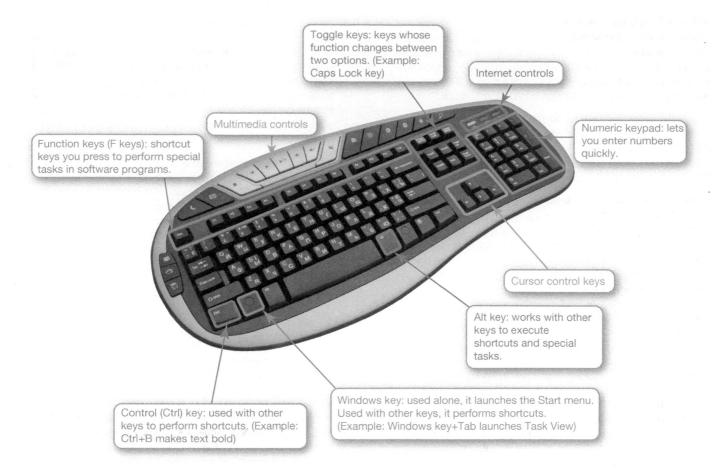

Toggle keys: keys whose function changes between two options. (Example: Caps Lock key)

Internet controls

Multimedia controls

Numeric keypad: lets you enter numbers quickly.

Function keys (F keys): shortcut keys you press to perform special tasks in software programs.

Cursor control keys

Alt key: works with other keys to execute shortcuts and special tasks.

Control (Ctrl) key: used with other keys to perform shortcuts. (Example: Ctrl+B makes text bold)

Windows key: used alone, it launches the Start menu. Used with other keys, it performs shortcuts. (Example: Windows key+Tab launches Task View)

Keyboards have a variety of keys that help you work more efficiently. (Note that on Macs, function keys are slightly different: The Control function is the Apple key or Command key, and the Alt function is the Option key.)

How can I use my keyboard most efficiently?

All keyboards have the standard set of alphabetic and numeric keys that you regularly use when typing. Many keyboards for laptop and desktop computers have additional keys that perform special functions. Knowing how to use the special keys will help you improve your efficiency.

Mice and Other Pointing Devices

Objective *Describe the main types of mice and pointing devices.*

What kinds of mice are there? A **mouse** is an input device used to enter user responses and commands. The mouse type you're probably most familiar with is the **optical mouse**. An optical mouse uses an internal sensor or laser to detect the mouse's movement. The sensor sends signals to the computer, telling it where to move the pointer on the screen. Optical mice don't require a mouse pad, though you can use one to enhance the movement of the mouse on an uneven surface or to protect your work surface from being scratched.

If you have special ergonomic needs or want to customize the functionality of your mouse, there are plenty of options. Most mice have two or three buttons that let you execute commands and open shortcut menus. (Mice for Macs sometimes have only one button.) Many customizable mice have additional programmable buttons and wheels

Customizable mice offer programmable buttons and adjustable fittings to meet most any need. *(kirill87/Fotolia)*

that let you quickly maneuver through web pages or games. These mice are also customizable to fit any size hand and grip style by allowing for length and width adjustments. Aside from gamers, many people use customizable mice to reduce susceptibility to repetitive strain injuries or if they suffer from physical limitations that prevent them from using standard mice.

How do wireless mice work? Wireless mice usually connect the same way that wireless keyboards do—either through Bluetooth or a receiver that plugs into a USB port. Wireless mice have receivers that often clip into the bottom of the mouse for easy storage when not in use.

Why would I want to use a mouse with a touch-screen device? If you're using a conventional keyboard with your touch-screen device, it's often easier to perform actions with a mouse rather than taking your hands off the keyboard and reaching to touch the screen. In addition, there are new kinds of mice, called *touch mice*, that are designed with touch-screen computers in mind. Unlike older mice, there are no specifically defined buttons. The top surface of a touch mouse is the button. You use one, two, or three fingers to perform touch-screen tasks such as scrolling, switching through open apps, and zooming. Touch mice also allow you to perform traditional mouse tasks, such as moving the cursor when you move the mouse.

What input devices do laptops use? Most laptops have an integrated pointing device, such as a **touch pad** (or **trackpad**)—a small, touch-sensitive area at the base of the keyboard. Mac laptops include multitouch trackpads, which don't have buttons but are controlled by various one-, two-, three-, and four-finger actions. For example, scrolling is controlled by brushing two fingers along the trackpad in any direction. Most touch pads are sensitive to taps, interpreting them as mouse clicks. Most laptops also have buttons under or near the pad to record mouse clicks.

What input devices are used with games? Game controllers such as joysticks, game pads, and steering wheels are also considered input devices because they send data to computing devices. Game controllers, which are similar to the devices used on gaming consoles such as the Xbox One and the PlayStation, are also available for use with computers. They have buttons and miniature pointing devices that provide input to the computer. Most game controllers, such as those for Rock Band and the Wii U, are wireless to provide extra mobility.

Image and Sound Input

Objective *Explain how images and sounds are input into computing devices.*

What are popular input devices for images? Digital cameras, camcorders, and cell phones are common devices for capturing pictures and video and are all

BITS&BYTES

Keystroke Shortcuts

Did you know that you can combine certain keystrokes to take shortcuts within an application, such as Microsoft Word, or within the operating system itself? The following are a few of the most helpful Windows-based shortcuts. For more, visit **support.microsoft.com**. For a list of shortcuts for Macs, see **apple.com/support**.

TEXT FORMATTING	FILE MANAGEMENT	CUT/COPY/PASTE	WINDOWS CONTROLS
Ctrl+B applies (or removes) **bold** formatting to/from selected text.	**Ctrl+O** opens the Open dialog box.	**Ctrl+X** cuts (removes) selected text and stores it in the Clipboard.	**Windows key+Arrow key** snaps active windows to corner or side.
Ctrl+I applies (or removes) *italic* formatting to/from selected text.	**Ctrl+N** opens a new document.	**Ctrl+C** copies selected text to the Clipboard.	**Alt+Tab** switches between apps and windows using Task view.
Ctrl+U applies (or removes) underlining to/from selected text.	**Ctrl+S** saves a document.	**Ctrl+V** pastes selected text (previously cut or copied) from the Clipboard.	**Windows key+Ctrl+D** creates a new virtual desktop.
	Ctrl+P opens the Print page (backstage view) in Office 2016.		**Windows key+Ctrl+F4** closes the current virtual desktop.

Touch-screen technology was developed in 1971 and used primarily with ATMs and fast-food order displays. The technology for monitors and other displays was made popular by the iPod Touch in 2007 and is now in smartphones, tablets, and laptop and desktop monitors. But how do touch-screen monitors know where you're touching? How do they know what you want them to do?

The basic idea behind touch screens is pretty straightforward—when you place your finger or stylus on a screen, it changes the physical state of the screen and registers your touch. The location of your touch is then translated into a command. Three basic systems are used to recognize a person's touch: *resistive*, *capacitive*, and *surface acoustic wave*. All of these systems require the basic components of a touch-responsive glass panel, controller, and software driver, combined with a display and computer processor.

The *resistive system* maps the exact location of the pressure point created when a user touches the screen. The *capacitive system* uses the change in the electrical charge on the glass panel of the monitor, which is created by the user's touch, to generate a location. The third technology, *surface acoustic wave system*, uses two transducers (electrical devices that convert energy from one form to another) that are placed along the x and y axes of the monitor's glass plate. Reflectors, which are also placed on the glass, are used to reflect an electric signal sent from the sending transducer to the receiving transducer. The receiving transducer determines whether the signal has been disturbed by a touch event and locates the touch instantly. With all three systems, the display's software driver then translates the touch into something the operating system can understand, similar to how a mouse driver translates a mouse's movements into a click or drag.

Because the resistive system uses pressure to register a touch, it doesn't matter if the touch is created by a finger or another device. On the other hand, a capacitive system must have conductive input, so generally a finger is required. The surface acoustic wave system allows touches by any object.

The iPhone introduced another complexity to the touch-screen system—a multitouch user interface. In addition to just pressing the screen in one location, multitouch technology can process multiple simultaneous touches on the screen. For example, pinching or spreading out your thumb and finger together makes the display zoom out and in,

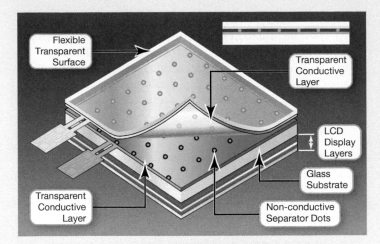

Some basic touch screens use a capacitive system to detect touches and translate them into meaningful commands that are understood by the computer's operating system.

respectively. The features of each touch, such as size, shape, and location, are also determined.

A touch-sensitive screen, like the one used with the iPhone and iPad and with many other smartphones and tablets, arranges the capacitors in a coordinate system so the circuitry can sense changes at each point along the grid.

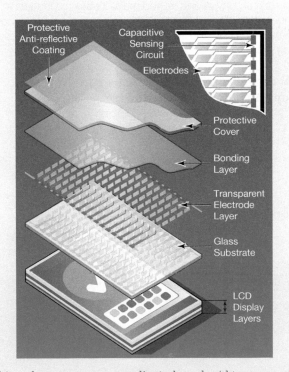

Multitouch screens use a coordinate-based grid to arrange the capacitors so the circuitry can detect and respond to multiple touches occurring at the same time.

Consequently, every point on the grid generates its own signal when touched and can do so even as another signal is being generated simultaneously. The signals are then relayed to the device's processor. This allows the device to determine the location and movement of simultaneous touches in multiple locations.

After detecting the position and type of touch occurring on the display, the device's processor combines this information with the information it has about the application in use and what was being done in the application when the touch occurred. The processor relays that information to the program in use, and the command is executed. All this happens seemingly instantaneously.

considered input devices. These devices can connect to your computer with a cable, transmit data wirelessly, or transfer data automatically through the Internet. **Scanners** can also input images. They work similarly to a photocopy machine; however, instead of generating the image on paper, they create a digital image, which you can then print, save, or e-mail.

How do I capture live video from my computing device? A **webcam** is a front-facing camera that attaches to a desktop computer or is built into a laptop, tablet, smartphone, or desktop monitor. Although webcams are able to capture still images, they're used mostly for capturing and transmitting live video. Videoconferencing software lets a person using a device equipped with a webcam and a microphone transmit video and audio across the Internet. Video apps such as Skype and ooVoo make it easy to videoconference with multiple people. With many apps, you can also exchange files, swap control of computers, and text message during calls.

How do my computing devices benefit from accepting sound input? In addition to letting others hear you in a videoconference, equipping your device to accept sound input opens up a variety of possibilities. You

can conduct audio conferences with work colleagues, chat with friends or family over the Internet, record podcasts, and even control computing devices with your voice. Inputting sound to your computer requires using a **microphone (or mic)**—a device that lets you capture sound waves (such as your voice) and transfer them to digital format on your computer. Laptops, tablets, and smartphones come with built-in microphones.

How can I use my voice to control my computing device? Voice recognition software allows you to control your computing devices by speaking into the device's microphone instead of using a keyboard or mouse. Apps like Dragon Naturally Speaking are available as stand-alone apps but voice recognition features are built into the Windows and OS X operating systems as well.

Popular extensions of voice recognition software are **intelligent personal assistants** such as Apple's Siri and Microsoft's Cortana. These

Just tap the microphone icon and ask Microsoft's intelligent personal assistant Cortana a question. She communicates using natural language processing techniques. *(Microsoft Cortana, Windows 10, Microsoft Corporation)*

Videoconferencing relies on two input devices: a *webcam* and a *microphone*. *(Rocketclips/Shutterstock)*

so-called *software agents* respond to voice commands and then use your input, access to the Internet, and location-aware services to perform various tasks, such as finding the closest pizza parlor to your present location.

What types of add-on microphones are available?
For specialized situations, built-in microphones don't always provide the best performance. You may want to consider adding other types of microphones. ■

Types of Microphones

MICROPHONE TYPE	ATTRIBUTES	BEST USED FOR	MICROPHONE TYPE	ATTRIBUTES	BEST USED FOR
Close Talk	• Attached to a headset (allows for listening) • Leaves hands free	• Video conferencing • Phone calls • Speech recognition software	**Unidirectional**	• Picks up sounds from only one direction	• Recordings with one voice (podcasts)
Omnidirectional	• Picks up sounds equally well from all directions	• Conference calls in meeting rooms	**Clip-On (Lavalier)**	• Clips to clothing • Available as wireless	• Presentations requiring freedom of movement • Leaves hands free for writing on whiteboards

(Fotolia, Joseph Branston/PC Format Magazine/Future/ Getty Images, Summersgraphicsinc/Fotolia, Feliks Gurevich/Shutterstock)

BITS&BYTES

Near Field Communication (NFC): Now Pay (or Get Paid) Anywhere with Your Phone

Paid for anything in a retail store with your phone lately? To accomplish this, your phone (and other devices) use a set of communication protocols called **near field communication (NFC)**. Devices equipped with NFC can communicate with each other when they are held in close proximity. When paying with your phone, NFC enables the input of payment information (your credit/debit card number) into a merchant's computer system.

But how can an artist selling his or her work at an art show in a park, for example, accept mobile payments? Now companies like Square are deploying readers that connect wirelessly to Apple and Android devices (like phones or tablets) and allow customers to pay using

NFC-enabled devices. Now you can sell your products and services anywhere and still accept all the latest payment technologies!

Portable NFC communication devices for accepting payments are now available. *(Mika Images/Alamy)*

output DEVICES

An **output device** lets you send processed data out of your computer in the form of text, pictures (graphics), sounds (audio), or video. Let's look at some popular output devices you'll encounter at school and in the workplace.

Monitors

Objective *Name common types of monitors, and identify important aspects of their quality.*

What are the different types of monitors? The most common output device is a **monitor** (sometimes referred to as a **display screen**), which displays text, graphics, and videos as soft copies (copies you can see only on screen). The most common type of monitor is a **liquid crystal display (LCD)**. An LCD monitor, also called a flat-panel monitor, is light and energy efficient. Some newer monitors use **light-emitting diode (LED)** technology, which is more energy efficient and may have better color accuracy and thinner panels than LCD monitors. LCD flat-panel monitors have replaced cathode ray tube (CRT) monitors. CRT monitors are considered **legacy technology**, or computing devices that use techniques, parts, and methods that are no longer popular. Although legacy technology may still be functional, it has been replaced by newer technological advances.

Organic light-emitting diode (OLED) displays use organic compounds that produce light when exposed to an electric current. Unlike LCDs and LEDs, OLEDs do not require a backlight to function and therefore draw less power and have a much thinner display, sometimes as thin as 3 mm. They are also brighter and more environmentally friendly than LCDs. Because of their lower power needs, OLED displays run longer on a single battery charge than do LEDs, which is why OLED technology is probably the technology used in your cell phone, iPod, and digital camera.

Companies like LG are now working on transparent and flexible OLED display screens. These screens allow you to see what is behind the screen while still being able to display information on the screen. These types of screens present interesting possibilities for augmented reality. *Augmentative reality (AR)* is a view of a real-world environment whose elements are *augmented* (or supplemented) by some type of computer-generated sensory input such as video, graphics, or GPS data. For instance, if you had a transparent screen on your smartphone and held it up to view street signs that were in English, you could possibly have your phone display the signs in another language. Currently, applications like this exist but require the use of a camera as well as your screen. But transparent screens will eliminate the need for the camera.

How do LCD monitors work? Monitor screens are grids made up of millions of tiny dots, called **pixels**. When

Because they don't need a backlight, OLED displays can be made transparent and flexible. *(Yonhap/EPA/Newscom)*

these pixels are illuminated by the light waves generated by a fluorescent panel at the back of your screen, they create the images you see on the screen or monitor. Each pixel on the newest 4K resolution TVs and monitors is actually made up of four yellow, red, blue, and green subpixels. (Older devices don't have yellow subpixels.) Some newer TVs further split the subpixels into upper and lower, which can brighten and darken independently. LCD monitors are made of two or more sheets of material filled with a liquid crystal solution. A fluorescent panel at the back of the LCD monitor generates light waves. When electric current passes through the liquid crystal solution, the crystals move around and either block the fluorescent light or let the light shine through. This blocking or passing of light by the crystals causes images to form on the screen. The various combinations of yellow, red, blue, and green make up the components of color we see on our monitors.

What factors affect the quality of an LCD monitor? When choosing an LCD monitor, the most important factors to consider are aspect ratio and resolution. The **aspect ratio** is the width-to-height proportion of a monitor. Traditionally, aspect ratios have been 4:3, but newer monitors are available with an aspect ratio of 16:9 to accommodate HD format video. The screen **resolution**, or the clearness or sharpness of the image, reflects the number of pixels on the screen. An LCD monitor may have a native (or maximum) resolution of 1600 × 1200, meaning it contains 1600 vertical

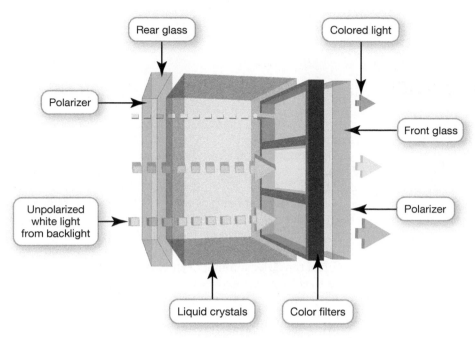

A magnification of a single pixel in a conventional LCD monitor. (The newest 4K resolution TVs and monitors also have a yellow subpixel.)

a monitor with the highest resolution available for the screen size (measured in inches). Lists these and other factors to consider when judging the quality of an LCD monitor.

Is a bigger screen size always better? The bigger the monitor, the more you can display, and depending on what you want to display, size may matter. In general, the larger the panel, the larger number of pixels it can display. For example, a 27-inch monitor can display 2560 × 1440 pixels, whereas a 21.5-inch monitor may only be able to display 1680 × 1050 pixels. However, most new monitors have at least the 1920 × 1080 resolution required to display Blu-ray movies.

Larger screens can also allow you to view multiple documents or web pages at the same time, creating the effect of using two separate monitors side by side. However, buying two smaller monitors might be cheaper than buying one large monitor. For either option—a big screen or two separate screens—check that your computer has the appropriate video hardware to support these display devices.

columns with 1200 pixels in each column. The higher the resolution, the sharper and clearer the image will be, but generally, the resolution of an LCD monitor is dictated by the screen size and aspect ratio. Although you can change the resolution of an LCD monitor beyond its native resolution, the images will become distorted. Generally, you should buy

What other features should I look for in an LCD monitor? Some monitors, especially those on laptop computers, come with built-in features such as speakers,

Factors to Consider When Shopping for a Monitor

FACTOR	POSSIBLE PROBLEMS	LOOK FOR
Aspect Ratio: Width-to-height proportion of a screen	• An odd aspect ratio may make images look distorted	• Ratios of 4:3 or 16:9 (HDTV)
Screen Resolution: Number of pixels displayed on the screen	• Low screen resolution = unclear image • High resolution on a small size monitor results in image being too small	• Highest resolution monitor is capable of displaying (make sure you are comfortable viewing that size image)
Contrast Ratio: Difference in light intensity between brightest white and darkest black a monitor can produce	• Ratio too low results in colors fading when adjusting brightness	• Ratios between 400:1 and 1,000:1
Viewing Angle: Distance in degrees from which you can move to the side of (or above or below) a monitor before the image degrades	• Angle too low means people not sitting directly in front of the monitor will see a poor image	• 150 degrees or more is preferable
Brightness: Greatest amount of light showing when the monitor is displaying pure white (measured in candelas per square meter [cd/m^2] or *nits*)	• Image will be hard to see in bright rooms if brightness level is too low	• $300 \ cd/m^2$ or greater
Response Time: Time it takes for a pixel to change color (in milliseconds)	• High response time results in images appearing jerky	• Seek lowest possible response time if viewing live action sports

webcams, and microphones. A built-in multiformat memory card reader is convenient for displaying images directly on the monitor or for downloading pictures quickly from a camera memory card to your PC. Another nice feature to look for in a desktop LCD monitor is built-in USB ports. This feature lets you connect extra peripherals easily without reaching around the back of the PC.

How do I show output to a large group of people? A **projector** lets you project images from your computing device onto a wall or viewing screen. Projectors are commonly used in business and education settings such as conference rooms and classrooms. Many projectors are small and lightweight and some are small enough to fit in the palm of your hand. These portable projectors are ideal for businesspeople who have to make presentations at client locations. *Entertainment projectors* include stereo speakers and an array of multimedia connectors, making them a good option for use in the home to display TV programs, DVDs, digital images, or video games in a large format. If your computing device is equipped with an HDMI port, you can also choose to connect your computer directly to an HDTV using an HDMI cable. Full size (or type A) connectors are found on most TVs and laptops. Tablets and phones are more likely to have a mini (type C) or micro (type D) HDMI port.

Printers

Objective *Describe various types of printers, and explain when you would use them.*

What are the different types of printers? In addition to monitors, another common output device is the **printer**, which creates hard copies (copies you can touch) of text and graphics. There are two primary categories of printers: inkjet and laser, both of which are considered nonimpact printers. A **nonimpact printer** such as an inkjet printer sprays ink or

HDMI (Full Size) TYPE A

HDMI Mini TYPE C

HDMI Micro TYPE D

Cables with the appropriate connectors are available to facilitate connection of your mobile devices to your HDTV for enhanced viewing. *(Tether Tools)*

uses laser beams to transfer marks onto the paper. An **impact printer** has tiny hammer-like keys that strike the paper through an inked ribbon to make marks on the paper. For most users, impact printers are legacy technology.

What are the advantages of inkjet printers? An **inkjet printer** Is the type of printer found in many homes. These printers are popular because they're affordable and produce high-quality printouts quickly and quietly. Inkjet printers work by spraying tiny drops of ink onto paper and are great for printing black-and-white text as well as color images. In fact, when loaded with the right paper, higher-end inkjet printers can print images that look like professional-quality photos. One thing to consider when buying an inkjet printer is the type and cost of the ink cartridges the printer needs. Some printers use two cartridges: black and color. Others use four or more cartridges: typically, cyan, magenta, yellow, and black. The four-color printing process many inkjets use is known as **CMYK** (this acronym stands for cyan, magenta, yellow, and key, which is usually represented by black). The inks are layered onto a lighter (usually white) surface to partially or entirely mask different colors. The layering reduces the brightness of the white so this process is known as a *subtractive color model*.

Why would I want a laser printer? A **laser printer** uses laser beams and static electricity to deliver toner (similar to ink) onto the correct areas of the page. Heat is used to fuse the toner to the page, making the image permanent. Laser printers are often used in office or classroom settings because they print faster than inkjet printers and produce higher-quality printouts. Black-and-white laser printers have also been common in homes for a decade. Over the past few years, the price of color laser printers has fallen dramatically, making them price competitive with high-end inkjet printers. Thus, color laser printers are a viable option for the home. If you print a high volume of pages, consider a laser printer. When you include the price of ink or toner in

Laser printers print quickly and offer high-quality printouts. *(Xerox Corporation)*

the overall cost, color laser printers can be more economical than inkjets.

What's the best way to print from portable devices such as tablets and smartphones? Wireless printers are a good option for home networks as they let several people print to the same printer from different devices and any location in the home. There are two types of wireless printers: WiFi and Bluetooth. Both WiFi and Bluetooth printers have a range of up to approximately 300 feet. WiFi, however, sends data more quickly than Bluetooth.

Wireless printers are also great for printing from portable devices. If you're using a device running Apple's iOS (such as an iPhone), AirPrint makes printing easy. AirPrint is a feature of iOS that facilitates printing to AirPrint-compatible wireless printers, and many printers produced today are AirPrint compatible.

For non-Apple mobile devices (or if your printer isn't compatible with AirPrint), you can try other solutions, such as Presto by Collobos Software and ThinPrint Cloud Printer by Cortado. Once you install one of these apps on your portable device, you can send documents to printers that are connected to PCs and Macs on your home network. It makes printing from mobile devices as simple as hitting print on your laptop.

Can I carry my printer with me? Although some inkjet printers are small enough to be considered portable, you may want to consider a printer designed for portability. These compact printers can connect to your computer, tablet, or smartphone via Bluetooth technology or through a USB port. Portable printers are often compact enough to fit in a briefcase

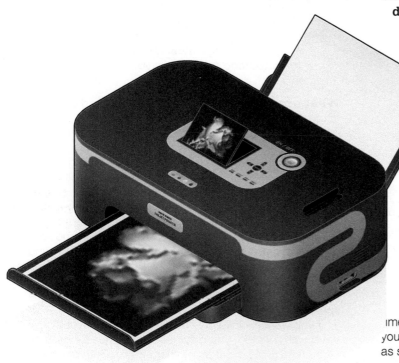

Inkjet printers are popular among home users, especially with the rise of digital photography. Many inkjet printers are optimized for printing photos from digital cameras. *(TheVectorminator/Shutterstock)*

a

b

c

Specialty printers: (a) all-in-one printer, (b) large format printer, (c) thermal printer. *(Image reprinted courtesy of Epson America, Inc.; Image reprinted courtesy of Epson America, Inc.; Vetkit/Fotolia)*

or backpack, are lightweight, and can run on batteries as well as AC power.

Are there any other types of specialty printers? Although you'll probably use laser or inkjet printers most often, you might also encounter several other types of printers:

- An **all-in-one printer** combines the functions of a printer, scanner, copier, and fax into one machine. Popular for their space-saving convenience, all-in-one printers may use either inkjet or laser technology.
- A **large format printer** generates oversize images such as professional graphics, high resolution photographs, banners, posters, and infographics that require more sophisticated color detail. Some of these printers use up to 12 different inks to achieve high-quality realistic color images.
- A **thermal printer** works either by melting wax-based ink onto ordinary paper (a process called *thermal wax transfer printing*) or by burning dots onto specially coated paper (a process called *direct thermal printing*). Thermal printers are used in stores to print receipts and in airports for electronic ticketing, and many models feature wireless technology. Thermal printers are also popular for mobile printing in conjunction with smartphones and tablets.

How do I choose the best printer? Your first step is to decide what your primary printing need is. If you're planning to print color photos and graphics, an inkjet printer or color laser printer is a must, even though the cost per page will be higher. If you'll be printing mostly black-and-white text-based documents or will be sharing your printer with others, a black-and-white laser printer is best because of its speed and overall economy for volume printing. It's also important to determine whether you want just a printer or a

device that prints and scans, copies, or faxes (an all-in-one). In addition, you should decide whether you need to print from mobile devices.

Once you have narrowed down the *type* of printer you want, you can use the criteria help you determine the best model to meet your needs.

Sound Output

Objective *Discuss options for outputting sound from your computing devices.*

What are the output devices for sound? Most computers include inexpensive **speakers**, which are the output devices for sound. These speakers are sufficient to play the standard audio clips you find on the web and usually for letting you participate in videoconferencing or phone calls over the Internet. However, if you plan to digitally edit audio files or are particular about how your music sounds, you may want a more sophisticated speaker system, such as one that includes subwoofers (special speakers that produce only low bass sounds) and surround-sound speakers. A **surround-sound system** is a set of speakers and audio processing that envelops the listener in a 360-degree field of sound. In addition, wireless speaker systems are available to help you avoid cluttering up your rooms with speaker wires.

If you work in close proximity to other employees or travel with a laptop, you may need to use headphones or earbuds to avoid distracting other people. Both devices plug into the same jack on your computing device to which speakers connect. Studies of users of portable media players have shown that hearing might be damaged by excessive volume, especially when using earbuds because they fit into the ear canals. Exercise caution when using these devices. ∎

BITS&BYTES

Does It Matter What Paper I Print On?

The quality of your printer is only part of what controls the quality of a printed image. The paper you use and the printer settings that control the amount of ink used are equally important.

- If you're printing text-only documents for personal use, using low-cost paper is fine. You also may want to consider selecting draft mode in your printer settings to conserve ink. However, if you're printing more formal documents, such as business correspondence, you may want to choose a higher-quality paper (determined by the paper's weight, whiteness, and brightness) and adjust your print setting to "normal" or "best."
- The weight of paper is measured in pounds, with 20 pounds being standard. A heavier paper may be best for projects such as brochures, but be sure to check that your printer can handle the added thickness of the paper.
- The degree of paper whiteness is a matter of personal preference. Generally, the whiter the paper, the brighter the printed color. However, for documents that are more formal, you may want to use a creamier color.
- The brightness of paper usually varies from 85 to 94. The higher the number, the brighter the paper, and the easier it is to read printed text.
- Opacity, or the "show through" of ink from one side of the paper to the other, is especially important if you're printing on both sides of the paper.

If you're printing photos, paper quality can have a big impact on your results. Photo paper is more expensive than regular paper and comes in a variety of textures ranging from matte to high gloss. For a photo-lab look, high-gloss paper is the best choice. Semigloss (often referred to as satin) is good for formal portraits, while a matte surface is often used for black-and-white photo printing.

Major Printer Attributes

ATTRIBUTE	CONSIDERATIONS
Speed	• Print speed is measured in *pages per minute (PPM)*. • Black-and-white documents print faster than color documents. • Laser printers often print faster than inkjets.

Resolution	• Resolution refers to a printer's image clarity.
	• Resolution is measured in *dots per inch (dpi)*.
	• Higher dpi = greater level of detail and clarity.
	• Recommended dpi:
	  • Black-and-white text: 300
	  • General purpose images: 1200
	  • Photos: 4800

Color Output	• Printers with separate cartridges for each color produce the best quality output. • Inkjet and laser color printers generally have four cartridges (black, cyan, magenta, and yellow). • Higher-quality printers have six cartridges (the four above plus light cyan and light magenta). • With separate cartridges, you only need to replace the empty one.
Cost of Consumables	• Consumables are printer cartridges and paper. • Printer cartridges can exceed the cost of some printers. • Consumer magazines such as *Consumer Reports* can help you research costs.

(Freshidea/Fotolia, Michael Nivelet/Fotolia, Thomas Amby/Fotolia, Tomislav Forgo/Fotolia)

Before moving on to Part 2:
1. **Watch Replay Video 2.1 .**
2. **Then check your understanding of what you've learned so far.**

check your understanding // review & practice

For a quick review to see what you've learned so far, answer the following questions.

multiple choice

1. Which of the following is NOT one of the four major functions of a computer?

   a. input

   b. processing

   c. indexing

   d. storage

2. Which of the following can be both an input and an output device?

   a. mouse

   b. keyboard

   c. monitor

   d. laser printer

3. Which of the following display screens does not require a backlight to function?

   a. organic light-emitting diode (OLED) display

   b. liquid crystal display (LCD)

   c. light-emitting diode (LED) display

   d. cathode ray tube (CRT)

4. What type of printer sprays tiny drops of ink onto paper?

   a. inkjet

   b. impact

   c. thermal

   d. laser

5. When buying a monitor, which factor is NOT important to consider?

   a. screen resolution

   b. viewing angle

   c. color depth

   d. aspect ratio

TECHBYTES WEEKLY

Stay current with the TechBytes Weekly Newsletter.

Processing, Storage, and Connectivity

Learning Outcome **You will be able to describe how computers process and store data and how devices connect to a computer system.**

So far, we have explored the components of your computer that you use to input and output data. But where does the processing take place, and where is the data stored? And how does your computer connect with peripherals and other computers?

processing and memory on the
MOTHERBOARD

The main processing functions of your computer take place in the CPU and memory, both of which reside on your computer's motherboard. In the following sections, we'll explore the components of the motherboard and how memory helps your computer process data.

The Motherboard and Memory

Objective *Define motherboard and RAM.*

What exactly is a motherboard? The **motherboard** is the main circuit board that contains the central electronic components of the computer, including the computer's processor (CPU), its memory, and the many circuit boards that help the computer function. On a desktop, the motherboard is located inside the system unit, the metal or plastic case that also houses the power source and all the storage devices (CD/DVD drive and hard drive). In a laptop or all-in-one computer, the system unit is combined with the monitor and the keyboard into a single package.

What's on the motherboard besides the CPU and memory? The motherboard also includes slots for **expansion cards (**or **adapter cards)**, which are circuit boards that provide additional functionality. Typical expansion cards found in the system unit are sound and video cards. A **sound card** provides a connection for the speakers and microphone, whereas a **video card** provides a connection for the monitor. Laptops and tablets have video and sound capabilities integrated into their motherboards.

High-end desktops use expansion cards to provide video and sound capabilities.

Other expansion cards provide a means for network and Internet connections. A **network interface card (NIC)**, which enables your computer to connect with other computers or to a cable modem to facilitate a high-speed Internet connection, is often integrated into the motherboard. Lastly, some expansion cards provide additional USB and Thunderbolt ports.

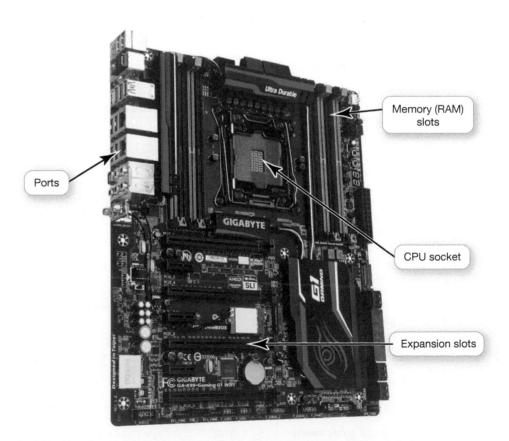

A motherboard contains the socket for the computer's processor (CPU), slots for memory (RAM) modules, ports, and slots for expansion cards. *(GIGA-BYTE Technology Co., Ltd.)*

What exactly is RAM? Random access memory (RAM) is the place in a computer where the programs and data that the computer is currently using, are stored. RAM is much faster to read from and write to than the hard drive and other forms of storage. The processor can request the RAM's contents, which can be located, opened, and delivered to the CPU for processing in a few nanoseconds (billionths of a second). If you look at a motherboard, you'll see RAM as a series of small cards (called *memory cards* or *memory modules*) plugged into slots on the motherboard.

Because the entire contents of RAM are erased when you turn off the computer, RAM is a temporary or **volatile storage** location. To save data permanently, you need to save it to your hard drive or to another permanent storage location such as a flash drive or cloud storage.

Does the motherboard contain any other kinds of memory besides RAM? In addition to RAM, the motherboard contains a form of memory called **read-only memory (ROM)**. ROM holds all the instructions the computer needs to start up when it's powered on. Unlike data stored in RAM, which is volatile storage, the instructions stored in ROM are permanent, making ROM a **nonvolatile storage** location, which means the data isn't erased when the power is turned off.

processor performance, CPU performance is also affected by other factors. One factor is the number of *cores*, or processing paths, a processor has. Initially, processors could handle only one instruction at a time. Now, processors have been designed so that they can have two, four, or even ten different paths, allowing them to process more than one instruction at a time. Applications such as virus protection software and the operating system, which are always running behind the scenes, can have their own processor paths, freeing up the other paths to run other applications such as a web browser, Word, or iTunes more efficiently.

Besides the number of cores, what other factors determine processing power? The "best" processor will depend on your particular needs and is not always the processor with the highest processor speed and the greatest number of cores. Intel, one of the leading manufacturers of computer processor chips, has created a pictorial rating system for CPU chips. Intel provides a website (**ark.intel.com**) that assists in comparing the performance of different models of CPUs. ∎

Processing

Objective *Explain the main functions of the CPU.*

What is the CPU? The **central processing unit (CPU or processor)** is sometimes referred to as the "brains" of the computer because it controls all the functions performed by the computer's other components and processes all the commands issued to it by software instructions. Modern CPUs can perform as many as tens of billions of tasks per second without error, making them extremely powerful components.

How is processor speed measured? Processor speed is measured in units of hertz (Hz). *Hertz* is a measurement of machine cycles per second. A *machine cycle* is the process of the CPU getting the data or instructions from RAM and decoding the instructions into something the computer can understand. Once the CPU has decoded the instructions, it executes them and stores the result back in system memory. Current systems run at speeds measured in **gigahertz (GHz)** or billions of machine cycles per second. Therefore, a 3.8 GHz processor performs work at a rate of 3.8 billion machine cycles per second. It's important to realize, however, that CPU processor speed alone doesn't determine the performance of the CPU.

What else determines processor performance? Although speed is an important consideration when determining

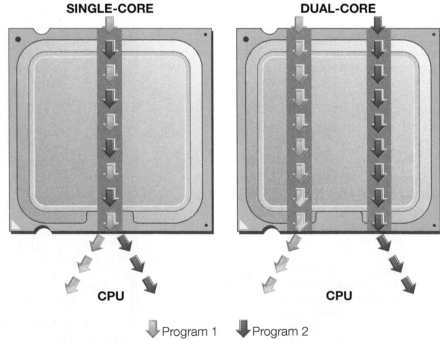

With multi-core processors, CPUs can work in parallel, processing two or more separate programs at the same time instead of switching back and forth between them.

storing data and
INFORMATION

Because RAM is volatile storage, it can't be used to store information indefinitely. To save your data and information permanently, you need to save it to a nonvolatile storage device, such as a hard drive, cloud storage location, DVD, or flash drive.

Hard Drives

Objective *List the various types of hard drives.*

Are there different kinds of hard drives? The **hard disk drive (HDD, or hard drive)** is your computer's primary device for permanent storage of software and documents. The hard drive is a nonvolatile storage device. An **internal hard drive** resides within the system unit and usually holds all permanently stored programs and data. Today's internal hard drives have capacities of as much as 8 TB or more. **External hard drives** offer similar storage capacities but reside outside the system unit and connect to the computer via a port.

The most common type of hard drive has moveable parts—spinning platters and a moving arm with a read/write head—that can fail and lead to devastating disk failure. However, the **solid-state drive (SSD)** has recently become a popular option for ultrabooks and laptop storage. SSDs have no moving parts, so they're more efficient, run with no noise, emit little heat, and require little power. In addition, they're less likely to fail after being bumped or dropped.

Permanent storage devices are located in your desktop or laptop computer in a space called a **drive bay**. There are two kinds of drive bays:

1. *Internal drive bays* cannot be seen or accessed from outside the system unit. Generally, internal drive bays are reserved for internal hard drives.

2. *External drive bays* can be seen and accessed from outside the system unit. External drive bays house DVD

Internal hard drives (shown here open—normally, they are sealed) are a computer's primary nonvolatile storage. *(Mbongo/ Fotolia)*

and Blu-ray drives, for example. On desktop computers, sometimes there are empty external drive bays that can be used to install additional drives. These extra spaces are covered by a faceplate on the front panel. Laptop computers generally do not give you the ability to add additional drives. Such expansion is done by attaching an external drive to the computer through a USB port.

Cloud Storage

Objective *Define cloud storage, and explain how to use it.*

How can I easily access my files if I constantly switch between devices? You may find yourself using multiple devices, such as a smartphone, laptop, and a tablet, at different times during the day. Invariably, you'll find you need access to a current version of a file that is stored on a device other than the one you're using. If your devices are connected to the Internet, cloud storage provides a convenient option.

Cloud storage refers to using a service that keeps your files on the Internet (in the "cloud") rather than storing your files solely on a local device. Using a cloud storage service requires that you install software or an app on your device. A popular web-based application for storing files on the cloud is Dropbox. Dropbox supports computers running Windows, OS X, and Linux as well as many smartphones and tablets. After installing the Dropbox software on your devices, any files you save in the Dropbox folder are accessible by all your other devices via the Internet. You can also share folders in Dropbox with other Dropbox users, making it ideal for group projects.

For example, when you save a history term paper to Dropbox on your laptop, the Dropbox software also copies the paper onto a computer attached to the web. Now when you grab your smartphone and head off to class, you can access the paper created on your laptop through the Internet connection on your smartphone and make changes to it if necessary.

Dropbox storage capacity is limited to between 2 GB and 18 GB for free accounts. Other cloud storage alternatives include Microsoft OneDrive and Google Drive, each of which provide 15 GB of free space, and Apple iCloud, which offers 5 GB of free storage.

Portable and Optical Storage Options

Objective *Describe the various portable and optical storage options.*

How can I take my files with me without relying on cloud storage? For large portable storage needs, there are portable external hard drives, which are small enough to fit into your pocket and have storage capacities of 4 TB

You've probably heard news stories about people using computers to unleash viruses or commit identity theft. You may also have read about students who were prosecuted for illegally sharing copyrighted material, such as songs and videos. These are both examples of *unethical* behavior while using a computer. However, what constitutes *ethical* behavior while using a computer?

Loosely defined, *ethics* is a system of moral principles, rules, and accepted standards of conduct. So what are the accepted standards of conduct when using computers? The Computer Ethics Institute has developed the Ten Commandments of Computer Ethics, which is widely cited as a benchmark for companies developing computer usage and compliance policies for employees. These guidelines are applicable for schools and students, as well. The following ethical computing guidelines are based on the Computer Ethics Institute's work:

There are different ways to define ethics, but they all apply to a common code of behavior for groups or individuals. *(Marek/Fotolia)*

Ethical Computing Guidelines

1. Avoid causing harm to others when using computers.
2. Do not interfere with other people's efforts at accomplishing work with computers.
3. Resist the temptation to snoop in other people's computer files.
4. Do not use computers to commit theft.
5. Agree not to use computers to promote lies.
6. Do not use software (or make illegal copies for others) without paying the creator for it.
7. Avoid using other people's computer resources without appropriate authorization or proper compensation.
8. Do not claim other people's intellectual output as your own.
9. Consider the social consequences of the products of your computer labor.
10. Only use computers in ways that show consideration and respect for others.

The United States has enacted laws that support some of these guidelines, such as Guideline 6, the breaking of which would violate copyright laws, and Guideline 4, which is enforceable under numerous federal and state larceny laws. Other guidelines, however, require more subtle interpretation as to what behavior is unethical because there are no laws designed to enforce them.

Consider Guideline 7, which covers unauthorized use of resources. The school you attend probably provides computer resources for you to use for coursework. But if your school gives you access to computers and the Internet, is it ethical for you to use those resources to run an online business on the weekends? Although it might not be technically illegal, you're tying up computer resources that other students could use for their intended purpose: learning and completing coursework. (This behavior also violates Guidelines 2 and 10.)

Throughout the chapters in this book, we touch on many topics related to these guidelines. So keep them in mind as you study, and think about how they relate to the actions you take as you use computers in your life.

Smaller, portable external hard drives enable you to take a significant amount of data and programs on the road with you. *(Inga Nielsen/Shutterstock)*

(or larger). These devices are lightweight and enclosed in a protective case. They attach to your computer via a USB port.

A **flash drive** (sometimes referred to as a **jump drive, USB drive,** or **thumb drive**) uses solid-state flash memory, storing information on an internal memory chip. When you plug a flash drive into your computer's USB port, it appears in the operating system as another disk drive. You can write data to it or read data from it as you would a hard drive. Because a flash drive contains no moving parts, it's quite durable. It's also tiny enough to fit in your pocket. Despite their size, flash drives can have significant storage capacity—currently as much as 1 TB. Often, flash drives are combined with other devices such as pens or keychains for added convenience.

Wireless flash drives are available that make transferring files from portable devices easier. Although they look like normal flash drives, these wireless drives can connect to your portable devices via WiFi after installing the appropriate app. Up to eight devices can be connected to the flash drive at once, and the drive can even stream media to three devices simultaneously. So your friend could be watching a movie stored on the flash drive while you're uploading pictures from your phone.

Another convenient means of portable storage is a **flash memory card**, such as an SD card. Like the flash drive, memory cards use solid-state flash memory. Most desktops and laptops include slots for flash memory cards, but if your computer is not equipped, there are memory card readers that you can plug into a USB port. Flash memory cards let you transfer digital data between your computer and devices such as digital cameras, smartphones, tablets, video cameras, and printers. Although incredibly small—some are even smaller than the size of a postage stamp—these memory cards have capacities that exceed the capacity of a DVD. Compares the storage capacities of hard drives and flash drives.

What other kinds of storage devices are available? Most desktop and all-in-one computers come

with at least one **optical drive** that can read from and maybe even write to CDs, DVDs, or Blu-ray discs. As we have moved toward streaming media services and cloud-based delivery of software, optical drives have not been included in laptops and ultrabooks to save weight and space. However, if you still have the need (or desire) to use optical drives, inexpensive portable drives that attach via USB ports are readily available.

Data is saved to optical discs as tiny pits that are burned into the disc by a high-speed laser. **Compact discs (CDs)** were initially created to store audio files. **Digital video (**or

Flash drives are a convenient means of portable storage and come in many different shapes and sizes. *(Ekler/Shutterstock)*

Hard Drive and Flash Drive Storage Capacity

DRIVE TYPE	IMAGE	TYPICAL CAPACITY	DRIVE TYPE	IMAGE	TYPICAL CAPACITY
Solid-state drive (SSD)		1 TB or more	Flash drive		256 GB or more
External portable hard drive		4 TB or more	Flash memory card		128 GB or more
Mechanical internal hard drive		8 TB or more			

(Oleksiy Mark/Shutterstock, Julia Ivantsova/Shutterstock, D. Hurst/Alamy, Cphoto/Fotolia, ZUMA Press, Inc/Alamy)

versatile) **discs (DVDs)** are the same size and shape as CDs but can store up to 14 times more data than CDs.

What if you want even more storage capacity? Blu-ray is the latest incarnation of optical storage. **Blu-ray discs (BDs)**, which are similar in size and shape to CDs and DVDs, can hold as much as 50 GB of data—enough to hold approximately 4.5 hours of movies in high-definition (HD) digital format. Many desktop systems are now available with BD-ROM drives and Blu-ray burners. External BD drives are another inexpensive way to add HD storage capacity to your system. ■

Optical Storage Media Capacities

MEDIUM TYPE	TYPICAL CAPACITY
Blu-ray (dual layer)	50 GB
Blu-ray	25 GB
DVD DL (dual layer)	8.5 GB
DVD	4.7 GB
CD	700 MB

 # connecting peripherals to the
COMPUTER

Throughout this chapter, we have discussed peripheral devices that input, store, and output data and information. We will now look at how these types of devices are connected to computers so they can exchange data.

Computer Ports

Objective *List the common types of ports used today.*

What is a port? A **port** is a place through which a peripheral device attaches to the computer so that data can be exchanged between it and the operating system. Although peripherals may connect to devices wirelessly, ports are still often used for connections.

What is the fastest data transfer port available on today's computing devices? Thunderbolt is the newest input/output technology on the market. It was developed by Intel using fiber optic technology and Thunderbolt 2 ports can achieve

trends in IT Green Computing (Green IT)

"Going green" is a goal for many modern businesses. **Green computing (or green IT)** is a movement to encourage environmentally sustainable computing. The main goal is to reduce the overall carbon footprint of a company through the strategic use of computing resources and environmentally friendly computing devices. A business's *carbon footprint* is the total amount of greenhouse gases produced directly and indirectly to support the activities of the business. Carbon footprints are expressed in equivalent tons of carbon dioxide (CO_2). CO_2 is the main greenhouse gas that is contributing to global warming. Reduction of greenhouse gas emissions is critical to sustaining a healthy environment.

The main goals of green computing are

1. Reducing the use of hazardous processes or materials in the production of computing equipment
2. Promoting the use of recyclable or biodegradable materials to facilitate safe disposal of products
3. Buying products that use energy efficiently
4. Using technology to reduce employee travel

(Weerapat1003/Fotolia)

5. Reducing the use of energy and consumption of materials through shared computing resources

Sharing computing resources can make a vast difference in the consumption of resources and electricity. This is one of the reasons cloud storage is becoming so popular. Rather than having 20 individual companies each maintaining a large group of computers to hold data, savings can be achieved by having one company maintain computer resources that are able to serve the 20 other companies. However, it's not all up to businesses to practice green computing.

Green Computing Problems and Solutions

ISSUE	ELECTRICITY	COMMUTING	USE TECHNOLOGY LONGER

Problems	• Electricity is often generated using fossil fuels, which produce greenhouse gas emissions • Devices are not energy efficient	• Cars generate greenhouse gases • Many people commute to work alone	• Items are replaced before their useful life is over • Old items are discarded instead of continuing to be used • Technology is not disposed of or recycled properly
Solutions	• Buy energy efficient computing equipment with high Energy Star ratings • Turn off computing devices when not in use • Use appropriate power management settings to use less power when operating devices	• Use technology to telecommute to your job • Use public transportation to commute, which uses energy more efficiently than cars • Use a green vehicle (bicycle, electric car) for your commute	• Only upgrade your technology when absolutely necessary • Donate your old technology to someone who will continue to use it (friends, family, charitable organization) • Only dispose of electronic devices at approved e-waste recycling facilities

(kovalto1/Fotolia, Berc/Fotolia, Marek/Fotolia)

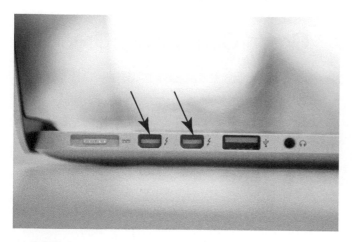

Thunderbolt ports are slim and speedy, making them popular on today's ultrabooks and laptops. *(David Paul Morris/Bloomberg/Getty Images)*

blazingly fast transfer speeds of up to 20 Gb/s (the upcoming Thunderbolt 3 protocol should double this to 40 Gb/s). **Thunderbolt ports** are very useful for laptops and ultrabooks because one Thunderbolt port can allow you to connect up to six different peripherals to your computer. Apple was the first computer maker to integrate the ports into their hardware although other manufacturers are now following suit.

What is the most common port on digital devices?
A **universal serial bus (USB) port** is the port type most commonly used to connect input and output devices to the computer. This is mainly because of the ready availability of USB-compatible peripherals. USB ports can connect a wide variety of peripherals to computing devices, including keyboards, printers, mice, smartphones, external hard drives, flash drives, and digital cameras. The new USB 3.1 standard provides

transfer speeds of 10 Gbps and charges devices faster than previous USB ports. USB ports come in variety of standard and proprietary configurations, plus the new Type-C connector (and port), which is expected to supplant older connections as USB 3.1 continues to roll out.

Which ports help me connect with other computers and the Internet?
Another set of ports on your computer helps you communicate with other computers. A **connectivity port** can give you access to networks and the Internet. To find a connectivity port, look for a port that resembles a standard phone jack but is slightly larger. This port is called an **Ethernet port**. Ethernet ports transfer data at speeds up to 10,000 Mbps. You can use an Ethernet port to connect your computer to either a cable modem or a network.

How do I connect monitors and multimedia devices?
Other ports on the back and sides of the computer include audio and video ports. Audio ports are where you connect headphones, microphones, and speakers to the computer. Whether you're attaching a monitor to a desktop computer, or adding a second, larger display to a laptop computer, you'll use a video port. HDMI ports are now the most common video port on computing devices.

A **high-definition multimedia interface (HDMI) port** is a compact audio–video interface that allows both HD video and uncompressed digital audio to be carried on one cable. Because HDMI can transmit uncompressed audio and video, there's no need to convert the signal, which could ultimately reduce the quality of the sound or picture. All currently available monitors, DVD players, televisions, and game consoles have at least one HDMI port.

What ports might I encounter on older computers and peripherals?
The **video graphics array (VGA) port** and the **digital video interface (DVI) port** are two ports to which older LCD monitors and televisions connect.

USB connectors come in a wide variety of styles. *(TaraPatta/Shutterstock)*

Some Apple computers now feature the new USB-C port that supports data transfer, video output, and charging all in a single port. *(EPA/Alamy)*

HDMI is the latest digital connector type for HD monitors, televisions, and home theater equipment. *(Feng Yu/Shutterstock)*

Older Apple computers feature a Mini DisplayPort for connection of video peripherals. Adapters are available for the Mini DisplayPort that allow the connection of older DVI and VGA devices.

Adding Ports: Expansion Cards and Hubs

Objective *List the options for adding ports to your device.*

What if I don't have all the ports I need? If you're looking to add the newest ports to an older desktop computer or to expand the number of ports on it, you can install special

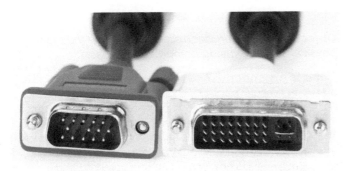

DVI (left) and VGA (right) cables are used to connect older LCD monitors and televisions to computing devices. *(Marek Kosmal/ Fotolia)*

expansion cards into an open expansion slot on the motherboard to provide additional ports.

Another alternative is adding an expansion hub. An expansion hub is a device that connects to one port, such as a USB port, to provide additional ports. It works like the multiplug extension cords used with electrical appliances. ∎

Expansion cards fit into slots on the motherboard in a desktop computer. *(Andrew Kitching/Alamy)*

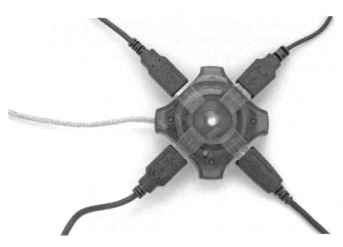

If you don't have enough USB ports to support your USB devices, consider getting an expansion hub, which can add four or more USB ports to your system. *(Norman Chan/Fotolia)*

power controls and
ERGONOMICS

Conserving energy and setting up workspaces so they are comfortable for employees are goals of many businesses. However, these are also excellent goals to strive for at your house. In the next two sections, we will explore optimizing the power consumption of computing devices as well as the proper workspace setup to minimize injuries.

Power Controls

Objective *Describe how to manage power consumption on your computing devices.*

What's the best way to turn my computer on and off? The **power supply**, which is housed inside the system unit, transforms the wall voltage to the voltages required by computer chips. Powering on your computer from a completely turned off state, such as when you start your computer in the morning, is called a **cold boot**. In Windows 10, you can turn your computer off by displaying the Start menu, selecting Power, and then choosing the Shut down option.

Should I turn off my computer every time I'm done using it? Some people say you should leave your computer on at all times. They argue that turning your computer on and off throughout the day subjects its components to stress because the heating and cooling process forces the components to expand and contract repeatedly. Other people say you should shut down your computer when you're not using it. They claim that it's not as environmentally friendly and that you'll end up wasting money on electricity from the computer running all the time.

Modern operating systems include power-management settings that allow the most power-hungry components of the system (the hard drive and monitor) to shut down after a short idle period. With the power-management options of Windows 10, for example, you only need to shut down your computer completely when you need to repair or install hardware in the system unit or move it to another location. However, if you use your computer only for a little while each day, it would be best to power it off completely after each daily use.

Can I "rest" my computer without turning it off completely? In Windows 10, the main method of power management is Sleep. When your computer enters **Sleep mode**, all of the documents, applications, and data you were using remain in RAM (memory), where they're quickly accessible when you restart your computer.

In Sleep mode, the computer enters a state of greatly reduced power consumption, which saves energy. To put your computer into Sleep mode in Windows 10, display the Start menu, select Power, then select the Sleep option. To wake up your computer, press a key or the physical power button. In a few seconds, the

computer will resume with exactly the same programs running and documents displayed as when you put it to sleep.

If you don't ever want to completely turn off your computer, you can change what happens when you press the power button or close the lid on your laptop. By accessing the Power Options System Settings window, you can decide if you want your computer to Sleep, Hibernate, or Shut down when you press the power button. The **Hibernate** option is similar to Sleep except that your data is stored on your hard drive instead of in RAM and your computer is powered off. This uses much less battery power than Sleep and is a good choice if you won't be using your laptop for a long time and won't have the opportunity to charge it. However, Sleep is still a good option to choose if you just won't be using your computer for a short time. You may want to set your computer so it sleeps when you close the lid but hibernates when you press the power button, giving you quick access to either option.

What's the Restart option in Windows for? If you're using Windows 10, you have the option to restart the computer when you access the Power option on the Start menu. Restarting the system while it's powered on is called a **warm boot**. You might need to perform a warm boot if the operating system or other software application stops responding or if you've installed new programs. It takes less time to perform a warm boot than to power down completely and then restart all your hardware.

Setting It All Up: Ergonomics

Objective *Define ergonomics, and discuss the ideal physical setup for using computing devices.*

What is ergonomics? It's important that you understand not only your computer's components and how they work together but also how to set up these components safely. **Ergonomics** is the science that deals with the design and location of machines and furniture so that the people using them aren't subjected to an uncomfortable or unsafe experience. In terms of computing, ergonomics refers to how you set up your computer and other equipment to minimize your risk of injury or discomfort.

Why is ergonomics important? Studies suggest that teenagers, on average, spend 7.5 hours per day using computing devices. When you factor in other computer uses such as playing video games, there is great potential for injury. The repetitive nature of long-term computing activities can place too much stress on joints and pull at the tendons and muscles, causing repetitive stress injuries such as carpal tunnel syndrome and tendonitis. These injuries can take months or years to develop to a point where they become painful, and by the time you notice the symptoms, the damage has already taken

You can determine what happens when you click the power button on your computer or close the lid through the Power Options System Settings screen. *(Windows 10, Microsoft Corporation)* >*To access Power Options System Settings, from the Start Menu, select* **Settings**, *select* **System**, *select* **Power & sleep**, *click the* **Additional power settings link**, *then select* **Choose what the power button does**.

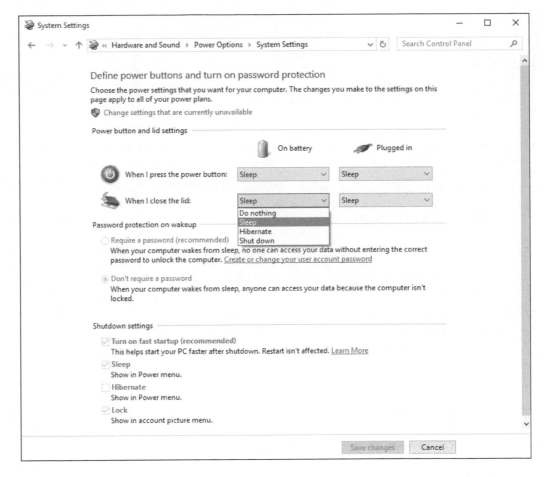

place. If you take precautionary measures now, you may prevent years of unnecessary pain later.

How can I avoid injuries when I'm working at my computer?
It's important to arrange your monitor, chair, body, and keyboard in ways that will help you avoid injury, discomfort, and eyestrain. The following additional guidelines can help keep you comfortable and productive:

- **Position your monitor correctly.** Studies suggest it's best to place your monitor at least 25 inches from your eyes. Experts recommend that you position your monitor either at eye level or at an angle 15–20 degrees below your line of sight.

- **Purchase an adjustable chair.** Adjust the height of your chair so that your feet touch the floor (or use a footrest to get the right position). The back support needs to be adjustable so that you can position it to support your lumbar (lower back) region. You should also be able to move the seat or adjust the back so that you can sit without exerting pressure on your knees. If your chair doesn't adjust, place a pillow behind your back to provide support.

- **Assume a proper position while typing.** Improperly positioned keyboards are one of the leading causes of repetitive stress

The Power option on the Windows 10 Start menu presents several power options. *(Windows 10, Microsoft Corporation)* >*For a warm boot, choose* **Restart**. *To power down the computer completely, choose* **Shut down**. *To put your computer into a lower power mode, select* **Sleep**.

Top of monitor at or below eye level

Adjustable monitor

Lumbar support

Adjustable-height keyboard tray and wrist rest

Fully adjustable chair

Footrest if needed

Using proper equipment that is adjusted correctly helps prevent repetitive strain injuries while working at a computer.

- **Take breaks.** Remaining in the same position for long periods of time increases stress on your body. Shift your position in your chair and stretch your hands and fingers periodically. Likewise, staring at the screen for long periods can lead to eyestrain, so rest your eyes by periodically taking them off the screen and focusing them on an object at least 8 feet away.
- **Ensure the lighting is adequate.** Ensuring that you have proper lighting in your work area minimizes eyestrain. Eliminate sources of direct glare (light shining directly into your eyes) or reflected glare (light shining off the computer screen) and ensure there is enough light to read comfortably. If you still can't eliminate glare from your computer screen, you can buy an antiglare screen to place over your monitor.

injuries in computer users. Your wrists should be flat (not bent) with respect to the keyboard, and your forearms should be parallel to the floor. Additionally, your wrists should not be resting on the keyboard while typing. You can adjust the height of your chair or install a height-adjustable keyboard tray to ensure a proper position.

Is ergonomics important when using mobile devices? Working with mobile computing devices presents interesting challenges when it comes to injury prevention. For example, many users work with laptops resting on their laps, placing the monitor outside of the optimal line of sight and thereby increasing neck strain.

So, whether you're computing at your desk or on the road, consider the ergonomics of your work environment. Doing so will help you avoid injury and discomfort.

BITS&BYTES

Save Power and Avoid Eyestrain: Use Blackle

Your computer uses less energy when it displays black as opposed to white (or other lighter colors). Also, bright colors such as white tend to increase eyestrain when viewing a computer screen. For a quick fix, try using an alternative search engine called Blackle (**blackle. com**). Powered by Google, this customized search engine displays a predominantly black screen instead of white. Since most modern monitors don't backlight the black parts of a display, you save a little bit of energy when using this alternative search engine. Yes, it's a small amount of energy—but every little bit helps!

Want to save energy while reducing eyestrain? Using apps or websites that use less white and more black helps. *(Grgroup/ Fotolia)*

Ergonomic keyboards have curved keyboards and wrist rests to help you maintain the proper hand position while typing to reduce the risk of repetitive strain injuries. *(Dmitriy Melnikov/Fotolia)*

What devices are available for people with disabilities? People who have physical challenges sometimes need special devices to access computers. **Assistive** (or **adaptive**) **technology** are products, devices, equipment, or software that are used to maintain, increase, or improve the functional capabilities of individuals with disabilities. For visually impaired users and individuals who can't type with their hand, voice recognition is a common input option. For those users whose visual limitations are less severe, keyboards with larger keys are available.

People with motor control issues may have difficulty with pointing devices. To aid such users, special trackballs are available that can be easily manipulated with one finger and can be attached to almost any surface, including a wheelchair. When arm motion is severely restrained, head-mounted pointing devices can be used. Generally, these involve a camera mounted on the computer monitor and a device attached to the head (often installed in a hat). When the user moves his or her head, the camera detects the movement and moves the cursor. In this case, mouse clicks are controlled by a switch that can be manipulated by the user's hands or feet or even by using an instrument that fits into the mouth and senses the user blowing into it. ∎

Preventing Injuries While on the Go

	SMARTPHONE REPETITIVE STRAIN INJURIES	PORTABLE MEDIA PLAYER HEARING DAMAGE	SMALL-SCREEN VISION ISSUES	LAP INJURIES	TABLET REPETITIVE STRAIN INJURIES
					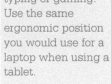
Malady	Repetitive strain injuries (such as DeQuervain's tendonitis) from constant typing of instant messages	Hearing loss from high-decibel sound levels in earbuds	Blurriness and dryness caused by squinting to view tiny screens on mobile devices	Burns on legs from heat generated by laptop	Pain caused from using tablets for prolonged periods in uncomfortable positions
Preventative Measures	Restrict length and frequency of messages, take breaks, and perform other motions with your thumbs and fingers during breaks to relieve tension.	Turn down volume (you should be able to hear external noises, such as people talking), use software that limits sound levels (not to exceed 60 decibels), and use external, over-ear style headphones instead of earbuds.	Blink frequently or use eye drops to maintain moisture in eyes, after 10 minutes take a break and focus on something at least 8 feet away for 5 minutes, use adequate amount of light, and increase the size of fonts.	Place a book, magazine, or laptop cooling pad between your legs and laptop.	Restrict the length of time you work at a tablet, especially typing or gaming. Use the same ergonomic position you would use for a laptop when using a tablet.

trends in IT

With the advent of the computer, many speculated that ours would become a paperless society. Instead of saving printed documents and other output as was done prior to the PC, information would be saved in a digital state: hard drives replacing filing cabinets, online photo buckets replacing photo albums and scrapbooks, and e-books replacing our favorite texts. Hard drive capacities do enable us to save more content, and online storage systems enable us to save pictures and other files to the "cloud." Additionally, e-book readers have increased in popularity. But has this push toward digital content begun to make the printer obsolete? Surprisingly, no. People still have a deep-rooted need to see, feel, mark, share, or use their digital images or information in a physical form. New technologies that push the boundaries of printing, such as printing from the cloud and 3-D printing, are being developed and refined.

Cloud Printing

To print a document from a desktop or laptop computer, you must have a printer associated with your computer. Usually, this is not a problem because at home, at school, or in the office, there is generally one printer, and all the PCs connected to it have the software and cables or wireless capabilities needed to use it. But what happens if you want to print something from your smartphone or tablet? Common solutions have been to e-mail the document to yourself or transfer the document to a web-based storage service such as Dropbox so that a printer-connected computer could access it. Another solution is Google Cloud Print, a service that lets you configure your printers so you can access them from mobile devices.

Google Cloud Print uses cloud-ready printers that are now available from manufacturers such as HP, Kodak, and Epson. These printers connect directly to the Internet and register themselves with Google Cloud Print without needing to be connected to a computer. Once a printer is registered with Cloud Print, printing jobs can be sent to it from mobile devices (such as tablets and smartphones) using the Internet. Conventional printers that you already own can also be registered with Cloud Print, although they require connection to the Internet through a computer.

Cloud-ready printers only need an Internet connection to be accessed from any mobile device.

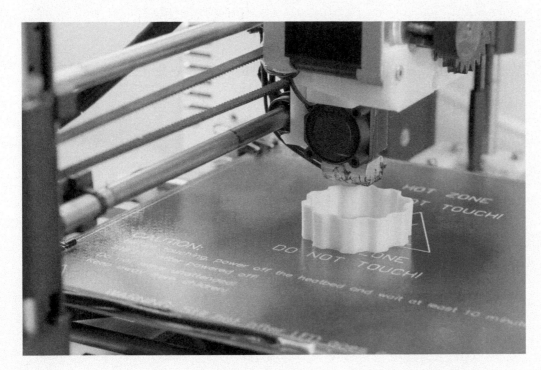

3-D printing is being used to fabricate parts for all sorts of devices on demand. *(Hopsalka/Fotolia)*

3-D Printing

Printing a 3-D model of a proposed building or new prototype is common for architects and engineers. The process builds a model one layer at a time from the bottom up. The procedure begins by spreading a layer of powder on a platform. Then, depending on the technology, the printer uses nozzles similar to those in an inkjet printer to spray tiny drops of glue at specific places to solidify the powder, or the powder is solidified through a melting process. The printer repeats solidifying layers of powder until the model is built to specifications. This technology has spurred the manufacturing of a variety of consumer goods, from toys to clothing. Shapeways (**shapeways.com**) uses 3-D printing to enable anyone to turn his or her 3-D designs into real physical models. Then, those models can be personalized, bought, or sold through Shapeways's online community.

3-D printing is being used in the medical community as well. Hearing aids are now being produced using 3-D printers and allow manufacturers to not only offer a custom fit but individual skin color matching as well (to make the devices less visible). And researchers at Wake Forest Institute for Regenerative Medicine have developed a way to use similar inkjet technologies to build heart, bone, and blood vessel tissues in the lab. They have also developed a way to "print" restorative cells directly into a soldier's wound at the site where the injury occurred, thus significantly improving the soldier's chances of survival.

Taking traditional technologies, such as inkjet printing, and applying them to solve current human struggles is a long and tedious process, but without these pioneers experimenting with different applications, society would advance a lot more slowly.

Before moving on to the Chapter Review:
1. Watch Replay Video 2.2 ☐.
2. Then check your understanding of what you've learned so far.

check your understanding // review & practice

For a quick review to see what you've learned so far, answer the following questions.

multiple choice

1. Which of the following is NOT found on a motherboard?

   a. RAM

   b. CPU

   c. sound card

   d. hard drive

2. Which of these is an example of optical storage media?

   a. DVD

   b. SSD

   c. thumb drive

   d. a flash memory card

3. Which of the following is the fastest data transfer port?

   a. HDMI

   b. VGA

   c. USB 3.1

   d. Thunderbolt

4. Which of these is considered volatile storage?

   a. SSD

   b. ROM

   c. RAM

   d. thumb drive

5. Which power control option performs a warm boot?

   a. Restart

   b. Sleep

   c. Log off

   d. Shut down

TECHBYTES WEEKLY

Stay current with the TechBytes Weekly Newsletter.

1 Chapter Review

summary //

Understanding Digital Components

Learning Outcome **You will be able to describe the devices that make up a computer system.**

Understanding Your Computer

Objective *Describe the four main functions of a computer system and how they interact with data and information.*

- The computer's four major functions are:
  (1) input: gather data or allow users to enter data;
  (2) process: manipulate, calculate, or organize that data; (3) output: display data and information in a form suitable for the user; and (4) storage: save data and information for later use.
- Data is a representation of a fact or idea. The number 3 and the words *televisions* and *Sony* are pieces of data.
- Information is data that has been organized or presented in a meaningful fashion. An inventory list that indicates that 3 Sony televisions are in stock is processed information. It allows a retail clerk to answer a customer query about the availability of merchandise. Information is more powerful than raw data.

Objective *Define bits and bytes, and describe how they are measured, used, and processed.*

- To process data into information, computers need to work in a language they understand. This language, called *binary language*, consists of two numbers: 0 and 1. Each 0 and each 1 is a binary digit or bit. Eight bits create one byte.
- In computers, each letter of the alphabet, each number, and each special character consists of a unique combination of eight bits (one byte)—a string of eight 0s and 1s.
- For describing large amounts of storage capacity, the terms *megabyte* (approximately 1 million bytes), *gigabyte* (approximately 1 billion bytes), *terabyte* (approximately 1 trillion bytes), and *petabyte* (1,000 terabytes) are used.

Objective *List common types of computers, and discuss their main features.*

- A tablet computer is a portable computer integrated into a flat multitouch-sensitive screen.
- A laptop or notebook computer is a portable computer that has a keyboard, monitor, and other devices integrated into a single compact case.
- An ultrabook is a lightweight laptop computer featuring low-power processors and solid-state drives.
- Chromebook computers use the Google Chrome OS. Documents and apps are stored primarily in the cloud.
- Desktop computers consist of a separate case (called the system unit) that houses the main components of the computer plus peripheral devices.

Input Devices

Objective *Identify the main types of keyboards and touch screens.*

- You use keyboards to enter typed data and commands. Most keyboards use the QWERTY layout.
- Touch screens are display screens that respond to commands initiated by a touch with a finger or a stylus.
- Wireless keyboards mainly use Bluetooth connectivity and provide alternatives to on-screen keyboards.

Objective *Describe the main types of mice and pointing devices.*

- Mice are used to enter user responses and commands.
- Optical mice use a laser to detect mouse movement.
- Some mice can be adjusted to provide better ergonomics for users.
- Laptops have integrated pointing devices called touch pads (trackpads).

Objective *Explain how images and sounds are input into computing devices.*

- Images are input into the computer with scanners, digital cameras, camcorders, and smartphones.
- Live video is captured with webcams and digital video recorders.
- Microphones capture sounds. There are many different types of microphones, including desktop, headset, and clip-on models.

Output Devices

Objective *Name common types of monitors, and identify important aspects of their quality.*

- Monitors display soft copies of text, graphics, and video.
- Liquid crystal display (LCD) and light-emitting diode (LED) are the most common types of computer monitors.
- OLED displays use organic compounds to produce light and don't require a backlight, which saves energy.
- Aspect ratio, screen resolution, contrast ratio, viewing angle, brightness, and response time are key aspects to consider when choosing a monitor.

Objective *Describe various types of printers, and explain when you would use them.*

- Printers create hard copies of text and graphics.
- There are two primary categories of printers: inkjet and laser. Laser printers usually print faster and deliver higher-quality output than inkjet printers. However, inkjet printers can be more economical for casual printing needs.
- Specialty printers are also available such as all-in-one printers, large format printers, and thermal printers.
- When choosing a printer, you should be aware of factors such as speed, resolution, color output, and cost of consumables.

Objective *Discuss options for outputting sound from your computing devices.*

- Speakers are the output devices for sound. Most computers include basic speakers.
- More sophisticated systems include subwoofers and surround sound.
- Headphone or earbuds are useful to avoid disturbing others.

Processing, Storage, and Connectivity

Learning Outcome **You will be able to describe how computers process and store data and how devices connect to a computer system.**

Processing and Memory on the Motherboard

Objective *Define motherboard and RAM.*

- The motherboard, the main circuit board of the system, contains a computer's CPU, which coordinates the functions of all other devices on the computer.
- The motherboard also houses slots for expansion cards, which have specific functions that augment the computer's basic functions. Typical expansion cards are sound and video cards.
- RAM, the computer's volatile memory, is also located on the motherboard. RAM is where all the data and instructions are held while the computer is running.

Objective *Explain the main functions of the CPU.*

- The CPU controls all the functions performed by the computer's other components. The CPU also processes all commands issued to it by software instructions.
- The performance of a CPU is affected by the speed of the processor (measured in GHz), the amount of cache memory, and the number of processing cores.

Storing Data and Information

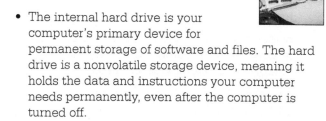

Objective *List the various types of hard drives.*

- The internal hard drive is your computer's primary device for permanent storage of software and files. The hard drive is a nonvolatile storage device, meaning it holds the data and instructions your computer needs permanently, even after the computer is turned off.

- SSD drives have no moving parts so they are more energy efficient and less susceptible to damage.
- External hard drives are essentially internal hard drives that have been made portable by enclosing them in a protective case and making them small and lightweight.

Objective *Define cloud storage, and explain how to use it.*

- Cloud storage refers to nonvolatile storage locations that are maintained on the Internet (in the "cloud"). Examples are OneDrive, Google Drive, and Dropbox.
- Storing your data in the cloud allows you to access it from almost any computing device that is connected to the Internet.

Objective *Describe the various portable and optical storage options.*

- Optical drives that can read from and write to CD, DVD, or Blu-ray discs are another means of permanent, portable storage. Data is saved to CDs, DVDs, and Blu-ray discs as pits that are burned into the disc by a laser.
- Flash drives are another portable means of storing data. Flash drives plug into USB ports.
- Flash memory cards let you transfer digital data between your computer and devices such as digital cameras, smartphones, video cameras, and printers.

Connecting Peripherals to the Computer

Objective *List the common types of ports used today.*

- The fastest type of port used to connect devices to a computer is the Thunderbolt port.
- The most common type of port used to connect devices to a computer is the USB port.
- Connectivity ports, such as Ethernet ports, give you access to networks and the Internet.

- HDMI ports are the most common multimedia port. They are used to connect monitors, TVs, and gaming consoles to computing devices and handle both audio and video data.
- Audio ports are used to connect headphones, microphones, and speakers to computing devices.

Objective *List the options for adding ports to your device.*

- Expansion cards can be plugged into the motherboard on desktop computers to add ports.
- Expansion hubs can be plugged into existing ports to provide additional ports of the same type.

Power Controls and Ergonomics

Objective *Describe how to manage power consumption on your computing devices.*

- Turning off your computer when you won't be using it for long periods of time saves energy. In Windows 10, you can turn your computer off by accessing the Power option on the Start menu, then selecting Shut down.
- If you are not using your computer for short periods of time, selecting the Sleep option will help your computer save energy but allows it to be quickly "awakened" for use.

Objective *Define ergonomics, and discuss the ideal physical setup for using computing devices.*

- Ergonomics refers to how you arrange your computer and equipment to minimize your risk of injury or discomfort.
- Achieving proper ergonomics includes positioning your monitor correctly, buying an adjustable chair, assuming a proper position while typing, making sure the lighting is adequate, and not looking at the screen for long periods. Other good practices include taking frequent breaks and using specially designed equipment such as ergonomic keyboards.
- Ergonomics is also important to consider when using mobile devices.

key terms //

chapter quiz // assessment

For a quick review to see what you've learned, answer the following questions. Submit the quiz as requested by your instructor. If you are using **MyITLab**, the quiz is also available there.

multiple choice

1. What is a gigabyte?

   a. one billion bytes

   b. one trillion bytes

   c. one billion bits

   d. one million bits

2. Which of the following is NOT an output device?

   a. touch-screen monitor

   b. optical mouse

   c. speakers

   d. laser printer

3. Monitor screens are made up of millions of tiny dots known as

   a. bytes.

   b. resolution points.

   c. pixels.

   d. bits.

4. Which of these is located on the motherboard?

   a. SSD drive

   b. RAM

   c. Hard drive

   d. DVD drive

5. Which of these is an optical storage device?

   a. flash drive

   b. SSD drive

   c. External hard drive

   d. Blu-ray drive

6. Ergonomics is an important consideration

   a. only for desktop computers.

   b. only for laptop computers.

   c. only for laptop and desktop computers, but never for mobile devices.

   d. for all computing devices.

true/false

1. Data and information are interchangeable terms.

2. Microsoft Word is a type of application software.

3. The fastest data transfer port is an HDMI port.

4. A typical CPU can complete billions of machine cycles in one second.

critical thinking

1. **Computers of the Future**

   Embedded computers keep turning up in new places. They can be found in cars, household appliances, smoke detectors, and thermostats too, enabling us to interact with even more of these "smart" devices every day. What common objects do you think might benefit from an embedded computer? What capabilities can you envision?

2. **New Display Features**

   The display screen of the future may be paper-thin, flexible, and transparent. Companies like Samsung and LG are already working on it. What uses can you envision for this new technology? What advantages and disadvantages do you foresee? Do you have any suggestions for the manufacturers to help make this successful?

Data Storage Options

Problem

You've joined a small business that's beginning to evaluate its technology setup. Because of the addition of several new sales representatives and other administrative employees, the company needs to reconsider the various ways its data is stored. You've been asked to evaluate options for on-site and off-site data storage.

Task

Split your class into teams of three and assign the following tasks:

- Member A explores the benefits and downfalls of cloud storage.
- Member B explores the benefits and downfalls of external hard drives.
- Member C explores the benefits and downfalls of portable storage devices.

Process

1. Think about what the storage needs are for the company and what information and resources you will need to tackle this project.

2. Research and then discuss the components of each method you're recommending. Are any of these options better suited for the particular needs of certain types of employees (sales representatives versus administrative staff)? Consider the types of data to be stored. Is some data confidential? How long should it be retained?

3. Consider the different types of employees in the company. Would a combination of methods be better than a single solution? If so, what kinds of employees would use which type of storage?

4. As a team, write a summary position paper. Support your recommendation for the company. Each team member should include why his or her data storage option will or will not be part of the solution.

Conclusion

There are advantages and disadvantages to any data storage option. Being aware of the pros and cons and knowing which method is best for a particular scenario or employee will help you to become a better consumer as well as a better computer user.

Green Computing

Ethical conduct is a stream of decisions you make all day long. In this exercise, you'll research and then role-play a complicated ethical situation. The role you play may or may not match your own personal beliefs, but your research and use of logic will enable you to represent whichever view is assigned. An arbitrator will watch and comment on both sides of the arguments, and together, the team will agree on an ethical solution.

Background

Green computing—conducting computing needs with the least possible amount of power and impact on the environment—is on everyone's minds. Although it's hard to argue with an environmentally conscious agenda, the pinch to our pocketbooks and the loss of some comforts sometimes make green computing difficult. Businesses, including colleges, need to consider a variety of issues and concerns before jumping into a complete green overhaul.

Research Areas to Consider

End-of-life management: e-waste and recycling

- Energy-efficient devices
- Renewable resources used in computer manufacturing
- Costs of green computing
- Government funding and incentives

Process

1. Divide the class into teams.
2. Research the areas cited above and devise a scenario in which your college is considering modifying its current technology setup to a more green information technology (IT) strategy.
3. Team members should write a summary that provides background information for their character—for example, environmentalist, college IT administrator, or arbitrator—and that details their character's behaviors to set the stage for the role-playing event. Then, team members should create an outline to use during the role-playing event.
4. Team members should arrange a mutually convenient time to meet, using a virtual meeting tool or by meeting in person.
5. Team members should present their case to the class or submit a PowerPoint presentation for review by the rest of the class, along with the summary and resolution they developed.

Conclusion

As technology becomes ever more prevalent and integrated into our lives, more and more ethical dilemmas will present themselves. Being able to understand and evaluate both sides of the argument, while responding in a personally or socially ethical manner, will be an important skill.

Technology Wish List

You are in need of a significant technology upgrade, and your parents have told you they will help you finance your purchases by loaning you the money. You will need to repay them with a modest 2.5% interest rate over two years. The only catch is that they want you to create a list of all the new devices that you need, note the cost, and provide a website for each device where they can find more information. Then, they want you to calculate how much you will need to give them each month to pay them back.

You will use the following skills as you complete this activity:

- Merge and Center
- Modify Workbook Themes
- Apply Number Formats
- Use the SUM, PMT, and COUNTA Functions

- Modify Column Widths
- Insert a Hyperlink
- Create a Formula
- Wrap Text

Instructions:

1. Open *TIA_Ch2_Start* and save as **TIA_Ch2_LastFirst**.

2. Format the title in cell A1 with the **Title Cell Style**, and format the column headers in cells A3:F3 with the **Heading 3 Cell Style**.
   a. Hint: To format cell styles, on the Home tab, in the Styles group, click **Cell Styles**.

3. **Merge and Center** cell A1 across columns A through F, and **Center align** the column headers in cells A3:F3.
   a. Hint: To Merge and Center text, on the Home tab, in the Alignment group, click **Merge & Center**.

4. Modify column widths so that Column A is **25** and Column D is **45**.
   a. Hint: To modify column widths, on the Home tab, in the Cells group, click **Format**, and then select **Column Width**.

5. In cells B4:F9, fill in the table with the Brand and Model of the six devices that you would like to purchase. The device type is filled out for you. In the *Reason* column, write a brief note as to why this device will help you. (You'll format the text so it all displays later.) Enter the cost of the device in the Cost column. Don't include tax and/or shipping.

6. Change the Workbook Theme to **Integral**.
   a. Hint: To apply the Theme, on the Page Layout tab, in the Themes group, click **Themes**.

7. In cells F4:F9, create a **Hyperlink** to a webpage that features each respective product so your grandparents can have access to more information if they need it. Ensure that each hyperlink includes the URL to the exact webpage for the device in the Address, but displays the Make/Model of the device in the worksheet.
   a. Hint: To insert a hyperlink, on the Insert tab, in the Links group, click **Hyperlink**. In the Insert Hyperlink dialog box, enter the URL in the Address: box and enter the Make/Model in the Text to display box.

8. Wrap the text in cells C4:C9, D4:D9, and F4:F9 so all text displays.
   a. Hint: To wrap text, on the Home tab, in the Alignment group, click **Wrap Text**.

9. Format the values in cells E4:E9 with the **Accounting Number format with two decimals**.

10. In cell A10, type **Subtotal**, then in cell E10, use a **SUM function** to calculate the total cost of all devices. Format the results in the **Accounting Number format with two decimals**.

11. In cell A11, type **Estimated Tax**, then in cell E11, create a formula that references the subtotal in cell E10 and multiplies it by a tax of 6%. Format the results in the **Accounting Number format with two decimals**.

12. In cell A12, type **Estimated Shipping**, then in cell E12, create a formula to calculate the shipping charge by using the **COUNTA function** to determine the number of devices being purchased and then multiplying that by a $10 shipping charge. Format the results in **Accounting Number Format with two decimals**.

13. In cell A13, type **Total Cost**, then in cell E13, use the **SUM function** to create a formula that adds up the *Subtotal*, *Estimated Tax*, and *Estimated Shipping* costs. Format the results in **Accounting Number Format with two decimals**. Format the cells A13:E13 with the **Total Cell Style**.

14. **Right align** cells A10:A13.

15. In cell D14, type **Estimated Monthly Payment**, and then in cell E14, use the **PMT function** to calculate the monthly payment owed to your parents to pay back the total purchase amount in two years at a 2.5% annual interest rate.

16. Save the workbook and submit based on your instructor's directions.

CHAPTER 2

Create Letters and Memos

▶ Microsoft Office Word is one of the most common productivity programs that individuals use on a computer.

▶ Word is used to create documents such as memos, reports, letters, and mailing labels. These documents can include tables and graphics.

▶ To work efficiently with Word, entering text, formatting text, and navigating within a Word document are the first basic skills you need.

▶ You can change the font and font size and add emphasis to text, but use caution not to apply too many different formats to your text. This can be distracting to the reader.

▶ It is never acceptable to have errors in spelling, grammar, or word usage in your documents; you can use Word spelling and grammar tools to prevent this.

▶ Business letters and memos are often structured and formatted in a formal manner as described in *The Gregg Reference Manual* by William A. Sabin.

Aspen Falls City Hall

In this chapter, you will assist Evelyn Stone, Human Resources Director, to create a letter to Dr. George Gato of Aspen Falls Community College. The purpose of the letter is to establish an internship program between City Hall and the students in the Information Systems Department chaired by Dr. Gato.

Microsoft Word is used often to write business letters and memos. You can quickly type, edit, and format text. Because business communication documents should be free of mistakes, spelling and grammar errors are flagged as you type. Most businesses apply a standard business letter format to all letters coming from the organization.

In this project, you will write a one-page business letter using the block style as defined by *The Gregg Reference Manual* by William A. Sabin. The **block style**, also called the **full-block style**, typically begins all lines at the left margin except for letterheads, tables, and block quotes. You will add a second page detailing the various internship positions available with City Hall.

Julien Eichinger/Fotolia

Introduction

Time to complete all 10
skills — 60 to 75 minutes

Outcome

Using the skills in this chapter, you will be able to create, edit, and save documents, apply styles, modify a document using copy, cut and paste, and confirm correct spelling and grammar.

Objectives

Create and edit a Word document

Use styles and advanced font settings

Adjust settings and review a document for printing

Create PDF files

SKILLS

At the end of this chapter you will be able to:

Skill 1 Type Letter Text

Skill 2 Apply Styles and Set Grammar and Spelling Options

Skill 3 Select and Insert Text

Skill 4 Copy, Cut, and Paste Text

Skill 5 Check Spelling and Grammar

Skill 6 Insert Synonyms

Skill 7 Use Format Painter

Skill 8 Apply Advanced Font Settings

Skill 9 Create Document Footers

Skill 10 Save Documents as PDF Files

MORE SKILLS

Skill 11 Manage Document Properties

Skill 12 Insert Screen Shots into Documents

Skill 13 Split and Arrange Windows

Skill 14 Insert Symbols

Student data file needed for this chapter:

wrd01_InternPositions

You will save your files as:

Last_First_wrd01_Interns (Word)
Last_First_wrd01_Interns (PDF)

ASPEN FALLS HUMAN RESOURCES
500 S Aspen Street
Aspen Falls, CA 93463

May 8, 2018

Dr. George Gato
Aspen Falls Community College
1 College Drive
Aspen Falls, CA 93464

Dear Dr. Gato:

Subject: City Hall Internships

Thank you so much for your letter offering the services of your Information Systems Department students. We currently have several projects that might benefit both City Hall and your students.

I have attached a description of the positions we are currently seeking. Please call me at (805) 555-1016 to discuss this further.

We have several positions open for students with skills in the four Office applications: Word, Excel, PowerPoint, and Access. We also need students capable of working with our IT Services Help Desk.

Sincerely,

Evelyn Stone
Human Resources Director

Last_First_wrd01_Interns

Word 2016, Windows 10, Microsoft Corporation

SKILL 1: Type Letter Text

▶ When working with Word documents, a paragraph can be a single line containing a heading or several lines of sentences.

▶ To see where paragraphs begin and end, it is helpful to display *formatting marks*—characters that display in your document to represent nonprinting characters such as paragraphs, spaces, and tabs.

1. Start **Word 2016**, and then on the Start screen, click **Blank document**.

2. On the **Home tab**, in the **Paragraph group**, click the **Show/Hide button** ¶ to display the nonprinting formatting marks. If the Navigation pane is open, Close ✕ it.

   The Show/Hide button is a *toggle button*—a button used to turn a feature both on and off. The paragraph mark (¶) indicates the end of a paragraph and will not print.

   Because many elements in the Word window adjust to your monitor size and personal settings, you may need to change your window size, exit Reading Mode, or disable Full Screen Mode to match the figures in this book.

3. With the insertion point in the blank paragraph, type Aspen Falls Human Resources and press Enter. Type 500 S Aspen Street and press Enter. Type Aspen Falls, CA 93463 and press Enter two times.

4. Type May 8, 2018 Press Enter three times, and then compare your screen.

   The letter has eight paragraphs—three for the letterhead, one for the date, and four blank paragraphs.

■ **Continue to the next page to complete the skill**

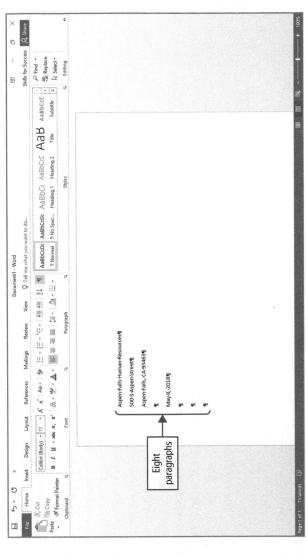

Word 2016, Windows 10, Microsoft Corporation

Word 2016, Windows 10, Microsoft Corporation

5. Type Dr. George Gato and press `Enter`; type Aspen Falls Community College and press `Enter`; type 1 College Drive and press `Enter`; and type Aspen Falls, CA 93464 and press `Enter`.

The word *Gato* is flagged as a spelling error, but it is spelled correctly.

6. Type Dear Dr. Gato: and press `Enter`. Type Subject: City Hall Internships and press `Enter`.

7. Type the following, inserting only one space after each sentence: Thank you so much for your letter offering the services of your Information Systems Department students. We currently have several projects that might benefit both us and your students. **Compare your screen.**

8. Press `Enter`, and then type We have several positions open for students with skills in the four Office applications: Word, Excel, PowerPoint, and Access. We also need students very capable of working with our IT Services Help Desk.

9. Press `Enter`, and type Sincerely, and then press `Enter` two times. Type Evelyn Stone Press `Enter`, and then type Human Resources Director

10. Click **Save** 🖫, and then on the **Save As** page, click the location and folder where you are saving your work. If necessary, click Browse.

11. In the **Save As** dialog box, click **New folder**, type Word Chapter 1 and then press `Enter` two times to open the new folder. Name the file Last_First_wrd01_Interns Click **Save**, and then compare your screen.

■ **You have completed Skill 1 of 10**

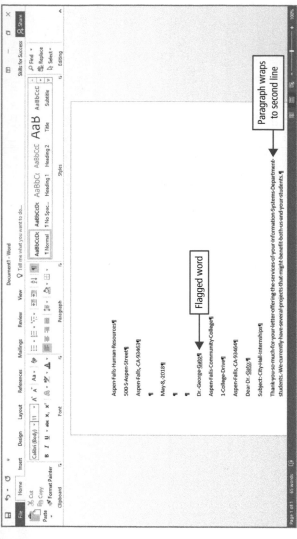

Flagged word

Paragraph wraps to second line

Word 2016, Windows 10, Microsoft Corporation

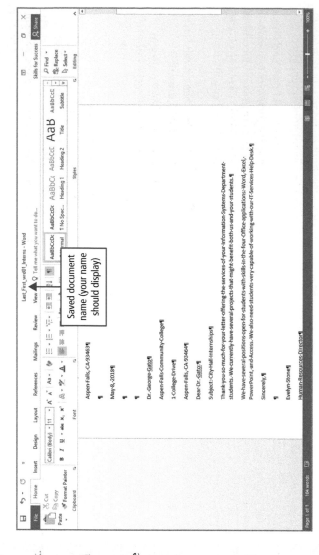

Saved document name (your name should display)

Word 2016, Windows 10, Microsoft Corporation

SKILL 2: Apply Styles and Set Grammar and Spelling Options

▲ You can format text quickly by applying *styles*—pre-built collections of formatting settings that can be assigned to text.

▲ During the writing process, it is a good idea to look for *flagged errors*—wavy lines indicating spelling or grammar errors. You can right-click these flagged errors to see a list of suggestions for fixing them.

1. In the inside address, right-click the word *Gato*, and then compare your screen.

   Red wavy lines indicate words that have been flagged as possible spelling errors, and the shortcut menu provides suggested spellings.

2. From the shortcut menu, click **Ignore All**, and verify that both instances of the word *Gato* are no longer flagged as spelling errors.

3. Hold down Ctrl and then press Home to move the insertion point to the beginning of the document.

4. Move the pointer to the left of the first line of the document to display the pointer. Drag down to select the first two lines of the document. On the **Home tab**, in the **Styles group**, click the **No Spacing** thumbnail. Compare your screen.

   The Normal style has extra space after each paragraph. The No Spacing style does not apply this extra space after each paragraph, and the extra space between the lines of the letterhead have been removed.

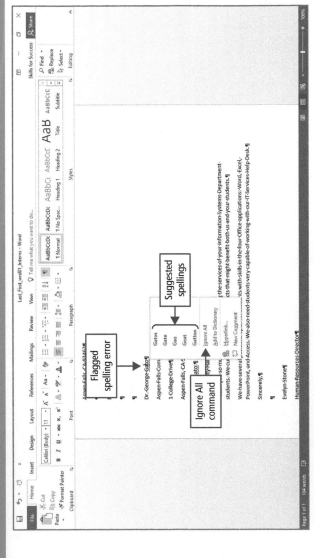

Word 2016, Windows 10, Microsoft Corporation

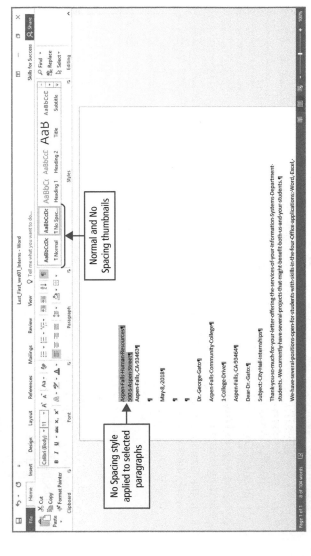

Word 2016, Windows 10, Microsoft Corporation

MOS Obj

■ **Continue to the next page to complete the skill**

MOS
Obj

5. Click the **File tab**, and then click **Options**. On the left pane of the **Word Options** dialog box, click **Proofing**.

6. Under **When correcting spelling and grammar in Word**, verify that the first four check boxes are selected.

7. To the right of **Writing Style**, click the **Settings** button.

8. In the **Grammar Settings** dialog box, verify the **Subject Verb Agreement** check box is selected. Compare your screen, and then click **OK**.

   In this manner, you can customize the types of errors that should be flagged as you work with a document.

9. Click **OK** to close the **Word Options** dialog box.

10. Click the **Save** button. Alternately, press Ctrl + S.

■ **You have completed Skill 2 of 10**

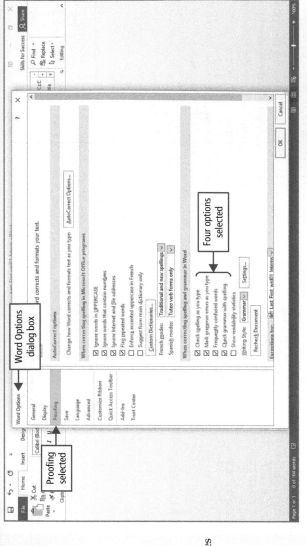

Word 2016, Windows 10, Microsoft Corporation

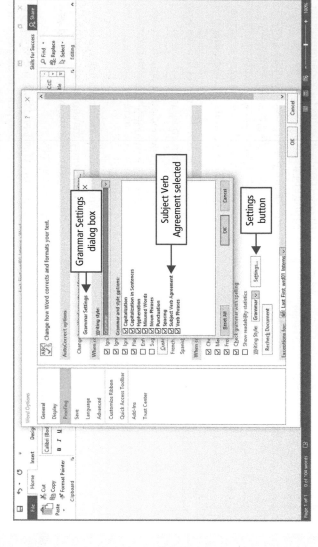

Word 2016, Windows 10, Microsoft Corporation

▶ You can select a single word by double-clicking and a single paragraph by triple-clicking.

▶ The amount of space between letter elements is specified by the style rules that your letter is following.

1. Click anywhere in the first paragraph of the document, *Aspen Falls Human Resources.*

2. On the **Home tab**, in the **Paragraph group**, click the **Center button** ≡ to center the paragraph.

   When you apply paragraph formatting, you do not need to select the paragraph. However, to apply paragraph formatting to two or more paragraphs at the same time, you will need to select all the paragraphs.

3. Repeat the technique just practiced to center the letterhead's second and third lines.

4. In the paragraph that begins *We have*, in the second sentence, point to the word *very*, and then double-click to select the word and display the Mini toolbar. Compare your screen.

5. With the word *very* selected, press Delete .

   When you double-click to select and delete a word, the selected word is deleted, along with the space following the word.

6. Move the insertion point in the margin to the left of *Dr. George Gato.* When the ⬧ pointer displays, drag straight down to select the paragraph and the two paragraphs below it. With the three paragraphs selected, on the **Home tab**, in the **Styles group**, click the **No Spacing** thumbnail. Compare your screen.

■ **Continue to the next page to complete the skill**

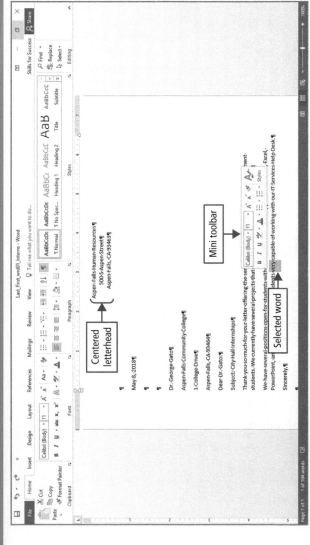

Word 2016, Windows 10, Microsoft Corporation

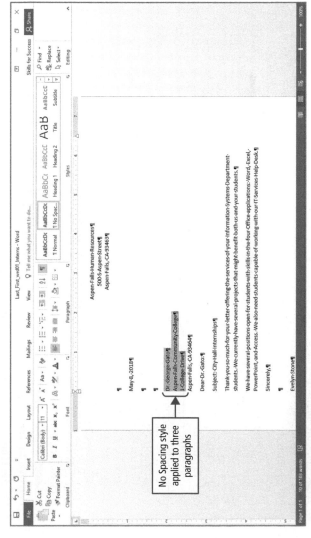

Word 2016, Windows 10, Microsoft Corporation

7. Triple-click the signature, *Evelyn Stone*, to select the paragraph, and then apply the **No Spacing** style.

8. In the paragraph that begins *Thank you,* double-click the word *us* to select it, and then type City Hall

9. In the paragraph that begins *Thank you,* click to position the insertion point at the end of the paragraph—following the period after *students*.

10. Press Enter one time, and then type I have attached a description of the positions we are currently seeking. Please call me at (805) 555-1016 to discuss this further. **Compare your screen.**

11. On the **Home tab**, in the **Editing group**, click **Select**, and then click **Select All** to select all of the text in the document. Alternately, press Ctrl + A.

12. On the **Home tab**, in the **Font group**, click the **Font arrow**. Scroll down the list of fonts, and then click **Cambria.**

13. Press Ctrl + Home and then on the Quick Access Toolbar, click the **Undo button** one time to change the font back to Calibri. **Compare your screen.**

As you work with a document, you need to be aware when text is selected. For example, if you start typing when the entire document is selected, all the text will be replaced with whatever new text you type. You can use the Undo button to fix this type of mistake.

14. Click anywhere in the document to deselect the text, and then **Save** the changes.

■ **You have completed Skill 3 of 10**

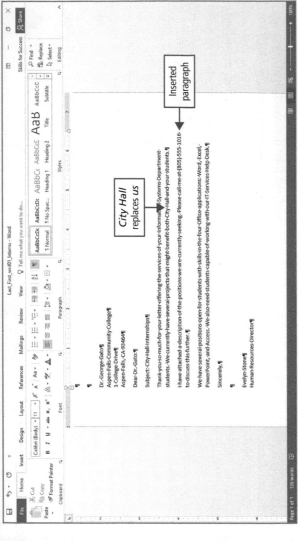

City Hall replaces us

Inserted paragraph

Word 2016, Windows 10, Microsoft Corporation

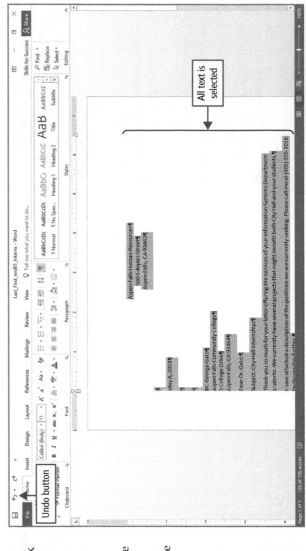

Undo button

All text is selected

Word 2016, Windows 10, Microsoft Corporation

▶ The copy command places a copy of the selected text or object in the *clipboard*—a temporary storage area that holds text or an object that has been cut or copied.

1. Press Ctrl + End to move the insertion point to the end of the document.

2. Click the **Layout tab**. In the **Page Setup group**, click **Breaks**, and then click **Page**. Alternately, press Ctrl + Enter. Compare your screen.

   A *manual page break*—forcing a page to end at a location you specify—is added at the end of Page 1.

3. On the **File tab**, click **Open**. On the **Open** page, click the **Browse** button.

4. In the **Open** dialog box, navigate to the student files for this chapter. Click **wrd01_InternPositions**, and then click **Open**.

5. On the **Home tab**, in the **Editing group**, click **Select**, and then click **Select All**.

6. With the text selected, on the **Home tab**, in the **Clipboard group**, click the **Copy** button. Alternately, press Ctrl + C.

7. On the taskbar, point to the **Word** button. Click the **Last_First_wrd01_Interns** thumbnail to make it the active window.

8. With the insertion point still at the end of the document, click the **Home tab**. In the **Clipboard group**, click the **Paste arrow**, and then compare your screen.

   The Paste button has two parts—the Paste button and the Paste arrow that displays paste options.

■ **Continue to the next page to complete the skill**

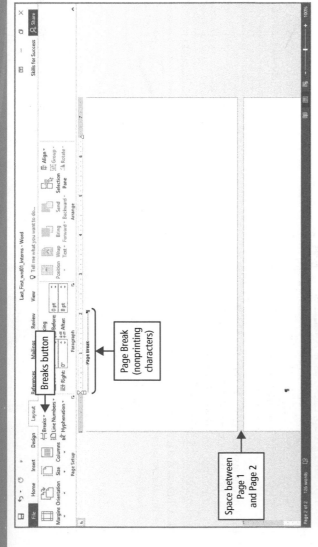

Word 2016, Windows 10, Microsoft Corporation

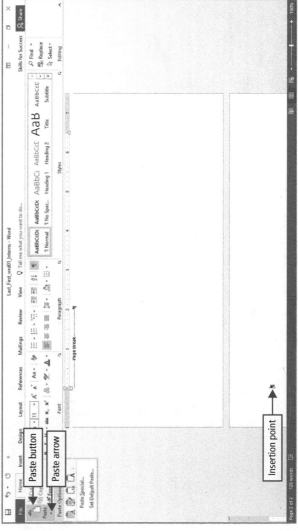

Word 2016, Windows 10, Microsoft Corporation

9. Click the **Paste** button, and then compare your screen.

When you paste, you insert a copy of the text or object stored in the clipboard and the Paste Options button displays near the pasted text. The spelling and grammar errors in the pasted text will be corrected in the next skill.

10. Press [Esc] to hide the Paste Options button. In the bulleted text, select the paragraph *Using the Internet* including the paragraph mark.

11. On the **Home tab**, in the **Clipboard group**, click the **Cut** button. Alternately, press [Ctrl] + [X].

The *cut* command deletes the selected text or object and places a copy in the Office clipboard.

12. In the bulleted list, click to place the insertion point to the left of the text *Microsoft Word* and to the right of the bullet and tab formatting mark. In the **Clipboard group**, click **Paste**. Alternately, press [Ctrl] + [V]. Compare your screen.

In this manner, you can move text by cutting it and then pasting it somewhere else.

13. On the taskbar, point to the **Word button** point to the **wrd01_InternPositions** thumbnail, and then click the thumbnail's **Close button** [X].

14. Click in the letter document to make it the active window, and then **Save** [💾] the changes.

■ **You have completed Skill 4 of 10**

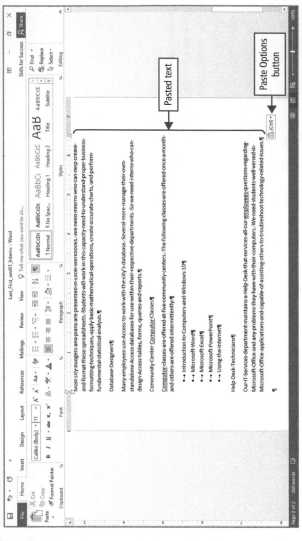

Pasted text

Paste Options button

Word 2016, Windows 10, Microsoft Corporation

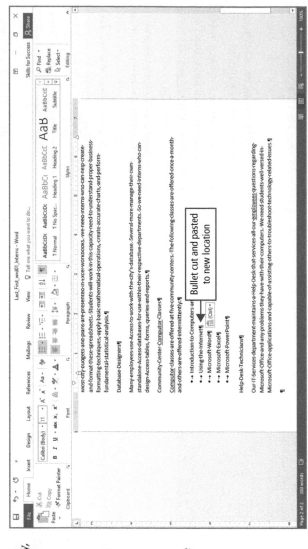

Bullet cut and pasted to new location

Word 2016, Windows 10, Microsoft Corporation

SKILL 5: Check Spelling and Grammar

▲ WATCH SKILL 1.5

▶ When you are done typing the text of a document, it is a good idea to run the Spelling and Grammar checker to check for potential errors.

1. Press Ctrl + Home to place the insertion point at the beginning of the document.

2. Click the **Review tab**, and then in the **Proofing group**, click **Spelling & Grammar**. Alternately, press F7. Compare your screen.

   Spelling and grammar errors display in a task pane on the right side of the window. The first error is a grammar error indicating the verb *has* is not in the correct form. The checker suggests that the verb be changed to *have*.

3. In the **Grammar** pane, click the **Change** button to accept the suggested verb form change and move to the next error.

4. In the **Spelling** pane, click the **Delete** button to remove the repeated word *the*, and then compare your screen.

   When a misspelled word is encountered, you can replace it with one of the suggested spellings or add it to the custom dictionary. Words added to the custom dictionary will not be flagged as spelling errors. If you accidentally add a misspelled word to the dictionary, you can open the dictionary from the Options dialog box and delete the word.

   The Spelling task pane often displays definitions to help you decide if the suggested spelling is the correct choice. By signing in to your Microsoft account, you can access additional online dictionaries.

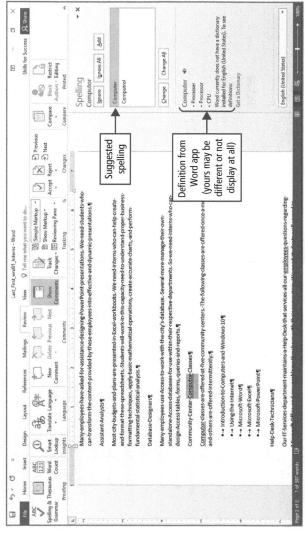

Word 2016, Windows 10, Microsoft Corporation

Word 2016, Windows 10, Microsoft Corporation

■ **Continue to the next page to complete the skill**

5. In the **Spelling** pane, click the **Change All** button to change both instances of the misspelled word, and then compare your screen.

   Many grammar errors are explained in the Grammar pane so that you can make an informed decision to ignore or accept the suggested change. Here, the word *employees* should have an apostrophe to indicate possessive use—*employees'*.

6. In the **Grammar** pane, click **employees'**, and then click the **Change** button to add the apostrophe. Compare your screen.

   When all flagged errors have been changed or ignored, a message displays indicating that the spelling and grammar check is complete. If you did not receive this message after completing this step, you may have typing errors, and you should fix them before continuing.

7. In the message indicating that the spelling and grammar check is complete, click **OK**, and then **Save** 🖫 the file.

■ **You have completed Skill 5 of 10**

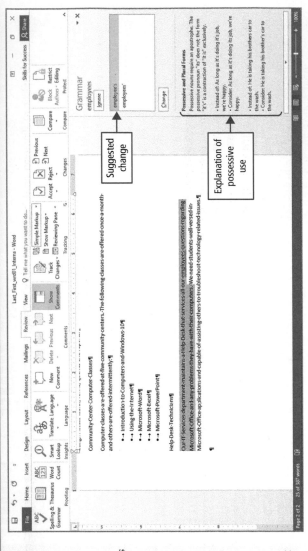

Word 2016, Windows 10, Microsoft Corporation

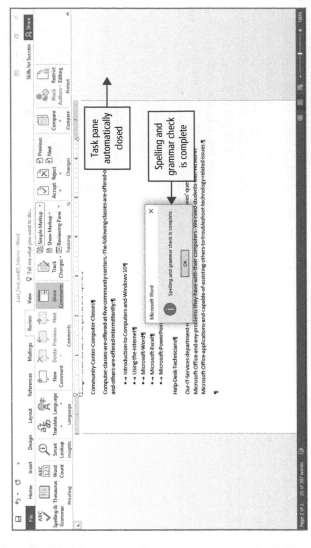

Word 2016, Windows 10, Microsoft Corporation

▶ You can insert a synonym to replace a word with a different word.

1. On the **File tab**, click **Options**. In the **Word Options** dialog box, click **Proofing** to display the spelling and grammar options.

2. In the **Word Options** dialog box, click the **Recheck Document** button. Read the message that displays, and then click **Yes**. Compare your screen.

3. In the **Word Options** dialog box, click **OK**.

4. Press **Ctrl** + **Home**, and then notice that *Gato* is again flagged as a potential spelling error.

   By clicking the Recheck Document button, you can run the Spelling & Grammar checker again, and previously ignored errors will again be flagged.

5. Scroll as needed to display the heading *Database Designers*.

6. Under the heading *Database Designers*, right-click the word *So*, point to **Synonyms**, and then compare your screen.

7. From the shortcut menu, click **Therefore**, and then notice that *Therefore* is flagged as a potential error. Right-click *Therefore*, and from the shortcut menu, click **Therefore**, to insert a comma.

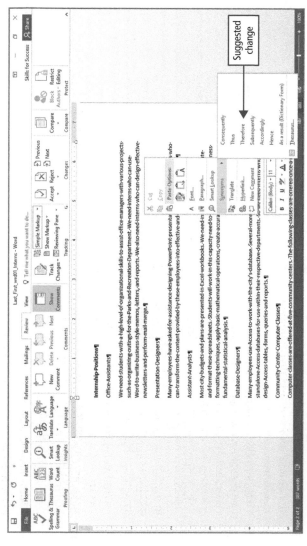

Suggested change

Word 2016, Windows 10, Microsoft Corporation

Word 2016, Windows 10, Microsoft Corporation

■ **Continue to the next page to complete the skill**

8. Point to the left of the paragraph starting *Computer classes are offered,* and then when the 🔎 pointer displays, double-click to select the entire paragraph.

9. With the entire paragraph selected, type the following: The five community centers offer the following computer classes once a month:

10. In the bulleted list, click to the right of *PowerPoint,* and then press [Enter]. On the **Home tab,** in the **Styles group,** click **Normal** to apply the default document formatting. Type We offer other classes intermittently. and then compare your screen.

11. Right-click the word *intermittently,* and then from the shortcut menu, point to **Synonyms.** Compare your screen.

The Synonyms command displays a submenu with alternate word choices. In this manner, Word Thesaurus can be accessed quickly. A *thesaurus* lists words that have the same or similar meaning to the word you are looking up.

12. From the **Synonyms** submenu, click **occasionally** to replace the word *intermittently.*

13. Save 💾 the file.

■ **You have completed Skill 6 of 10**

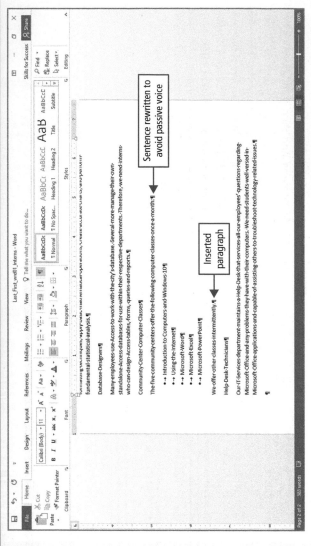

Word 2016, Windows 10, Microsoft Corporation

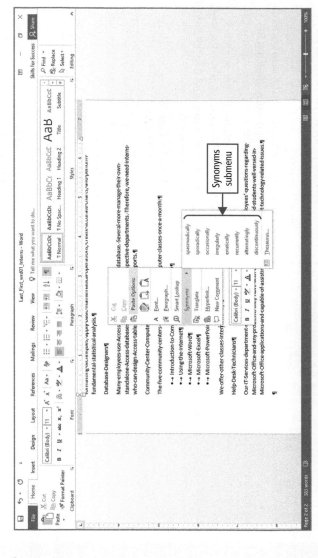

Word 2016, Windows 10, Microsoft Corporation

▶ Formatting document text should help organize the document visually without detracting from its message.

▶ A set of formatting choices can be applied with Format Painter quickly and consistently.

1. Select the first paragraph of the letterhead, *Aspen Falls Human Resources.* On the **Home tab,** in the **Font group,** click the **Font Size arrow,** and then click **16.**

2. With the first paragraph still selected, click the **Font arrow,** click **Cambria,** and then apply **Bold** B.

3. In the letterhead, drag to select the two paragraphs beginning with *500* and ending with *93463.* In the **Font group,** click the **Italic button** I, and then compare your screen.

4. In the letterhead, click in the text *Aspen Falls Human Resources.* On the **Home tab,** in the **Clipboard group,** click the **Format Painter button.**

5. Press PageDown as needed to display the top of Page 2. With the icon, drag through the heading *Internship Positions.* Compare your screen, and then release the left mouse button.

   In this manner, you can copy a collection of formatting settings to other text in the document. When you release the left mouse button, Format Painter will no longer be active.

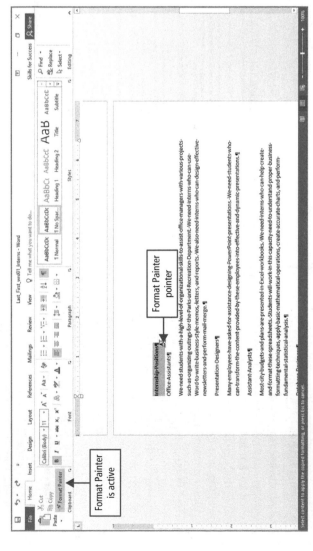

Word 2016, Windows 10, Microsoft Corporation

Word 2016, Windows 10, Microsoft Corporation

■ **Continue to the next page to complete the skill**

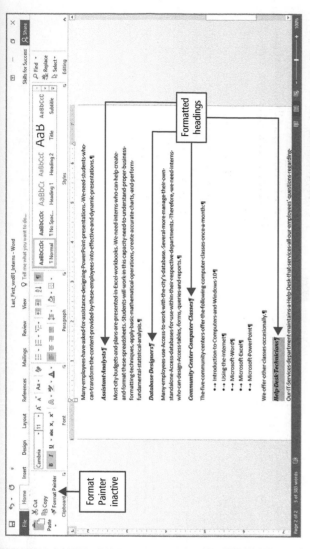

Word 2016, Windows 10, Microsoft Corporation

6. Near the top of Page 2, select the heading *Office Assistants*, and then apply the **Cambria** font, **Bold** B, and **Italic** I.

7. With the heading *Office Assistants* still selected, in the **Clipboard group**, double-click the **Format Painter** button. Drag through the *Presentation Designers* heading, and then notice that Format Painter remains active.

8. Drag through the *Assistant Analysts* heading to apply the formatting, and then repeat this technique to apply the formatting to the three remaining headings on Page 2.

9. In the **Clipboard group**, click the **Format Painter** button to release it, and then compare your screen.

   In this manner, you can use Format Painter multiple times to format headings and other document elements. You can also release Format Painter by pressing Esc.

10. **Save** the file, and then take a moment to review the common formatting options as described in the table.

▪ **You have completed Skill 7 of 10**

Common Formatting Options	
Format	**Description**
Font	A set of characters with a common design.
Font size	The size of the characters typically measured in points.
Bold	Extra thickness applied to characters to emphasize text.
Italic	A slant applied to characters to emphasize text.
Underline	A line under characters used to emphasize text.
Text efects	A set of decorative formatting applied to characters.
Highlight color	Shading applied to the background of characters.
Font color	The color applied to the characters.

▶ Dialog boxes often contain commands that are not on the ribbon. Many of these dialog boxes can be launched from their Ribbon group. For example, the Font dialog box can be opened by clicking the Dialog Box Launcher in the Font group.

1. At the beginning of the letter, select the first paragraph, *Aspen Falls Human Resources.*

2. On the **Home tab**, in the **Font group**, point to—do not click—the **Font Dialog Box Launcher** 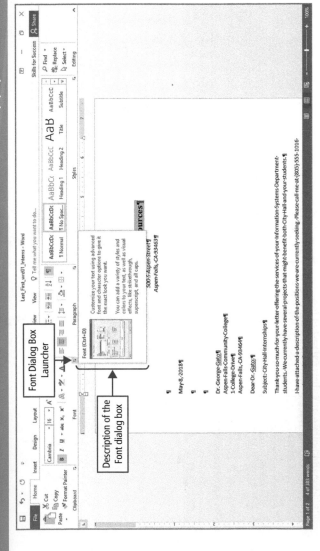, and then compare your screen.

    When you point to a Dialog Box Launcher, the name of the dialog box and the name of the keyboard shortcut that opens it display. A thumbnail of the dialog box displays next to its description.

3. Click the **Font Dialog Box Launcher** 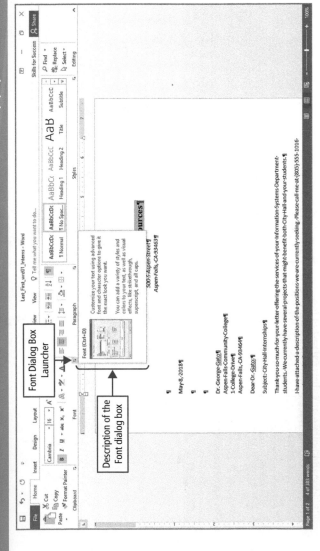 to open the Font dialog box.

4. In the **Font** dialog box, under **Font style**, click **Regular** to remove the Bold font style.

5. Under **Effects**, select the **Small caps** check box, and then compare your screen.

    The *small caps* effect displays all characters in uppercase while making any character originally typed as an uppercase letter taller than the ones typed as lowercase characters. Small caps is an alternate to using bold or italic to emphasize text. A preview of the effect displays at the bottom of the Font dialog box.

MOS
Obj

■ **Continue to the next page to complete the skill**

Word 2016, Windows 10, Microsoft Corporation

Word 2016, Windows 10, Microsoft Corporation

6. In the **Font** dialog box, click the **Advanced tab**.

7. On the **Advanced tab** of the **Font** dialog box, under **Character Spacing**, click the **Scale arrow**, and then click **150%**.

8. Under **Character Spacing**, click the **Spacing arrow**, and then click **Expanded**.

9. To the right of **Spacing**, in the **By** box, replace the value *1 pt* with *3 pt*.

10. Press Tab, and then compare your screen.

    Font sizes and the spacing between characters are measured in *points*—a unit of measure with 72 points per inch. Here, the characters will have an additional 3 points of space between them.

11. Click **OK** to accept the changes and close the dialog box.

12. Click anywhere in the document to deselect the text, and then compare your screen.

    An organization's letterhead is typically formatted differently than the rest of the letter to make it stand out. Here, the text is centered and the department's name has been expanded and stretched.

13. Save the file.

■ **You have completed Skill 8 of 10**

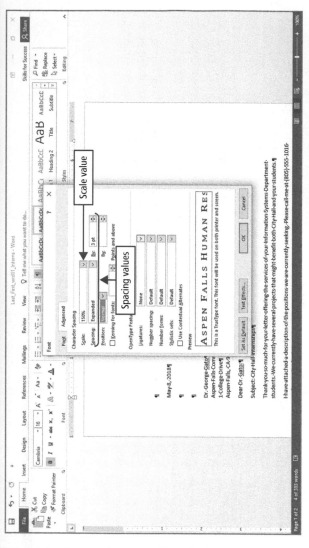

Word 2016, Windows 10, Microsoft Corporation

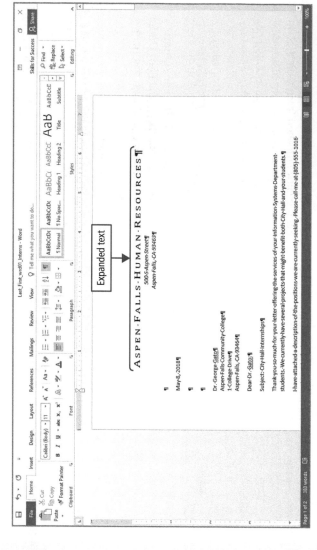

Word 2016, Windows 10, Microsoft Corporation

► A **header** and **footer** are reserved areas for text, graphics, and fields that display at the top (header) or bottom (footer) of each page in a document.

► You can insert a built-in header or footer, or you can create your own custom header or footer.

► Throughout this book, you will insert the document file name in the footer of each document.

1. Press Ctrl + Home to move to the beginning of the document. On the **Insert tab**, in the **Header & Footer group**, click the **Footer button**.

2. Compare your screen, and then in the Footer gallery scroll down to view the built-in footers.

   You can quickly insert a footer by selecting a built-in footer from the Footer gallery.

3. Below the **Footer gallery**, click **Edit Footer**. Notice that at the bottom of Page 1, below **Footer**, the insertion point is blinking in the footer, and the **Header & Footer Tools Design tab** displays on the Ribbon.

   When you want to create or edit your own custom footer, you need to make the footer area active. You can do this using the Edit Footer command or by double-clicking in the footer area.

4. On the **Header & Footer Tools Design tab**, in the **Insert group**, click the **Quick Parts** button. From the displayed list, click **Field**.

   A **field** is a category of data—such as a file name, a page number, or the current date—that can be inserted into a document.

MOS
Obj

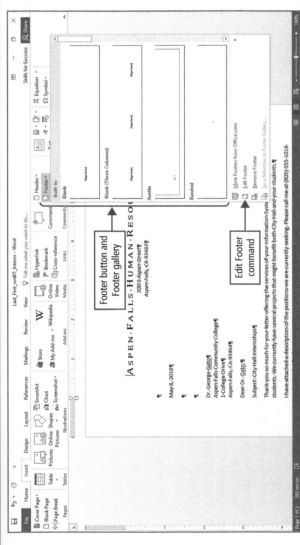

Footer button and Footer gallery

Edit Footer command

Word 2016, Windows 10, Microsoft Corporation

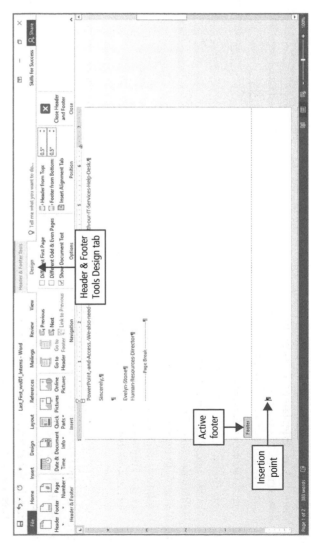

Header & Footer Tools Design tab

Active footer

Insertion point

Word 2016, Windows 10, Microsoft Corporation

■ **Continue to the next page to complete the skill**

5. Under **Field names**, scroll down to see what types of fields are available, and then click the **FileName** field. Compare your screen.

   Spaces between multiple words in field names are removed to create a single word.

6. Under **Format**, be sure that **(none)** is selected, and then at the bottom of the **Field** dialog box, click **OK** to insert the file name in the footer.

7. Scroll to display the bottom of Page 2, click the **FileName** field one time to select it, and then compare your screen.

   By default, footers are inserted on each page of the document. When you select a field, it is shaded in gray.

8. On the **Header & Footer Tools Design tab**, click the **Close Header and Footer** button. Scroll to display the bottom of Page 1 and the top of Page 2, and then notice that the header and footer areas are inactive as indicated by the dimmed file name.

   While the document text is active, the footer text cannot be edited. When the footer area is active, the footer text is black, and the document text is dimmed and cannot be edited.

9. Save the file.

■ **You have completed Skill 9 of 10**

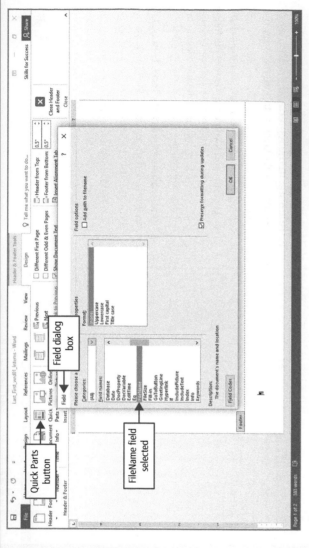

Word 2016, Windows 10, Microsoft Corporation

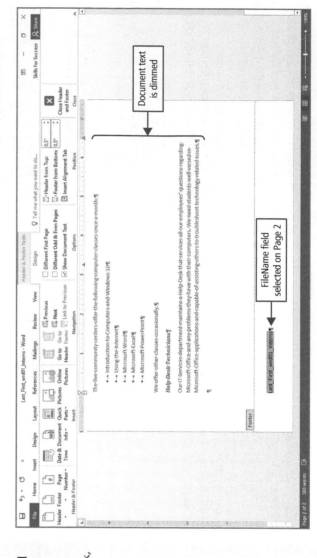

Word 2016, Windows 10, Microsoft Corporation

► Before printing, it is a good idea to set the zoom level to view one or more pages without scrolling.

► You can save documents in different formats so that people who do not have Word can read them.

1. Press **Ctrl** + **Home** to move to the beginning of the document. On the **Home tab**, in the **Paragraph group**, click the **Show/Hide button** ¶ so that the formatting marks do not display.

   Because formatting marks do not print, hiding them gives you a better idea of how the printed page will look.

2. On the **View tab**, in the **Zoom group**, click **Multiple Pages**, and then compare your screen.

   When you zoom to display multiple pages, a best fit is calculated based on your monitor size. Here, two pages are displayed with a zoom level of 47 percent. If you have a different-sized monitor, your zoom percentage may be different.

3. In the **Zoom group**, click the **100%** button to return to your original zoom level.

4. On the **File tab**, click **Print**. On the **Print** page, click the **Next Page button** ▲ to preview, and then compare your screen.

5. If you are printing your work for this project, click the **Print button** to print the letter. Otherwise, click the **Back button** ⊕.

6. Click **Save** 🖫. Click the **File tab**, and then click **Export**. On the **Export** page, click the **Create PDF/XPS** button.

■ **Continue to the next page to complete the skill**

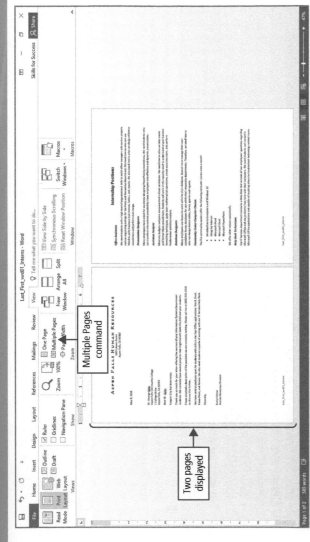

Word 2016, Windows 10, Microsoft Corporation

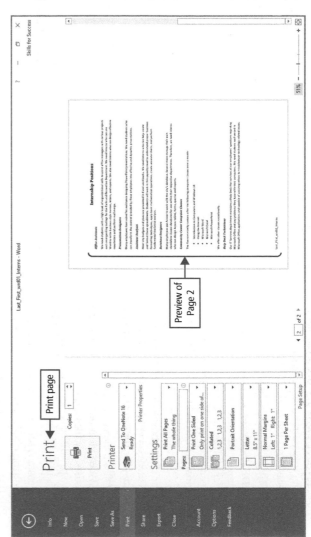

Word 2016, Windows 10, Microsoft Corporation

7. In the **Publish as PDF or XPS** dialog box, navigate to your **Word Chapter 1** folder. Notice that the Word document is not listed and the suggested file name is identical to the Word file name.

A *PDF document* is an image of a document that can be viewed using a PDF reader such as Adobe Acrobat Reader instead of the application that created the original document.

Here, you can use the file name suggested in the dialog box because a PDF document file extension will be *.pdf* instead of *.docx*—the file extension assigned to Word documents.

The Word file is not listed in the dialog box because only files with the extensions .pdf and .xps will be listed. The original Word file is in the folder and will not be altered.

8. If necessary, select the **Open file after publishing** check box, and then click **Publish.**

9. Wait a few moments for the document to publish and display in your default PDF viewer. Compare your screen.

10. **Close** your PDF viewer application window.

11. **Close** ☒ Word. If you are prompted to save changes, click Save. Submit your printout or files as directed by your instructor.

▶ **DONE! You have completed Skill 10 of 10, and your file is complete!**

Word 2016, Windows 10, Microsoft Corporation

Word 2016, Windows 10, Microsoft Corporation

PDF document open in Reader

More Skills 11

Manage Document Properties

To complete this project, you will need the following file:

- wrd01_MS11Memo

You will save your file as:

- Last_First_wrd01_MS11Memo

▶ *Document properties* are information about a document that can help you identify or organize your files, such as the name of the document author, the file name, and key words.

1. Start **Word 2016**, and then open the student data file **wrd01_MS11Memo. Save** the file in your chapter folder as Last_First_wrd01_MS11Memo

2. Click the **File tab**, and then on the Info page, notice the Properties.

3. On the **Info** page, click the **Check for Issues** button, and then click **Inspect Document**. Compare your screen.

    Document Inspector looks for comments that you may have forgotten to remove, headers or footers that you may not have intended to include, and *metadata*—information and personal data that is stored with your document. It also looks for features that may not work correctly on another computer.

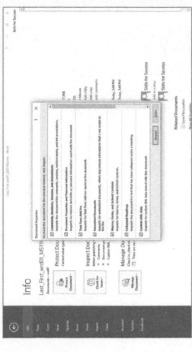

Word 2016, Windows 10, Microsoft Corporation

4. In the **Document Inspector** dialog box, be sure all of the check boxes are selected, and then click **Inspect**. To the right of **Comments, Revisions, Versions, and Annotations**, click the **Remove All** button.

    A check mark indicates that the information has been successfully removed.

5. To the right of **Document Properties and Personal Information**, click the **Remove All** button, and then **Close** the Document Inspector dialog box.

6. On the **Info** page, in the **Properties** pane, click in the **Title** box. Type City Parks and then at the top of the **Properties** list, click the **Properties** button, and then click **Advanced Properties**.

    Notice the title *City Parks* displays in the Properties dialog box.

7. Click in the **Subject** box, and then type Park Benefits Click in the **Keywords** box, and then type parks, ecology and then in the **Comments** box, type We need an in-depth report for the new park. Compare your screen, and then click **OK**.

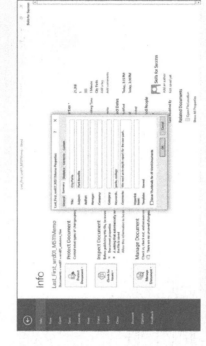

Word 2016, Windows 10, Microsoft Corporation

8. At the bottom of the **Properties** list, click **Show All Properties**.

    On the Info page, some properties are displayed automatically and others display only when you click the Show All Properties command.

9. Click the **Back** button, and then add the **FileName** field to the footer. **Save** the file, **Close** Word, and then submit the file as directed by your instructor.

- **You have completed More Skills 11**

More Skills 12

Insert Screen Shots into Documents

To complete this project, you will need the following file:

- wrd01_MS12Sites

You will save your file as:

- Last_First_wrd01_MS12Sites

▶ A *screen shot* is a picture of your computer screen, a window, or a selected region saved as a file that can be printed or shared electronically.

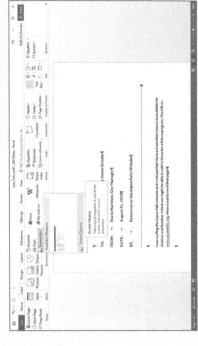

Word 2016, Windows 10, Microsoft Corporation

MOS
Obj

1. Start **Word 2016**, and then open the student data file **wrd01_MS12Sites**. Save the file in your chapter folder as Last_First_wrd01_MS12Sites

2. On the **Insert tab**, in the **Header & Footer group**, click the **Footer** button, and then click **Edit Footer**. On the **Header & Footer Tools Design tab**, in the **Insert group**, click the **Document Info** button, and then click **File Name**.

   In the **Close group**, click the **Close Header and Footer** button.

3. In the memo, locate the hyperlink *www.aspenfalls.org*. Press and hold Ctrl point to *www.aspenfalls.org*, and then with the 🖑 pointer, click the hyperlink to open the page in a web browser. If necessary, Maximize the browser window.

4. On the taskbar, click the **Word** button to return to the Word document. Press Ctrl + End to move to the blank line at the end of the document.

MOS
Obj

5. Click the **Insert tab**, and then in the **Illustrations group**, click the **Screenshot** button. In the gallery, point to **Screen Clipping**, and then compare your screen.

6. Click **Screen Clipping**. Point at the top left corner of the window, and then drag from the top left corner to the bottom right corner to select and insert the clip.

7. **Save** the file, **Close** the open windows, and then submit the file as directed by your instructor.

■ **You have completed More Skills 12**

More Skills 13

Split and Arrange Windows

To complete this project, you will need the following files:

- wrd01_MS13Donations
- wrd01_MS13EstatePlanning

You will save your files as:

- Last_First_wrd01_MS13Snip1
- Last_First_wrd01_MS13Snip2

▶ In Word, you can split the screen, which lets you look at two different parts of the same document at the same time. This is useful in a long document, for example, when you are writing a summary. The split bar indicates the location of the border between the windows.

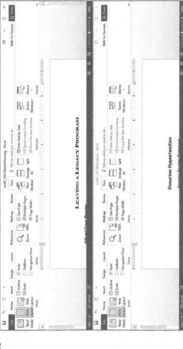

Word 2016, Windows 10, Microsoft Corporation

MOS
Obj

1. Start **Word 2016**, and then open the student data file **wrd01_MS13Donations**.

2. On the **View tab**, in the **Show group**, verify that the **Ruler** check box is selected. In the **Window group**, click the **Split** button.

3. Near the middle of the screen, point to the *split bar*—a bar that splits a document into two windows—and then compare your screen.

4. With the ⬍ pointer, drag down to move the split bar below the line that ends *how to avoid spreading them*.

5. In the lower window, scroll down to display the *Wildlife Viewing Blinds* subtitle.

6. Click ⊞ type snip and then press Enter. In the **Snipping Tool window**, click the **New arrow**, and then click **Full-screen Snip**.

7. In the **Snipping Tool mark-up window**, click the **Save Snip button** 🖫. In the **Save As** dialog box, navigate to your chapter folder, and then **Save** the snip as Last_First_wrd01_MS13Snip1 **Minimize** the Snipping Tool mark-up window.

8. On the **View tab**, in the **Window group**, click the **Remove Split** button. Alternately, drag the split bar to the top or the bottom of the document window.

9. Open the student data file **wrd01_MS13EstatePlanning**.

10. On the **View tab**, in the **Window group**, click the **Arrange All** button. Notice that both documents display in their own window, and each window has a Ribbon.

You can view two different documents side by side to make comparisons between the two, use one as a source of information, or copy text from one document to another.

11. On the taskbar, click the **Snipping Tool button**. Click the **New button** 🖉, and then create a **Full-screen Snip**. **Save** the snip in your chapter folder with the name Last_First_wrd01_MS13Snip2 and then **Close** the Snipping Tool mark-up window.

12. **Close** Word, and then submit the files as directed by your instructor.

■ **You have completed More Skills 13**

More Skills 14

Insert Symbols

To complete this document, you will need the following file:

■ wrd01_MS14Training

You will save your file as:

■ Last_First_wrd01_MS14Training

▶ When you insert a symbol, it is inserted at the position of the insertion point and the Symbol dialog box remains open.

▶ Symbols are inserted characters that are formatted in the same manner as letters you type.

▶ An *em dash* is the word processing name for a long dash in a sentence, which marks a break in thought, similar to a comma but stronger. An em dash is slightly wider than the width of the capital letter M in the existing font and font size.

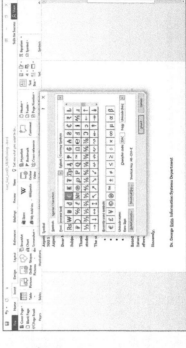

Word 2016, Windows 10, Microsoft Corporation

1. Start **Word 2016**, and then open the student data file **wrd01_MS14Training**. Save the file in your chapter folder as Last_First_wrd01_MS14Training and then add the **FileName** field to the footer.

2. In the bulleted list, click to the right of *Microsoft Word*. On the **Insert tab**, in the **Symbols group**, click the **Symbol** button to display the Symbol gallery.

3. Below the **Symbol** gallery, click **More Symbols** to open the Symbol dialog box, and then compare your screen.

    Each font has a separate set of associated symbols. You can view and search for additional symbols by changing the font. Your symbols may be different.

4. In the **Symbol** dialog box, click the **Special Characters tab** to display a list of common characters and symbol characters.

5. Click the **Registered** symbol ®, and then at the bottom of the dialog box, click **Insert**.

6. If necessary, move the **Symbol** dialog box so that you can see the bulleted list.

7. Click to the right of *Microsoft Excel*, and then insert a **Registered** symbol.

8. Move the **Symbol** dialog box so that you can see the two hyphens following the word *sessions*. Double-click the two hyphens to select them.

9. In the **Symbol** dialog box, click the **Em Dash**, and then click **Insert**.

10. In the same paragraph, select the double hyphens to the right of *adults*, and then insert another em dash. **Close** the Symbol dialog box.

11. **Save** the file, **Close** Word, and then submit the file as directed by your instructor.

■ **You have completed More Skills 14**

The following table summarizes the **SKILLS AND PROCEDURES** covered in this chapter.

Skills Number	Task	Step	Icon	Keyboard Shortcut
1	Display formatting marks	Home tab → Paragraph group → Show/Hide	¶	Ctrl + *
2	Apply styles	Home tab → Styles group → click desired style		
2	Ignore flagged words	Right-click the word, and click Ignore All		
2	Change spelling and grammar options	File tab → Options → Proofing page → Settings button		
3	Select paragraphs	Triple-click the paragraph, or with the ⌐ pointer, double-click		
3	Undo an action	Quick Access Toolbar → Undo (repeat as needed)	↶	Ctrl + Z
3	Select all	Home tab → Editing group → Select → Select All		Ctrl + A
3	Move to beginning of document			Ctrl + Home
4	Move to end of document			Ctrl + End
4	Copy text	Select text, then Home tab → Clipboard group → Copy	📋	Ctrl + C
4	Cut text	Select text, then Home tab → Clipboard group → Cut	✂	Ctrl + X
4	Paste text	Position insertion point, then Home tab → Clipboard group → Paste		Ctrl + V
5	Check spelling and grammar	Review tab → Proofing group → Spelling & Grammar		F7
7	Use Format Painter	Select formatted text, then Home → Clipboard group → Format Painter Click once for one time, double-click for multiple times		
8	Open the Font dialog box	Home tab → Font group → Dialog Box Launcher	⌐	Ctrl + D
8	Apply small caps	In Font dialog box, select Small caps check box		
8	Expand or stretch text	Font dialog box → Advanced tab		
9	Make footers active	Insert tab → Header & Footer group → Footer → Edit Footer		
9	Insert file names in footers	With footer active → Header & Footer Tools Design tab → Insert group → Quick Parts		
10	View two pages	View tab → Zoom group → Multiple Pages		
10	Save as PDF documents	File tab → Export → Create PDF/XPS		
MS12	Insert screen shot	Insert tab → Illustrations group → Screenshot		
MS13	Show the ruler	View tab → Show group → Ruler check box selected		
MS13	Split the window	View tab → Window group → Split		
MS14	Insert symbol	Insert tab → Symbols group → Symbol		

Review

Project Summary Chart

Project	Project Type	Project Location
Skills Review	Review	In Book & MIL
Skills Assessment 1	Review	In Book & MIL
Skills Assessment 2	Review	Book
My Skills	Problem Solving	Book
Visual Skills Check	Problem Solving	Book
Skills Challenge 1	Critical Thinking	Book
Skills Challenge 2	Critical Thinking	Book
More Skills Assessment	Review	In Book & MIL
Collaborating with Google	Critical Thinking	Book

MOS Objectives Covered

Create a blank document

Inspect a document for hidden properties or personal information

Insert headers and footers

Cut, copy and paste text

Customize views by using zoom settings

Insert special characters

Split the window

Apply font formatting

Add document properties

Apply formatting by using Format Painter

Show or hide formatting symbols

Apply built-in styles to text

Save documents in alternative file formats

Insert a screen shot or screen clipping

Print all or part of a document

Utilize global content standards

Key Terms

BizSkills Video

1. What is a professional network, and how would you build one?

2. What are some of the best sources for job leads?

Online Help Skills

1. With Word 2016 open, on the **File tab**, in the upper right corner of the screen, click the **Microsoft Word Help** ? button, or press F1.

2. In the **Word Help** window **Search** box, type Start up and then press Enter.

3. In the search results list, click **Word options (General)**. Maximize the Word **Help** window, and then compare your screen.

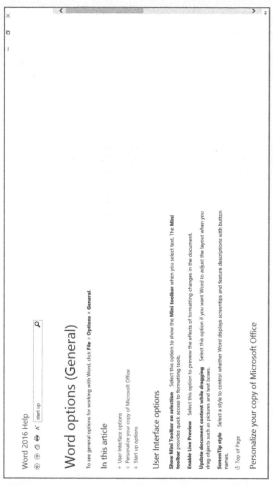

Word 2016, Windows 10, Microsoft Corporation

4. Read the article, and then see if you can answer the following question: What are some ways you can personalize your copy of Office?

Matching

Match each term in the second column with its correct definition in the first column by writing the letter of the term on the blank line in front of the correct definition.

___ **1.** A character that indicates a paragraph, tab, or space on your screen, but that does not print when you print a Word document.

___ **2.** A pre-built collection of formatting settings that can be assigned to text.

___ **3.** A red wavy line indicates this type of error.

___ **4.** Forces a page to end, and places subsequent text at the top of the next page.

___ **5.** A command that deletes the selected text or object and places a copy in the Office Clipboard.

___ **6.** A reference that lists words that have the same or similar meaning to the word you are looking up.

___ **7.** A unit of measurement for font sizes.

___ **8.** A reserved area for text, graphics, and fields that displays at the top of each page in a document.

___ **9.** A category of data—such as a file name, the page number, or the current date—that can be inserted into a document.

___ **10.** An image of a document that can be viewed using a reader such as Adobe Acrobat Reader instead of the application that created the original document.

A Cut

B Field

C Formatting mark

D Header

E Manual page break

F PDF document

G Point

H Spelling

I Style

J Thesaurus

Multiple Choice

Choose the correct answer.

1. A button used to turn a feature both on and off.
   A. Dialog Box Launcher
   B. Spin button
   C. Toggle button

2. To change Proofing settings, first display the:
   A. File tab
   B. Home tab
   C. Reference tab

3. In the Grammar Settings dialog box, which is a category that can be enabled or disabled?
   A. Check spelling as you type
   B. Small caps
   C. Subject Verb Agreement

4. A wavy line indicating a possible spelling, grammar, or style error.
   A. AutoComplete error
   B. Flagged error
   C. ScreenTip

5. This keyboard shortcut places the insertion point at the beginning of the document.
   A. Ctrl + A
   B. Ctrl + PageUp
   C. Ctrl + Home

6. The Spelling & Grammar button is located on this Ribbon tab.
   A. Home
   B. References
   C. Review

7. The Undo button is located here.
   A. Quick Access Toolbar
   B. Ribbon Home tab
   C. Ribbon Review tab

8. A font effect that displays all characters in uppercase while making any character originally typed as an uppercase letter taller than the ones typed as lowercase characters.
   A. CamelCase
   B. Small caps
   C. Uppercase

9. To view two pages at the same time, on the View tab, in the Zoom group, click this command.
   A. Fit Two
   B. Multiple Pages
   C. Two Pages

10. The typical file extension assigned to a Word document.
   A. .docx
   B. .pdf
   C. .xps

Topics for Discussion

1. Many organizations have professionally designed letterhead printed on sheets of paper. When writing a letter such as the one in this chapter, what would you need to do differently to accommodate stationery that already has your organization's name and address printed at the top? What might you need to do differently to print the letter?

2. When you check the spelling in a document, one of the options is to add unrecognized words to the dictionary. If you were working for a large company, what types of words do you think you would add to your dictionary?

Skills Review

To complete this project, you will need the following file:

- wrd01_SRParkDonations

You will save your files as:

- Last_First_wrd01_SRParks (Word)
- Last_First_wrd01_SRParks (PDF)

May 17, 2018

¶

¶

Mr. Fred Ashkenazy
2279 Shoreline Dr.
Aspen Heights, CA 93449

¶

Dear Mr. Ashkenazy:
Subject: Donation to Aspen Falls Lake Conservation Area

Word 2016, Windows 10, Microsoft Corporation

Word 2016, Windows 10, Microsoft Corporation

1. Start a blank Word document. On the **Home tab**, click the **Show/Hide** button as needed to display the formatting marks. Type Aspen Falls Parks and Recreation Department and press Enter . Type 500 S Aspen Street and press Enter . Type Aspen Falls, CA 93463 and press Enter two times. Complete the beginning of the letter with the information.

2. Press Enter , and then type Thank you for your interest in making a donation to the Aspen Falls Lake Conservation Area. You asked about projects for which we need additional resources, so I have attached a list of possible projects.

3. Press Enter , type Sincerely, and then press Enter two times. Type Leah Kim Press Enter , type Parks and Recreation Director and then apply the No Spacing style to the paragraph *Leah Kim*.

4. Select the first two lines of the letterhead. On the **Home tab**, in the **Styles group**, click the **No Spacing** button. Repeat this procedure with the first two lines of the inside address.

5. Click at the end of the paragraph that ends *possible projects*. Press Enter , and then type All donations made to the Friends of the Aspen Falls Conservation Areas (FAFCA) are tax deductible. Compare your screen.

6. **Save** the document in your **Word Chapter 1** folder as Last_First_wrd01_SRParks

7. **Open** the student data file wrd01_SRParkDonations. On the **Home tab**, in the **Editing group**, click **Select**, and then click **Select All**. On the **Home tab**, in the **Clipboard group**, click **Copy**. **Close** the document.

8. In **Last_First_wrd01_SRParks**, press Ctrl + End . On the **Layout tab**, in the **Page Setup group**, click **Breaks**, and then click **Page**.

9. On the **Home tab**, in the **Clipboard group**, click **Paste**.

▪ **Continue to the next page to complete this Skills Review**

10. Select the heading *Land Acquisitions Trust Fund* and the paragraph that follows it. On the **Home tab**, in the **Clipboard group**, click **Cut** to remove the two paragraphs.

11. Click to the left of the heading *Invasive Species Abatement*, and then in the **Clipboard group**, click **Paste**.

12. In the paragraph starting *The Land Acquisitions*, select the text *is used to expand*, and then type expands In the same sentence, change *purchase* to purchases

13. Move to the beginning of the document. On the **Review tab**, in the **Proofing group**, click the **Spelling & Grammar** button. Use the **Spelling and Grammar** task panes to fix all spelling and grammar errors in the document.

14. In the paragraph below the *Wildlife Viewing Blinds* heading, right-click *inhabitants*, and then use the **Synonyms** submenu to change the word to **populations.**

15. Using the **Format Painter**, apply the formatting in the *Land Acquisitions Trust Fund* heading to the five other headings on the page. Compare your screen.

16. In the letterhead, select the paragraph starting *Aspen Falls Parks*. On the **Home tab**, in the **Font group**, click the **Font Dialog Box Launcher.**

17. In the Font dialog box, select **Small caps,** and then click the **Advanced tab.** Change the **Spacing** to **Expanded,** leave the **By** value at **1 pt,** and then click **OK**. Apply the **Cambria** font and font size **16.**

18. On the **Insert tab,** in the **Header & Footer group,** click the **Footer** button, and then click **Edit Footer.**

19. On the **Design tab,** in the **Insert group,** click the **Quick Parts** button, and then click **Field.** Under **Field names,** scroll down and click **FileName.** Click **OK,** and then click **Close Header and Footer.** Move to the beginning of the document, and then compare your screen.

20. On the **File tab,** click **Export.** On the **Export** page, click the **Create PDF/XPS** button.

21. In the **Publish as PDF or XPS** dialog box, navigate to your **Word Chapter 1** folder. Be sure the **Open file after publishing** check box is selected, and then click **Publish.**

22. View the document in a PDF viewer, and then **Close** the window.

Word 2016, Windows 10, Microsoft Corporation

23. **Save** the file, **Close Word,** and then submit the files as directed by your instructor.

 **DONE! You have completed the Skills Review**

Skills Assessment

To complete this project, you will need the following files:

- wrd01_SA1Land
- wrd01_SA1Legacy

You will save your files as:

- Last_First_wrd01_SA1Land (Word)
- Last_First_wrd01_SA1Land (PDF)

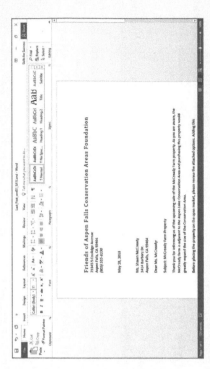

Word 2016, Windows 10, Microsoft Corporation

Word 2016, Windows 10, Microsoft Corporation

1. Start **Word 2016**, and then open the student data file **wrd01_SA1Land**. Save the file in your chapter folder as Last_First_wrd01_SA1Land Add the **FileName** field to the footer.

2. After the date, insert two blank lines and the following inside address: Ms. Shawn McCready; 1414 Barbary Dr; Aspen Falls, CA 93464

3. For the first three lines of the letterhead, apply the **No Spacing** style. Repeat this procedure with the first two lines of the inside address.

4. For the letterhead's first line, apply the **Cambria** font, font size **16**, and then set the **Character Spacing** to **Expanded** by **1.3 pt**.

5. Below the inside address, add the salutation Dear Ms. McCready:

6. After the salutation, insert a new paragraph with the text Subject: McCready Farm Property Compare your screen.

7. Open the student data file **wrd01_SA1Legacy**. Copy all of the text, and then **Close** the document.

8. At the end of **Last_First_wrd01_SA1Land**, insert a manual page break, and then at the top of Page 2, paste the contents of the clipboard.

9. On Page 2, below *Gift and Estate Planning*, replace the word *various* with the suggested synonym **several**.

10. Use **Cut** and **Paste** to move the *Outright Gift* heading and its two bullets so that the section comes before the *Life Estate Gift Annuity* heading.

11. Use the **Spelling & Grammar** checker to fix all spelling and grammar errors in the document.

12. Use **Format Painter** to apply the formatting in the *Gift and Estate Planning* heading to the five other headings on Page 2.

13. Compare your screen, and then **Save** the file.

14. Save the file as a PDF document in your chapter folder with the file name Last_First_wrd01_SA1Land **Close** Word, and then submit the files as directed by your instructor.

 DONE! You have completed Skills Assessment 1

Skills Assessment

To complete this project, you will need the following files:

- wrd01_SA2Memo
- wrd01_SA2Topics

You will save your files as:

- Last_First_wrd01_SA2Memo (Word)
- Last_First_wrd01_SA2Memo (PDF)

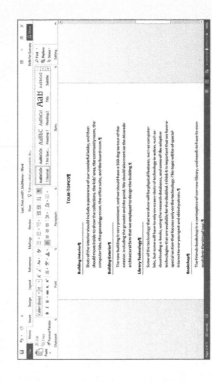

Word 2016, Windows 10, Microsoft Corporation

Word 2016, Windows 10, Microsoft Corporation

1. Start **Word 2016**, and then open the student data file **wrd01_SA2Memo**. Save the file in your chapter folder as Last_First_wrd01_SA2Memo Add the **FileName** field to the footer.

2. With the insertion point in the blank paragraph at the top of the document, apply the **No Spacing** style, and then press Enter five times. Type Memorandum

3. For the word *Memorandum*, set the **Font Size** to **36** and the **Character Spacing** to Expanded by **2.5 pt.**

4. In the last blank line of the document, type Jamie:

5. Press Enter, and then type the following paragraph: I have been thinking about the suggestion made at the Board of Trustees meeting the other night that we hire an outside company to design a virtual tour of the library. The virtual tour might consist of several modules featuring different topics. I have listed some of the topics on the next page.

6. Press Enter, and then type Let me know what you think. Press Enter two times, type Doug, and then compare your screen.

7. At the end of the document, insert a manual page break, and then on Page 2, copy and paste all of the text from the student data file **wrd01_SA2Topics.**

8. Cut the heading *Building Interior* and the paragraph that follows it, and then paste it before the *Building Exterior* heading.

9. Use the **Spelling & Grammar** checker to fix all spelling, grammar, and style errors in the document.

10. In the paragraph below *Building Exterior*, replace the word *striking* with the suggested synonym **prominent.**

11. Use **Format Painter** to apply the formatting in the *Building Interior* heading to the other four headings on Page 2.

12. Compare your screen, and then **Save** the file.

13. **Save** the file as a PDF document in your chapter folder with the name Last_First_wrd01_SA2Memo **Close** Word, and then submit the files as directed by your instructor.

▶ **DONE! You have completed Skills Assessment 2**

My Skills

To complete this project, you will need the following file:

- Blank Word document

You will save your file as:

- Last_First_wrd01_MyLetter

1. Create a blank Word document, and then save the file in your chapter folder as Last_First_wrd01_MyLetter Add the **FileName** field to the footer.

2. Type your First and Last names and then press Enter. On the next two lines of the letterhead, type your own address information. At the beginning of the document, enter the information.

3. Press Enter, and then type One of my instructors at Aspen Falls Community College, Dr. Gato, suggested that I contact you regarding internships at Aspen Falls City Hall. My studies at the college qualify me for such a position starting as early as next term.

4. Press Enter, and then type As you review the enclosed resume, please notice my training in Microsoft Office and my organizational skills. Specifically, my experience with Word and my work-study position with Dr. Gato indicate a successful internship as an Office Assistant.

5. Press Enter, and then using your e-mail address, type If you have any questions, or if you want to schedule an interview, please contact me at (805) 555-3355 or e-mail me at youremail@address.

6. Press Enter, and then type Sincerely, Press Enter two times, and then type your name.

7. Select the first two lines of the letterhead, and then apply the **No Spacing** style. Repeat this procedure with the first three lines of the inside address.

8. Using the techniques practiced in this chapter, format the letterhead to make it stand out slightly from the rest of the letter, and then compare your screen.

9. Save the file, **Close** Word, and then submit the file as directed by your instructor.

 DONE! You have completed My Skills

June 11, 2018

Evelyn Stone
Aspen Falls City Hall
500 S Aspen St
Aspen Falls, CA 93464

Dear Mrs. Stone:
Subject: City Hall Internships

Word 2016, Windows 10, Microsoft Corporation

Y o u r   N a m e
1234 N Your St
Your City, State 99999

June 11, 2018

Evelyn Stone
Aspen Falls City Hall
500 S Aspen St
Aspen Falls, CA 93464

Dear Mrs. Stone:

Subject: City Hall Internships

One of my instructors at Aspen Falls Community College, Dr. Gato, suggested that I contact you regarding internships at Aspen Falls City Hall. My studies at the college qualify me for such a position starting as early as next term.

As you review the enclosed resume, please notice my training in Microsoft Office and my organizational skills. Specifically, my experience with Word and my work-study position with Dr. Gato indicate a successful internship as an Office Assistant.

If you have any questions, or if you want to schedule an interview, please contact me at (805) 555-3355 or e-mail me at youremail@address.

Sincerely,

Your Name

Last_First_wrd01_MyLetter

Word 2016, Windows 10, Microsoft Corporation

Visual Skills Check

To complete this project, you will need the following file:

- Blank Word document

You will save your file as:

- Last_First_wrd01_VSCenter

Using the skills practiced in this chapter, create the document. **Save** the file as Last_First_wrd01_VSCenter in your chapter folder. Format the first line of the letterhead using the **Cambria** font sized at **24 points**, small caps, and expanded by **1.5 points**. Format the rest of the document using the **Calibri** font and font size **11**. Maintain the space between paragraphs. Insert the **FileName** field in the footer. **Save** the file, **Close** Word, and then submit the file as directed by your instructor.

 DONE! You have completed Visual Skills Check

ASPEN FALLS COMMUNITY CENTERS

500 S Aspen Street
Aspen Falls, CA 93463

July 13, 2018

Mrs. Natalie Lee
3947 Strong Rd
Aspen Heights, CA 93464

Dear Mrs. Lee:

Subject: Community Center Closings for the 2015 Calendar Year

Thank you for your inquiry about next year's community center closings. Please refer to the following:

Holidays: We will be closed on New Year's Day, Easter, Memorial Day, the Fourth of July, Labor Day, Thanksgiving, and Christmas.

In-Service Days: We will be closed on April 15th for a session on library security, and on November 7th for a session that will focus on streamlining the material handling process.

Close Early: We will close early on New Year's Eve, the day before Easter, the day before Thanksgiving, and Christmas Eve.

If you have any question, feel free to contact me again.

Sincerely,

Lorrine Deely
Community Center Supervisor

Last_First_wrd01_VSCenter

Word 2016, Windows 10, Microsoft Corporation

Skills Challenge 1

To complete this project, you will need the following file:

- wrd01_SC1Trustees

You will save your file as:

- Last_First_wrd01_SC1Trustees

Open the student data file **wrd01_SC1Trustees**, and then save it in your chapter folder as Last_First_wrd01_SC1Trustees

For the entire document, apply a single font that is more appropriate than Comic Sans MS. Correct or ignore all flagged spelling, grammar, and style errors as appropriate to their context. Insert a page break so the letter ends on Page 1 and the report starts on Page 2.

On Page 1, correct the paragraph alignment and paragraph spacing so that it follows the block style business letter modeled in Skills 1–10. Format the letterhead so that *Aspen Falls Public Library* stands out from the rest of the letter.

On Page 2, use cut and paste to arrange the headings and their paragraphs in alphabetical order by heading. Format the heading and side headings to visually organize the report. Be sure to apply the same formatting to all five headings.

Insert the FileName field in the footer. Save the file, close Word, and then submit the file as directed by your instructor.

 DONE! You have completed Skills Challenge 1

Skills Challenge 2

To complete this project, you will need the following file:

- **Blank Word document**

You will save your file as:

- Last_First_wrd01_SC2Recommendation

Deborah Davidson, Public Information Specialist at Aspen Falls City Hall, needs to know if the current format for city letters is still the best choice. She specifically needs to know if the *block style, modified-block style, or modified-block style with indented paragraphs* should be used.

Use a business correspondence guide from your library or search online to compare the three styles under consideration. Summarize your findings in a letter addressed to Deborah Davidson, Public Information Specialist, Aspen Falls City Hall, 500 S Aspen Street, Aspen Falls, CA 93463.

For each of the three styles, write a short paragraph describing its features and comparative advantages and disadvantages. In a fourth paragraph, recommend which style the city should use, and then justify your decision. Finally, format the letter using the style you recommended. Insert the FileName field in the footer, and save the file as Last_First_wrd01_SC2Recommendation Close Word, and then submit the file as directed by your instructor.

 DONE! You have completed Skills Challenge 2

More Skills Assessment

To complete this project, you will need the following file:

- wrd01_MSAMemo

You will save your files as:

- Last_First_wrd01_MSAMemo
- Last_First_wrd01_MSASnip1
- Last_First_wrd01_MSASnip2

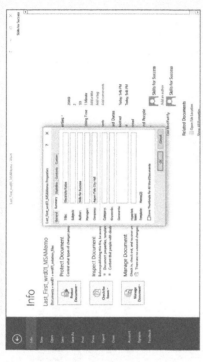

Word 2016, Windows 10, Microsoft Corporation

Word 2016, Windows 10, Microsoft Corporation

1. Start **Word 2016**, and then open the student data file **wrd01_MSAMemo**. **Save** the file in your chapter folder as Last_First_wrd01_MSAMemo

2. Open the **Document Inspector** dialog box. Verify all of the check boxes are selected, and then click **Inspect**. To the right of **Comments, Revisions, Versions, and Annotations**, click the **Remove All** button, and then **Close** the dialog box.

3. Open the **Document Properties** dialog box. Click in the **Title** box, and then type Electricity Rates Click in the **Company** box, type Aspen Falls City Hall and then compare your screen.

4. Click ▦, type snip and then press [Enter] to start the **Snipping Tool**. Click the **New arrow**, and then click **Full-screen Snip**. In the **Snipping Tool** mark-up window, click the **Save Snip** button ▦. In the **Save As** dialog box, navigate to your Word Chapter 1 folder. Be sure the **Save as type** box displays **JPEG file**. Name the file Last_First_wrd01_MSASnip1 **Minimize** the Snipping Tool mark-up window.

5. In the **Document Properties** dialog box, click **OK**.

6. On Page 2, locate the hyperlink *http://www.loc.gov/*. Press and hold [Ctrl], and then with the ⬛ pointer, click the hyperlink. If necessary, Maximize the browser window.

7. On the taskbar, click the **Word** button, and then move the insertion point to the end of the document.

8. Insert a screen clipping of the browser window.

9. On the **View tab**, verify the ruler displays, and then split the window. In the upper window, display the top of Page 1, and in the lower window, display the top of Page 2.

10. On the taskbar, click the **Snipping Tool** button. Click the **New** button ✂, and then create a **Full-screen Snip**. Save the snip in your chapter folder as Last_First_wrd01_MSASnip2 **Close** the Snipping Tool mark-up window.

11. Remove the split from the Word window.

12. On Page 1, in the paragraph above the table, replace the two hyphens with the **Em Dash** symbol.

13. Add the **FileName** field to the footer.

14. **Save** the file, **Close** Word, and then submit the files as directed by your instructor.

➤ **DONE! You have completed More Skills Assessment**

Collaborating with Google

To complete this project, you will need a Google account (refer to the Common Features chapter)

You will save your files as:

- Last_First_wrd01_GPSnip1
- Last_First_wrd01_GPSnip2

City Engineer Position

The position vacancy for the City Engineer position will need to be revised. I'm including the list of areas you will need to update. For the current working area, please refer to the City Engineer description at the HR portal.
Minimum qualifications
Salary grade
Salary range
Number of employees supervised

1. Open a web browser. Log into your Google account, and then click the **Google Apps button** .

2. Click the **Drive** button to open Google Drive. If you receive a pop-up message, read the message, and then click **Next**. Read each message, and then close the dialog box.

3. Click the **New** button, and then click **Google Docs** to open a blank document.

4. Type City Engineer Position press Enter twice, and then type the information.

5. Select *City Engineer Position*. Click the **Styles** button, and then click **Title.** Click the **Center** button .

6. Select the text *Minimum qualifications*. On the **Edit tab**, click **Cut.** Click in front of *Salary grade*. On the **Edit tab**, click **Paste,** and then press Enter .

7. On the **Insert tab**, click **Footer.** In the footer, type Last_First_wrd01_GoogleProject and then click in the document to close the footer area.

8. On the **Tools tab**, click **Spelling,** and then correct any spelling errors.

9. Click the document title, **Untitled document**. Verify **City Engineer Position** displays as the name of the document, and then press Enter .

10. Click the **Share** button, and then in the **Share with others** dialog box, type AspenFallsEvents@gmail.com to share the sheet with another user.

11. In the **Add a note** text box, type I have been informed that Human Resources now has other items that need to be updated. Please add the other items to this document. Compare your screen.

12. Click , type snip and then press Enter to start the Snipping Tool. Click the **New arrow,** and then click **Full-screen Snip.** In the Snipping

Tool mark-up window, click the **Save Snip button** . In the **Save As** dialog box, navigate to your Word Chapter 1 folder. Be sure the **Save as type** box displays **JPEG file**. Name the file Last_First_wrd01_GPSnip1 and then **Minimize** the Snipping Tool mark-up window.

13. In the **Share with others** dialog box, click **Send.**

14. On the taskbar, click the **Snipping Tool** button. Click the **New** button , and then create a **Full-screen Snip.** Save the snip in your chapter folder as Last_First_wrd01_GPSnip2

15. **Close** all windows, and then submit the files as directed by your instructor.

DONE! You have completed Collaborating with Google

CHAPTER 3

Create Business Reports

- Informal business reports are often formatted using guidelines in *The Gregg Reference Manual* by William A. Sabin. These guidelines specify the way the text is formatted, the way notes display, and the types of citations used.

- A footnote or endnote can be inserted when you have supplemental information that does not fit well in the document.

- When you use quotations or paraphrase information created by someone else, you need to cite your sources in the document and list them at the end of the document.

- Report style guidelines specify how headings and side headings should be formatted. Your guidelines should also specify how much space should be above and below paragraphs, how the first line should be indented, and how much space should be between each line.

- Document margins are the spaces that display on the outer edges of a printed page. All four page margins can be adjusted independently.

- Lists make information easier to understand. Use numbered lists when information is displayed in a sequence, and use bulleted lists when information can appear in any order.

Aspen Falls City Hall

In this chapter, you will finish a report for Richard Mack, Aspen Falls Assistant City Manager. The report provides a cost-benefit analysis regarding LED lights and makes recommendations based on that analysis. The study was conducted at the request of the city in cooperation with the Durango County Museum of History located in Aspen Falls.

If someone has requested that you write a report for them, you should ask them for guidelines regarding length, style, and format. Academic reports typically follow a set of guidelines such as MLA or Chicago, whereas the guidelines for business reports vary. Reports are either formal or informal. Formal reports include front matter, such as a separate title page and a table of contents, and back matter, such as bibliographies and appendixes. Informal reports do not contain front matter, are short in length, and may have an optional bibliography.

In this project, you will edit and format an informal business report using the guidelines from *The Gregg Reference Manual* by William A. Sabin. You will edit text and then insert comments in footnotes. Following *The Chicago Manual of Style*, you will add sources to the document, cite those sources, and then insert a bibliography. Finally, you will format the document following standard guidelines for informal business reports.

Gam16/Fotolia

Time to complete all 10
skills — 60 to 75 minutes

Student data file needed for this chapter:

wrd02_LEDs

You will save your file as:

Last_First_wrd02_LEDs

Outcome

Using the skills in this chapter, you will be able to create and modify a report; insert footnotes, citations, bibliographies, and bulleted and numbered lists; and modify paragraph formatting.

Objectives

Create an informal report

Organize a report using bulleted and numbered lists, and insert custom headers and footers

Insert and modify footnotes, citations, and bibliographies

Format a report using paragraph indents, line spacing, and page margins

SKILLS

At the end of this chapter you will be able to:

Skill 1 Find and Replace Text

Skill 2 Insert and Modify Footnotes

Skill 3 Add Sources

Skill 4 Insert Citations and Bibliographies

Skill 5 Format Bulleted and Numbered Lists

Skill 6 Set Paragraph Indents

Skill 7 Modify Line and Paragraph Spacing

Skill 8 Set Line and Page Break Options and Modify Styles

Skill 9 View Multiple Pages and Set Margins

Skill 10 Create Custom Headers and Footers

MORE SKILLS

Skill 11 Record AutoCorrect Entries

Skill 12 Use AutoFormat to Create Numbered Lists

Skill 13 Format and Customize Lists

Skill 14 Create Standard Outlines

LED LIGHTS

A Museum Exhibit Case Study

By Your Name

July 20, 2018

In April 2014, the Durango County Museum of History installed a small exhibit titled *Our heritage: Pictures from the past*. The collection consists of five daguerreotypes and several silver albumen prints. A study was made to measure the benefits and costs of using LED lights instead of traditional halogen lamps.

RISKS OF LIGHTING HISTORIC PHOTOGRAPHS

All lighting harms photographs. (Lavedrine 2003) It is the task of the conservator to minimize this harm so that the photographs can be viewed for a significant span of time, typically 50 to 100 years. For these reasons, historical photographs are displayed only periodically in rooms with significantly reduced lighting. These practices minimize the visitor experience and according to Hunt, reducing light levels diminishes color saturation and contrast. (Hunt 1952, 192)

In all lighting systems, ultraviolet light (UV) must be eliminated as that spectrum harms photographs the most. Halogen lights must have UV filters installed which adds to their cost and effectiveness. LED lamps do not emit UV light and do not need extra filters. According to a study by the Getty Conservation Institute, fading from LED lamps does not result in any more damage than conventional halogen lamps with ultraviolet filtering. They found that it is likely using LED lamps results in less fading of photographic materials. (Druzik and Miller 2015)

METHODOLOGY

In the new exhibit, 12 watt PAR38 20° lamps were utilized. The temperature rating for these lamps was 2700 Kelvin. Although the LED light output was significantly less than traditional halogen lamps, some screening was still needed. UV filters were not installed because LED lights do not emit any significant levels of ultra-violet light. This simplified the installation process.

SKILL 1: Find and Replace Text

- The Navigation pane can be used to find text quickly.

- When you need to find and then replace several instances of the same words or phrases, you can use the Find and Replace dialog box.

1. Start **Word 2016**, and then open the student data file **wrd02_LEDs**. If necessary, display the formatting marks.

2. On the **File tab**, click **Save As**, and then click **Browse**. In the **Save As** dialog box, navigate to the location where you are saving your files. Create a folder named Word Chapter 2 and then save the file as Last_First_wrd02_LEDs

3. On the **View tab**, in the **Show group**, select the **Navigation Pane** check box, and then compare your screen.

4. With the insertion point at the top of the document, press Enter five times. On the **Home tab**, in the **Styles group**, click the **Heading 1** thumbnail. Type LED LIGHTS and then press Enter. Type A Museum Exhibit Case Study and then press Enter.

5. Using your own name, type By Your Name and then press Enter. Type the current date, and then press Enter.

6. Click to place the insertion point to the left of the title. Press and hold Shift while clicking to the right of the date to select the four lines.

7. In the **Paragraph group**, click the **Center** button and then compare your screen.

   In an informal report, there should be 2 inches of space above the title, and the title, subtitle, writer's name, and date should be centered.

■ **Continue to the next page to complete the skill**

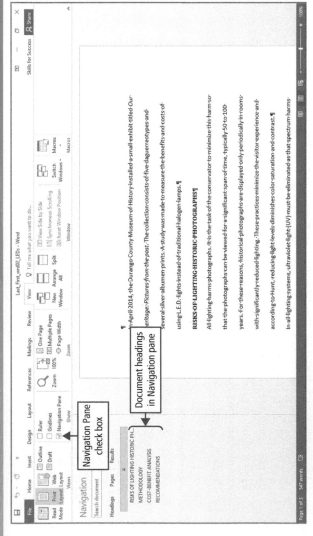

Word 2016, Windows 10, Microsoft Corporation

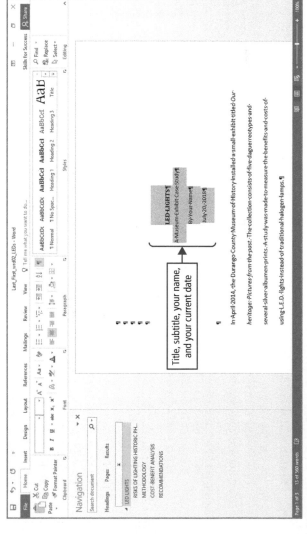

Word 2016, Windows 10, Microsoft Corporation

MOS
Obj

8. In the **Navigation** pane **Search document** box, type L.E.D. and then click **Results** to display the results.

9. Scroll to the bottom of the **Results** list, click the last search result, and then compare your screen.

   In this manner, you can quickly find and navigate to a word or phrase in a document. In the document, each instance of the searched text is highlighted.

MOS
Obj

10. Click in the document, and then press Ctrl + Home to move the insertion point to the beginning of the document. In the **Navigation** pane, click the **Search for more things arrow**, and then click **Replace** to open the Find and Replace dialog box.

11. Verify that the **Find what** box has the text *L.E.D.*, and then in the **Replace with** box, type LED Compare your screen.

   When you open the Find and Replace dialog box from the Navigation pane, the word or phrase you want to find is automatically entered into the *Find what* box.

12. Click the **Find Next** button to select the next occurrence of *L.E.D.* Click the **Replace** button to replace the initials and move to the next occurrence. Click **Replace** to replace another occurrence of *L.E.D.* with *LED*.

   In this manner, you can replace each instance one at a time.

13. Click the **Replace All** button to replace the eleven remaining occurrences. Read the message that displays, click **OK**, and then **Close** the Find and Replace dialog box. **Save** 🖫 the file.

■ **You have completed Skill 1 of 10**

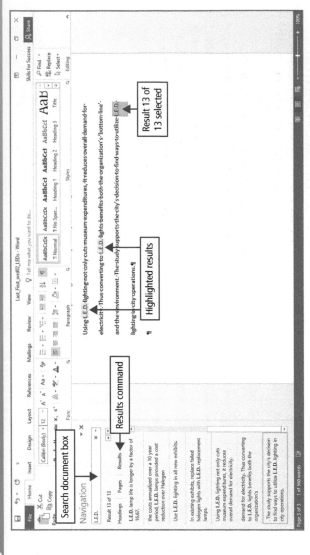

Word 2016, Windows 10, Microsoft Corporation

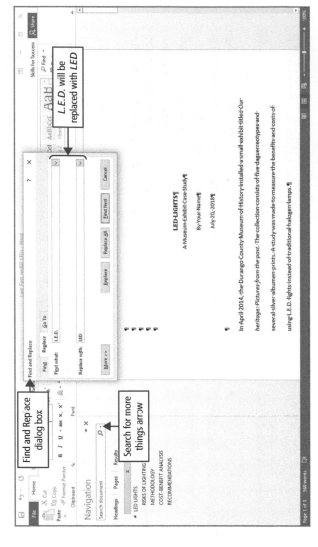

Word 2016, Windows 10, Microsoft Corporation

SKILL 2: Insert and Modify Footnotes

► A *footnote* is a note or comment placed at the bottom of the page. An *endnote* is a note or comment placed at the end of a section or a document.

1. In the **Navigation** pane, click the **Headings** command, and then click the **METHODOLOGY** heading to display that section of the report.

2. Click to the right of the period in the paragraph ending *output to the desired level*. Click the **References tab**, and then in the **Footnotes group**, click the **Insert Footnote** button.

   A footnote displays at the bottom of the page with a number 1 before the insertion point. A line is also inserted above the footnote area to separate it from the document text.

3. Type Screening is the process of installing layers of metal window screen. Compare your screen.

4. Navigate to the **COST-BENEFIT ANALYSIS** section, and then click to the right of the sentence ending *LED lamp life is longer by a factor of 16.67*.

5. Repeat the technique just practiced to insert a second footnote with the text Derived from industry standards. Compare your screen.

   Footnote numbers are inserted and formatted as *superscript*—text that is positioned higher and smaller than the other text.

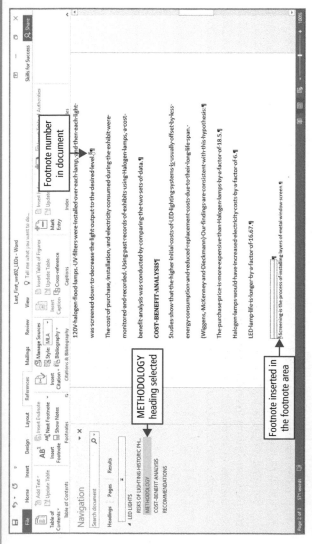

METHODOLOGY heading selected

Footnote number in document

Footnote inserted in the footnote area

Word 2016, Windows 10, Microsoft Corporation

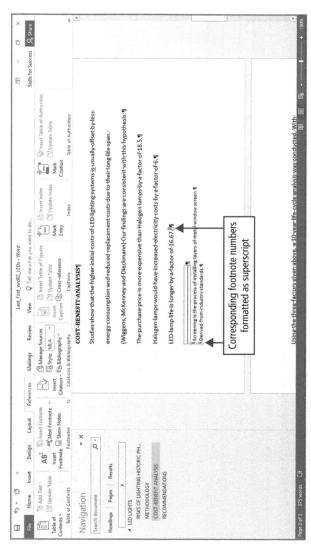

Corresponding footnote numbers formatted as superscript

Word 2016, Windows 10, Microsoft Corporation

■ **Continue to the next page to complete the skill**

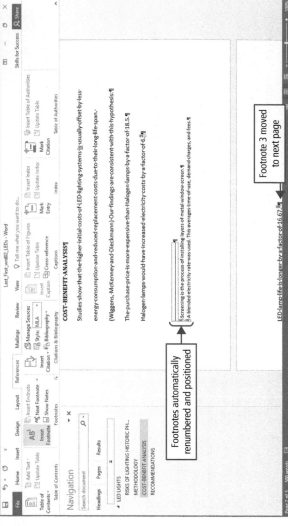

Footnotes automatically renumbered and positioned

Footnote 3 moved to next page

Word 2016, Windows 10, Microsoft Corporation

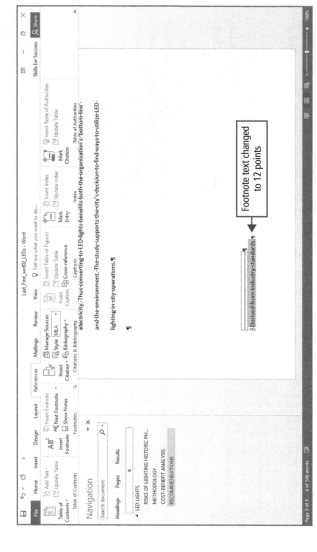

Footnote text changed to 12 points

Word 2016, Windows 10, Microsoft Corporation

6. Above the footnotes, click to the right of the sentence ending *increased electricity costs by a factor of 6.* Insert another footnote with the text A blended electricity rate was used. This averages time-of-use, demand charges, and fees. Compare your screen.

   Footnotes automatically position themselves at the bottom of the correct page and adjust so that they are renumbered sequentially.

7. At the bottom of Page 2, select the text of the first footnote without selecting the footnote number. Change the font size to **12.**

   Most style manuals call for the footer text to be the same size as the document text. Footnote numbers are typically smaller than the report text.

8. Repeat the technique just practiced to change the text of the second footnote to 12 points. Take care to format just the text and not the footnote number.

9. Scroll to the bottom of Page 3 to display the third footnote, and then change the footnote text to **12 points.**

10. Compare your screen and then **Save** 🔲 the file.

■ **You have completed Skill 2 of 10**

SKILL 3: Add Sources

▶ A ***source*** is the reference used to find information or data.

1. On the **References tab**, in the **Citations & Bibliography group**, click the **Style arrow**, and then click **Chicago Sixteenth Edition**.

2. In the **Citations & Bibliography group**, click **Manage Sources**, and then under **Current List**, click the source starting *Wiggens*. Compare your screen.

   The Master List sources are available for all your documents, and the Current List sources are available only for a single document. The Preview pane displays citations and bibliography entries in the format for the selected style—here, Chicago Sixteenth Edition. The check mark indicates that the source has been cited in the document.

3. Click the **New button**, and then verify the **Type of Source** is **Book**.

4. In the **Author box**, type Bertrand Lavedrine and then in the **Title box**, type A Guide to the Preventive Conservation of Photograph Collections

5. For the **Year**, type 2003 and for the **City**, type Los Angeles For the **Publisher**, type Getty Conservation Institute and then compare your screen.

   The Create Source dialog box displays the fields required by the Chicago style for the selected source type.

6. Click **OK**, and then in **Source Manager**, preview the new source's citation and bibliography entry.

   The author's last name followed by a comma was placed before the first name when you closed the dialog box.

7. Click the **New button**, and then change the **Type of Source** to **Journal Article**.

■ **Continue to the next page to complete the skill**

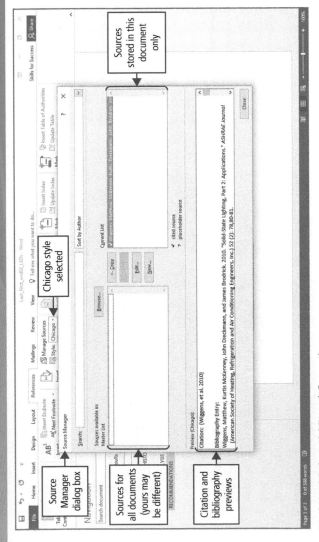

Word 2016, Windows 10, Microsoft Corporation

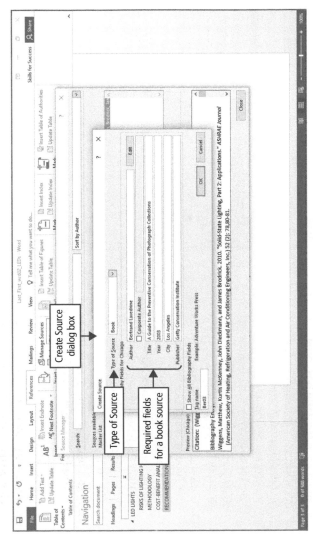

Word 2016, Windows 10, Microsoft Corporation

8. In the **Author** box, type Hunt, Robert W and then in the **Title** box, type Light and Dark Adaptation and Perception of Color

9. For the **Journal Name**, type Journal of the Optical Society of America and in the **Year** box, type 1952 In the **Pages** box, type 190-199 Compare your screen and then click **OK**.

10. Click the **New** button, and then change the **Type of Source** to **Web site.**

11. In the **Author** box, type Druzik, Jim; Miller, Naomi and then in the **Name of Web Page** box, type Guidelines for Selecting Solid State Lighting for Museums

12. In the **Year** box, type 2015 In the **Year Accessed** box, type 2018 The **Month Accessed** is April and the **Day Accessed** is 13

13. In the **URL** box, type http://www. getty.edu/conservation/our_projects/ science/lighting/lighting_component8. html Compare your screen and then click **OK.**

14. In the **Source Manager** dialog box **Master List,** select the first source created in this skill. Verify you selected the title in the **Master List**—*not* the one in the Current List—and then click the **Delete** button. Repeat to delete the other two sources created in this skill from the **Master List,** and then click the **Close** button.

When you add a new source, it is placed in both the Master and Current Lists. If you do not plan to use a source in other documents, it can be deleted from the Master List. However, take care to leave the sources in the Current List.

■ **You have completed Skill 3 of 10**

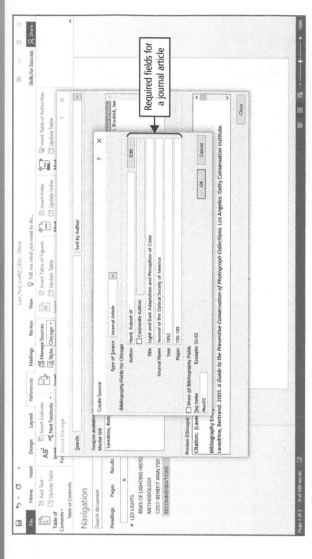

Word 2016, Windows 10, Microsoft Corporation

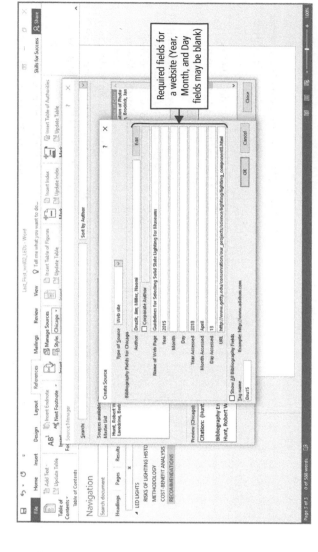

Word 2016, Windows 10, Microsoft Corporation

SKILL 4: Insert Citations and Bibliographies

► When you quote or refer to information from another source, you need to credit that source.

► A **bibliography** is a compilation of sources referenced in a report and listed on a separate page.

► A **citation** is a note in the document that refers the reader to a source in the bibliography.

1. Navigate to the **RISKS OF LIGHTING HISTORIC PHOTOGRAPHS** section.

2. Click to the right of the period ending the first sentence *All lighting harms photographs*. On the **References tab**, in the **Citations & Bibliography group**, click **Insert Citation**, and then compare your screen.

   When you insert a citation field, the sources stored in Source Manager display in the gallery.

3. In the **Citation** gallery, click the **Lavedrine, Bertand** source to insert the citation.

4. In the same paragraph, click to the right of the period of the sentence ending *saturation and contrast*. Repeat the technique just practiced to insert the citation for **Hunt, Robert W.**

5. Click the citation just inserted, click the field's **Citation Options arrow**, and then click **Edit Citation**. In the **Pages** box, type 192 click **OK**, and then compare your screen.

   Many business reports use the **author–date citation**, which contains the author's last name, the publication year, and the specific page number(s) if one is available.

■ **Continue to the next page to complete the skill**

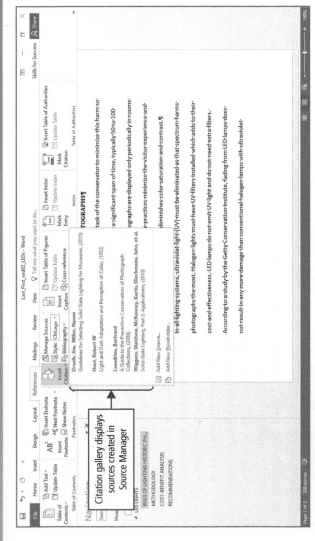

Word 2016, Windows 10, Microsoft Corporation

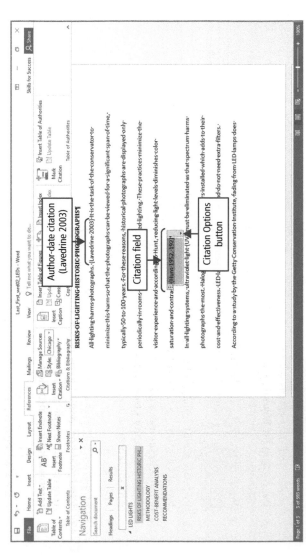

Word 2016, Windows 10, Microsoft Corporation

6. At the top of Page 2, click to the right of the period of the sentence ending *fading of photographic materials,* and then insert the citation for **Druzik, Jim, Miller, Naomi.**

7. Press Ctrl + End, and then press Ctrl + Enter to insert a manual page break and start a new page. Press Enter two times to create about 2 inches of space from the top of the page.

8. On the **References tab,** in the **Citations & Bibliography group,** click the **Bibliography** button, and then compare your screen.

9. From the gallery, click the **Bibliography** thumbnail to insert a bibliography field. If necessary, scroll up to display the inserted bibliography field.

   In the Chicago style, the Bibliography field displays each source using hanging indents. In a *hanging indent,* the first line extends to the left of the rest of the paragraph.

10. Double-click the *Bibliography* title, and then type BIBLIOGRAPHY In the Navigation pane, verify that the *BIBLIOGRAPHY* title has been added as a level 1 heading. Compare your screen.

    In an informal report, the first-level headings should be uppercase and centered. You will center this title in a later skill.

11. Save 🖫 the file.

    If you change the reference style or report sources, you can update the citation and bibliography fields by clicking the field and then selecting its update command.

■ **You have completed Skill 4 of 10**

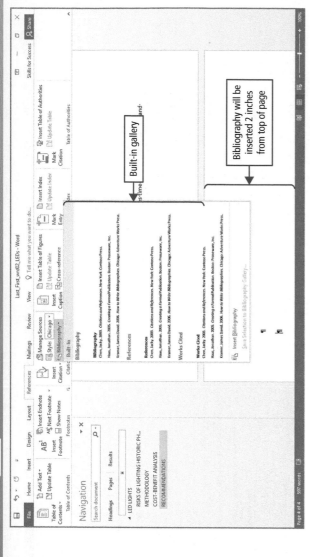

Word 2016, Windows 10, Microsoft Corporation

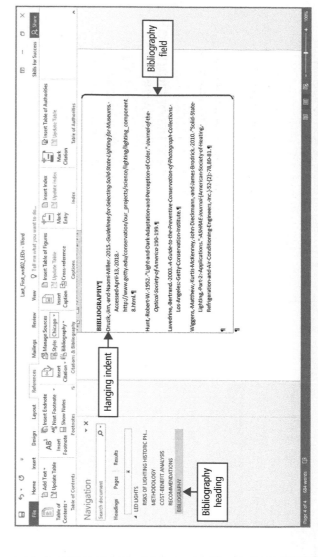

Word 2016, Windows 10, Microsoft Corporation

SKILL 5: Format Bulleted and Numbered Lists

▶ A **bulleted list** is a list of items with each item introduced by a symbol—such as a small circle or check mark—in which the list items can be presented in any order.

1. Navigate to the **COST-BENEFIT ANALYSIS** section.

2. If necessary, scroll down to display the bottom of Page 2 and the top of Page 3.

3. Point to the left of the paragraph that starts *The purchase price is more* to display the ⬈ pointer, and then drag straight down to select the three paragraphs starting *The purchase price* and ending with *factor of 16.67* including the footnote number and paragraph marks. Compare your screen.

   When you select text with footnotes, the text in the footnotes area will not be selected.

4. If your ruler does not display, on the **View tab**, in the **Show group**, select the **Ruler** check box.

5. On the **Home tab**, in the **Paragraph group**, click the **Bullets arrow** ⊞▾, and then in the **Bullets gallery**, click the solid circle bullet. **[MOS Obj]**

   The Bullets gallery displays commonly used bullet characters, and the most recently used bullet displays at the top.

6. In the **Paragraph group**, click the **Increase Indent button** ⬚ one time, and then compare your screen. **[MOS Obj]**

   In reports, lists are typically indented 0.5 inches on the left with a hanging indent set to 0.25 inches for the first line.

■ **Continue to the next page to complete the skill**

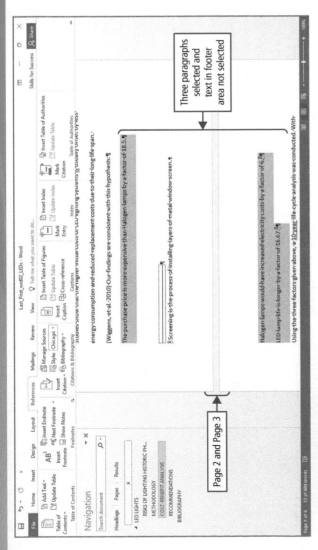

Word 2016, Windows 10, Microsoft Corporation

Three paragraphs selected and text in footer area not selected

Page 2 and Page 3

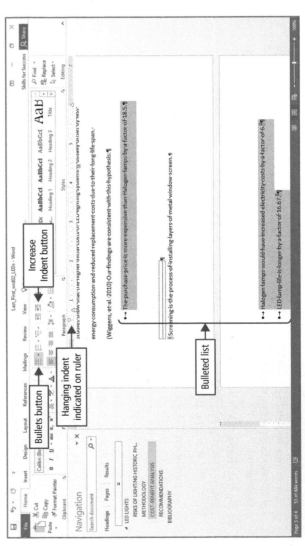

Word 2016, Windows 10, Microsoft Corporation

Bullets button

Hanging indent indicated on ruler

Increase Indent button

Bulleted list

7. Navigate to the **RECOMMENDATIONS** section, and then select the four paragraphs beginning *Use LED lighting in all new* and ending with *City Hall departments*.

8. On the **Home tab**, in the **Paragraph group**, click the **Numbering arrow**, and then compare your screen.

   A ***numbered list*** is a list of items with each item introduced by a consecutive number or letter to indicate definite steps, a sequence of actions, or chronological order.

   The Numbering gallery displays common formats that can be used to enumerate lists. For all lists, you should refer to the style guidelines specified for your report. Certain bullet characters may be specified or a different numbering system may need to be applied.

9. In the **Numbering** gallery, click the thumbnail with the **1. 2. 3.** formatting.

10. In the **Paragraph group**, click the **Increase Indent button** one time, and then compare your screen.

11. Save the file.

■ **You have completed 5 of 10**

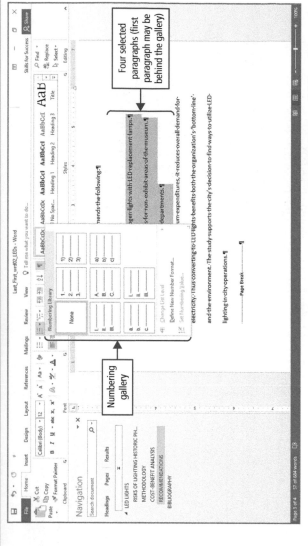

Numbering gallery

Four selected paragraphs (first paragraph may be behind the gallery)

Word 2016, Windows 10, Microsoft Corporation

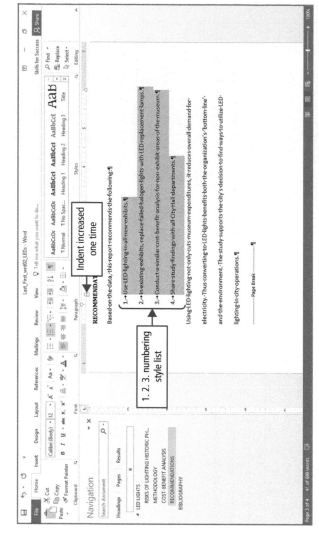

1. 2. 3. numbering style list

Indent increased one time

Word 2016, Windows 10, Microsoft Corporation

SKILL 6: Set Paragraph Indents

▶ An *indent* is the position of paragraph lines in relation to a page margin.

1. Navigate to the **LED LIGHTS** heading, and then click in the body paragraph that starts *In April 2014.*

2. On the **Home tab**, in the **Paragraph group**, click the **Paragraph Dialog Box Launcher** ◻.

   The Paragraph dialog box has commands and settings that are not available in the Paragraph group.

3. Under **Indentation**, click the **Special arrow**, and then click **First line**. Compare your screen.

   The *first line indent* is the location of the beginning of the first line of a paragraph in relation to the left edge of the remainder of the paragraph. In this case, the *By* box displays *0.5″*, which will indent the first line of the current paragraph one-half inch.

4. Click **OK** to indent the first line of the paragraph. On the ruler, verify that the **First Line Indent** marker is now at the **0.5 inch** mark.

5. Click in the paragraph starting *All lighting harms photographs*. Press F4 to repeat the previous task.

   The F4 keyboard shortcut repeats the last command. If you performed an additional task after setting the previous indent, you will need to set the indent using the Paragraph dialog box.

6. Click in the next paragraph starting *In all lighting systems*, press F4, and then compare your screen.

■ **Continue to the next page to complete the skill**

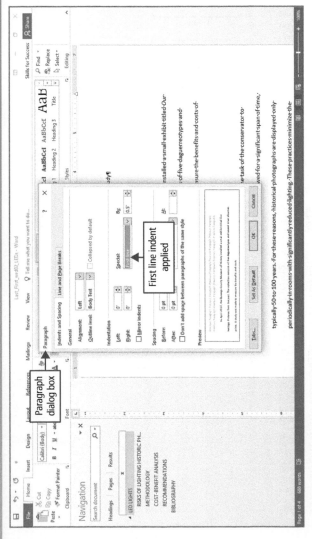

Word 2016, Windows 10, Microsoft Corporation

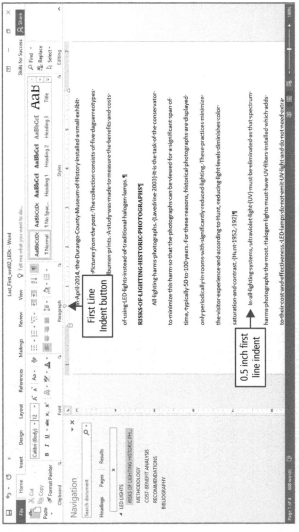

Word 2016, Windows 10, Microsoft Corporation

7. In the **METHODOLOGY** section, click in the first paragraph beginning *In the new exhibit.* On the ruler, drag the **First Line Indent** button to the **0.5 inch** mark on the ruler.

   In this manner, you can set the first line indent in the Paragraph dialog box or on the ruler.

8. Select the two paragraphs beginning *In the past* and *The cost of purchase*, and then repeat one of the techniques practiced in this skill to set a **0.5 inch** first line indent to both paragraphs.

9. Navigate to the **COST-BENEFIT ANALYSIS** section, and then apply a **0.5 inch** first line indent to the two paragraphs starting *Studies show that* and *Using the three factors.* Compare your screen.

   Recall that the bulleted list was indented to 0.5 inches in the previous skill and already has a hanging indent.

10. Navigate to the **RECOMMENDATIONS** section, and then apply a **0.5 inch** first line indent to the two paragraphs starting *Based on the data* and *Using LED lighting not only cuts.* Compare your screen.

    In a report, the paragraph first line indents and the bullets or numbers in a list should all align at the 0.5 inch mark.

11. **Save** 🖫 the file.

■ **You have completed Skill 6 of 10**

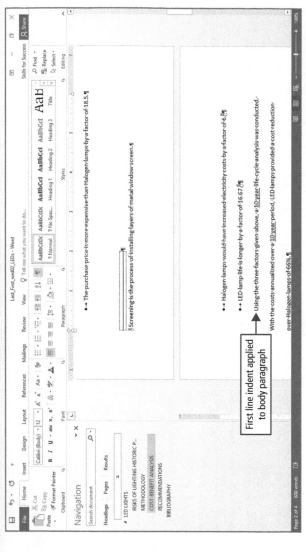

First line indent applied to body paragraph

Word 2016, Windows 10, Microsoft Corporation

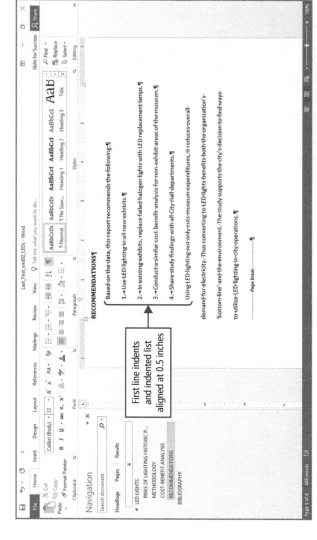

First line indents and indented list aligned at 0.5 inches

Word 2016, Windows 10, Microsoft Corporation

SKILL 7: Modify Line and Paragraph Spacing

▶ **Line spacing** is the vertical distance between lines of text in a paragraph, and **paragraph spacing** is the vertical distance above and below each paragraph. Both may need to be adjusted to match your report's style guide.

MOS
Obj

1. In the **Navigation** pane, click the **LED LIGHTS** heading. Select the title and the three paragraphs after it. On the **Home** tab, in the **Paragraph group**, click the **Paragraph Dialog Box Launcher** □.

2. In the **Paragraph** dialog box, under **Spacing**, click the **Before up spin arrow** one time to change the value to **0 pt**, and then change the **After** value to **12 pt**.

3. Click the **Line spacing arrow**, and then click **Single**. Compare your screen and then click **OK**.

Reports should have a blank line between each element. The style guide you follow should specify if this should be done by inserting a blank paragraph or by adjusting the paragraph spacing.

4. Click in the body paragraph that begins *In April 2014*. In the **Paragraph group**, click the **Line and Paragraph Spacing** button ‡=‡, and then compare your screen.

To increase readability in longer reports, the default line spacing should be 2.0, which is **double-spacing**—the equivalent of a blank line of text displays between each line of text.

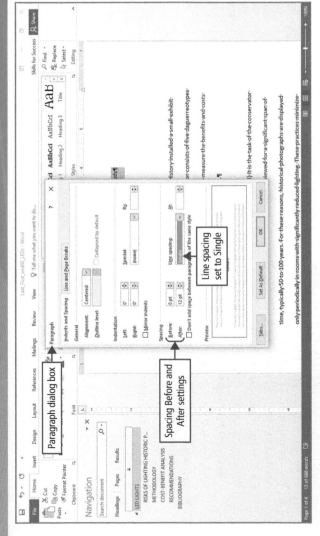

Word 2016, Windows 10, Microsoft Corporation

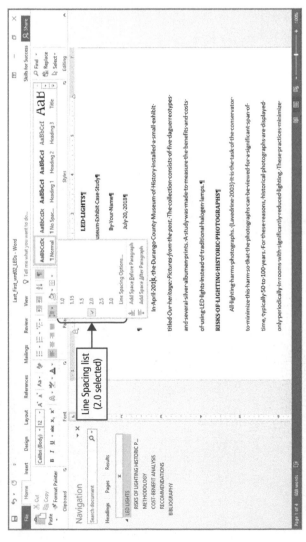

Word 2016, Windows 10, Microsoft Corporation

■ **Continue to the next page to complete the skill**

SKILL 7: Modify Line and Paragraph Spacing ▶ **WATCH** SKILL 3.7

5. In the **Line and Paragraph Spacing** list, point to **1.15** to preview the setting, and then click **1.15**.

In shorter, informal reports such as this report, you can reduce the amount of line spacing so that the report fits on fewer pages. Text with a line spacing of 1.15 has been found to be easier to read than single-spaced text.

6. Open the **Paragraph** dialog box, and then change the **After** setting to **12 pt**. Compare your screen and then click **OK**.

7. With the insertion point still in the paragraph, double-click the **Format Painter** button. With the **Format Painter** pointer, click one time in the nine remaining body paragraphs—do not drag—to apply the line and paragraph spacing formatting. Do not apply the formatting to the headings, bulleted list items, numbered list items, or bibliography items. When you are done, click the **Format Painter** button so it is no longer active.

8. Navigate to the **COST-BENEFIT ANALYSIS** section, and then select the first two bulleted list items. In the **Paragraph** group, click the **Line and Paragraph Spacing** button, and then click **1.15**.

9. In the **RECOMMENDATIONS** section, select the first three numbered list items, and then set the **Line Spacing** to **1.15**. Compare your screen.

10. Save the file.

■ **You have completed Skill 7 of 10**

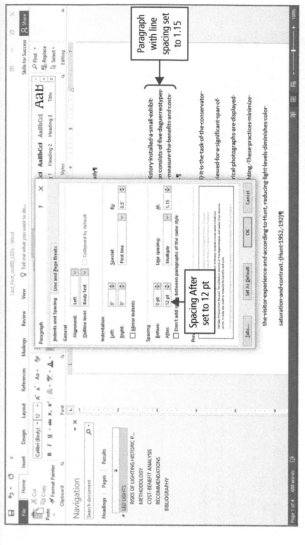

Word 2016, Windows 10, Microsoft Corporation

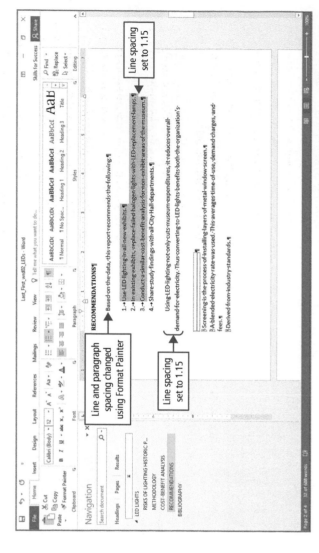

Word 2016, Windows 10, Microsoft Corporation

SKILL 8: Set Line and Page Break Options and Modify Styles

► You may need to adjust line and page break options to avoid problems when headings and paragraphs split across two pages.

► You can format elements quickly by modifying the styles assigned to them.

1. In the **Navigation** pane, click the **BIBLIOGRAPHY** header, and then compare your screen.

   The Bibliography header was assigned the Heading 1 style, but it does not have the same alignment and paragraph spacing as the document title.

2. Navigate to the document title, **LED LIGHTS**. With the insertion point in the title paragraph, on the **Home tab**, in the **Styles group**, right-click the **Heading 1** thumbnail. From the shortcut menu, click **Update Heading 1 to Match Selection**.

   Recall that for paragraph formatting, the paragraph does not actually need to be selected. Here, the Heading 1 style was updated based on the formatting of the paragraph the insertion point was in.

3. Navigate to the **BIBLIOGRAPHY** heading, and then compare your screen.

   The heading is now center aligned with 12 points of space below the paragraph. In this manner, you can format a document quickly by modifying its styles.

4. Navigate to the **METHODOLOGY** section. Click in the paragraph that begins *In the new exhibit*, and then open the **Paragraph** dialog box.

■ **Continue to the next page to complete the skill**

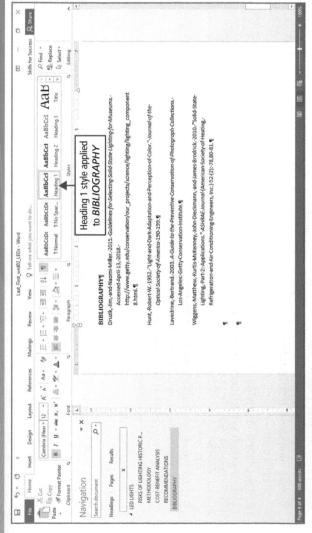

Word 2016, Windows 10, Microsoft Corporation

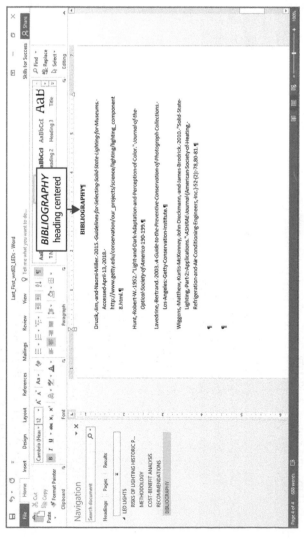

Word 2016, Windows 10, Microsoft Corporation

5. In the **Paragraph** dialog box, click the **Line and Page Breaks tab**, clear the **Widow/Orphan control** check box, and then click **OK**. Compare your screen.

   The top of Page 3 displays a *widow*—the last line of a paragraph displays as the first line of a page. An *orphan* is the first line of a paragraph that displays as the last line of a page. Both widows and orphans should be avoided.

6. On the **Quick Access Toolbar**, click the **Undo** button to enable widow and orphan control. Alternately, press Ctrl + Z.

7. Click to place the insertion point in the *METHODOLOGY* header. In the **Styles group**, right-click the **Heading 2** thumbnail, and then from the shortcut menu, click **Modify**.

8. In the lower corner of the **Modify Style** dialog box, click the **Format** button, and then click **Paragraph**.

9. On the **Line and Page Breaks tab** of the **Paragraph** dialog box, select the **Keep with next** check box, and then compare your screen.

10. Click **OK** two times to close the dialog boxes and update the Heading 2 style.

    Headings should have the *Keep with next* option selected so that at least two lines of the paragraph that follows them always display on the same page as the heading. Here, the setting has been applied to all the document's side headings—Heading 2.

11. **Save** the file.

■ **You have completed 8 of 10**

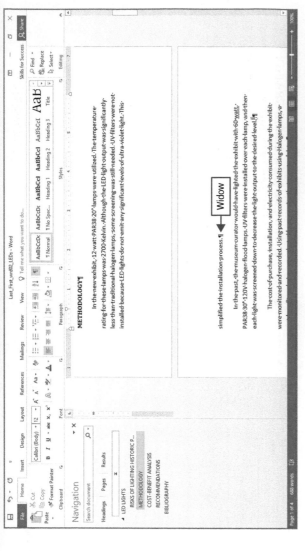

Word 2016, Windows 10, Microsoft Corporation

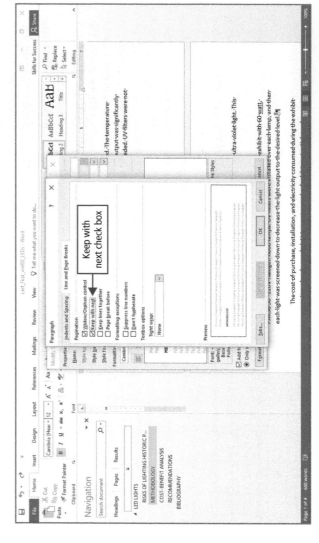

Word 2016, Windows 10, Microsoft Corporation

SKILL 9: View Multiple Pages and Set Margins

▶ **Margins** are the spaces between the text and the top, bottom, left, and right edges of the paper.

▶ Viewing multiple pages on a single screen is useful when you need to evaluate the overall layout of a document.

MOS
Obj

1. Navigate to the **LED LIGHTS** heading. On the **View tab**, in the **Zoom group**, click **Multiple Pages**. Compare your screen.

   The number of pages that display when you view multiple pages depends on the dimensions of your monitor or window. On large monitors, your window may be large enough to display three pages and the text may be large enough to edit and format.

2. In the **Navigation** pane, click the **BIBLIOGRAPHY** heading. **Close** ☒ the Navigation pane, and then compare your screen.

   Depending on the audience, you may want to reduce the length of a report to as few pages as possible. Here, the end of the report body uses a small portion of Page 3. Reducing the size of the side margins may fit the report on three pages instead of four.

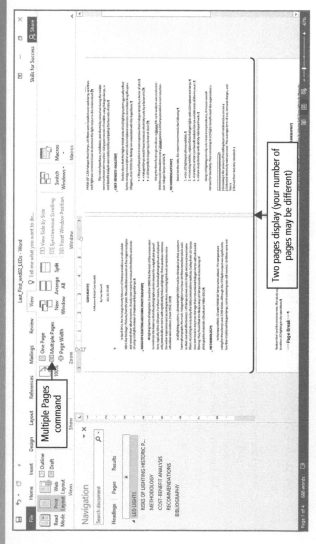

Multiple Pages command

Two pages display (your number of pages may be different)

Word 2016, Windows 10, Microsoft Corporation

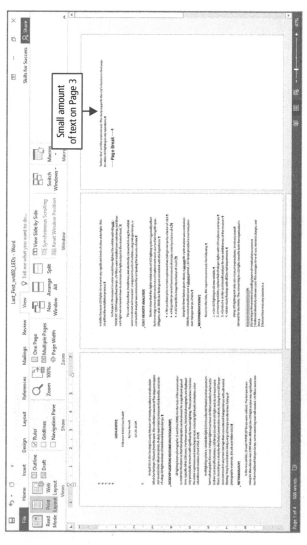

Small amount of text on Page 3

Word 2016, Windows 10, Microsoft Corporation

■ **Continue to the next page to complete the skill**

▶ **WATCH** SKILL 3.9

3. On the **Layout tab**, in the **Page Setup group**, click **Margins**, and then compare your screen.

The Margins gallery displays thumbnails and descriptions of common margin settings. Here, the report is set to the default margin sizes used in an older version of Word—Office 2003 Default.

In a report, the top and bottom margins are typically 1.0 inch each, and the side margins are 1.25 inches each. In a short informal report, you can change the side margins to 1 inch each if needed.

4. In the **Margins gallery**, click the **Normal** thumbnail to set the margins to 1 inch on all four sides. Compare your screen.

With the smaller margins, the report title and body now fit on two pages, and the Bibliography is on the third page. Before setting the margins on a report, you should check the assigned style guidelines for the dimensions that you should use.

5. Scroll up to view Page 1 and Page 2, and then on the **View tab**, in the **Zoom group**, click **100%** to return to the default view.

If you are working on a large monitor, you may still see two pages displayed with the 100% zoom level. If so, you can snap the window to either half of the screen to see only one page at a time.

6. Save 🖫 the file.

■ **You have completed Skill 9 of 10**

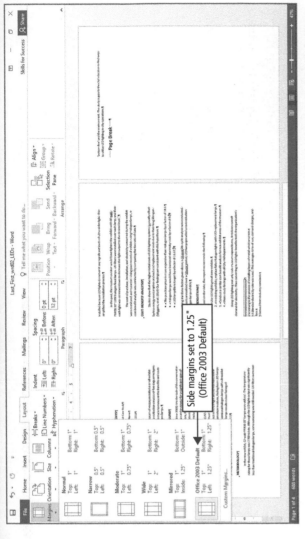

Side margins set to 1.25" (Office 2003 Default)

Word 2016, Windows 10, Microsoft Corporation

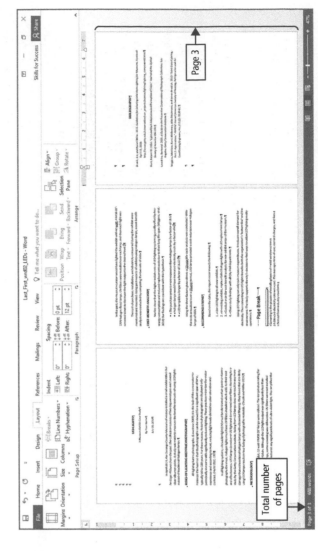

Total number of pages

Page 3

Word 2016, Windows 10, Microsoft Corporation

▶ Headers and footers can include text you type, fields, and graphics.

▶ On the first page of a document, you can set the headers and footers so that they do not display.

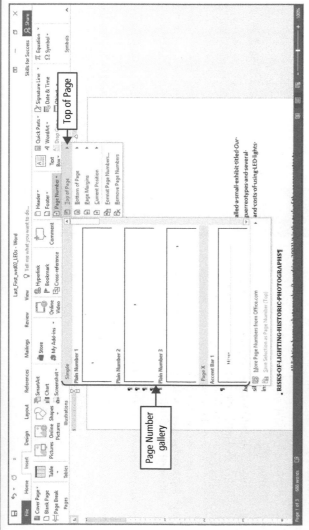

Word 2016, Windows 10, Microsoft Corporation

1. Press Ctrl + Home to move the insertion point to the beginning of the document. On the **Insert tab**, in the **Header & Footer group**, click **Page Number**. In the **Page Number** list, point to **Top of Page**, and then compare your screen.

2. In the **Page Number** gallery, use the vertical scroll bar to scroll through the page number options. When you are through, scroll to the top of the list. Under **Simple**, click **Plain Number 3** to insert the page number at the top and right margins.

When you insert a pre-built page number in this manner, the header and footer areas are activated so that you can continue working with them.

3. Under **Header & Footer Tools**, on the **Design tab**, in the **Options group**, select the **Different First Page** check box, and notice the page number on Page 1 is removed.

4. Scroll to the top of Page 2, and verify that the page number displays.

In reports where the body starts on the same page as the title, the page number is not included on the first page.

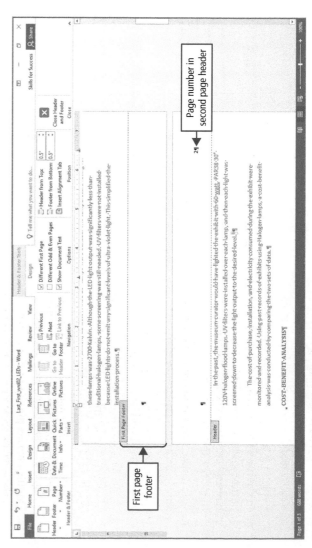

Word 2016, Windows 10, Microsoft Corporation

■ **Continue to the next page to complete the skill**

5. Scroll to the bottom of Page 2, and then click in the footer area. If you accidentally deactivated the header and footer areas, double-click the footer area.

6. In the **Insert group**, click the **Quick Parts** button, and then click **Field**. Under **Field names**, scroll down, click **FileName**, and then click **OK**.

7. Add a space, and then type (DRAFT) Be sure to include the parentheses.

    In this manner, headers and footers can contain both fields such as page numbers and file names and text that you type.

8. On the **Home tab**, in the **Paragraph group**, click the **Align Right** button , and then compare your screen.

    In a business setting, this footer would be removed before the report is published.

9. Double-click in the report body to deactivate the footer area. On the **File tab**, click **Print**, and then compare your screen.

10. If you are printing your work, print the report. Otherwise, click the **Back** button ⊕.

11. **Save** ⊞ the file, **Close** ✕ Word, and then submit the file as directed by your instructor.

📌 **DONE! You have completed Skill 10 of 10 and your document is complete!**

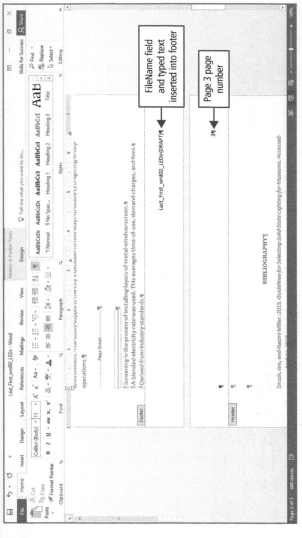

FileName field and typed text inserted into footer

Page 3 page number

Word 2016, Windows 10, Microsoft Corporation

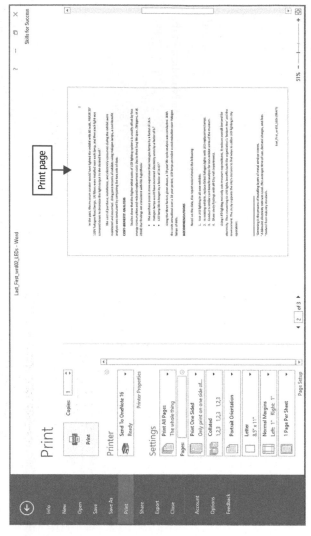

Print page

Word 2016, Windows 10, Microsoft Corporation

More Skills 11

Record AutoCorrect Entries

To complete this project, you will need the following file:

- wrd02_MS11Budget

You will save your file as:

- Last_First_wrd02_MS11Budget

▸ **AutoCorrect** corrects common spelling errors as you type; for example, *teh* is automatically corrected to *the*.

▸ AutoCorrect stores misspelled words in the Replace column and correct spellings in the With column.

1. Start **Word 2016**, and then open the student data file **wrd02_MS11Budget**. Save the file in your folder as Last_First_wrd02_MS11Budget and then add the **FileName** field to the footer.

2. On the **File tab**, click **Options**. In the **Word Options** dialog box, click **Proofing**, and then click the **AutoCorrect Options** button.

3. On the **AutoCorrect tab**, verify that the **Replace text as you type** check box is selected. In the **Replace** box, type shoud and in the **With** box, type should Compare your screen.

4. Near the bottom of the **AutoCorrect** dialog box, click the **Add** button, and then click **OK**. If you see the Replace button, click it instead. Click **OK** to close the **Word Options** dialog box.

   If someone else has already added a correction, a Replace button will display in place of the Add button.

5. In the paragraph that begins *I just received*, click to position the insertion point between *Council* and the period. Type a comma, add a space, then type the following text exactly as written, and watch your screen when you misspell *shoud*: and I thought you shoud see the plans

6. In the paragraph that begins *In accordance*, select the text *Aspen Falls Planning Department*.

7. Open the **AutoCorrect** dialog box again. Notice that the phrase automatically displays in the *With* box. In the **Replace** box, type afpdx. Click the **Add** button, and then click **OK**. If you see the Replace button, click it instead. Click **OK** to close the dialog box.

   When you create a shortcut, it is a good idea to use an acronym of the phrase, and then add another letter to create a word that will never be typed.

Word 2016, Windows 10, Microsoft Corporation

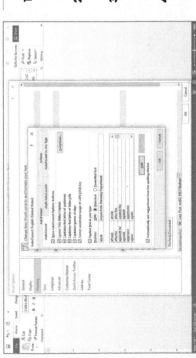

Word 2016, Windows 10, Microsoft Corporation

8. In the last paragraph, select and then delete the words *our own*. Type afpdx and then press [Spacebar] to use AutoCorrect to insert the text *Aspen Falls Planning Department*. If you have two spaces after the phrase, delete one.

9. Open the **AutoCorrect** dialog box again. In the **Replace** box, type afpdx to highlight the phrase in the list, and then click **Delete**. In the **Replace** box, type shoud and then click **Delete**. **Close** the dialog boxes.

10. **Save** the file, **Close Word**, and then submit the file as directed by your instructor.

■ **You have completed More Skills 11**

More Skills 12

Use AutoFormat to Create Numbered Lists

To complete this project, you will need the following file:

- wrd02_MS12Permits

You will save your file as:

- Last_First_wrd02_MS12Permits

▶ You can create a numbered list using existing text or create the list as you type.

▶ The Word AutoCorrect option to create lists automatically can be turned on or off as desired.

---

1. Start **Word 2016**, and then open the student data file **wrd02_MS12Permits**. Save the file in your chapter folder as Last_First_wrd02_MS12Permits and then add the **FileName** field to the footer.

2. On the **File tab**, click **Options**. On the left side of the **Word Options** dialog box, click **Proofing**. Under **AutoCorrect options**, click the **AutoCorrect Options** button.

3. In the **AutoCorrect** dialog box, click the **AutoFormat As You Type tab**. Under **Apply as you type**, verify that the **Automatic numbered lists** check box is selected.

   The other check boxes that are selected on your computer may vary and do not need to be changed.

4. Click **OK** two times to close the dialog boxes, and then position the insertion point in the blank line between the memo's two body paragraphs.

5. Type 1. (include the period), and then press SpaceBar . Notice that the number is indented, a tab is added after the number, and the AutoCorrect Options button displays.

6. Click the **AutoCorrect Options** button ⚡ to view the menu.

   In the AutoCorrect Options menu, you can turn off automatic numbering should you need that option.

7. Click the **AutoCorrect Options** button ⚡ again to hide the menu.

8. Type the following list. Press Enter after each item except the last one.

   1. Notify the Planning Department at least 60 days prior to the event.

   2. Fill out and submit a permit request at least 30 days prior to the event.

   3. Meet with a Planning Department representative at least 14 days prior to the event.

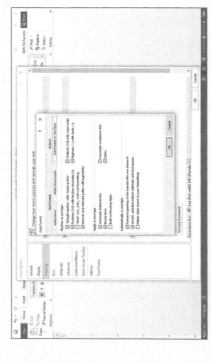

Word 2016, Windows 10, Microsoft Corporation

If you are typing a list and want the list to end, you can press Enter two times or click the Numbering button to turn off automatic numbering.

9. **Save** the file.

10. If you changed the Word Options settings in Step 3, repeat Steps 2–4 to clear the *Automatic numbered lists* check box. **Close** Word, and then submit the file as directed by your instructor.

■ **You have completed More Skills 12**

More Skills 13
Format and Customize Lists

To complete this project, you will need the following file:

- wrd02_MS13Garden

You will save your file as:

- Last_First_wrd02_MS13Garden

▶ Numbered lists separated by other text can be formatted to display continuous numbering.

1. Start Word 2016, and then open the student data file **wrd02_MS13Garden.** Save the file in your chapter folder as Last_First_wrd02_MS13Garden and then add the **FileName** field to the footer.

2. In the first numbered list—which uses capital letters instead of numbers—select list items *A–C.* On the **Home tab,** in the **Paragraph group,** click the **Numbering arrow,** and then click the numbering style *1) 2) 3).*

3. Use the same technique to change the second numbered list to the 1) 2) 3) numbering style.

   Because the two numbered lists are interrupted by a paragraph, the second list starts numbering from 1.

4. Right-click the first item in the second list, and then from the shortcut menu, click **Continue Numbering.** Compare your screen.

5. Select the three items in the first numbered list. In the **Paragraph group,** click the **Increase Indent** button one time.

   When you change the numbering to *Continuous,* formatting edits made to one list affect the other lists. Here, the indents for both numbered lists increased.

6. With the first three items still selected, in the **Paragraph group,** click the **Decrease Indent** button one time to move both lists to the left margin.

   When you decrease the indent of a list, it moves to the left 0.5 inches. When you increase the indent, the list moves to the right 0.25 inches.

7. With the first three items still selected, in the **Paragraph group,** click the **Increase Indent** button one time to move both lists to their original position.

8. In the bulleted list, click at the end of the last item ending *garden beds,* and then press Enter. Type Trellises

9. In the same list, click to the right of *Water source,* and then press Enter. Type Captured rainwater and then press Enter. Type Water tap on roof.

10. Select the two list items *Captured rainwater* and *Water tap on roof.* In the **Paragraph group,** click the **Increase Indent** button to assign a different level than the rest of the list items.

    When you indent part of a list, the indent moves 0.5 inches and the symbol or number assigned to that level displays. Here, the circle symbol is assigned to second-level items.

11. **Save** the file, **Close** Word, and then submit the file as directed by your instructor.

- **You have completed More Skills 13**

Word 2016, Windows 10, Microsoft Corporation

More Skills 14
Create Standard Outlines

To complete this project, you will need the following file:

- wrd02_MS14Outline

You will save your file as:

- Last_First_wrd02_MS14Outline

▶ **Outlines** are used to plan and organize longer documents such as formal reports.

1. Start **Word 2016**, and then open the student data file **wrd02_MS14Outline**. Save the file in your chapter folder as Last_First_wrd02_MS14Outline and then add the **FileName** field to the footer.

2. In the third paragraph, replace the words *Your Name* with your First and Last name.

3. On the **File tab**, click **Options**. In the **Word Options** dialog box, click **Proofing**, and then click the **AutoCorrect Options** button.

4. In the **AutoCorrect** dialog box, click the **AutoFormat As You Type tab**, and then under **Apply as you type**, clear the **Automatic numbered lists** check box.

5. Under **Automatically as you type**, clear the **Set left- and first-indent with tabs and backspaces** check box. Compare your screen and then click **OK** two times to close the dialog boxes.

   With these two AutoComplete features disabled, you can indent and number the outline following the standard outline format. You will enable these two settings at the end of the skill.

6. Click to the right of *Installation Procedures.*

7. Press `Enter` three times. Type IV. (include the period) press `Tab`, and then type COST BENEFIT ANALYSIS

8. Press `Enter` two times, and then press `Tab`. Type A. press `Tab`, and then type Initial Costs

9. Press `Enter`, and then press `Tab`. Type B. press `Tab`, and then type Long-Term Costs

10. Press `Enter`, and then press `Tab` two times. Type 1. press `Tab`, and then type Maintenance

11. Press `Enter`, and then press `Tab` two times. Type 2. press `Tab`, and then type Replacement

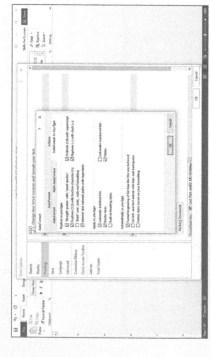

Word 2016, Windows 10, Microsoft Corporation

12. Press `Enter`, and then press `Tab`. Type C. press `Tab`, and then type Overall Costs and Benefits

13. Press `Enter` three times. Type V. press `Tab`, and then type RECOMMENDATIONS Verify your outline fits on one page and your list levels align with the items above.

14. Reopen the **AutoCorrect** dialog box, click the **AutoFormat As You Type tab**, and then if they were selected previous to this skill, select the **Automatic numbered lists** and **Set left- and first-indent with tabs and backspaces** check boxes. Click **OK** to close the dialog boxes.

15. **Save** the file, **Close** Word, and then submit the file as directed by your instructor.

- **You have completed More Skills 14**

The following table summarizes the **SKILLS AND PROCEDURES** covered in this chapter.

Skills Number	Task	Step	Icon	Keyboard Shortcut
1	Find text	In the Navigation pane, use the search box and click Results		Ctrl + F
1	Find and replace text	In the Navigation pane, click the Search for more things arrow		Ctrl + H
1	Navigate by headings	In the Navigation pane, click Headings		
2	Insert footnotes	References tab → Footnotes group → Insert Footnote		Alt + Ctrl + F
3	Add or edit sources	References tab → Citations & Bibliography group → Manage Sources		
3	Set reference styles	References tab → Citations & Bibliography group → Style		
4	Insert citations	References tab → Citations & Bibliography group → Insert Citation		
4	Insert a bibliography	References tab → Citations & Bibliography group → Bibliography		
5	Apply bullet lists	Home tab → Paragraph group → Bullets arrow		
5	Apply numbered lists	Home tab → Paragraph group → Numbering arrow		
5	Indent lists	Home tab → Paragraph group → Increase Indent		
6	Set first line indents	Paragraph group → Paragraph Dialog Box Launcher → Special → First Line		
7	Modify line and paragraph spacing	Paragraph group → Paragraph Dialog Box Launcher		
7	Repeat the last command			F4
8	Enable widow and orphan control	Paragraph group → Paragraph Dialog Box Launcher → Line and Page Breaks tab		
8	Set keep with next control	Paragraph group → Paragraph Dialog Box Launcher → Line and Page Breaks tab		
8	Modify styles	Right-click style thumbnail in Styles group, and then click Modify. Click the Format button and open desired dialog box.		
8	Update styles	Click or select text with desired style formatting. Right-click the style's thumbnail in Styles group, and then click Update command.		
9	Change margins	Layout tab → Margins		
10	Add page numbers	Insert tab → Header & Footer group → Page Number		
10	Apply different first page headers and footers	Header & Footer Tools → Design tab → Different first page		
MS11	Insert AutoCorrect text	File tab → Options → Proofing → AutoCorrect Options		
MS12	Apply numbered lists using AutoFormat	File tab → Options → Proofing → AutoCorrect Options → AutoFormat As You Type tab → Automatic numbered lists check box selected		
MS13	Insert continuous numbering	Right-click first list item → Continue Numbering		
MS14	Apply standard outline	File tab → Options → Proofing → AutoCorrect Options → AutoFormat As You Type tab → Automatic numbered lists check box not selected		

Review

Project Summary Chart

Project	Project Type	Project Location
Skills Review	Review	In Book & MIL
Skills Assessment 1	Review	In Book & MIL
Skills Assessment 2	Review	Book
My Skills	Problem Solving	Book
Visual Skills Check	Problem Solving	Book
Skills Challenge 1	Critical Thinking	Book
Skills Challenge 2	Critical Thinking	Book
More Skills Assessment	Review	In Book & MIL
Collaborating with Google	Critical Thinking	Book

MOS Objectives Covered

- Create a numbered or bulleted list
- Increase or decrease list levels
- or continue list numbering
- Insert footnotes and endnotes
- Create bibliography citations sources
- Insert citations for bibliographies
- Set paragraph pagination options

Search for text

Insert headers and footers

Insert page numbers

Change document views

Find and replace text

Replace text by using AutoCorrect

Set line and paragraph spacing and indentation

Key Terms

BizSkills Video

1. What are some actions that you should take when attending a job fair?

2. What actions should be avoided when attending a job fair?

Online Help Skills

1. With Word 2016 open, on the **File tab**, in the upper right corner of the screen, click the **Microsoft Word Help** ? button, or press F1.

2. In the **Word Help** window **Search** box, type word count and then press Enter.

3. In the search result list, click **Show the word count**. Maximize the **Word Help** window, and then compare your screen.

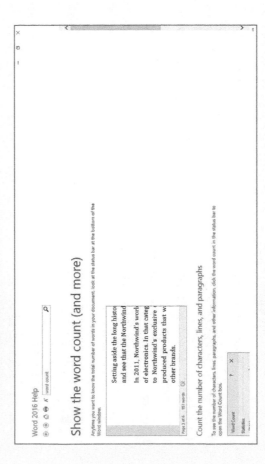

Word 2016, Windows 10, Microsoft Corporation

4. Read the article to see if you can find the answer to the following question: How can you find out how many words are in the document without counting the words in the footnotes?

Matching

Match each term in the second column with its correct definition in the first column by writing the letter of the term on the blank line in front of the correct definition.

A Author-date

B Bibliography

C Double-spacing

D Endnote

E First line indent

F Margin

G Navigation

H Numbered

I Paragraph spacing

J Source

_____ **1.** The pane used to find document text.

_____ **2.** A comment or notation added to the end of a section or document.

_____ **3.** The reference used to find information or data when writing a report.

_____ **4.** The citation type used for the Chicago style.

_____ **5.** A list of sources displayed on a separate page at the end of a report.

_____ **6.** The type of list used for items that are in chronological or sequential order.

_____ **7.** The equivalent of a blank line of text displayed between each line of text in a paragraph.

_____ **8.** The vertical distance above and below each paragraph in a document.

_____ **9.** The position of the first line of a paragraph relative to the text in the rest of the paragraph.

_____ **10.** The space between the text and the top, bottom, left, and right edges of the paper when you print the document.

Multiple Choice

Choose the correct answer.

1. To place a note on the same page as the comment or notation, which of the following should be used?
   A. Footnote
   B. Endnote
   C. Citation

2. This is placed in body paragraphs and points to an entry in the bibliography.
   A. Footnote
   B. Citation
   C. Endnote

3. The number of inches from the top edge of the paper to the beginning of the bibliography.
   A. 0.5 inches
   B. 1 inch
   C. 2 inches

4. In a Chicago style bibliography, this type of indent is used for each reference.
   A. Hanging indent
   B. First line indent
   C. Left alignment

5. Items that can be listed in any order are best presented using which of the following?
   A. Bulleted list
   B. Numbered list
   C. Outline list

6. The default line spacing in a long report.
   A. Custom
   B. Single
   C. Double

7. The vertical distance between lines in a paragraph.
   A. Spacing after
   B. Line spacing
   C. Text wrapping

8. The last line of a paragraph that displays as the first line of a page.
   A. Single
   B. Stray
   C. Widow

9. The pre-built setting that places all four margins at 1.0 inches.
   A. Narrow
   B. Normal
   C. Office 2003 Default

10. This type of alignment positions the text so that it is aligned with the right margin.
    A. Right
    B. Center
    C. Left

Topics for Discussion

1. You can build and save a list of master sources you have used in research papers and reports and display them using Manage Sources. What are the advantages of storing sources over time?

2. Paragraph text can be left aligned, centered, right aligned, or justified. Left alignment is most commonly used. In what situations would you use centered text? Justified text? Can you think of any situations where you might want to use right alignment?

Skills Review

To complete this project, you will need the following file:

- wrd02_SRWeb

You will save your file as:

- Last_First_wrd02_SRWeb

---

1. Start **Word 2016**, and then open the student data file **wrd02_SRWeb**. Save the file in your chapter folder as Last_First_wrd02_SRWeb If necessary, display the formatting marks and the Navigation pane.

2. Click to the right of *By*, add a space, and then type your name.

3. Click in the first body paragraph beginning *The city of Aspen Falls*. Click the **Paragraph Dialog Box Launcher**, and then in the **Paragraph** dialog box, under **Spacing**, change the **After** value to **12 pt**, and then click **OK**. Click in the paragraph beginning *Color blindness varies*, and then press F4 to repeat the formatting.

4. Click in the side heading beginning *DESIGN FOR*. In the **Styles group**, right-click **Heading 2**, and then click **Modify**. In the **Modify Style** dialog box, click the **Format** button, and then click **Paragraph**. In the **Paragraph** dialog box, click the **Line and Page Breaks tab**, and then select the **Keep with next** check box. Click **OK** two times. Compare your screen.

5. On the **References tab**, in the **Citations & Bibliography group**, verify that **Chicago** is selected, and then click **Manage Sources**.

6. Select the source for **Bennett, Jean**, and then click the **Edit** button. Change the **Type of Source** to **Journal Article**. Add the **Journal Name** The New England Journal of Medicine and the **Pages** 2483-2484

7. Click **OK**, and then **Close Source Manager**. In the *DESIGN FOR COLOR BLINDNESS* section, click to the right of the sentence ending *degree of color blindness*. In the **Citations & Bibliography group**, click **Insert Citation**, and then click the **Bennett, Jean** source.

8. Right-click the citation just inserted, and then click **Edit Citation**. In the **Edit Citation** dialog box, type 2483 and then click **OK**. Deselect the citation, and then compare your screen.

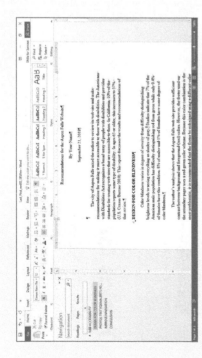

Word 2016, Windows 10, Microsoft Corporation

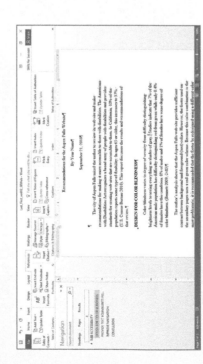

Word 2016, Windows 10, Microsoft Corporation

■ **Continue to the next page to complete this Skills Review**

9. In the **Navigation** pane search box, type web site and then click **Results**.

10. In the **Navigation** pane, click the **Search for more things arrow**, and then click **Replace**. In the **Replace with** box, type website Click **Replace All**. Click **OK**, and then **Close** the dialog box.

11. Navigate to the *IMPROVE NAVIGATION* section, and then click to the right of the sentence ending *link to the home page.* In the **Footnotes group**, click **Insert Footnote**, and then type This includes the logo on the home page itself.

12. In the footnote just inserted, select the text but not the footnote number, and then change the font size to **12**.

13. Select the four paragraphs beginning *The main logo* and ending with *using the keyboard.* Apply a numbered list with the **1. 2. 3.** format. In the **Paragraph group**, click the **Increase Indent** button one time.

14. In the *CONCLUSION* section, select the four paragraphs beginning *Anyone with a vision* and ending with *a portable device.* Apply a bulleted list with the solid round circle. On the **Home tab**, in the **Paragraph group**, click the **Increase Indent** button one time.

15. With the bulleted list still selected, in the **Paragraph group**, click the **Line and Paragraph Spacing** button, and then click **1.15**. Repeat this formatting for the paragraphs in the numbered list.

16. On the **Layout tab**, in the **Page Setup group**, click the **Margins** button, and then click **Normal**. Compare your screen.

17. Move to the end of the document, and then press Ctrl + Enter to insert a page break. At the top of Page 3, press Enter two times.

18. On the **References tab**, in the **Citations & Bibliography group**, click **Bibliography**, and then click the **Bibliography** thumbnail. Change the *Bibliography* heading to BIBLIOGRAPHY

19. On the **Insert tab**, in the **Header & Footer group**, click **Page Number**, point to **Top of Page**, and then click **Plain Number 3**. In the **Options group**, select the **Different First Page** check box.

20. Navigate to the Page 2 footer, and then click in the footer. Insert the **FileName** field, add a space, and then type (DRAFT) On the **Home tab**, in the **Paragraph group**, click the **Align Right** button, and then double-click in the document.

21. On the **View tab**, in the **Zoom group**, click **Multiple Pages**, and then compare your screen.

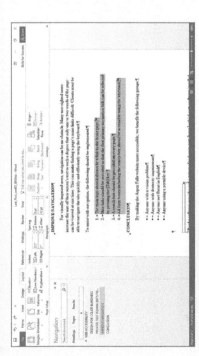

Word 2016, Windows 10, Microsoft Corporation

Word 2016, Windows 10, Microsoft Corporation

22. In the **Zoom group** click **100%**, and then **Close** the Navigation pane.

23. **Save** the file, **Close** Word, and then submit the file as directed by your instructor.

DONE! You have completed this Skills Review

Skills Assessment 1

To complete this project, you will need the following file:

- wrd02_SA1Tourism

You will save your file as:

- Last_First_wrd02_SA1Tourism

1. Start **Word 2016**, and then open the student data file **wrd02_SA1Tourism**. Save the file in your chapter folder as Last_First_wrd02_SA1Tourism

2. Click to the right of *By*, add a space, and then type your name.

3. Replace all occurrences of the phrase *City of Aspen Falls* with *Aspen Falls*

4. In the first body paragraph beginning *The Aspen Falls Tourism*, set a **0.5 inch** first line indent and the spacing after to **12 pt**. Repeat the same formatting to the paragraph beginning *The number of people visiting*.

5. Modify the **Heading 2** style so that **Keep with next** is enabled.

6. In the *DEMOGRAPHICS* section, apply a solid circle bullet to the four paragraphs beginning *Stay longer than* and ending with *drive to Aspen Falls*. Increase the list's indent to **0.5 inch** and set the line spacing to **1.15**.

7. Use **Source Manager** to edit the source for **Law, Christopher M.** Change the source type to **Journal Article**, and then add the **Journal Name** Urban Studies and the **Pages** 599-618

8. In the *DEVELOPMENT AREAS* section, after the sentence ending *is a recent practice*, insert a citation using **Law, Christopher M.** as the reference. Edit the citation field to include the pages 599-618

9. Apply a list with the **1. 2. 3.** format to the three paragraphs beginning *Agritourism* and ending with *Sports Tourism*. Increase the indent of the numbered list to **0.5 inch** and set the line spacing to **1.15**.

10. Insert a footnote after the list item *Agritourism* with the text Agritourism caters to those interested in visiting farms, ranches, and wineries. Change the font size of the footnote text to **12**.

11. In the blank paragraph below the *SUMMARY* section, insert a manual page break. Press [Enter] two times, and then insert the **Bibliography** built-in field. Change the bibliography's heading to BIBLIOGRAPHY

TRAVEL AND TOURISM

Trends for the Aspen Falls Metro Area

By Your Name

September 21, 2018

The Aspen Falls Tourism Department in cooperation with the Aspen Falls Chamber of Commerce surveyed random tourists' about their visit to Aspen Falls. Other key indicators were assembled from public records. These include airport arrivals and departures and room tax revenues. From this analysis trends, demographics, and recommendations are provided in this report.

TRENDS

The number of people visiting Aspen Falls grew about 10% last year, and for the first time topped the 1 million mark. Over the past 10 years, spending by convention and event attendees has risen consistently. However, this past year saw a decrease in business tourist spending of 4%. This decline was offset by an increase in spending from leisure visitors. Overall, spending by business and leisure tourists increased by over 9%.

DEMOGRAPHICS

The study shows that 60% of Aspen Falls tourists are from California — resident visitors. Further, non-resident tourists:

- Stay longer than resident visitors.
- Are slightly older than resident visitors.
- Have a higher average household income than resident visitors.
- Fly in instead of drive to Aspen Falls.

Other studies have shown that on average, leisure visitors travel with larger parties and stay longer than business visitors. (Tribe 2011) These demographics suggest that marketing to

¹ A tourist is any person staying for one or more nights in the Aspen Falls metro area outside of their regular residence. A tourist can be classified as either a business visitor or a leisure visitor.

wrd02_COfq02 (DRAFT)

non-resident leisure visitors would have th area.

DEVELOPMENT AREAS

Treating tourism as a growth indus in recent years that the classifications of to field. Currently, specialty tourism is seeing seeing robust potential.

Given its location and economy, th three specialty areas:

1. Agritourism²
2. Wildlife Tourism
3. Sports Tourism

According to the World Tourism O of international tourism growth. (World T leisure visitors from China is not mutually

SUMMARY

The economic benefits from promo would have a significant impact on the loc local organizations enhance the visitor exp conservation areas attract more visitors wh improving venues for playing sports and ou resident and non-resident visitors.

² Agritourism caters to those interested in visiting farms, ranches, and wineries.

---

12. In the header, insert the **Plain Number 3** page number so that it displays on all pages except for Page 1.

13. In the Page 2 footer, insert the **FileName** field, add a space, and then type (DRAFT) Align the footer paragraph with the right margin, and then close the footer.

14. Change the page margins to **Normal** (1 inch on all sides).

15. Compare your screen. **Save** the file, **Close Word**, and then submit the file as directed by your instructor.

 **DONE! You have completed Skills Assessment 1**

Skills Assessment 2

To complete this project, you will need the following file:

- wrd02_SA2Wildlife

You will save your file as:

- Last_First_wrd02_SA2Wildlife

---

1. Start Word 2016, and then open the student data file **wrd02_SA2Wildlife**. Save the file in your chapter folder as Last_First_wrd02_SA2Wildlife

2. Click to the right of *By*, add a space, and then type your name.

3. Replace all occurrences of the word *fisherman* with *angler* and then replace all occurrences of the word *fishermen* with *anglers*

4. In the first body paragraph beginning *This report summarizes*, set a **0.5 inch** first line indent and the spacing after to **12 pt**. Repeat the same formatting to the paragraph beginning *The 2017 survey was provided*.

5. Modify the **Heading 2** style so that **Widow/Orphan control and Keep with next** are enabled.

6. Use **Source Manager** to edit the source for **U.S. Fish & Wildlife Service**. Change the source type to **Document From Web site**, and then add the **URL** http://www.census.gov/prod/www/abs/fishing.html

7. In the *FINDINGS* section, after the sentence ending *with the state trend*, insert a citation using **U.S. Fish & Wildlife Service** as the reference.

8. In the same section, apply a solid circle bullet to the two paragraphs beginning *Each angler spent* and ending with *equipment and trip expenses*. Increase the list's indent to **0.5 inch** and set the line spacing to **1.15**.

9. At the end of the second bulleted list item, insert a footnote with the text *Equipment includes binoculars, clothing, tents, and backpacking equipment.* Change the footnote's text to **12 points**.

10. In the *RECOMMENDATIONS* section, apply a list with the **1. 2. 3.** format to the six paragraphs beginning *Maintain existing natural areas* and ending with *wildlife recreation areas*. Increase the indent of the numbered list to **0.5 inch** and set the line spacing to **1.15**.

11. In the blank paragraph below the numbered list, insert a manual page break. Press [Enter] two times, and then insert the

Bibliography built-in field. Change the bibliography's heading to BIBLIOGRAPHY

12. In the header, insert the **Plain Number 3** page number so that it displays on all pages except for Page 1.

13. In the Page 2 footer, insert the **FileName** field, add a space, and then type (DO NOT RELEASE YET) Align the footer paragraph with the right margin, and then close the footer.

14. Change the page margins to **Normal.**

15. Compare your screen. **Save** the file, **Close** Word, and then submit the file as directed by your instructor.

DONE! You have completed Skills Assessment 2

Document preview content:

ASPEN FALLS WILDLIFE RECREATION

An Analysis of the 2017 Visitor and Citizen Surveys

By Your Name

October 5, 2018

This report summarizes the findings of the annual survey of Durango County residents about their wildlife recreation. In the Aspen Falls area, wildlife recreation opportunities are limited to fishing and wildlife observation. The two activities are not mutually exclusive. Wildlife observation includes watching, photographing, or painting wildlife. Based on the annual survey, recommendations have been provided to assist Aspen Falls Parks and Recreation managers formulate policies and procedures.

METHODOLOGY

The 2017 survey was provided online and via a scripted interview process. The citizenry were invited via several media including mailings, Parks and Recreation catalogs and flyers, and public service announcements on radio and TV. A random selection of citizens were called and invited to complete the survey over the phone. Non-residents were also surveyed in the field using the interview process.

FINDINGS

An overall increase in wildlife recreation indicates that it is a significant source of enjoyment for residents and non-residents alike. However, only 23% of anglers are from out of the area and 11% are from out of state. A far higher percentage of wildlife viewers were from out of the area—nearly 45%. This indicates that the Aspen Falls area wildlife viewing opportunities attract a significant number of visitors to the area.

Over the past 10 year period, angling has decreased by 36% while wildlife viewing has increased by nearly 83%. Currently, anglers still outnumber wildlife observers nearly 2 to 1. If current trends continue, it will be several years before the number of days spent wildlife viewing will be on par with angling. This trend is consistent with the state trend. (U.S. Fish & Wildlife Service 2015)

The study found the following c...

- Each angler spent an average...
- Each wildlife watcher spent a...

RECOMMENDATIONS

Based on the survey results, city opportunities. Improving and expanding greatest increase in wildlife recreation. S habitat and healthy fish stocks. (Lau, La also increase native plantings and natura recreationists will be served.

To improve upland river habitat.

1. Maintain existing natural are areas. A natural area is a define open fields for the primary p
2. Maintain and introduce nativ and cover plants for the prim
3. Educate the populace on how species, and protect natural a
4. Provide wildlife photography raising tool.
5. Sponsor volunteer based ever invasive species, and plant na
6. Improve field guides and ma

¹ Trip expenses include food, fuel, and lodging. Angling equipment includes, clothing, and fishing gear.
² Equipment includes binoculars, clothing, tents, and backpacking equipment.

Last_First_wrd02_SA2Wildlife (DO NOT RELEASE YET)

My Skills

To complete this project, you will need the following file:

- wrd02_MYCosts

You will save your file as:

- Last_First_wrd02_MYCosts

1. Start Word 2016, and then open the student data file **wrd02_MYCosts.** Save the file in your chapter folder as Last_First_wrd02_MYCosts

2. Click to the right of *By*, add a space, and then type your name.

3. Replace all occurrences of the word *you* with students

4. In the first body paragraph beginning *In the previous year*, set a **0.5 inch** first line indent and the spacing after to **12 pt**. Repeat the same formatting to the paragraph beginning *Students should pursue.*

5. Update the **Heading 1** style to match the formatting of the report title.

6. Use **Source Manager** to edit the source for **U.S. Government**. Change the source type to **Web site**, and then add the **URL** https://studentaid2.ed.gov/getmoney/pay_for_college/cost_35.html

7. In the *STAY LOCAL* section, after the sentence ending *$6000 per year*, insert a citation using **U.S. Government Department of Education** as the reference.

8. In the *TEST OUT* section, after the last sentence ending *credit for life experiences,* insert a footnote with the text Contact the Distance Education and Training Council at 1601 18th Street, NW, Washington, DC 20009, or call (202) 234-5100 for more information.

9. In the footnote just inserted, change the footnote text font size to **12.**

10. At the end of the document, apply a solid circle bullet to the three paragraphs beginning *Take transferable summer and* ending with *semesters needed to graduate.* Increase the indent of the list items to **0.5 inch** and set the line spacing to **1.15.**

11. In the blank paragraph below the last bulleted list, insert a manual page break. Press Enter two times, and then insert the **Bibliography** built-in field. Change the bibliography's heading to BIBLIOGRAPHY

12. In the header, insert the **Plain Number 3** page number so that it displays on all pages except for Page 1.

13. In the Page 2 footer, insert the **FileName** field, align the footer paragraph with the right margin, and then close the footer.

14. Change the page margins to **Normal** (1 inch on all sides).

15. Compare your screen. **Save** the file, **Close** Word, and then submit the file as directed by your instructor.

DONE! You have completed My Skills

PAYING FOR COLLEGE

Techniques for Saving Money

By Your Name

March 14, 2018

In the previous year, college tuition and fees at public colleges increased by over 8%. Students at private colleges saw increases of 3.2 to 4.5%. (Education & the Workforce Committee 2014). To counter this rise, students can employ several strategies to reduce the cost of attending college.

PURSUE SCHOLARSHIPS

Students should pursue all scholarship opportunities, not just those that are based on need. Scholarships based on academic achievement have been increasingly awarded in past years. (Silverstein 2015) Nearly all colleges provide merit-based scholarships to prospective students. Most states offer scholarships through their education offices. Finally, many schools offer grants and scholarships in special areas such as music, technology, math, and science.

Many companies and associations offer scholarships. For example, banks often provide scholarships or grants for students planning to work in the finance industry. Alumni organizations typically have scholarship programs. Parents should check with their employers to see if they provide assistance to children of employees.

Students should pursue all avenues for funding. For example, many schools have special scholarships for students who do not qualify for federal or state funding. Others may offer discounted tuition to older students. Typically, financial aid counselors can help students find scholarships, grants, and discounts.

STAY LOCAL

Students who attend local colleges can save considerable money on both housing and tuition. Students who live at home can save as much as $6000 per year U.S. Government

---

2

Department of Education n.d.). Living at home also enables students to attend a community college for the first 1 or 2 years, which substantially lowers tuition costs. Tuition at local public colleges avoids the extra tuition typically charged to out-of-state residents.

WORK AND STUDY

Many students can leverage their income by working at a job coordinated through the college that they are attending. Some schools provide free room and board to students in exchange for the work they perform. Others provide discounts to student government leaders. Students should find their institution's placement office to find on and off campus jobs.

SERVE IN AN ARMED FORCE

Two programs pay for tuition and fees for those planning to be in a military service—Service Academy Scholarships and the Reserve Officers Training Corps (ROTC) Scholarship Program. Service Academy Scholarships are competitive scholarships that provide free tuition at a military academy. ROTC scholarships pay for tuition, textbooks, and a monthly living allowance. Both scholarships require a service commitment upon graduation.

TEST OUT

Receive college credit by testing through one of these test-out programs:

- Advanced Placement Program (APP)
- College-Level Examination Program (CLEP)
- Provenience Examination Program (PEP)

Some colleges give credit for life experiences.[1]

OTHER OPTIONS

Several other options include:

- Take transferable summer college courses at less expensive schools.
- Take advantage of accelerated 3-year programs when they are available
- Take the maximum number of allowed credits to reduce the number of quarters or semesters needed to graduate.

[1] Contact the Distance Education and Training Council at 1601 18th Street, NW, Washington, DC 20009, or call (202) 234-5100 for more information.

Visual Skills Check

To complete this project, you will need the following file:

- wrd02_VSSecurity

You will save your file as:

- Last_First_wrd02_VSSecurity

Open the student data file **wrd02_VSSecurity**, and then save the file in your chapter folder as Last_First_wrd02_VSSecurity

To complete this document, set the margins to Office 2003 Default. Format the three lists. The lists have been indented to 0.5 inch, line spacing is 1.15, and the spacing after is 12 pt.

The front matter is center aligned, the *By* line should display your own name, and the date should display your current date. The date paragraph's spacing after is set to 12 pt.

The body paragraph has a first line indent of 0.5 inches, spacing after of 12 pt, and line spacing of 1.15. At the end of the paragraph, a footnote has been inserted with the text *Federal Trade Commission. Protecting Personal Information: A Guide for Business. Washington, November 2015.* The footnote text is size 12, and the source title is italic.

Save the file, Close Word, and then submit the file as directed by your instructor.

 DONE! You have completed Visual Skills Check

SECURING DATA

A Summary for Aspen Falls City Government

By Your Name

October 12, 2018

Several laws require the city to keep sensitive data secure. Most notably are the Federal Trade Commission Act, Fair Credit Reporting Act, and the Gramm-Leach-Bliley Act. To comply with these laws and respect the rights of our citizens and those who do business with City Hall, the FTC recommends following these 5 key principles.[1]

1. Take stock. Know what personal information is stored on city systems.
2. Scale down. Keep only what we need to conduct city business.
3. Lock it. Prevent physical and virtual access to all information systems.
4. Pitch it. Dispose of all data that is no longer needed.
5. Plan ahead. Create an incident response plan.

PHYSICAL SECURITY

- Keep all paper documents, CDs, DVDs, and other storage medium in a locked room or locked file cabinet.
- Train employees to put away all files and log off their computer at the end of their shifts.
- Keep servers in locked rooms with access restricted only to authorized IT Department staff.
- Keep long term storage offsite and access should be limited only to those employees with a legitimate need for the data.
- Install alarms and institute a procedure for reporting unfamiliar persons on the premises.

VIRTUAL SECURITY

- Encrypt all sensitive information.
- Restrict employee privileges to install software.
- Keep anti-malware software up to date.
- Conduct periodic security audits including penetration testing.

---

[1] Federal Trade Commission. *Protecting Personal Information: A Guide for Business.* Washington, November 2015.

Critical Thinking

Skills Challenge 1

To complete this project, you will need the following file:

- wrd02_SC1Aging

You will save your file as:

- Last_First_wrd02_SC1Aging

Open the student data file **wrd02_SC1Aging**, and then save the file in your chapter folder as Last_First_wrd02_SC1Aging.

Format the report following informal business report rules modeled in Skills 1–10. Take care to apply the appropriate paragraph spacing, paragraph line spacing, paragraph alignment, and indents for front matter, headings, body paragraphs, and lists. Adjust the font size of the footnotes to those used in an informal business report. Apply one of the pre-built margins accepted in an informal business report, making sure that the report fits within a total of three pages.

Insert your name in the By line and the FileName field in the footer. Adjust the page numbers to the correct format and placement. Save the file, Close Word, and then submit the file as directed by your instructor.

 DONE! You have completed Skills Challenge 1

Skills Challenge 2

To complete this project, you will need the following file:

- New blank Word document

You will save your file as:

- Last_First_wrd02_SC2Parks

The Aspen Falls Planning Department is working with the Travel and Tourism Bureau to explore ways to use the city as the base of operation for tourists who want to visit important sites within a day's drive. Using the skills you practiced in this chapter, create a report on the nearby major nature attractions. These could include Yosemite National Park (250 miles), Death Valley National Park (200 miles), Sequoia National Forest (180 miles), and the Channel Islands National Park (40 miles). Research three of these sites, and write a report about the highlights of what a visitor might find at each. Include an introduction, a section for each of the three attractions, and a conclusion. Add your sources to Source Manager, and insert them in citations and a bibliography. Format the report as an informal business report.

Insert the FileName field in the footer, and check the entire document for grammar and spelling. Save the file in your chapter folder as Last_First_wrd02_SC2Parks Close Word, and then submit the file as directed by your instructor.

 DONE! You have completed Skills Challenge 2

More Skills Assessment

To complete this project, you will need the following file:

- wrd02_MSATours

You will save your file as:

- Last_First_wrd02_MSATours

1. Start **Word 2016**, and then open the student data file **wrd02_MSATours**. Save the file in your folder as Last_First_wrd02_MSATours Add the **FileName** field to the footer, and then verify the formatting marks display.

2. Open the **AutoCorrect** dialog box. On the **AutoCorrect tab**, in the **Replace** box, type *afx* and in the **With** box, type Aspen Falls and then click the **Add** button. Compare your screen

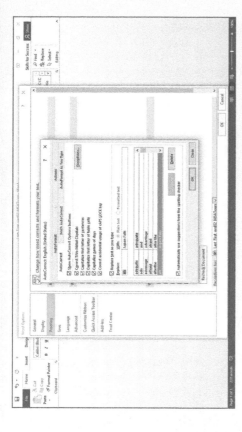

Word 2016, Windows 10, Microsoft Corporation

3. In the **AutoCorrect** dialog box, clear the **Automatic numbered lists** check box, and then clear the **Set left- and first-indent with tabs and backspaces** check box. Click **OK** two times to close the dialog boxes.

4. At the top of the document, in the paragraph beginning *The city wine region*, select and then delete the word *city*. Type afx and then press [SpaceBar] to replace *city* with *Aspen Falls*. At the end of the page, repeat this step in the paragraph beginning *For more information*.

5. Under the title *Wine Tours*, click in the blank line under the list item *Four hours*.

6. Type 2. (include the period) press [Tab], and then type Group Size

7. Press [Enter], and then press [Tab]. Type A. press [Tab], and then type Four people

8. Press [Enter], and then press [Tab]. Type B. press [Tab], and then type Six people Verify your file fits on one page and your list levels align with the items above. Compare your screen.

9. Reopen the **AutoCorrect** dialog box. On the **AutoCorrect tab**, delete the phrase *afx*. If they were selected previous to this skill, select the **Automatic numbered lists** and **Set left- and first-indent with tabs and backspaces** check boxes. Click **OK** to close the dialog boxes.

10. Under the title *Activities*, select list items *A–C*. Change the numbering style to 1. 2. 3.

Word 2016, Windows 10, Microsoft Corporation

11. **Save** the file, **Close** Word, and then submit the file as directed by your instructor.

 DONE! You have completed More Skills Assessment

Collaborating with Google

To complete this project, you will need a Google account (refer to the Common Features chapter) and the following file:

- wrd02_GPPlayground

You will save your file as:

- Last_First_wrd02_GPPlayground

1. Open a web browser. Log into your Google account, and then click the **Google Apps** button.

2. Click the **Drive** button to open Google Drive. If you receive a pop-up message, read the message, and then click **Next**. Read each message, and then close the dialog box.

3. Click the **New** button, click **Google Docs**, and then change the document title to Playground Proposal

4. In **Word 2016**, open the student data file **wrd02_GPPlayground**. Select and copy all the text and paste it in your Google Doc. At the top of the document, replace *Your Name* with your First and Last name.

5. Click the **Edit tab**, and then click **Find and replace**. In the **Find and replace** dialog box, **Find** all occurrences of play ground and **Replace** with playground

6. Click in the paragraph starting *The majority of*. On the **Format tab**, click **Line spacing**, and then click **Double**. Click to the right of the double quotes at the end of the paragraph. On the **Insert tab**, click **Footnote**, and then type StrongReach.com, Strong Reach, 2017, http://strongreach.org/ (accessed January 24, 2018). Compare your screen.

7. Under the title *ADA Compliance*, select the four requirements starting with *Wheelchair access*. On the **Format tab**, click **Lists**, and then click **Bulleted list**. In the gallery, click the first bullet style. Scroll down to the *Design Elements* title, and then repeat this technique to apply the bulleted list to the five ground covers. Compare your screen.

8. Under the document title *Playground Proposal*, click the **File tab**, click **Download as**, and then click **Microsoft Word (.docx)**. **Save** the file in your chapter folder as Last_First_wrd02_GPPlayground

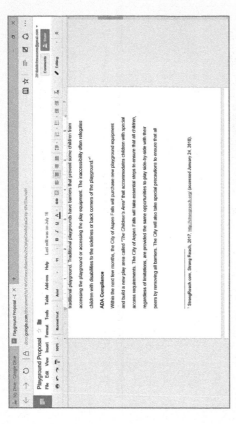

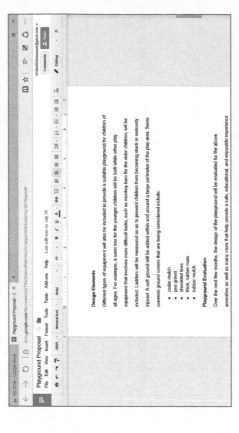

9. Start **Word 2016**, and then open the file **Last_First_wrd02_GPPlayground**. Insert the **FileName** field in the footer.

10. Save the file, **Close** the open windows, and then submit the file as directed by your instructor.

DONE! You have completed Collaborating with Google

CHAPTER 4

Create Workbooks with Excel 2016

▸ Microsoft Office Excel 2016 is used worldwide to create workbooks and to analyze data that is organized into columns and rows.

▸ After data is entered into Excel, you can perform calculations on the numerical data and analyze the data to make informed decisions.

▸ When you make changes to one or more number values, you can immediately see the effect of those changes in totals and charts that rely on those values.

▸ An Excel workbook can contain a large amount of data—up to 16,384 columns and 1,048,576 rows.

▸ The basic skills you need to work efficiently with Excel include entering and formatting data and navigating within Excel.

▸ When planning your worksheet, think about what information will form the rows and what information will form the columns. Generally, rows are used to list the items and columns to group or describe the items in the list.

Aspen Falls Outdoor Recreation

In this chapter, you will create a workbook for Amado Pettinelli, the Outdoor Recreation Supervisor. Mr. Pettinelli wants to know the attendance at each city attraction and the revenue each venue generates for the city. He plans to recommend to the Aspen Falls City Council that the busiest attractions receive more city funding in the next fiscal year.

A business spreadsheet can be used for many purposes including tracking budgets, manufacture measurements, or employees. The spreadsheet data can be manipulated using arithmetic and mathematical formulas commonly used in the modern-day business world. If you are asked to create a spreadsheet, you need to know if the results of the data manipulation will be presented in numerical or graphical format.

In this project, you will create a new Excel workbook and enter data that displays the total number of visitors at the various city attractions in Aspen Falls. You will format the data, construct formulas, and insert functions. You will calculate the percentage of weekday visitors at each of the locations and insert a footer. Finally, you will check the spelling in the workbook.

Vlad_g/Fotolia

Introduction

60-90 min.

Time to complete all 10 skills — 60 to 90 minutes

Outcome

Using the skills in this chapter, you will be able to create, edit, and save workbooks; create addition, subtraction, multiplication, and division formulas and functions; modify cell and worksheet formats; and apply print settings.

Objectives:

Create and enter data into worksheets

Construct basic functions and formulas

Apply cell formatting

Adjust settings and review worksheets for printing

Student data file needed for this chapter:

Blank Excel workbook

You will save your file as:

Last_First_exl01_Visitors

Aspen Falls Outdoor Recreation
Visitors to City Attractions

Location	Weekends	Weekdays	All Visitors	Difference	Entrance Fee	Total Fees
Zoo	3,169	1,739	4,908	1,430	$ 10	$ 49,080
Pool	5,338	3,352	8,690	1,986	10	86,900
Aquarium	9,027	3,868	12,895	5,159	12	154,740
Garden	4,738	2,788	7,526	1,950	4	30,104
Museum	3,876	913	4,789	2,963	11	52,679
Total	26,148	12,660	38,808			$ 373,503

Percent of Weekday Visitors	
Zoo	35.4%
Pool	38.6%
Aquarium	30.0%
Garden	37.0%
Museum	19.1%

Excel 2016, Windows 10, Microsoft Corporation

SKILLS

At the end of this chapter you will be able to:

Skill 1 Create and Save Workbooks

Skill 2 Enter Data and Merge and Center Titles

Skill 3 Construct Addition and Subtraction Formulas

Skill 4 Construct Multiplication and Division Formulas

Skill 5 Adjust Column Widths and Apply Cell Styles

Skill 6 Insert the SUM Function

Skill 7 AutoFill Formulas and Data

Skill 8 Format, Edit, and Check Spelling

Skill 9 Insert Footers and Adjust Page Settings

Skill 10 Display Formulas and Print Worksheets

MORE SKILLS

Skill 11 Set Print Areas

Skill 12 Fill Data with Flash Fill

Skill 13 Create Templates and Workbooks from Templates

Skill 14 Manage Document Properties

▲ An Excel **workbook** is a file that you can use to organize various kinds of related information. A workbook contains **worksheets**, also called **spreadsheets**—the primary documents that you use in Excel to store and work with data.

▲ The worksheet forms a grid of vertical columns and horizontal rows. The small box where one column and one row meet is a cell.

MOS
Obj

1. Start **Excel 2016**, and then click **Blank workbook**. In the lower right, notice the zoom level.

    Your zoom level should be 100%, but most figures in this chapter are zoomed to 120%.

2. Verify the cell in the upper left corner is the *active cell*.

    active cell—the cell outlined in green in which data is entered when you begin typing. In a worksheet, columns have alphabetical headings across the top, and rows have numerical headings down the left side. When a cell is active, the headings for the column and row in which the cell is located are shaded. The column letter and row number that identify a cell compose the **cell address**, also called the **cell reference**.

3. In cell **A1**, type Aspen Falls Outdoor Recreation and then press Enter to accept the entry.

4. In cell **A2**, type Visitors and then press Enter two times. Compare your screen.

5. In cell **A4**, type Location and press Tab to make the cell to the right—**B4**—active.

■ **Continue to the next page to complete the skill**

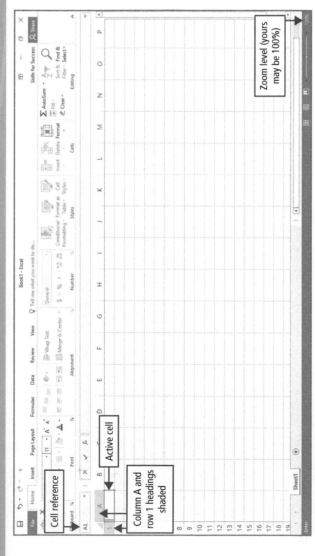

Cell reference

Active cell

Column A and row 1 headings shaded

Zoom level (yours may be 100%)

Excel 2016, Windows 10, Microsoft Corporation

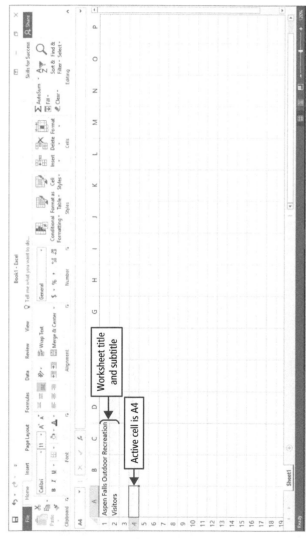

Worksheet title and subtitle

Active cell is A4

Excel 2016, Windows 10, Microsoft Corporation

6. With cell **B4** the active cell, type the following labels, pressing Tab between each label:

Weekends

Weekdays

All Visitors

Difference

Entrance Fee

Total Fees

Labels at the beginning of columns or rows help readers understand the data.

To correct typing errors, click a cell and retype the data. The new typing will replace the existing data.

7. Click cell **A5**, type Zoo and then press Tab. Type 3169 and then press Tab. Type 1739 and then press Enter. Compare your screen.

Data in a cell is called a *value*. You can have a *text value*—character data in a cell that usually labels number values, or a *number value*—numeric data in a cell. A text value is often used as a *label*. Text values align at the left cell edge, and number values align at the right cell edge.

8. Click **Save** [icon], and then on the **Save As** page, click the **Browse** button. In the **Save As** dialog box, navigate to the location where you are saving your files. Click **New folder**, type Excel Chapter 4 and then press Enter two times. In the **File name** box, name the file Last_First_exl01_Visitors and then press Enter.

9. Take a few moments to familiarize yourself with common methods to move between cells as summarized in the table.

■ **You have completed Skill 1 of 10**

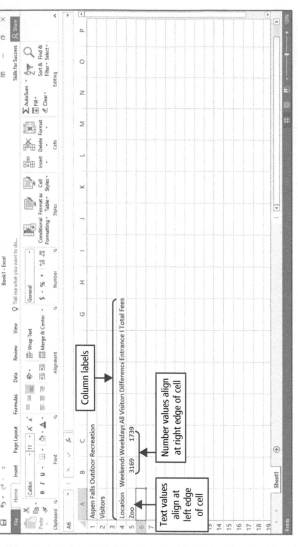

Excel 2016, Windows 10, Microsoft Corporation

Common Ways to Move or Scroll Through a Worksheet

Key	Description
Enter	Move down one row.
Tab	Move one column to the right.
Shift + Tab	Move one column to the left.
→ ↑ ← ↓	Move one cell in the direction of the arrow.
Ctrl + Home	Move to cell A1.
Ctrl + End	Move to the last row and last column farthest to the bottom right that contains data.

▶ To create an effective worksheet, you enter titles and subtitles and add labels for each row and column of data. It is a good idea to have the worksheet title and subtitle span across all the columns containing data.

1. In cell **A6**, type Aquarium and then press [Tab].

2. In cell **B6**, type 9027 and then press [Tab]. In cell **C6**, type 3868 and then press [Enter].

3. In row 7 and row 8, type the following data:

   Garden | 5738 | 2877
   Museum | 3876 | 913

4. In cell **A9**, type Total and then press [Enter]. Compare your screen.

5. Click cell **B1**, type Worksheet and then press [Enter]. Click cell **A1**, and then compare your screen.

   When text is too long to fit in a cell and the cell to the right of it contains data, the text will be *truncated*—cut off. Here, the text in cell A1 is truncated.

   The *formula bar* is a bar below the ribbon that displays the value contained in the active cell and is used to enter or edit values or formulas.

   Data displayed in a cell is the *displayed value*. Data displayed in the formula bar is the *underlying value*. Displayed values often do not match their underlying values.

6. On the Quick Access Toolbar, click the **Undo** button ↺ to remove the text in cell B1.

   Long text in cells overlaps into other columns only when those cells are empty. Here, A1 text now overlaps B1 because that cell is empty.

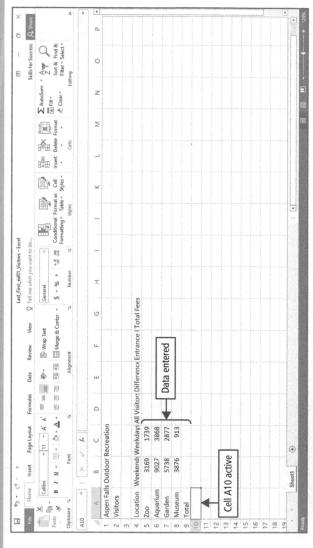

Excel 2016, Windows 10, Microsoft Corporation

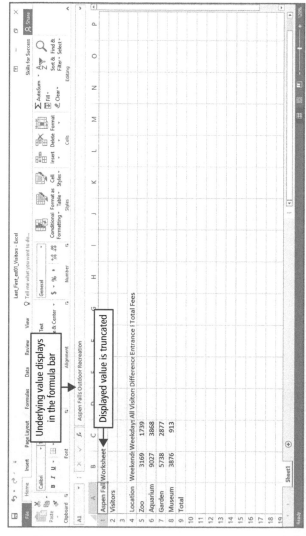

Excel 2016, Windows 10, Microsoft Corporation

■ **Continue to the next page to complete the skill**

MOS
Obj

7. Point to the middle of cell **A1** to display the ⊕ pointer. Hold down the left mouse button, and then drag to the right to select cells **A1** through **G1**. Compare your screen. To select a range on a touch screen, tap the cell, and then drag the selection handle.

The selected range is referred to as *A1:G1* (A1 through G1). A *range* is two or more cells in a worksheet that are adjacent (next to each other). A colon (:) between two cell references indicates that the range includes the two cell references and all the cells between them. When you select a range, a thick green line surrounds the range, and all but the first cell in the range are shaded. The first cell reference will be displayed in the *Name Box*—an area by the formula bar that displays the active cell reference.

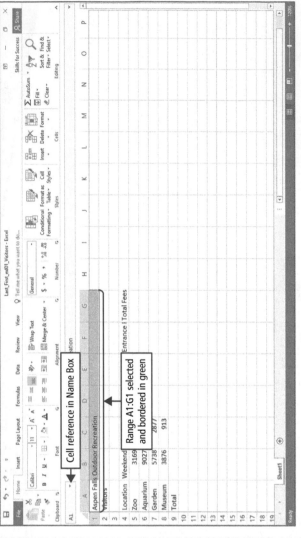

Excel 2016, Windows 10, Microsoft Corporation

MOS
Obj

8. On the **Home tab**, in the **Alignment group**, click the **Merge & Center** button ⊞.

The selected range, A1:G1, merges into one larger cell, and the data is centered in the new cell. The cells in B1 through G1 can no longer be selected individually because they are merged into cell A1.

9. Using the technique just practiced, merge and center the range **A2:G2.**

10. **Save** ⊞ the file, and then compare your screen.

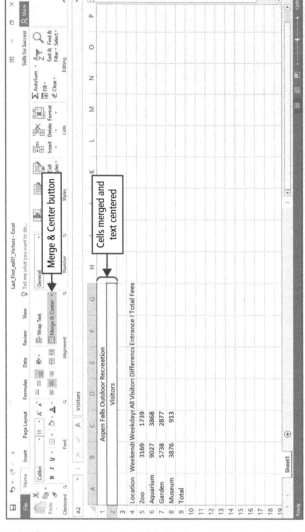

Excel 2016, Windows 10, Microsoft Corporation

■ **You have completed Skill 2 of 10**

Symbols Used in Excel for Arithmetic Operators

+ (plus sign)	Addition
- (minus sign)	Subtraction (also negation)
* (asterisk)	Multiplication
/ (forward slash)	Division
% (percent sign)	Percent
^ (caret)	Exponentiation

▶ A cell's underlying value can be a text value, a number value, or a *formula*—an equation that performs mathematical calculations on number values in the worksheet.

▶ Formulas begin with an equal sign and often include an *arithmetic operator*—a symbol that specifies a mathematical operation such as addition or subtraction.

1. Study the symbols that Excel uses to perform mathematical operations, as summarized in the table.

2. In cell **D5**, type =B5+C5 and then press Enter.

   When you include cell references in formulas, the values in those cells are inserted. Here, the total number of visitors for the zoo location equals the sum of the values in cells B5 and C5 (3169 + 1739 = 4908).

   When you type a formula, you might see a brief display of function names that match the first letter you type. This Excel feature, called *Formula AutoComplete*, suggests values as you type a function.

3. In cell **D6**, type the formula to add cells B6 and C6, =B6+C6 and then press Enter.

4. In cell **D7**, type = and then click cell **B7** to automatically insert B7 into the formula. Compare your screen.

   Cell B7 is surrounded by a moving border indicating that it is part of an active formula.

5. Type + Click cell **C7**, and then press Enter to display the result 8615.

   You can either type formulas or construct them by pointing and clicking in this manner.

■ **Continue to the next page to complete the skill**

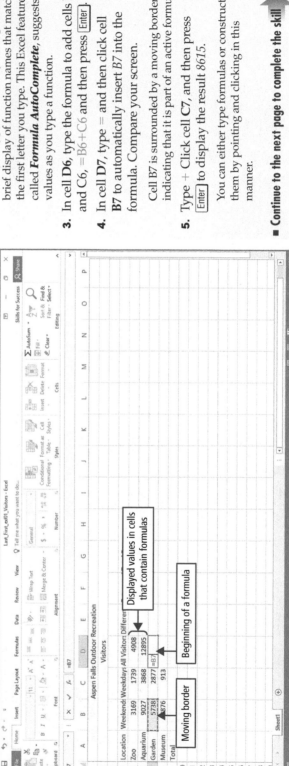

Excel 2016, Windows 10, Microsoft Corporation

6. In cell **D8**, use point and click to construct a formula that adds cells **B8** and **C8**. Press Enter when done.

7. In cell **E5**, type = B5-C5 On the formula bar, click the **Enter button** ✓ to confirm the entry while keeping cell **E5** the active cell, and then compare your screen.

   Here, the underlying value for cell E5 displays as a formula in the formula bar and displays as a value, *1430*, in the cell as a result of the formula.

   If you make an error entering a formula, you can click the Cancel button ✗ and then start over. Alternately, you can press the Esc key.

8. In cell **E6**, use point and click to enter the formula = B6-C6 to display the difference for the aquarium weekend and weekday visitors. (You will complete the column E formulas in Skill 7.)

9. In column **F**, type the following data as listed in the table below, and then compare your screen.

Cell	Value
F5	10
F6	12
F7	4
F8	11

10. **Save** 🖫 the file.

■ **You have completed Skill 3 of 10**

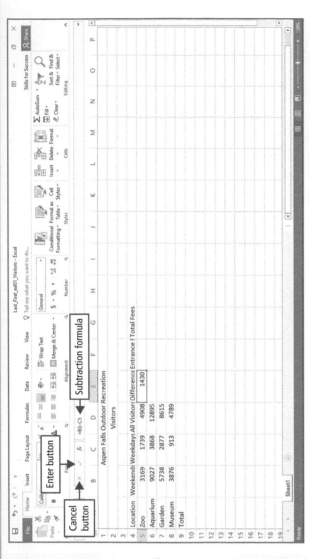

Subtraction formula

Enter button

Cancel button

Excel 2016, Windows 10, Microsoft Corporation

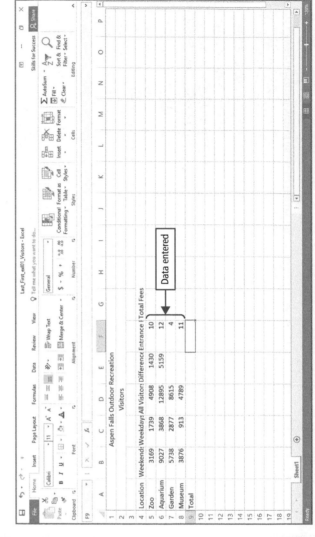

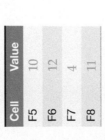

Data entered

Excel 2016, Windows 10, Microsoft Corporation

▶ The four most common operators for addition (+), subtraction (−), multiplication (*), and division (/) can be found on the number keypad at the right side of a standard keyboard or on the number keys at the top of a keyboard.

1. In cell **G5**, type **=D5*F5** This formula multiplies the total zoo visitors by its entrance fee. On the formula bar, click the **Enter** button ✓, and then compare your screen.

The **underlying formula**—the formula as displayed in the formula bar—multiplies the value in cell D5 (*4908*) by the value in cell F5 (*10*) and displays the result in cell G5 (*49080*).

2. In the range **G6:G8**, enter the following formulas:

Cell	Formula
G6	=D6*F6
G7	=D7*F7
G8	=D8*F8

3. In cell **A11**, type Percent of Weekday Visitors and then press Enter. Compare your screen.

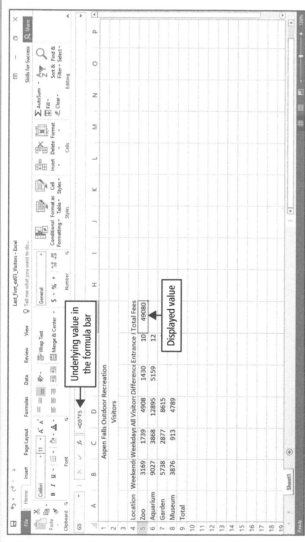

Excel 2016, Windows 10, Microsoft Corporation

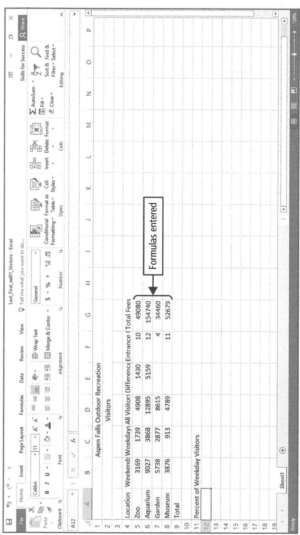

Excel 2016, Windows 10, Microsoft Corporation

■ **Continue to the next page to complete the skill**

Obj

4. Select the range **A5:A8**, and then on the **Home tab**, in the **Clipboard group**, click the **Copy** button. Click cell **A12**, and then in the **Clipboard group**, click the **Paste** button.

> The four location labels are copied to the range A12:A15.

5. Press [Esc] to remove the moving border around the copied cells.

6. In cell **B12**, construct the formula to divide the number of weekday zoo visitors by the total zoo visitors, =C5/D5 and then click the **Enter** button . Compare your screen.

> Percentages are calculated by taking the amount divided by the total and will be displayed in decimal format. Here, the underlying formula in B12 (=C5/D5) divides the weekday zoo visitors (1739) by the total zoo visitors (4908).

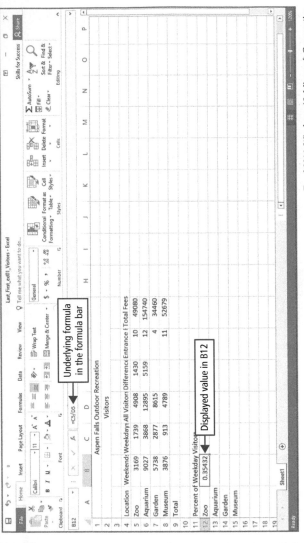

7. Construct the following formulas to calculate the percentage of weekday visitors for each location, and then compare your screen.

Cell	Formula
B13	=C6/D6
B14	=C7/D7
B15	=C8/D8

8. Save the file.

■ **You have completed Skill 4 of 10**

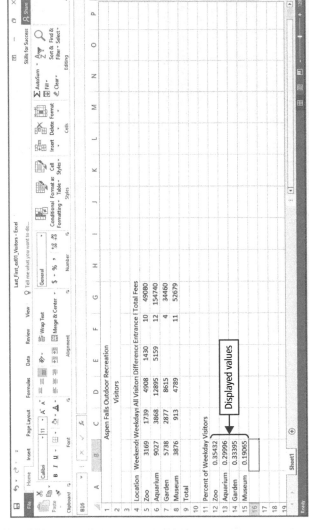

Excel 2016, Windows 10, Microsoft Corporation

Excel 2016, Windows 10, Microsoft Corporation

WATCH SKILL 1.5

▶ The *column heading* is the letter that displays at the top of a column. The number that displays at the left of a row is the *row heading*.

▶ *Formatting* is the process of specifying the appearance of cells or the overall layout of a worksheet.

MOS Obj

1. Click cell **A4**. On the **Home tab**, in the **Cells group**, click the **Format button**, and then click **Column Width**. In the **Column Width** dialog box, type 13

2. Compare your screen, and then click **OK**.

   The default column width will display as 8.43 characters when formatted in the standard font. Here, the width is increased to display more characters.

3. Select the range **B4:G4**. In the **Cells group**, click the **Format button**, and then click **Column Width**. In the **Column Width** dialog box, type 12 and then click **OK**.

   As an alternate method, you can select the column range to format the column widths.

4. Select cells **A11:B11**. On the **Home tab**, in the **Alignment group**, click the **Merge & Center arrow**, and then on the displayed list, click **Merge Across**. Compare your screen.

   Merge Across merges the selected cells without centering them.

MOS Obj

5. Click cell **A1** to select the merged and centered range A1:G1. In the **Cells group**, click the **Format button**, and then click **Row Height**. In the **Row Height** dialog box, type 22.5 and then click **OK**.

■ **Continue to the next page to complete the skill**

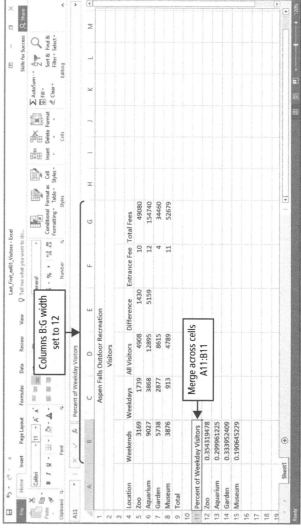

Excel 2016, Windows 10, Microsoft Corporation

Excel 2016, Windows 10, Microsoft Corporation

MOS
Obj

6. With **A1:G1** still selected, in the **Styles** group, click the **Cell Styles** button. In the Cell Styles gallery, under **Titles and Headings**, use Live Preview to view the title as you point to **Heading 1** and then **Heading 2**.

   A *cell style* is a prebuilt set of formatting characteristics, such as font, font size, font color, cell borders, and cell shading.

7. Under **Themed Cell Styles**, point to the **Accent1** style. Compare your screen, and then click **Accent1**.

MOS
Obj

8. In the **Font** group, click the **Font Size arrow** ⎸11 ▾⎸, and then click **16**.

9. Click cell **A2**, and then using the technique you just practiced, apply the **40% - Accent1** cell style. In the **Font** group, click the **Increase Font Size** button ⎸A^⎸ one time to change the font size to **12**.

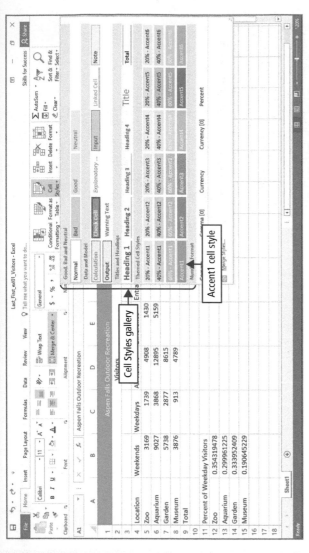

Excel 2016, Windows 10, Microsoft Corporation

10. Select the range **B4:G4**. Right-click the selected range to display a shortcut menu and the Mini toolbar. On the Mini toolbar, click the **Bold button** ⎸B⎸ and then click the **Center button** ⎸≡⎸ to apply bold and to center the text within each of the selected cells.

11. Select the range **A4:A9**. Display the Mini toolbar, and then apply **Bold** to the selected range. Click cell **A10**, and then compare your screen .

12. **Save** ⎸🖫⎸ the file.

■ **You have completed Skill 5 of 10**

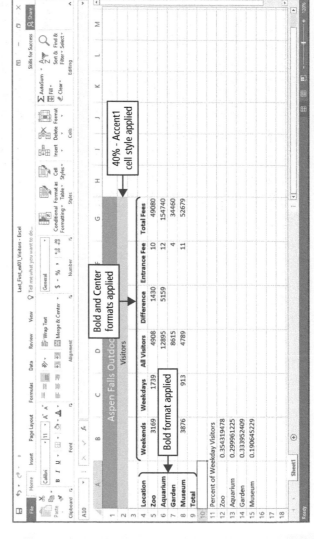

Excel 2016, Windows 10, Microsoft Corporation

▶ You can create your own formulas, or you can use a *function*—a prewritten Excel formula that takes a value or values, performs an operation, and returns a value or values.

▶ The AutoSum button is used to insert common summary functions into a worksheet.

▶ When cell references are used in a formula or function, the results are automatically recalculated whenever those cells are edited.

MOS Obj

1. Click cell **B9**. On the **Home tab**, in the **Editing group**, click the **AutoSum** button ∑ AutoSum ·, and then compare your screen.

   SUM is an Excel function that adds all the numbers in a range of cells. The range in parentheses, *(B5:B8)*, indicates the range of cells on which the SUM function will be performed.

   When the AutoSum button is used, Excel first looks *above* the selected cell for a range of cells to sum. If there is no data detected in the range above the selected cell, Excel then looks to the *left* and proposes a range of cells to sum. Here, the range B5:B8 is surrounded by a moving border, and =SUM(B5:B8) displays in cell B9.

2. Press Enter to display the function result—*21810*.

3. Select the range **C9:D9**. In the **Editing group**, click the **AutoSum button** ∑ AutoSum ·, and then compare your screen.

■ **Continue to the next page to complete the skill**

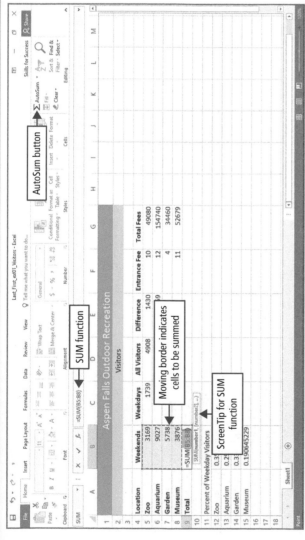

Excel 2016, Windows 10, Microsoft Corporation

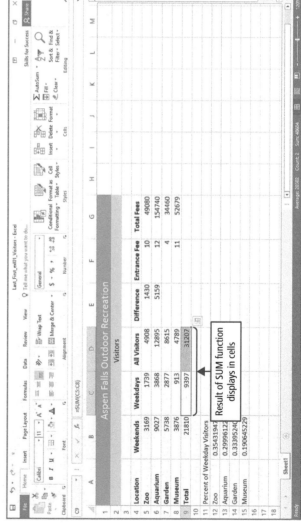

Excel 2016, Windows 10, Microsoft Corporation

4. Click cell **C9**, and then in the formula bar, verify that the SUM function adds the values in the range *C5:C8.*

5. Click cell **D9**, and then verify that the SUM function adds the values in the range *D5:D8.*

6. Using the technique just practiced, in cell **G9**, insert the SUM function to add the values in the range **G5:G8**. Select cell **G9**, and then compare your screen.

7. In cell **B7**, type 4738 Watch the total in cell **B9** update as you press Tab.

In cell B9, the displayed value changed to 20810, but the underlying formula remained the same.

8. In cell **C7**, type 2788 and then press Enter to update the totals in cells C9, G7, and G9. Compare your screen.

The amounts were recalculated when the data was changed because cell references were used in the functions.

9. Save ⊞ the file.

■ **You have completed Skill 6 of 10**

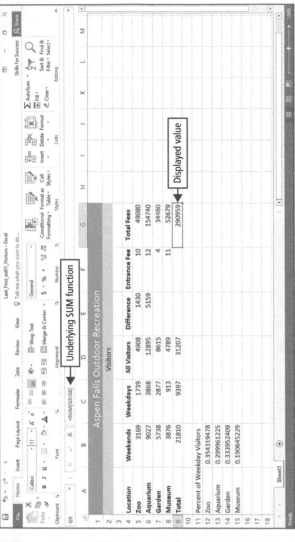

Excel 2016, Windows 10, Microsoft Corporation

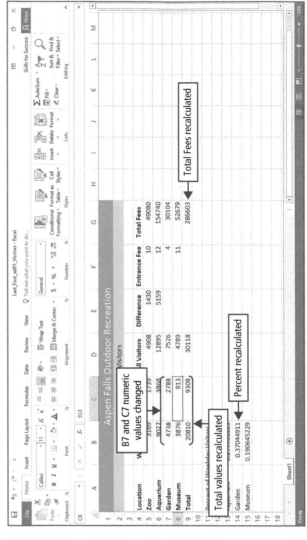

Excel 2016, Windows 10, Microsoft Corporation

▶ Text, numbers, formulas, and functions can be copied down rows and across columns to insert formulas and functions quickly.

▶ When a formula is copied to another cell, Excel adjusts the cell references relative to the new location of the formula.

MOS
Obj

1. Click cell **E6**. With cell **E6** selected, point to the **fill handle**—the small green square in the lower right corner of the selection—until the **+** pointer displays.

   To use the fill handle, first select the cell that contains the content you want to copy—here the formula =B6-C6.

2. Drag the **+** pointer down to cell **E8**, and then release the mouse button.

MOS
Obj

3. Click cell **E7**, and verify on the formula bar that the formula copied from E6 changed to =B7-C7. Click cell **E8**, and then compare your screen.

   In each row, the cell references in the formula adjusted *relative to* the row number—B6 changed to B7 and then to B8. This adjustment is called a **relative cell reference** because it refers to cells based on their position *in relation to* (relative to) the cell that contains the formula.

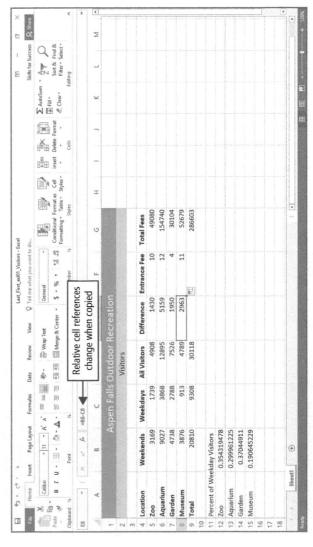

Excel 2016, Windows 10, Microsoft Corporation

Excel 2016, Windows 10, Microsoft Corporation

■ **Continue to the next page to complete the skill**

4. Click cell **A6**. In the **Cells** group, click the **Insert arrow**, and then click **Insert Sheet Rows**. Click cell **B10**, and then compare your screen.

When you insert a new row or column, the cell references and the ranges in formulas or in functions adjust to include the new row or column. Here, in cell B10, the range in the function automatically updated to include the new row in the range.

5. In cell **A6**, type Pool and then press Tab.

By default, formatting (bold) from the row above is applied to an inserted row.

6. In cell **B6**, type 5338 and then press Tab to enter the value and update the column total in cell B10 to 26148.

7. In cell **C6**, type 3352 and then press Tab.

8. Select cells **D5:G5**. Point to the fill handle until the + pointer displays, and then drag the + pointer down one row. Release the mouse button, and then click the **Auto Fill Options button** ⊞. Compare your screen.

Three formulas and a number are copied. When you copy number values using the fill handle, the numbers automatically increment for each row or column. Here, the number value in cell F5 increased by one when it was copied to cell F6.

9. In the **Auto Fill Options** menu, click **Copy Cells**.

With the Copy Cells option, number values are copied exactly and do not increment. Here, the number value in cell F6 changes to 10.

10. **Save** 🖫 the file.

■ **You have completed Skill 7 of 10**

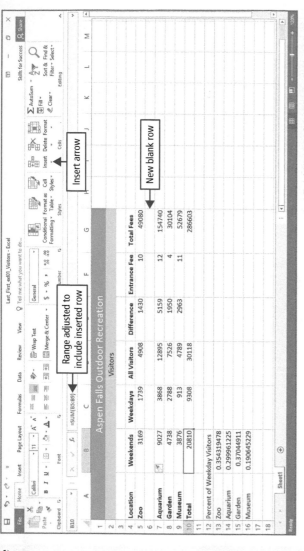

Excel 2016, Windows 10, Microsoft Corporation

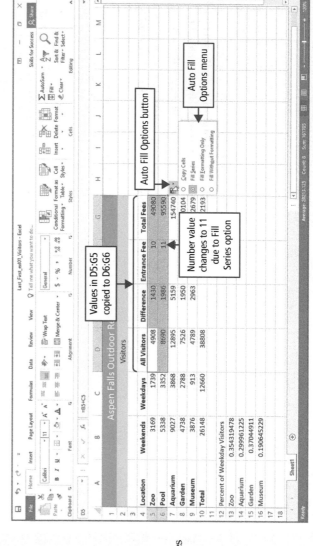

Excel 2016, Windows 10, Microsoft Corporation

Number Formats

Format	Description
Comma	Adds commas where appropriate and displays two decimals. Added character space in right margin for negative parenthetical numbers.
Comma [0]	Adds commas where appropriate and displays no decimals. Added character space in right margin for negative parenthetical numbers.
Currency	Adds the dollar sign, commas where appropriate, displays two decimals, and left justifies dollar symbol. Added character space in right margin for negative parenthetical numbers.
Currency [0]	Adds the dollar sign, commas where appropriate, displays no decimals, and left justifies dollar symbol. Added character space in right margin for negative parenthetical numbers.
Percent	Adds the percent sign and multiplies the number by 100.

▶ Always check spelling after you have completed formatting and editing worksheet data.

1. Click cell **A14**, and then repeat the technique used previously to insert a new row. In cell **A14**, type Pool and then press Enter.

2. Click cell **B13**, and then use the fill handle to copy the formula down to cell **B14**.

3. Double-click cell **A2** to edit the cell contents. Use the arrow keys to move to the right of the word *Visitors*. Add a space, type to City Attractions and then press Enter.

MOS
Obj

4. Select the range **F5:G5**. In the **Styles group**, click the **Cell Styles** button, and then under **Number Format**, click **Currency [0]**. Repeat this technique to apply the **Currency [0]** format to cell **G10**. Review Cell Style Number Formats as summarized in the table.

When applying number formats, general practice is to apply the currency symbol to the top and bottom amounts.

5. Select the range **B5:E10**. Click the **Cell Styles** button, and then under **Number Format**, click **Comma [0]**. Repeat the technique to apply the **Comma [0]** format to the range **F6:G9**.

6. Select the range **B13:B17**. In the **Number group**, click the **Percent Style** button [%], and then click the **Increase Decimal** button one time. Compare your screen.

The Increase Decimal and Decrease Decimal buttons do not add or remove decimals; they change how the decimal values *display* in the cells.

MOS
Obj

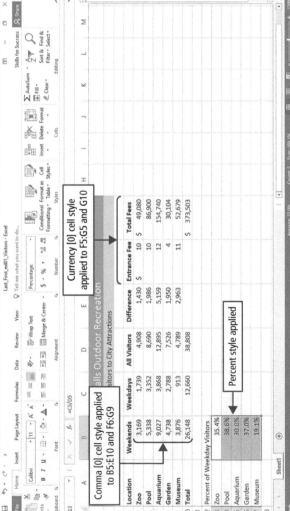

Excel 2016, Windows 10, Microsoft Corporation

■ **Continue to the next page to complete the skill**

MOS
Obj

7. Select the range **B10:D10**. Hold down Ctrl, and then click cell **G10**. Click the **Cell Styles** button. Under **Titles and Headings**, click the **Total** style.

8. Select cell **A12**, and then click the **Cell Styles** button. Under **Themed Cell Styles**, click **40% - Accent1**.

9. Press Ctrl + Home to make cell **A1** active. On the **Review tab**, in the **Proofing group**, click the **Spelling** button.

The Spelling checker starts with the active cell and moves to the right and down. Making cell A1 the active cell verifies the spreadsheet is checked from the beginning.

If the Spelling dialog box opens to reveal unrecognized words not in the Office dictionary, (your screen may be different), the words not in the dictionary are not necessarily misspelled. Many proper nouns or less commonly used words are not in the Office dictionary.

To correct a misspelled word and to move to the next word not in the Office dictionary, under Suggestions, verify that the correct spelling is selected, and then click the Change button.

10. Use the Spelling checker to correct any errors you may have made. When the **Spell check complete. You're good to go!** message box displays, click **OK**.

When words you use often are not in the Office dictionary, you can click *Add to Dictionary* to add them.

11. Save the file.

■ **You have completed Skill 8 of 10**

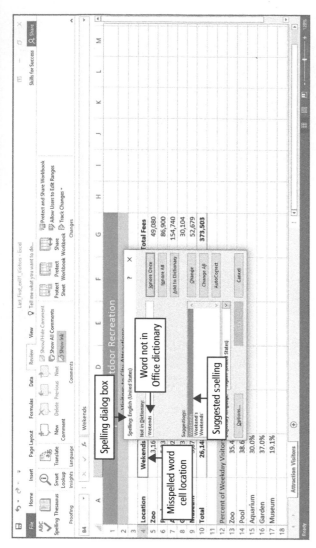

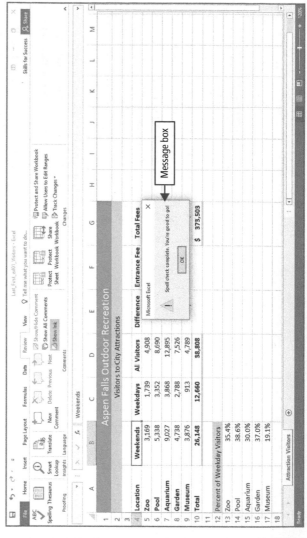

Excel 2016, Windows 10, Microsoft Corporation

Excel 2016, Windows 10, Microsoft Corporation

WATCH SKILL 1.9

▶ In Excel, *Page Layout view* is used to adjust how a worksheet will look when it is printed.

1. Click the **Insert tab**, in the **Text group**, click the **Header & Footer** button to switch to **Page Layout view** and to display the **Header & Footer Tools Design** contextual tab.

2. On the **Design tab**, in the **Navigation group**, click the **Go to Footer** button to move to the Footer area. Click just above the word **Footer** to place the insertion point in the left section of the Footer area. Compare your screen.

3. In the **Header & Footer Elements group**, click the **File Name** button, and then click any cell in the workbook to view the file name, if necessary.

   Predefined headers and footers insert placeholders with instructions for printing. Here, the *&[File]* placeholder instructs Excel to insert the file name when the worksheet is printed.

4. At the bottom of your worksheet, right-click the **Sheet1** worksheet tab, and then from the shortcut menu, click **Rename**. Type **Attraction Visitors** and then press **Enter** to change the worksheet tab name. Compare your screen.

5. Click in the middle section of the Footer area, click the **Header & Footer Tools tab**, and then click the **Current Date** button. Click the right section of the Footer area, and then click the **Sheet Name** button. Click in a cell just above the footer to exit the Footer area, and then press **Ctrl** + **Home**.

■ **Continue to the next page to complete the skill**

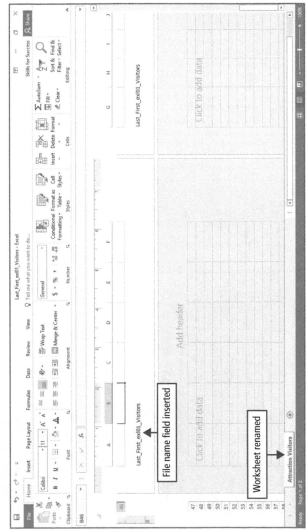

Header & Footer Tools Design contextual tab

File Name button

Left Footer section

Edges of paper if worksheet is printed

Excel 2016, Windows 10, Microsoft Corporation

File name field inserted

Worksheet renamed

Add header

Excel 2016, Windows 10, Microsoft Corporation

MOS
Obj

6. Click the **Page Layout tab**. In the **Sheet Options group**, under **Gridlines**, select the **Print** check box.

7. In the **Page Setup group**, click the **Margins** button. Below the **Margins** gallery, click **Custom Margin**, and then type 0.5 in the **Left** and **Right** margins.

8. In the **Page Setup** dialog box, under **Center on page**, click to select the **Horizontally** and **Vertically** check boxes, and then compare your screen.

9. In the **Page Setup** dialog box, click **Print Preview**, and then compare your screen.

MOS
Obj

10. Click the **Back button** ⬅. On the lower right side of the status bar, click the **Normal button** ⊞ to return to Normal view.

    Normal view maximizes the number of cells visible on the screen. The page break—the dotted line between columns G and H—indicates where one page ends and a new page begins.

11. Save 💾 the file.

■ **You have completed Skill 9 of 10**

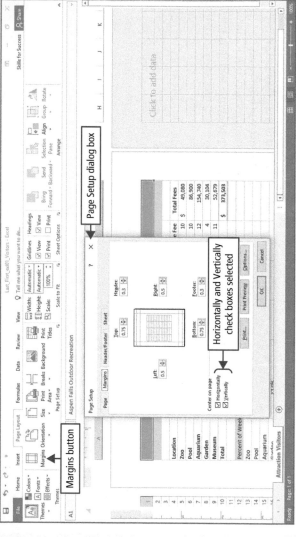

Excel 2016, Windows 10, Microsoft Corporation

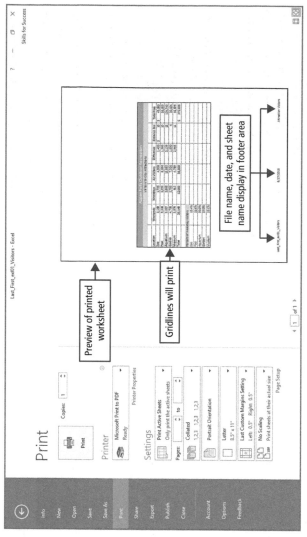

Excel 2016, Windows 10, Microsoft Corporation

SKILL 10: Display Formulas and Print Worksheets

▶ Underlying formulas and functions can be displayed and printed.

▶ When formulas are displayed in cells, the orientation and worksheet scale may need to be changed so that the worksheet prints on a single page.

1. Click the **Formulas tab**. In the **Formula Auditing group**, click the **Show Formulas** button to display the underlying formulas in the cells. Compare your screen.

Columns often become wider when formulas are displayed. Here, the printed worksheet extends to a third page.

2. Click the **File tab**, and then click **Print**.

Below the preview of the printed page, *1 of 3* indicates that the worksheet will print on three pages.

3. In **Backstage** view, on the bottom of the **Print page**, click the **Next Page** button two times to view the second and third pages, and then compare your screen.

4. Click the **Back button**. On the **Page Layout tab**, in the **Page Setup group**, click the **Orientation** button, and then click **Landscape** so that the page orientation will be wider than it is tall.

■ **Continue to the next page to complete the skill**

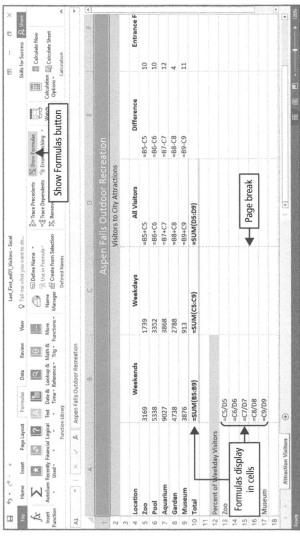

Excel 2016, Windows 10, Microsoft Corporation

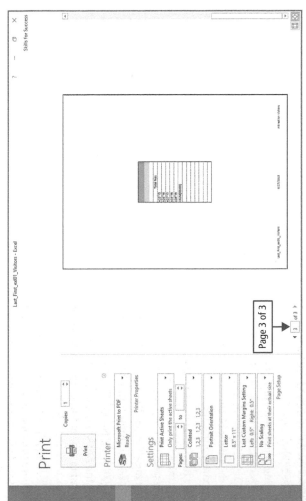

Excel 2016, Windows 10, Microsoft Corporation

MOS
Obj

5. In the **Scale to Fit** group, click the **Width** arrow, and then click **1 page**. Compare your screen.

   Scaling adjusts the size of the printed worksheet to fit on the number of pages that you specify.

6. Click the **File tab**, and then click **Print**. Compare your screen.

   1 of 1 displays at the bottom of the Print page to notify you that the worksheet will now print on one page.

7. If you are directed by your instructor to submit a printout with your formulas displayed, click the Print button.

8. Click the **Back button** ⬅ On the **Formulas tab**, in the **Formula Auditing group**, click the **Show Formulas** button to hide the formulas.

MOS
Obj

9. If you are printing your work, print the worksheet with the values displayed and formulas hidden.

10. **Save** 🖫 the file, and then **Close** ✕ Excel. Submit the file as directed by your instructor.

 **DONE! You have completed Skill and your file is complete!**

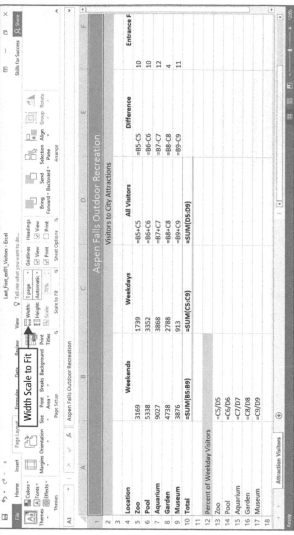

Excel 2016, Windows 10, Microsoft Corporation

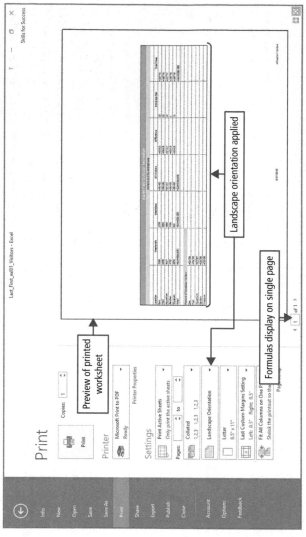

Excel 2016, Windows 10, Microsoft Corporation

More Skills 11
Set Print Areas

To complete this project, you will need the following file:

- exl01_MS11Business

You will save your file as:

- Last_First_exl01_MS11Business

▶ If the same portion of a worksheet needs to be printed repeatedly, you can save time by setting a print area.

MOS
Obj

1. Start Excel 2016, open the student data file **exl01_MS11Business,** and then save the file in your chapter folder as Last_First_exl01_MS11Business

2. Select the range **A4:C12.** On the **Page Layout tab,** in the **Page Setup group,** click the **Print Area** button, and then click **Set Print Area.**

3. Click cell **A1,** and notice that a border surrounds the print area.

MOS
Obj

4. Click the **Name Box arrow** above column A, and then click **Print_Area.**

   When a print area is set, the range of selected cells is named Print_Area.

5. Verify that the range A4:C12 is selected, and then compare your screen.

6. Click the **File tab,** and then click **Print.** Verify that only the print area displays.

   To print a worksheet portion only once, select the cells, and then on the File tab, click Print. Under Settings, select Print Selection.

7. Compare your screen, and then click **Save** 🖫.

   The print area setting is saved when the workbook is saved.

8. **Close** ✕ Excel. Submit the file as directed by your instructor.

■ **You have completed More Skills 11**

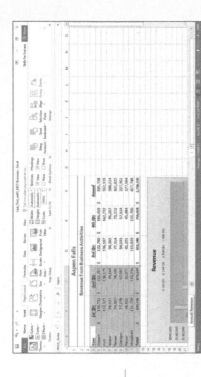

Excel 2016, Windows 10, Microsoft Corporation

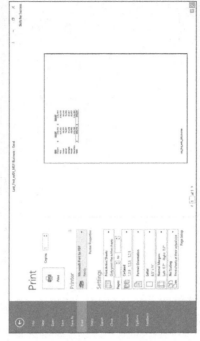

Excel 2016, Windows 10, Microsoft Corporation

More Skills 12

Fill Data with Flash Fill

To complete this project, you will need the following file:

- exl01_MS12Employees

You will save your file as:

- Last_First_exl01_MS12Employees

▶ *Flash Fill* recognizes a pattern in data and automatically enters the rest of the data.

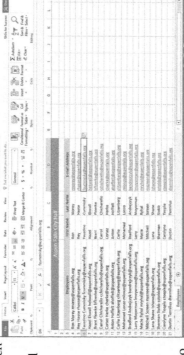

Excel 2016, Windows 10, Microsoft Corporation

1. Start Excel 2016, open the student data file **exl01_MS12Employees**, and then save the file in your chapter folder as Last_First_exl01_MS12Employees

2. Add the file name in the worksheet's left footer, and then return to **Normal** view. Press Ctrl + Home.

   Often, data imported from a database will place spaces between data instead of placing each field in a separate column.

   MOS
   Obj

3. Click cell **B4**, type Ron and then press Enter. In cell **B5**, type Re and then pause to preview all the employee first names in column B.

   Flash Fill recognizes the first name pattern in your data.

4. Press Enter to automatically fill all employee first names.

5. Using the technique just practiced, use Flash Fill to enter the last names into column C and the e-mail addresses into column D. Compare your screen.

6. **Save** 🔲 the file, and then **Close** ✕ Excel. Submit the file as directed by your instructor.

■ You have completed More Skills 12

More Skills 13

Create Templates and Workbooks from Templates

To complete this project, you will need the following file:

- Blank Excel workbook

You will save your files as:

- Last_First_exl01_MS13Timecard
- Last_First_exl01_MS13Template

▶ A **template**—a prebuilt workbook used as a pattern for creating new workbooks—is used to build workbooks without having to start from a blank workbook.

▶ When a template is opened, a copy of the file is created to keep the original template.

▶ A workbook submitted on a regular basis, such as a time card or an expense report, can be saved as a template.

1. Start **Excel 2016**. At the top of the window, in the search box, type time card and then press [Enter]. If necessary, scroll to find the **Time card** template.

2. Click the **Time card** template, and then click the **Create** button.

   If you are not able to locate this template, navigate to your student data files and open exl01_MS13Timecard.

3. With cell **C7** the active cell, type the following data using your name where indicated.

Title	Cell	Data
Employee	C7	Your First Last Name
[Street Address]	C9	500 S Aspen Street
[City, ST ZIP Code]	C13	Aspen Falls, CA 93463
Manager	G7	Maria Martinez
Employee phone	G9	(805) 555-9080

4. On the **File tab**, click **Save As**, and then in **Backstage** view, click the **Browse** button. In the **Save As** dialog box, click the **Save as type arrow**, and then click **Excel Template**. Save the file in your chapter folder as Last_First_exl01_MS13Template **MOS Obj**

   By default, Excel saves templates in the Templates folder.

5. Click **Save** 🖫 and then **Close** ☒ Excel.

6. Navigate to your chapter folder, and then open the file Last_First_exl01_MS13Template to create a new workbook. **MOS Obj**

7. In cell **C16**, type 11/16/2018 and then press [Enter]. Scroll down to display row **30**.

   When a date is entered in cell C16, functions in C21:C27 automatically display the corresponding dates.

8. In cell **D21**, type 8 and then, on the formula bar, click the **Enter button** ✓. Fill the number 8 down through the cells **D22:D25**. Click the **Auto Fill Options button** 🖳 and then click **Fill Without Formatting**. In cell **D29**, type 25 and then press [Enter]. Compare your screen. **MOS Obj**

   When the regular hours are entered in cells D21:D25, the total hours in cell D28 are automatically calculated.

   Formatting symbols, such as the dollar sign in cell D29, are already formatted in a template.

9. Save the file as Last_First_exl01_MS13Timecard and then **Close** ☒ Excel. Submit the files as directed by your instructor.

■ **You have completed More Skills 13**

Excel 2016, Windows 10, Microsoft Corporation

More Skills 14

Manage Document Properties

To complete this project, you will need the following file:

- exl01_MS14Revenue

You will save your files as:

- Last_First_exl01_MS14Revenue
- Last_First_exl01_MS14Snip

▶ *Document properties* are details about a file that describe or identify the file, such as title, author, and keywords.

▶ The document properties are stored as part of the Excel file.

Excel 2016, Windows 10, Microsoft Corporation

1. Start **Excel 2016**, open the student data file **exl01_MS14Revenue**, and then save the file in your chapter folder as Last_First_exl01_MS14Revenue

2. Click the **File tab**. In **Backstage** view, on the right side of the **Info** page, click the **Title** box, and then type Park Revenue

3. In the **Tags** box, type first half, park, revenue, chart

4. In the **Author** box, replace the existing text with your First and Last names.

5. Select the **Show All Properties** link.

6. In the **Status** box, type Draft

MOS
Obj

7. At the top of the right panel, click **Properties**, click **Advanced Properties**, and then ensure the **Summary tab** is selected.

8. In the **Company** box, type Aspen Falls In the **Comments** box, type Need to increase marketing effort

9. In the **Properties** dialog box, click **OK**.

10. Start the **Snipping Tool**, click the **New arrow**, and then click **Full-screen Snip**.

11. Click the **Save Snip button**. In the **Save As** dialog box, navigate to your chapter folder. **Save** the file as Last_First_exl01_MS14Snip and then **Close** ⊠ the Snipping Tool window. Compare your screen.

12. **Close** the Document Information Panel. **Save** 🔲 the file, and then **Close** ⊠ Excel. Submit the files as directed by your instructor.

- **You have completed More Skills 14**

The following table summarizes the **SKILLS AND PROCEDURES** covered in this chapter.

Skills Number	Task	Step	Icon	Keyboard Shortcut
2	Merge cells	Home tab → Alignment group → Merge & Center	[Merge icon]	
3	Accept a cell entry	Formula bar → Enter	[✓]	Enter
5	Adjust column width	Home tab → Cells group → Format → Column Width		
5	Adjust row height	Home tab → Cells group → Format → Row Height		
5	Apply Cell Styles	Home tab → Styles group → Cell Styles		
6	Insert SUM function	Home tab → Editing group → AutoSum	Σ AutoSum ▾	Alt + =
7	Insert a row	Home tab → Cells group → Insert → Insert Sheet Rows		
8	Check spelling	Review tab → Proofing group → Spelling		F7
8	Edit inside cells	Double-click		F2
8	Increase decimals	Home tab → Number group → Increase Decimal	[.00 →.0]	
8	Decrease decimals	Home tab → Number group → Decrease Decimal	[.00 →.0]	
9	Display workbook in Normal View	Status bar → Normal	[grid icon]	
9	Move to cell A1			Ctrl + Home
9	Insert text and fields into footers	Insert tab → Text group → Header & Footer		
9	Rename a worksheet tab	Right-click worksheet tab → Rename		
10	Display formulas	Formulas tab → Formula Auditing group → Show Formulas	[icon]	Ctrl + [']
10	Scale to print on one page	Page Layout tab → Scale to Fit group → Width / Height		
10	Change page orientation	Page Layout tab → Page Setup group → Orientation		
MS 11	Set print area	Page Layout tab → Page Setup group → Print Area		
MS 12	Flash Fill	Type Text → Home tab → Editing group → Fill		
MS 13	Create template	Excel Start Screen → Search box → Create		
MS 14	Document properties	File tab → Backstage view → Info		

Project Summary Chart

Project	Project Type	Project Location
Skills Review	Review	In Book & MIL
Skills Assessment 1	Review	In Book & MIL
Skills Assessment 2	Review	Book
My Skills	Problem Solving	Book
Visual Skills Check	Problem Solving	Book
Skills Challenge 1	Critical Thinking	Book
Skills Challenge 2	Critical Thinking	Book
More Skills Assessment	Review	In Book & MIL
Collaborating with Google	Critical Thinking	Book

MOS Objectives Covered

Create a workbook	Set a print area
Navigate to a named cell, range, or workbook element	Save workbooks in alternative file formats
Rename a worksheet	Set print scaling
Modify page setup	Copy and paste data
Adjust column width	Fill cells by using AutoFill
Adjust row height	Merge cells
Insert headers and footers	Apply number formats
Change workbook views	Apply cell styles
Modify document properties	Insert references
Display formulas	Perform calculations by using the SUM function

Key Terms

BizSkills Video

1. What are the best ways to network online?

2. What are some of the biggest pitfalls in using social media to communicate a personal brand?

Online Help Skills

1. Start **Excel 2016**, and then in the upper right corner of the start page, click the **Help button** ?.

2. In the **Excel Help** window **Search help** box, type broken formula and then press Enter.

3. In the search result list, click **How to avoid broken formulas**, **Maximize** the Help window, and then compare your screen.

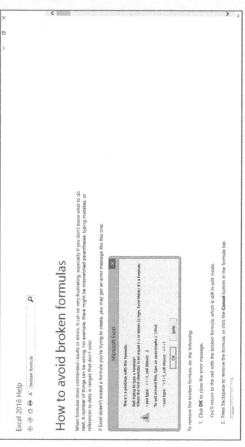

Excel 2016, Windows 10, Microsoft Corporation

4. Read the article to answer the following questions: How do you remove a broken formula? What sign does every function start with?

Matching

Match each term in the second column with its correct definition in the first column by writing the letter of the term on the blank line in front of the correct definition.

___ 1. An Excel file that contains one or more worksheets.

___ 2. The primary document that you use in Excel to store and work with data.

___ 3. The cell, surrounded by a green border, ready to receive data or be affected by the next Excel command.

___ 4. The identification of a specific cell by its intersecting column letter and row number.

___ 5. Data in a cell—text or numbers.

___ 6. Data in a cell made up of text only.

___ 7. Data in a cell made up of numbers only.

___ 8. Two or more cells on a worksheet.

___ 9. The Excel window area that displays the address of a selected cell.

___ 10. An Excel feature that suggests values as you type a function.

A Active cell

B Cell reference

C Formula AutoComplete

D Name Box

E Number value

F Range

G Text value

H Value

I Workbook

J Worksheet

Multiple Choice

Choose the correct answer.

1. An Excel window area that displays the value contained in the active cell.
   A. Formula bar
   B. Workbook
   C. Name Box

2. The column letter and row number that identify a cell.
   A. Cell window
   B. Cell address
   C. Cell file name

3. The data displayed in a cell.
   A. Viewed value
   B. Inspected value
   C. Displayed value

4. An equation that performs mathematical calculations on number values.
   A. Method
   B. Formula
   C. System

5. Page headers and footers can be changed in this view.
   A. Print preview
   B. Page Layout view
   C. Normal view

6. Symbols that specify mathematical operations such as addition or subtraction.
   A. Hyperlinks
   B. Bookmarks
   C. Arithmetic operators

7. The number that displays at the left of a row.
   A. Row heading
   B. Row name
   C. Row border

8. A prewritten Excel formula.
   A. Method
   B. Function
   C. Exponent

9. The small green square in the lower right corner of the active cell.
   A. Border
   B. Fill handle
   C. Edge

10. A view that maximizes the number of cells visible on the screen.
    A. Page Layout view
    B. Standard view
    C. Normal view

Topics for Discussion

1. What is the advantage of using cell references instead of actual number values in formulas and functions?

2. What are some things you can do to make your worksheet easier for others to read and understand?

3. According to the introduction to this chapter, how do you decide which information to put in columns and which to put in rows?

Skills Review

To complete this project, you will need the following file:

- Blank Excel document

You will save your file as:

- Last_First_exl01_SRFitness

1. **Start Excel 2016.** In cell **A1**, type Aspen Falls Fitness Events and then in cell **A2**, type Number of Participants In cell **A4**, type Department and then pressing [Tab] after each label, type Spring | Fall | Total Participants | Difference

2. In rows **5** through **9**, enter the following data starting in cell **A5**:

City Hall	185	140
Finance	147	136
IT Services	130	117
Engineering	169	147
City Council	195	152

3. In cell **D5**, type =B5+C5 and then in cell **E5**, type =B5-C5 Select the range **D5:E5**. Point to the fill handle, and then drag down through row **9**. Compare your screen.

4. **Save** the file in your chapter folder with the name Last_First_exl01_SRFitness

5. On the **Insert tab**, in the **Text group**, click the **Header & Footer** button. In the **Navigation group**, click the **Go to Footer** button, and then click in the left footer. In the **Header & Footer Elements group**, click the **File Name** button. Click in a cell just above the footer. On the lower right side of the status bar, click the **Normal** button, and then press [Ctrl] + [Home].

6. In cell **A10**, type Total and then select the range **B10:D10**. On the **Home tab**, in the **Editing group**, click the **AutoSum** button.

7. Click cell **A7**. In the **Cells group**, click the **Insert arrow**, and then click **Insert Sheet Rows**. In the new row **7**, type the following data in columns **A:C**: Public Works | 95 | 87

8. Select the range **D6:E6**, and then use the fill handle to copy the formulas down one row.

9. In cell **A13**, type Fall Participants as Percent of Total

10. Select the range **A5:A10**, and then on the **Home tab**, in the **Clipboard group**, click the **Copy** button. Click cell **A14**, and then in the **Clipboard group**, click the **Paste** button. Press [Esc] and then compare your screen.

➤ **Continue to the next page to complete this Skills Review**

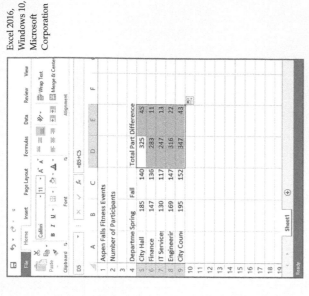

Excel 2016, Windows 10, Microsoft Corporation

Excel 2016, Windows 10, Microsoft Corporation

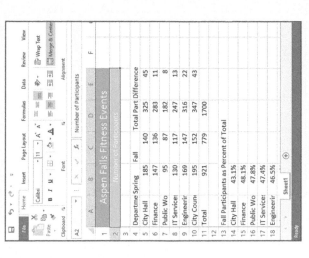

Excel 2016, Windows 10, Microsoft Corporation

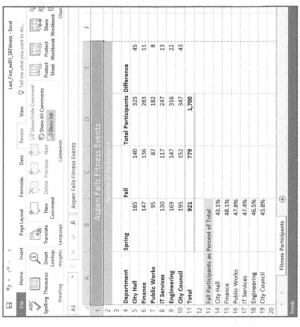

Excel 2016, Windows 10, Microsoft Corporation

11. In cell B14, type =C5/D5 and then on the formula bar, click the **Enter** button. In the **Number** group, click the **Percent Style** button, and then click the **Increase Decimal** button one time. With cell **B14** still the active cell, use the fill handle to copy the formula down through row **19**.

12. Select the range **A1:E1**, and then on the **Home tab**, in the **Alignment group**, click the **Merge & Center** button. In the **Styles** group, click the **Cell Styles** button, and then click **Accent6**. In the **Font** group, click the **Font Size arrow**, and then click **16**. Select the range **A2:E2**, and then click the **Merge & Center** button. Click the **Cell Styles** button, and then click **60% - Accent6**. Compare your screen.

13. Select the range **A4:E4**. On the **Home tab**, in the **Cells group**, click the **Format** button, and then click **Column Width**. In the **Column Width** dialog box, type **16** and then click **OK**.

14. With the range **A4:F4** still selected, hold down Ctrl and then select the range **A5:A11**. In the **Font group**, click the **Bold** button.

15. Select range **B5:E11**. In the **Styles group**, click the **Cell Styles** button, and then click **Comma [0]**. Select the range **B11:D11**. Click the **Cell Styles** button, and then click the **Total** style.

16. Select the range **A13:B13**. In the **Alignment group**, click the **Merge & Center** arrow, and then click **Merge Across**. Click the **Cell Styles** button, and then click **40% - Accent6**.

17. On the **Page Layout tab**, in the **Page Setup group**, click the **Margins** button. Below the **Margins** gallery, click **Custom Margins**. In the **Page Setup** dialog box, under **Center on page**, select the **Horizontally** check box, and then click **OK**.

18. Press Ctrl + Home. On the **Review tab**, in the **Proofing group**, click the **Spelling** button, and then correct any spelling errors.

19. Right-click the **Sheet1** worksheet tab, and then from the shortcut menu, click **Rename**. Type Fitness Participants and then press Enter. Press Ctrl + Home. Compare your screen. If directed by your instructor, display and format the worksheet formulas as described in Skill 10, and then print the worksheet.

20. **Save** the file, and then **Close** Excel. Submit the file as directed by your instructor.

 **DONE! You have completed the Skills Review**

Skills Assessment 1

To complete this project, you will need the following file:

- exl01_SA1Path

You will save your file as:

- Last_First_exl01_SA1Path

Aspen Falls
Bike Path Construction Costs

Location	Brush Clearing	Paving	Landscaping	Total Cost
Cornish Forest	$ 5,883	$ 15,580	$ 3,271	$ 24,734
Haack Center	6,234	18,916	1,697	26,847
Aspen Lakes	4,763	18,846	1,498	25,107
Hamilton Hills Park	4,981	17,169	1,805	23,955
Hansen Hills	4,209	14,062	2,437	20,708
Plasek Park	3,247	12,691	3,971	19,909
Price Lakes	3,648	19,387	2,927	25,962
Rodman Creek	4,515	13,120	1,934	19,569
Schroder Brook	3,862	19,166	2,036	25,064
Terry Park	2,569	17,506	1,756	21,831
Total	$ 43,911	$ 166,443	$ 23,332	$ 233,686

Location	Increase	Cost Increase
Cornish Forest	3%	$ 742.02
Haack Center	3%	805.41
Aspen Lakes	5%	1,255.35
Hamilton Hills Park	5%	1,197.75
Hansen Hills	6%	1,242.48
Plasek Park	6%	1,194.54
Price Lakes	6%	1,557.72
Rodman Creek	6%	1,174.14
Schroder Brook	6%	1,503.84
Terry Park	6%	1,309.86
Total		$ 11,983.11

---

1. Start Excel 2016. From your student data files, open **exl01_SA1Path**. Save the file in your chapter folder as Last_First_exl01_SA1Path Rename the **Sheet1** worksheet tab as Path Costs

2. Add the file name to the worksheet's left footer, add the current date to the center footer, and then in the right footer, insert the sheet name. Return to **Normal** view.

3. For the range **A1:E1**, merge and center and apply the **Accent5** cell style. Increase the font size to **18** points. For the range **A2:E2**, merge and center and apply the **40% - Accent5** cell style. Increase the width of column **A** to **20**. For all column and row labels **A4:E4**, **A5:A14**, and **A17:C17**, apply **Bold**.

4. For the range **E5:E13**, insert the **SUM** function to add the three costs for each row. In the range **B14:E14**, insert the **SUM** function to provide totals for each column.

5. Select the nonadjacent ranges **B5:E5** and **B14:E14**. Apply the **Currency [0]** cell style.

6. Select the range **B6:E13**, and then apply the **Comma [0]** cell style. Select the range **B14:E14**, and then apply the **Total** cell style.

7. Insert a new row above row **7**. In cell **A7**, type Aspen Lakes and as the costs for the new location, type 4763 | 18846 | 1498 Use the fill handle to copy the formula in cell **E6** to cell **E7**.

8. Copy the location names from the range **A5:A14** to the range **A19:A28**. In cell **A29**, type Total

9. In cells **B19** and **B20**, type .03 In cells **B21** and **B22**, type .05 In cell **B23**, type .06 Use the fill handle to copy the value in cell **B23** down through cell **B28**. Select the range **B19:B28**, and then apply the **Percent Style** cell style.

10. In cell **C19**, enter a formula that calculates the cost increase by multiplying cell **E5** by cell **B19**. Fill the formula in cell **C19** down through cell **C28**.

11. In cell **C29**, insert the **SUM** function to add the total cost increase, and then apply the **Total** cell style.

12. Select the range **C20:C28**, apply the **Comma [0]** cell style, and then increase the decimal two times.

13. Use **Page Setup** to center the worksheet **Horizontally**. Set the **Gridlines** to print.

14. Review and correct any spelling errors, ignoring proper names. Press [Ctrl] + [Home].

15. Save the file, and then compare your screen.

16. **Close** the file, and then submit the file as directed by your instructor.

 DONE! You have completed Skills Assessment 1

Skills Assessment 2

To complete this project, you will need the following file:

- exl01_SA2Guests

You will save your file as:

- Last_First_exl01_SA2Guests

Aspen Lake Recreation Area

| | Number of Guests | | | | |
Ages	1st Quarter	2nd Quarter	Total Guests	2nd Quarter Increase	2nd Quarter as Percent of Total
Over 70	14,102	15,216	29,318	1,114	51.9%
65 to 70	15,125	17,854	32,979	2,729	54.1%
60 to 65	11,175	18,273	29,448	7,098	62.1%
55 to 60	15,110	16,572	31,682	1,462	52.3%
50 to 55	19,114	19,841	38,955	727	50.9%
45 to 50	18,475	21,418	39,893	2,943	53.7%
40 to 45	12,064	13,242	25,306	1,178	52.3%
35 to 40	14,628	16,232	30,860	1,604	52.6%
30 to 35	14,543	19,975	34,518	5,432	57.9%
25 to 30	17,933	19,724	37,657	1,791	52.4%
20 to 25	17,196	19,133	36,329	1,937	52.7%
15 to 20	30,516	32,597	63,113	2,081	51.6%
10 to 15	13,469	17,439	30,908	3,970	56.4%
Under 10	17,876	19,599	37,475	1,723	52.3%
Total	231,326	267,115	498,441		

Projected 2nd Half Guests

Ages	Projected Percentage Increase	Projected Increase in Guests
Over 70	2%	586
65 to 70	8%	2,638
60 to 65	4%	1,178
55 to 60	1%	317
50 to 55	5%	1,948
45 to 50	6%	2,394
40 to 45	9%	2,278
35 to 40	3%	926
30 to 35	6%	2,071
25 to 30	15%	5,649
20 to 25	14%	5,086
15 to 20	18%	11,360
10 to 15	21%	6,491
Under 10	23%	8,619

1. Start **Excel 2016**. From the student data files, open **exl01_SA2Guests**. Save the file in your chapter folder as Last_First_exl01_SA2Guests

2. Rename the worksheet tab Aspen Lake Guests Add the file name to the worksheet's left footer, and then add the current date to the right footer. Return to **Normal** view.

3. In cell **D5**, construct a formula to add the *1st Qtr.* and *2nd Qtr.* guests who are *Over 70*. In cell **E5**, construct a formula to calculate the increase of guests from the *1st Qtr.* to the *2nd Qtr.* who are *Over 70*.

4. In cell **F5** for the *Over 70* row, construct a formula to divide *2nd Qtr.* guests by the *1st Half Total Guests*. Fill the formulas in **D5:F5** down through row **17**.

5. In cell **A18**, type Total and then in row **18**, insert the function to total columns **B:D**.

6. Insert a new row above row **15**, and then using the other rows as an example, enter the following data: 20 to 25 | 17196 | 19133

7. For the range **B5:E19**, apply the **Comma [0]** cell style, and then for the range **F5:F18**, apply the **Percent** cell style and display one decimal.

8. Merge and center the range **A1:F1**, and then apply the **Accent6** cell style. Increase the font size to **18**. Merge and center the range **A2:F2**, and then apply the **40% - Accent6** cell style. Increase the font size to **14**.

9. Increase the column widths of **A:C** to **11.00**, and then increase the column widths of **D:F** to **14.00**.

10. For the column and row labels, apply **Bold**. In the range **B19:D19**, apply the **Total** cell style.

11. For the range **A21:C21**, apply the **Merge Across** alignment and the **40% - Accent6** cell style.

12. In cell **C23**, construct a formula to multiply *Total Guests* in the *Over 70* row by the *Projected Percent Increase* in cell **B23**. Apply the **Comma [0]** cell style. Fill the formula down through row **36**.

13. Review and correct any spelling errors.

14. Use **Page Setup** to center the page **Horizontally**, and then set the **Gridlines** to print.

15. If you are instructed to do so, display the worksheet formulas, scale the worksheet to print on one page, and then print with the formulas displayed.

16. Compare your screen. Save the file, and then **Close** Excel. Submit the file as directed by your instructor.

 DONE! You have completed Skills Assessment 2

My College Enrollment				
Course Name	Fall	Spring	Summer	Course Total
Algebra	1,173	938	415	2,526
Intro to Computers	1,043	857	497	2,397
Biology	578	311	253	1,142
World History	688	549	372	1,609
American History	824	598	397	1,819
Management	367	228	103	698
English	1,292	1,125	573	2,990
Semester Total	5,965	4,606	2,610	13,181

Summer as a Percent of Total	
Algebra	16.4%
Intro to Computers	20.7%
Biology	22.2%
World History	23.1%
American History	21.8%
Management	14.8%
English	19.2%

My Skills

To complete this project, you will need the following file:

- exl01_MYCollege

You will save your file as:

- Last_First_exl01_MYCollege

1. Start **Excel 2016**. From the student data files, open **exl01_MYCollege**. Save the file in your chapter folder as Last_First_exl01_MYCollege Rename the **Sheet1** worksheet tab as Enrollment

2. Add the file name to the worksheet's left footer, insert the sheet name in the right footer, and then return to **Normal** view.

3. For the range **A1:E1**, merge and center and apply the **Accent3** cell style, and then change the font size to 16

4. Increase the width of column **A** to 20 and then increase the width of columns **B:E** to 12

5. For the range **B3:E3**, center the labels. For all column and row labels, apply **Bold**.

6. For cell **E4**, insert the **SUM** function to provide the total for the row. Fill the formula in cell **E4** down through cell **E9**.

7. Insert the **SUM** function for the range **B10:E10** to provide totals for each column. With the range **B10:E10** still selected, apply the **Total** cell style.

8. For the range **B4:E10**, apply the **Comma [0]** cell style.

9. Insert a new row above row 7. In cell **A7**, type World History and then as the

10. enrollment for the new course, type 688 | 549 | 372 Fill the formula in cell **E6** to cell **E7**.

11. **Copy** the course names from the range **A4:A10** to the range **A15:A21**.

12. In cell **B15**, create a formula that calculates the summer semester as a percentage of the total course enrollment by dividing cell **D4** by cell **E4**. Apply the **Percent Style** cell style, and then display one decimal. Fill the formula in cell **B15** down through cell **B21**.

13. For the range **A14:B14**, merge across and apply the **40% – Accent3** cell style.

14. Use **Page Setup** to center the worksheet **Horizontally**.

15. Check and correct any spelling errors.

16. Compare your screen. If you are instructed to do so, display the worksheet formulas, and scale the worksheet to print on one page.

17. **Save** the file, and **then Close** Excel. Submit the file as directed by your instructor.

 DONE! You have completed My Skills

Visual Skills Check

To complete this project, you will need the following file:

- Blank Excel workbook

You will save your file as:

- Last_First_exl01_VSWorkers

Start Excel 2016. Open a blank workbook, and then **Save** the file in your chapter folder as Last_First_exl01_VSWorkers Create the worksheet. The width of column **A** is **20** and the width of columns **B:F** is **13**. Construct formulas that display the results shown in columns **D** and **F**, row **13**, and the range **B16:B23**. The title uses the **Accent4** cell style, and the font size is **20**. The subtitle uses the **40% – Accent4** cell style, and the font size is **16**. The title and subtitle should be merged and centered. As your guide, apply the **Currency [0]** cell style, the **Comma [0]** cell style, the **Total** cell style, the **Percent** cell style with one decimal place, and the **Bold** format. On the range **A15:C15**, use **Merge Across** and apply the **20% – Accent4** cell style. Rename the Sheet1 worksheet tab as Park Workers Check and correct any spelling errors. Add the file name to the left footer. **Save** the file, **Close** Excel, and then submit the file as directed by your instructor.

DONE! You have completed Visual Skills Check

Aspen Falls					
Park Workers					
	Price Park	Silkwood Park	Total Workers	Wage	Total Wages
Ticket Sellers	75	52	127	$ 15	$ 1,905
Security	92	79	171	25	4,275
Landscapers	19	11	30	20	600
Life Guards	23	23	46	15	690
Cashiers	73	58	131	15	1,965
Parking Attendants	15	11	26	15	390
Maintenance	21	28	49	20	980
Cleaning	29	17	46	18	828
Total	347	279	626		$ 11,633
Price Park as Percent of Total Workers					
Ticket Sellers	59.1%				
Security	53.8%				
Landscapers	63.3%				
Life Guards	50.0%				
Cashiers	55.7%				
Parking Attendants	57.7%				
Maintenance	42.9%				
Cleaning	63.0%				

Skills Challenge 1

To complete this project, you will need the following file:

- exl01_SC1Employees

You will save your file as:

- Last_First_exl01_SC1Employees

Start Excel 2016, and then from the student data files, open **exl01_SC1Employees**. Save the file in your chapter folder as Last_First_exl01_SC1Employees Duncan Chueng, the Park Operations Manager for Aspen Falls, wants to total and compare the number of employees at the city recreation areas. Using the skills you practiced in this chapter, correct the SUM function for each row and column. Format the worksheet using cell styles as practiced in this chapter. Merge and center the title across the correct columns. Correct the number formats. No decimals should display in rows 5:11. Adjust column widths as necessary to display all data. Set the gridlines to print, and then center the data horizontally on the page. Add the file name in the worksheet's left footer, and check for spelling errors. Save the file, and then close Excel. Submit the file as directed by your instructor.

 DONE! You have completed Skills Challenge 1

Skills Challenge 2

To complete this project, you will need the following file:

- exl01_SC2Painting

You will save your file as:

- Last_First_exl01_SC2Painting

Start Excel 2016, and then from the student data files, open **exl01_SC2Painting**. Save the file in your chapter folder as Last_First_exl01_SC2Painting The Art Center wants to total and compare the number of students enrolled in the painting classes in the different neighborhoods. Using the skills you practiced in this chapter, insert appropriate formulas and functions. Adjust column widths and row heights as necessary to display all data. Format the worksheet as appropriate. Add the file name in the worksheet's left footer, and check for spelling errors. Save the file, and then close Excel. Submit the file as directed by your instructor.

 **DONE! You have completed Skills Challenge 2**

More Skills Assessment

To complete this project, you will need the following files:

- Blank Excel workbook
- exl01_MSAAnalysis

You will save your files as:

- Last_First_exl01_MSATemplate
- Last_First_exl01_MSACalendar
- Last_First_exl01_MSAAnalysis

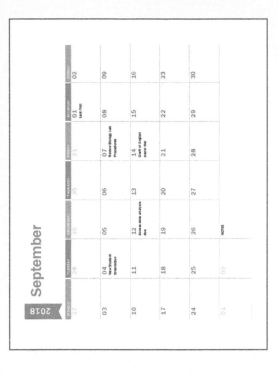

1. Start **Excel 2016**. At the top of the screen, in the search box, type Academic calendar

2. Select the template, and then Create the template file. If necessary, scroll through and find the Academic calendar template. If you do not have an Internet connection, navigate to your student data files and open exl01_MSAAssessment.

3. Save your workbook as an Excel template in your chapter folder as Last_First_exl01_MSATemplate Create a new workbook using the template, and then save your workbook in your chapter folder as Last_First_exl01_MSACalendar

4. In cell **B1**, click the **spinner arrow** to change the start year to **2018**.

5. Click the merged cell **C1**, and then click the **arrow** in the lower right corner to display the months.

6. From the displayed list, click **September**. In the worksheet, scroll down to view the months that follow.

7. Select the four sample calendar entries in the nonadjacent range **E7:F7** and cells **B9** and **F13**. Delete the four entries.

8. Click cell **G5**, the cell for September 1. Enter your name, Last First

9. Enter or replace the following data in the cells.

Date	Cell	Data
September 4	C7	New Student Orientation
September 7	F7	Review Biology Lab Procedures
September 12	D9	Access data analysis due
September 14	F9	Draft of English paper due

10. Set the print area for the range **A1:H15**, and then **Save** the workbook. Preview the document, and then compare your screen.

11. On the right side of the **Info** page, revise the **Title** to Calendar 2018

12. Enter calendar, academic, 2018 as **Tags**.

13. In the **Author** box, replace the existing text with your First and Last names, and then **Save** the workbook.

14. Open the student data file **exl01_MSAAnalysis**, and then save the file in your chapter folder as Last_First_exl01_MSAAnalysis

15. In cell **B4**, enter Anten In cell **B5**, enter Boy and then flash fill the list of first names in column B.

16. Repeat this technique to enter the last names into column C and the e-mail addresses into column **D**.

17. **Save** the file. Close all open windows, and then submit the files as directed by your instructor.

 DONE! You have completed the More Skills Assessment

Collaborating with Google

To complete this project, you will need a Google account (refer to the Common Features chapter) and the following file:

- exl01_GPCityFees

You will save your file as:

- Last_First_exl01_GPSnip

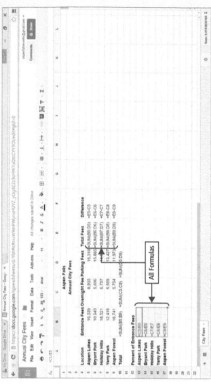

All Formulas

1. Open the Google Chrome web browser. Log into your Google account, and then click **Google Apps**.

2. Click **Drive** to open Google Drive. If you receive a pop-up message, read the message, and then click **Next**. Read each message, and then close the dialog box.

3. Click **New**, and then click **Google Sheets** to open a blank spreadsheet.

4. Open the workbook from the student data file **exl01_GPCityFees**. Copy the range **A1:F17** from the *City Fees* worksheet, and then paste it in cell **A1** of the blank Google worksheet.

5. Click the spreadsheet title, **Untitled spreadsheet**. Type Annual City Fees as the name of the spreadsheet, and then click **OK**. Rename the *Sheet1* worksheet tab as City Fees

6. Select the range **A1:F1**, click **Merge**, and then click **Center**. Repeat this process to apply the same formatting to the range **A2:F2**.

7. Select the range **B10:D10**, and then insert the SUM function to calculate total fees. Repeat this technique to apply the SUM function to the range **E5:E9** to calculate the total for each location.

8. In the range **F5:F9**, enter a formula to calculate the difference, subtracting Overnight Fees from Total Fees.

9. Select the range **B5:F10**. Click **Format**. Point to **Number**, click the **Financial** number format, and then select **Decrease decimal places** two times.

10. Apply **Bold** format to all worksheet headings and row and column headings.

11. In the range **B13:B17**, enter a formula to calculate Overnight Fees divided by Total Fees for each location. With the range **B13:B17** still selected, point to **Format**, point to **Number**, and then click **Percent**.

12. Click **View**, select **All Formulas**, and then compare your screen.

13. Click **Share** , and then in the **Share with others** dialog box, type AspenFallsEvents@gmail.com

14. In the **Add a note** text box, type Please review and contact me with any questions.

15. Click **Send**. Press 🪟 type snip and then press Enter to start the **Snipping Tool**. Click the **New arrow**, and then click **Window Snip**. Point to the Windows Explorer window, and then when a red border displays around the window, click one time.

16. In the **Snipping Tool** mark-up window, click the **Save Snip** button. In the **Save As** dialog box, navigate to your Excel Chapter 1 folder. Be sure the **Save as type** box displays **JPEG file**. Name the file Last_First_exl01_GPSnip and then press Enter.

17. Close all windows, and then submit the file as directed by your instructor.

▶ **DONE! You have completed Collaborating with Google**

CHAPTER 5

Insert Summary Functions and Create Charts

- ▶ Functions are prewritten formulas that have two parts—the name of the function and the arguments that specify the values or cells to be used by the function.
- ▶ Functions analyze data to answer financial, statistical, or logical questions. Summary functions are used to recap information.
- ▶ Excel provides various types of charts that can make your data easier to understand.

- ▶ Column charts show data changes over a period of time or illustrate comparisons among items.
- ▶ Pie charts illustrate how each part relates to the whole. Pie charts display the relative sizes of items in a single data series.
- ▶ Charts can be enhanced with effects such as 3-D and soft shadows to create compelling graphical summaries.

Aspen Falls City Hall

In this chapter, you will finish a workbook for Thelma Perkins, a Risk Management Specialist in the Finance Department. The workbook displays the department expenditures for Aspen Falls. The City Council requires that the Finance Department present the departmental information annually for review and approval.

Companies use formulas and statistical functions to manipulate and summarize data to make better decisions. Summary results can include the data totals or averages. Results can be displayed graphically as charts, providing a visual representation of data. Commonly used chart types include line charts to illustrate trends over time or bar charts to illustrate comparisons among individual items. Based on the type of data selected, the Quick Analysis tools provide chart type options.

In this project, you will open an existing workbook, construct formulas containing absolute cell references, and AutoFill the formulas to other cells. You will insert the statistical functions AVERAGE, MAX, and MIN. You will create and format column charts and pie charts and insert WordArt. Finally, you will prepare the chart sheet and the worksheet to meet printing requirements.

Djile/Fotolia

Introduction

Time to complete all 10 skills — 60 to 90 minutes

60-90 min.

Outcome

Using the skills in this chapter, you will be able to modify cell and number formats; create formulas using absolute cell references and average, minimum, and maximum functions; create, edit, and format pie and column charts; and update print settings for multiple worksheets.

Objectives

Construct statistical functions

Generate formulas using absolute cell references

Apply cell and number formatting

Create, edit, and format basic charts

Modify workbook print settings

Student data file needed for this chapter:

exl02_Expenditures

You will save your file as:

Last_First_exl02_Expenditures

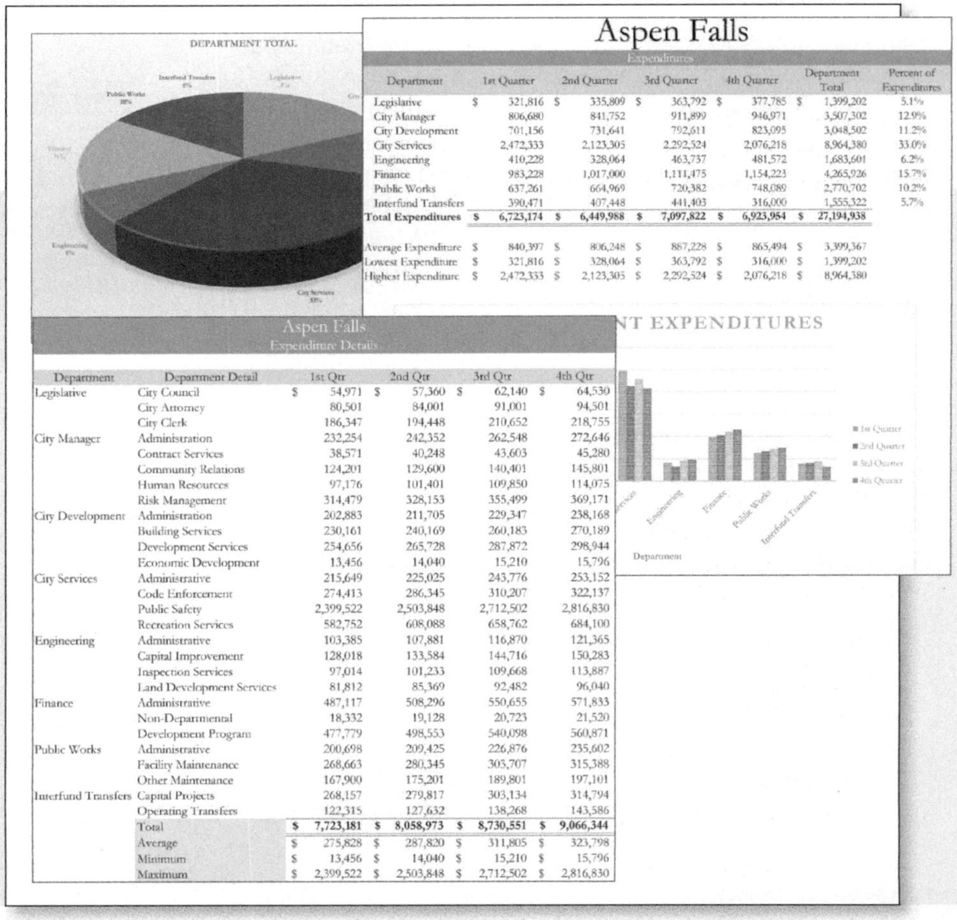

SKILLS

At the end of this chapter you will be able to:

Skill 1 Align and Wrap Text
Skill 2 Apply Absolute Cell References
Skill 3 Format Numbers
Skill 4 Insert the AVERAGE Function
Skill 5 Insert the MIN and MAX Functions
Skill 6 Create Column Charts
Skill 7 Format Column Charts
Skill 8 Create and Format Pie Charts
Skill 9 Update Charts and Insert WordArt
Skill 10 Preview and Print Multiple Worksheets

MORE SKILLS

Skill 11 Validate Workbooks for Accessibility
Skill 12 Change Chart Types
Skill 13 Copy Excel Data to Word Documents
Skill 14 Create Line Charts

▶ The **Text wrap** format displays text on multiple lines within a cell.

1. Start Excel 2016, open the student data file **exl02_Expenditures**, and then compare your screen.

   When columns in a worksheet are not wide enough, the labels in the cells will be truncated and values will display as # characters.

2. On the **File tab**, click **Save As**. On the **Save As** page, click the **Browse** button. Navigate to the location where you are saving your files. Click **New folder**, type Excel Chapter 2 and then press Enter two times. In the **File name** box, name the workbook Last_First_exl02_Expenditures and then press Enter.

3. Verify **Expenditures** is the active worksheet. Click the **Insert tab**, and then in the **Text group**, click the **Header & Footer button**. In the **Navigation group**, click the **Go to Footer button**. Click just above the word **Footer**, and then in the **Header & Footer Elements group**, click the **File Name button**. Click a cell above the footer. On the status bar, click the **Normal button**, and then press Ctrl + Home.

4. Click cell **B2**. Point at the fill handle to display the + pointer, and then drag right through cell E2 to AutoFill the labels. Compare your screen.

   Excel's AutoFill feature can generate a series of values into adjacent cells. A **series** is a group of numbers, text, dates, or time periods that come one after another in succession. For example, the months *January, February, March* are a series. Likewise, *1st Quarter, 2nd Quarter, 3rd Quarter,* and *4th Quarter* form a series.

■ **Continue to the next page to complete the skill**

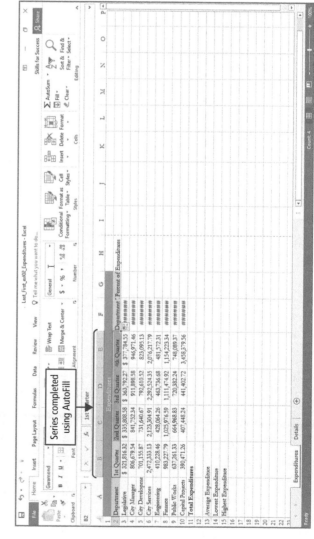

Excel 2016, Windows 10, Microsoft Corporation

Column is too narrow to display values

Truncated label

Excel 2016, Windows 10, Microsoft Corporation

Series completed using AutoFill

MOS
Obj

5. Select the range **A2:G2**. On the **Home tab**, in the **Alignment group**, click the **Wrap Text button** 🔲, the **Middle Align button** 🔲, and the **Center button** 🔲.

MOS
Obj

6. In the column heading area, point to the right boundary of column **A** to display the 🔛 pointer.

7. With the 🔛 pointer displayed, double-click to **AutoFit** the column.

   AutoFit—automatically change the column width to accommodate the longest entry.

8. In the column heading area, click the column **B** heading, and then drag right through column **G** to select columns **B:G**. Right-click the boundary of column G to display the Column Width box, type 14 in the box, and then compare your screen. Click OK to change the width.

9. Select the range **A3:A10**, and then in the **Alignment group**, click the **Increase Indent button** 🔲.

10. **Save** 🔲 the file.

■ **You have completed Skill 1 of 10**

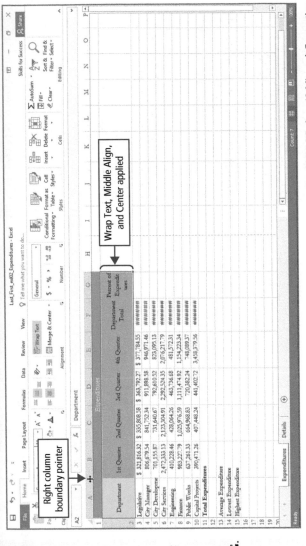

Excel 2016, Windows 10, Microsoft Corporation

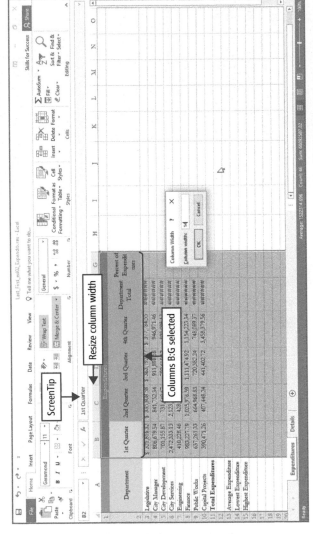

Excel 2016, Windows 10, Microsoft Corporation

WATCH SKILL 2.2

▲ The Quick Analysis button is used to apply conditional formatting or to insert charts and totals.

▲ Excel uses rules to check for formula errors. When a formula breaks a rule, the cell displays an *error indicator*—a green triangle that indicates a possible error in a formula.

▲ An *absolute cell reference* is a cell reference address that remains the same when it is copied or filled to other cells. To make a cell reference absolute, insert a dollar sign ($) before the row and column references.

1. Select **B3:F10**, click the **Quick Analysis** button 📊, and then compare your screen.

2. In the **Quick Analysis** gallery, click **Totals**, and then click the first option—**SUM**—to insert column totals.

3. Click cell **G3**, and then type =F3/F11 On the formula bar, click the **Enter** button ✓. Double-click cell **G3** to display the range finder, and then compare your screen.

The *range finder* outlines all of the cells referenced in a formula. It is useful for verifying which cells are used in a formula and for editing formulas.

4. Press **Esc** to close the range finder. Point to the **G3** fill handle, and then AutoFill the formula down through **G10** to display error values.

Error values—messages that display whenever a formula or function cannot perform its calculations. The #DIV/0! error value displays in a cell whenever the underlying formula attempts to divide by zero.

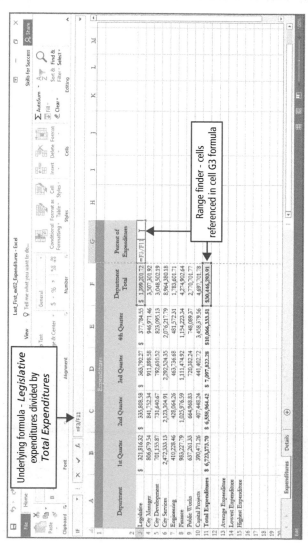

Excel 2016, Windows 10, Microsoft Corporation

■ **Continue to the next page to complete the skill**

5. Click cell **G4**. To the left of the cell, point to the **Error Message** button to display the ScreenTip—*The formula or function used is dividing by zero or empty cells.*

6. Double-click cell **G4** to display the range finder.

   The formula was copied with a relative cell reference. In the copied formula, the cell reference to cell F4 is correct, but the formula is dividing by the value in cell F12, an empty cell. In this calculation, the divisor must be cell F11.

7. Press **Esc**, and then double-click cell **G3**. In the formula, click after the reference to cell F11, and then press **F4** to insert a dollar sign ($) before the column reference *F* and the row reference *11*.

   The dollar signs are used to indicate an absolute cell reference.

8. On the formula bar, click the **Enter** button, and then AutoFill the formula in cell **G3** down through cell **G10**.

9. Click cell **G4**, and verify that the divisor refers to cell **F11**.

   The cell reference for the row *City Manager Department Total* changed relative to its row; however, the value used as the divisor—*Total Expenditures* in cell F11—remains absolute.

10. Press the **↓** two times and verify the contents of each cell. Notice that the divisor remains constant—**F11**—while the dividend changes relative to the row.

11. **Save** the file.

■ **You have completed Skill 2 of 10**

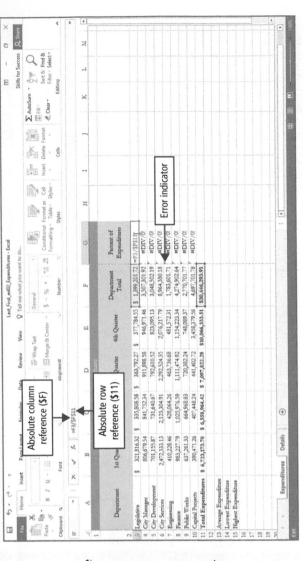

Error indicator

Absolute column reference ($F)

Absolute row reference ($11)

Excel 2016, Windows 10, Microsoft Corporation

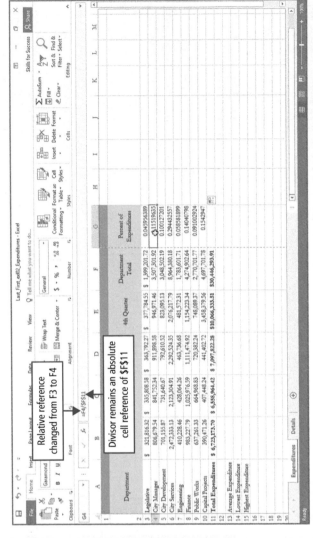

Relative reference changed from F3 to F4

Divisor remains an absolute cell reference of F11

Excel 2016, Windows 10, Microsoft Corporation

▶ A **number format** is a specific way that Excel displays numbers; for example, the number of decimals or whether commas and special symbols, such as dollar signs, display.

▶ By default, Excel displays the **General format**—a number format that does not display commas or trailing zeros to the right of a decimal point.

1. Click cell **B2**, and then on the **Home tab**, in the **Number group**, notice that *General* displays. Compare your screen.

2. Select the range **B3:F3**, press Ctrl, and then select the range **B11:F11**. In the **Number group**, click the **Decrease Decimal button** 📉 two times to round the number and hide the decimals. Select the range **B4:F10**. In the **Number group**, click the **Decrease Decimal button** 📉 two times. Click cell **B6**, and then compare your screen.

   The Decrease Decimal button hides the displayed value decimals. The underlying value shows the decimals.

3. Select the range **G3:G10**. In the **Number group**, click the **Percent Style button** %, and then click the **Increase Decimal button** 📈 one time to add one decimal to the applied Percent Style. In the **Alignment group**, click the **Center button** ▤.

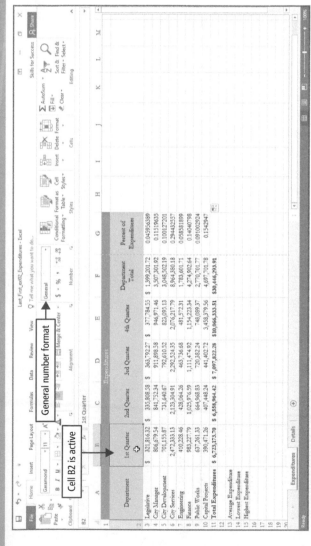

Excel 2016, Windows 10, Microsoft Corporation

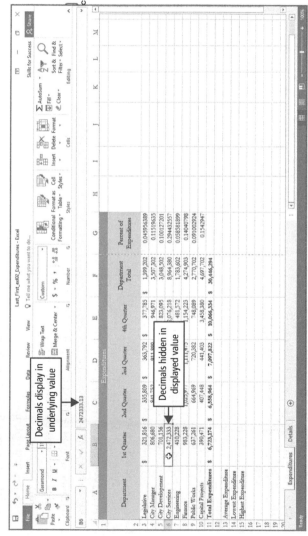

Excel 2016, Windows 10, Microsoft Corporation

■ **Continue to the next page to complete the skill**

4. Select the range **B11:F11**. In the **Styles** group, click the **Cell Styles** button, and then under **Titles and Headings**, click **Total**. Click cell **B13**, and then compare your screen.

5. Along the bottom of the Excel window, notice the worksheet tabs. Click the **Details** worksheet tab to make it the active worksheet.

Worksheet tabs, the labels along the lower border of the workbook window that identify each worksheet.

6. Click cell **C5**. Hold down the (Ctrl) + (Shift) keys. With both keys held down, press the ↓ one time and the → one time to select the range C5:F32.

7. With the range **C5:F32** selected, click the **Quick Analysis** button. In the **Quick Analysis** gallery, click **Totals**, and then click the first option—**SUM**.

8. Select the range **C5:F5**, press (Ctrl) and then select the range **C33:F33**. In the **Number group**, click the **Decrease Decimal** button two times. Select the range **C6:F32**. In the **Number group**, click the **Decrease Decimal** button two times.

9. Select the range **C33:F33**, and then apply the **Total** cell style. Click cell **F35**, and then compare your screen.

10. Save the file.

■ **You have completed Skill 3 of 10**

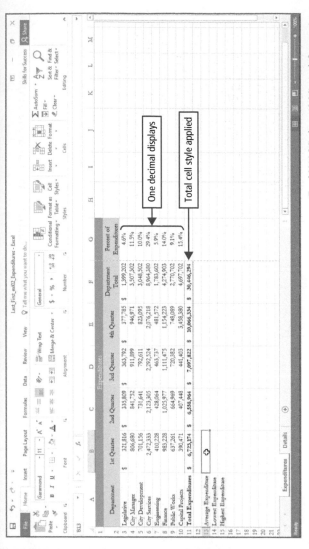

Excel 2016, Windows 10, Microsoft Corporation

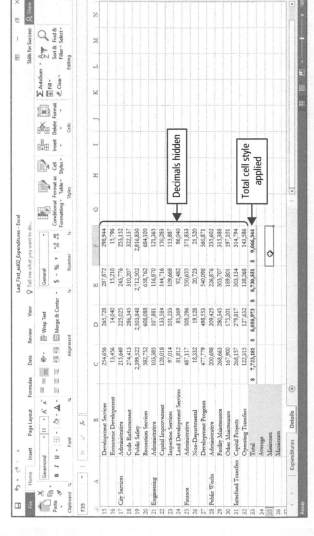

Excel 2016, Windows 10, Microsoft Corporation

▶ **Statistical functions** are predefined formulas that describe a collection of data—for example, averages, maximums, and minimums.

▶ The **AVERAGE function** adds a group of values and then divides the result by the number of values in the group.

1. Click the **Expenditures** worksheet tab, and then click cell **B13**. On the **Home tab**, in the **Editing group**, click the **AutoSum arrow**, and then in the list of functions, click **Average**. Look in the formula bar and in cell B13 to verify that the range *B3:B12* is the suggested range of cells that will be averaged.

   The range in parentheses is the function **argument**—the values that a function uses to perform operations or calculations. The arguments each function uses are specific to that function. Common arguments include numbers, text, cell references, and range names.

   When data is above or to the left of a selected cell, the function argument will automatically be entered. Often, you will need to edit the argument range.

2. With the function argument still active in cell B13, click cell **B3**. On the range finder, click a bottom corner sizing handle, and then drag down to select the argument range **B3:B10**, to exclude the *Total Expenditures* value in cell B11. On the formula bar, click the **Enter button** ✓ to display the result *$840,397*. Compare your screen.

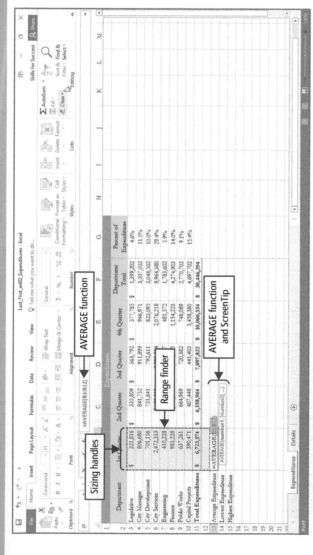

Excel 2016, Windows 10, Microsoft Corporation

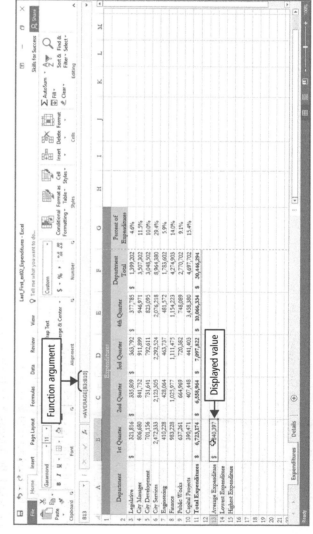

Excel 2016, Windows 10, Microsoft Corporation

■ **Continue to the next page to complete the skill**

3. Click cell **C13**. In the **Editing group**, click the **AutoSum arrow**, and then in the list of functions, click **Average**. In the formula bar and in the cell, notice that Excel proposes to average the value in cell *B13*, not the values in column C.

4. With cell reference **B13** highlighted in the function argument, click cell **C3**, and then use the range finder sizing handle to select the range **C3:C10**. On the formula bar, click the **Enter button** ✓ to display the result *$819,871*.

5. Click cell **D13**. Using the techniques just practiced, enter the **AVERAGE** function using the argument range **D3:D10**, and then on the formula bar, click the **Enter** button ✓.

6. Verify that cell *D13* is the active cell, and then AutoFill the function to the right through cell **F13**. Compare your sheet.

7. Click the **Details** worksheet tab, and then click cell **C34**. Enter the **AVERAGE** function using the argument range **C5:C32**. Do not include the *Total* value in cell C33 in the function argument. Compare your sheet.

8. Display the worksheet footers, click in the left footer, and then click the **File Name** button. Click in the right footer, and then click the **Sheet Name** button. Click in a cell above the footer, and then press Ctrl + Home. Return to **Normal** view.

9. Save ⊟ the file.

■ **You have completed Skill 4 of 10**

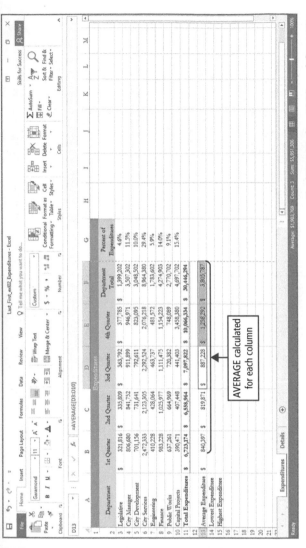

AVERAGE calculated for each column

Excel 2016, Windows 10, Microsoft Corporation

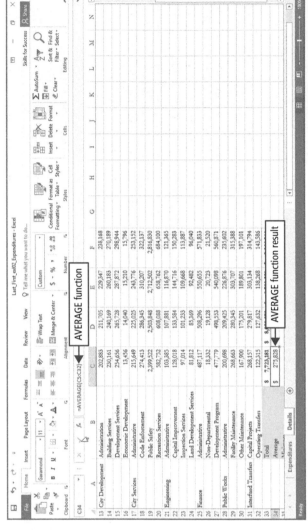

AVERAGE function

AVERAGE function result

Excel 2016, Windows 10, Microsoft Corporation

▶ The **MIN function** returns the smallest value in a range of cells.

▶ The **MAX function** returns the largest value in a range of cells.

MOS
Obj

1. On the **Details** worksheet, click cell C35. Type =Mi and then in the **Formula AutoComplete** list, double-click **MIN**. With the insertion point blinking in the function argument, click cell C32, and then use the range finder top corner sizing handles to drag up and select the range **C5:C32**. Press Enter to display the result *$13,456.*

The MIN function evaluates the range provided in the function argument—C5:C32—and then returns the lowest value—*$13,456.* Here, the *Total* and *Average* values in cells C33 and C34 should not be included in the argument range.

MOS
Obj

2. Verify that **C36** is the active cell. Type =Ma and then in the **Formula AutoComplete** list, double-click **MAX**. Using the technique just practiced, select the range **C5:C32**, and then on the formula bar, click the **Enter** button ✓ to display the result *$2,399,522.* Compare your screen.

The MAX function evaluates all of the values in the range C5:C32 and then returns the highest value found in the range.

3. Select the range **C34:C36**. AutoFill the formulas to the right through column **F**, and then compare your screen.

In this manner, you can AutoFill several different functions or formulas at the same time. Here, the different functions are at the beginning of each row are filled across the columns.

Excel 2016, Windows 10, Microsoft Corporation

(Screenshot: MAX function in formula bar; =MAX(C5:C32); MIN function result; MAX function result)

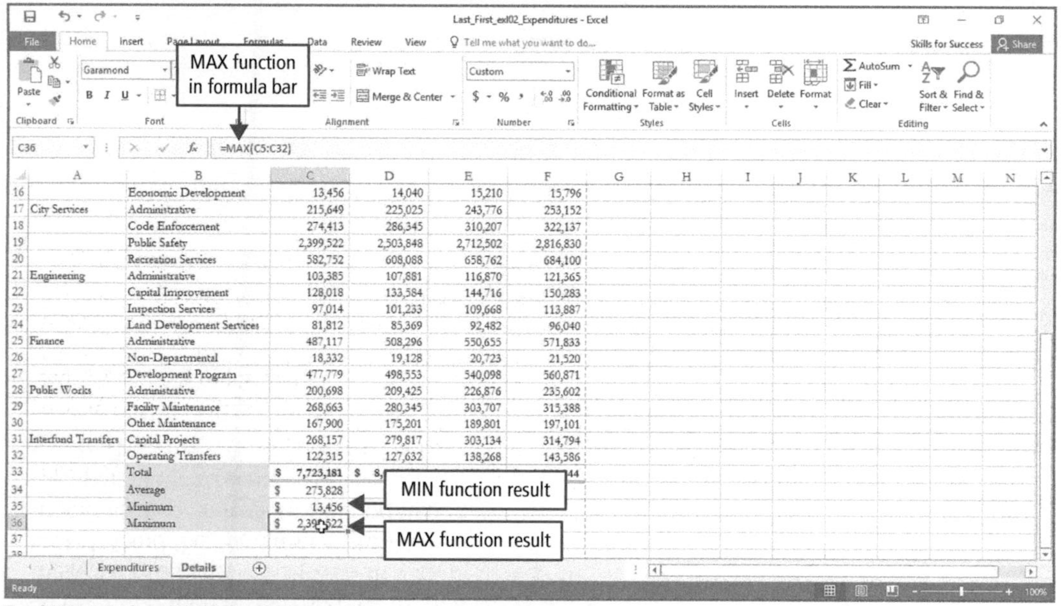

Excel 2016, Windows 10, Microsoft Corporation

(Screenshot: =AVERAGE(C5:C32); Formulas AutoFilled across the columns)

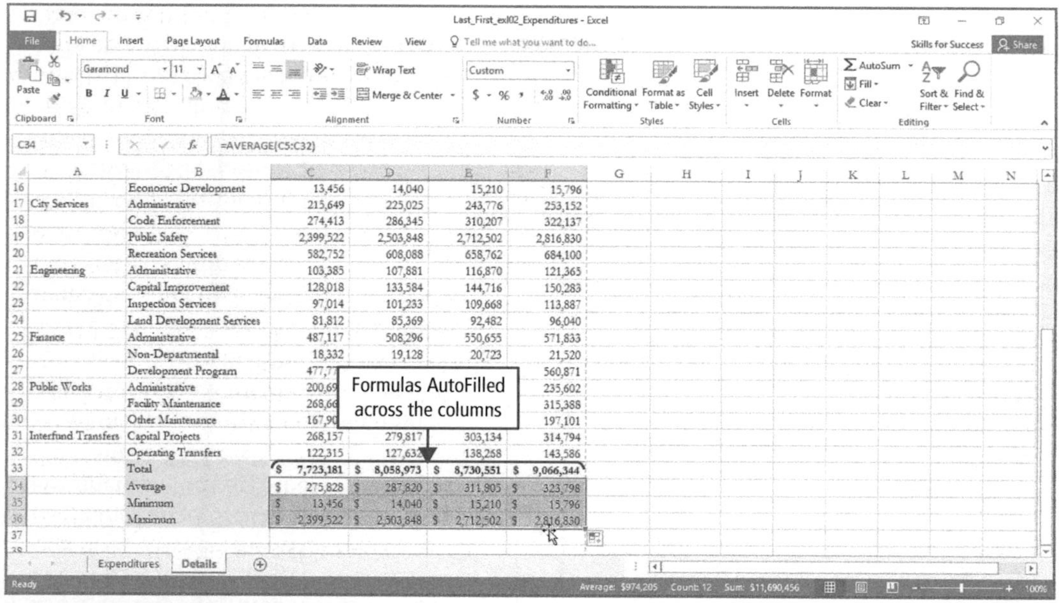

■ **Continue to the next page to complete the skill**

4. Click the **Expenditures** worksheet tab. In cell **B14**, repeat the technique just practiced to insert the **MIN** function using the range **B3:B10** as the function argument in the parentheses. Verify that the result is *$321,816*.

5. In cell **B15**, insert the **MAX** function using the range **B3:B10** as the function argument. Verify that the result is *$2,472,333*. Take care that the argument range does not include the cells with the total expenditures or average expenditures.

6. AutoFill the formulas in **B14:B15** to the right through column **F**. Review the functions, and verify that the lowest and highest values in each column were selected from each of the ranges for the MIN and MAX functions. Click cell **C7**, and then compare your screen.

7. With cell **C7** as the active cell, type 328064 and then press [Enter]. In cell **C8**, type 4025977 and then press [Enter]. Verify that the MIN and MAX values in cells **C14** and **C15** and the SUM and AVERAGE functions were automatically updated. Compare your screen.

8. Save the file.

■ **You have completed Skill 5 of 10**

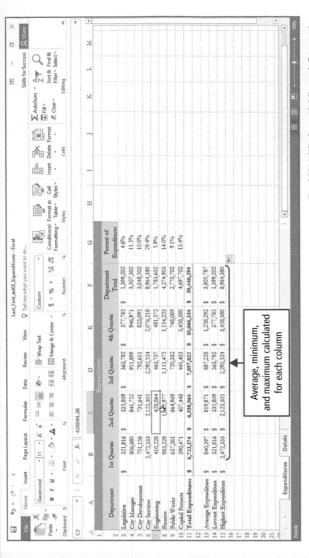

Average, minimum, and maximum calculated for each column

Excel 2016, Windows 10, Microsoft Corporation

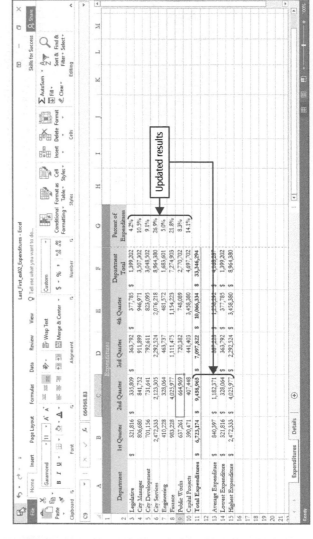

Updated results

Excel 2016, Windows 10, Microsoft Corporation

WATCH SKILL 2.6

▶ A *chart* is a graphical representation of data used to show comparisons, patterns, and trends.

▶ A *column chart* is useful for illustrating comparisons among related numbers.

MOS Obj

1. On the **Expenditures** worksheet, select the range A2:E10—do *not* include the *Department Total* column or the *Total Expenditures* row in your selection. Click the **Quick Analysis button**, and then in the **Quick Analysis gallery**, click **Charts.** Compare your screen.

2. In the **Quick Analysis** gallery, click the third chart—**Clustered Column**—to insert the chart and display the *Chart Tools* contextual tabs. Compare your screen.

MOS Obj

When you insert a chart in this manner, an *embedded chart*—a chart that is placed on the worksheet containing the data—is created. Embedded charts are beneficial when you want to view or print a chart with its source data.

An *axis* is a line bordering the chart plot area that is used as a frame of reference for measurement. The *category axis* is the axis that displays the category labels. A *category label* is nonnumeric text that identifies the categories of data. Here, the worksheet's row labels—the department names in A3:A10—are used for the category labels.

The *value axis* is the vertical axis of a chart that displays the worksheet's numeric data.

The *y-axis* is the vertical axis of a chart, and the *x-axis* is the horizontal axis of a chart.

■ **Continue to the next page to complete the skill**

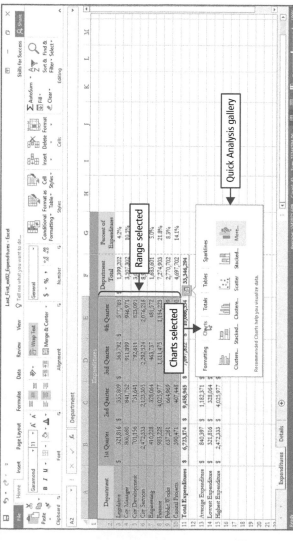

Excel 2016, Windows 10, Microsoft Corporation

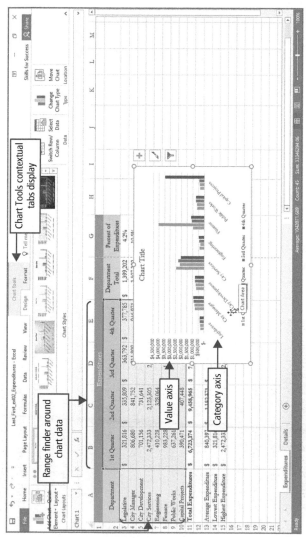

Excel 2016, Windows 10, Microsoft Corporation

3. On the left side of the chart, locate the numerical scale, and then on the bottom, locate the quarters displayed in the legend. Compare your screen.

In the worksheet, each cell in the blue range finder is referred to as a *data point*—a chart value that originates in a worksheet cell. Each data point is represented in a chart by a *data marker*—a column, a bar, an area, a dot, a pie slice, or another symbol that represents a single data point.

Data points that are related to one another form a *data series*, and each data series has a unique color or pattern represented in the chart *legend*—a box that identifies the patterns or colors that are assigned to the data series or categories in the chart. Here, each quarter is a different data series, and the legend shows the color assigned to each quarter.

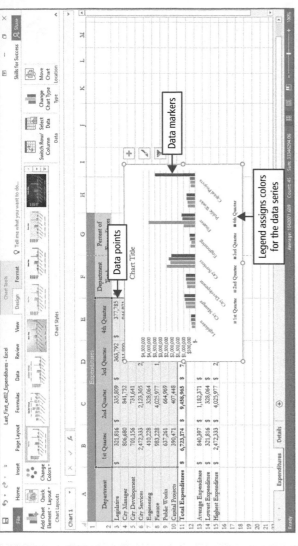

Excel 2016, Windows 10, Microsoft Corporation

4. With the chart selected, point to the upper border of the chart to display the ⯐ pointer, and then move the chart to position its upper left corner in the middle of cell **A17**. If you are working with a touch screen, you can touch the chart and slide it to the correct position.

5. Scroll down to display row **36**. Point to the lower right corner of the chart to display the ⬉ pointer, and then drag to resize the chart until the lower right chart corner is in the middle of cell **G36**. Click cell **G15**, and then compare your screen.

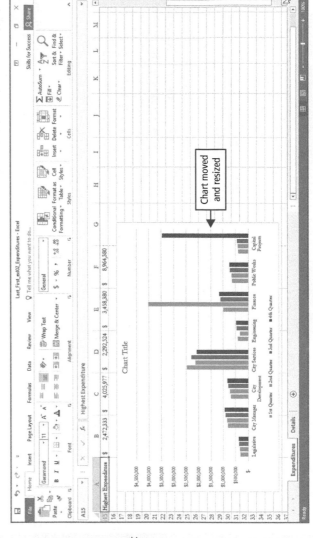

Excel 2016, Windows 10, Microsoft Corporation

6. **Save** 🖫 the file.

■ **You have completed Skill 6 of 10**

▲ You can modify the overall look of a chart by applying a **chart layout**—a prebuilt set of chart elements that can include a title, a legend, or labels.

▲ You can modify the overall look of a chart by applying a **chart style**—a prebuilt chart format that applies an overall visual look to a chart by modifying its graphic effects, colors, and backgrounds.

1. Click the border of the chart to select the chart and display the chart buttons.

2. To the right of the chart, click the **Chart Styles** button, and then click **Style 3**. At the top of the **Chart Styles** gallery, click the **Color tab**, and then under **Colorful**, click **Color 3**. Compare your screen.

3. Click the **Chart Styles** button to close the gallery.

4. On the **Design tab**, in the **Chart Layouts group**, click the **Quick Layout** button. Point at the different layouts to preview the layouts on the chart. Point at **Layout 9**, and then compare your screen.

5. In the **Quick Layout** gallery, click **Layout 9** to add the axes titles and to move the legend to the right side of the chart.

Excel 2016, Windows 10, Microsoft Corporation

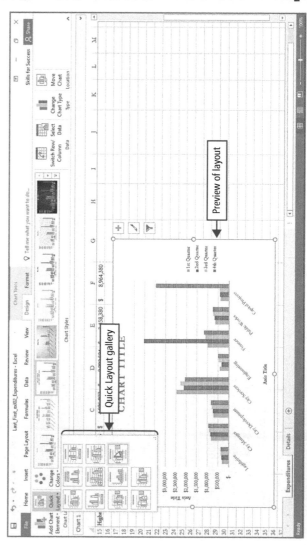

Excel 2016, Windows 10, Microsoft Corporation

■ **Continue to the next page to complete the skill**

6. At the top of the chart, click the text *Chart Title*, and then type Department Expenditures to insert the text into the formula bar. Press Enter to accept the text. Verify that your text replaced any text in the chart title.

7. Below the horizontal axis, click the text *Axis Title*, type Department and then press Enter.

8. To the left of the vertical axis, click the text *Axis Title*, type Cost and then press Enter.

9. Click cell **G15** to deselect the chart. **Save** the file, and then compare your screen.

10. Take a moment to examine the various types of charts available in Excel.

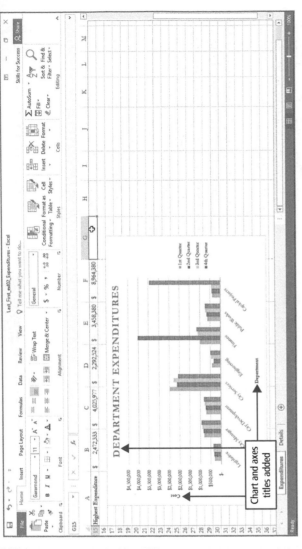

Excel 2016, Windows 10, Microsoft Corporation

■ **You have completed Skill 7 of 10**

Chart Types Commonly Used in Excel	
Chart type	**Used to**
Column	Illustrate data changes over a period of time or illustrate comparisons among items.
Line	Illustrate trends over time, with time displayed along the horizontal axis and the data point values connected by a line.
Pie	Illustrate the relationship of parts to a whole.
Bar	Illustrate comparisons among individual items.
Area	Emphasize the magnitude of change over time.

▶ A *pie chart* displays the relationship of parts to a whole.

▶ A *chart sheet* is a workbook sheet that contains only a chart and is useful when you want to view a chart separately from the worksheet data.

1. Verify that *Expenditures* is the active sheet. Select the range A2:A10. Hold down Ctrl, and then select the nonadjacent range F2:F10.

2. On the **Insert tab**, in the **Charts group**, click the **Recommended Charts button**, and then compare your screen.

3. In the **Insert Chart** dialog box, click the **Pie thumbnail**, and then click **OK**.

   Here, the row labels identify the slices of the pie chart, and the department totals are the data series that determine the size of each pie slice.

4. On the **Design tab**, in the **Location group**, click the **Move Chart button**. In the **Move Chart** dialog box, select the **New sheet option button**. In the **New sheet box**, replace the highlighted text *Chart1* with Expenditure Chart.

5. In the **Move Chart** dialog box, click **OK** to move the pie chart to a chart sheet.

6. On the **Design tab**, in the **Type group**, click the **Change Chart Type button**. In the **Change Chart Type** dialog box, click the **3-D Pie thumbnail**, and then click **OK**.

   The chart is changed from a two-dimensional chart to a three-dimensional chart. *3-D*, which is short for *three-dimensional*, refers to an image that appears to have all three spatial dimensions—length, width, and depth.

■ **Continue to the next page to complete the skill**

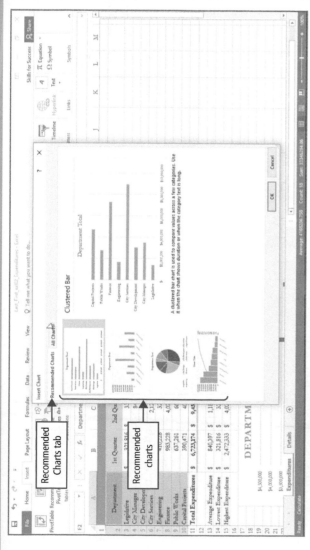

Excel 2016, Windows 10, Microsoft Corporation

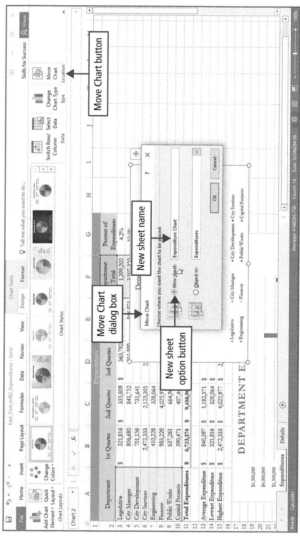

Excel 2016, Windows 10, Microsoft Corporation

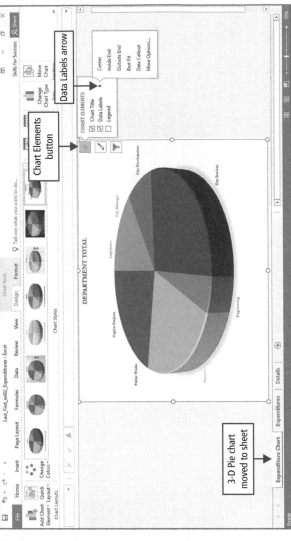

Excel 2016, Windows 10, Microsoft Corporation

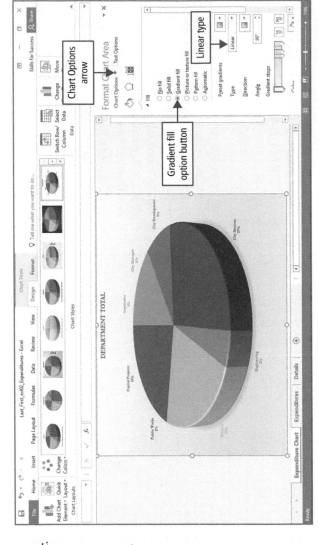

Excel 2016, Windows 10, Microsoft Corporation

MOS
Obj

7. To the right of the chart, click the **Chart Styles** button. In the **Chart Styles** gallery, scroll down, and then click **Style 8**.

MOS
Obj

8. To the right of the chart, click the **Chart Elements** button. Under **Chart Elements**, point at **Data Labels**, and then click the **Data Labels arrow**. Compare your screen.

9. In the **Data Labels** list, click **More Options** to open the Format Data Labels pane.

10. In the **Format Data Labels** pane, under **Label Contains**, select the **Percentage** check box. Verify that the **Category Name** check box is selected, and then clear any other check boxes.

11. At the top of the pane, click the **Label Options arrow**, and then click **Chart Area** to open the Format Chart Area pane. In the **Format Chart Area** pane, click the **Fill & Line** button, and then click **Fill**. Click the **Gradient fill** option button, and verify that the Type is Linear. Compare your screen.

12. **Close** the Format Chart Area pane.

13. On the **Insert tab**, in the **Text group**, click the **Header & Footer** button. In the **Page Setup** dialog box, click the **Custom Footer** button. Verify that the insertion point is in the **Left section** box, and then click the **Insert File Name** button. Click in the **Right section** box, and then click the **Insert Sheet Name** button. Click **OK** two times.

14. **Save** the file.

■ **You have completed Skill 8 of 10**

▶ A chart's data series and labels are linked to the source data in the worksheet. When worksheet values are changed, the chart is automatically updated.

1. Click the **Expenditures** worksheet tab to display the worksheet. Scroll as necessary to display row 8 at the top of the window and the chart at the bottom of the window. In the column chart, note the height of the *Finance* data marker for the 2nd Quarter and the *Capital Projects* data marker for the 4th Quarter.

2. Click cell **C8**. Type 1017000 and then press Enter to accept the new value. Notice the animation in the chart when changes are made to its source data. Compare your screen.

3. Click cell **E10**, type 316000 and then press Enter. In cell G10, the *Capital Projects* expenditure now represents 5.7% of the projected total.

4. Click the **Expenditure Chart** worksheet tab to display the pie chart. Verify that in the pie chart, the slice for *Capital Projects* displays 6%.

   When underlying data is changed, the pie chart percentages and pie slices are automatically recalculated and resized. On the chart, 5.7% is rounded up to 6%.

5. Right-click the *Capital Projects* data label to select all of the data labels, and then in the shortcut menu, click **Font**. In the **Size** box, type 11 Compare your screen, and then click **OK**.

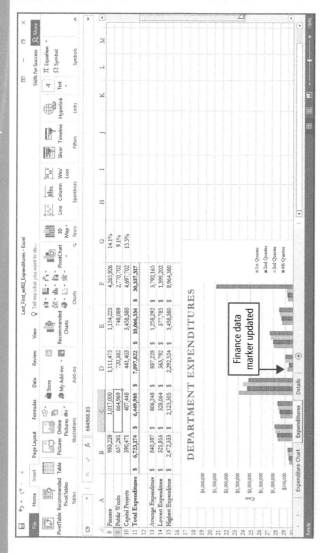

Excel 2016, Windows 10, Microsoft Corporation

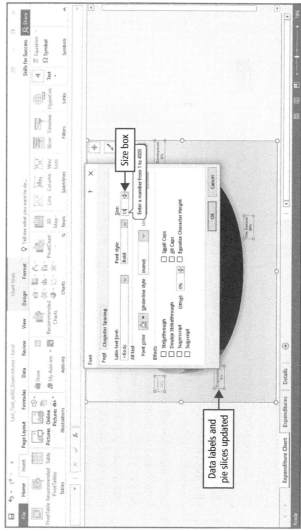

Excel 2016, Windows 10, Microsoft Corporation

■ **Continue to the next page to complete the skill**

6. Click the **Expenditures** worksheet tab, and then in cell **A10**, change *Capital Projects* to *Interfund Transfers* Press **Enter**, and then scroll down to verify that the column chart category label changed. Compare your screen.

7. Click the **Expenditure Chart** worksheet tab, and verify that the data label on the pie chart displays as *Interfund Transfers*.

8. Click the **Expenditures** worksheet tab. Scroll up, and then select the range **A1:G3**. On the **Home tab**, in the **Cells group**, click the **Insert arrow**, and then click **Insert Sheet Rows** to insert three blank rows.

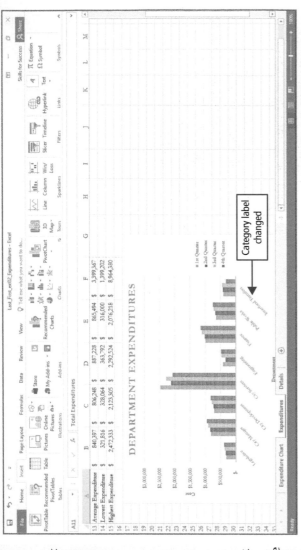

Excel 2016, Windows 10, Microsoft Corporation

9. On the **Insert tab**, in the **Text group**, click the **Insert WordArt button** . In the **WordArt** gallery, click the first style in the first row—**Fill - Black, Text 1, Shadow.** Immediately type Aspen Falls

10. Select the WordArt text. On the Mini toolbar, click the **Font Size button** , and then click **32.**

11. Point to the bottom border of the WordArt box, and then with the pointer, drag to position the WordArt object to approximately the range **C1:E3.** Click cell **A1** to deselect the WordArt, and then compare your screen.

12. **Save** the file.

■ **You have completed Skill 9 of 10**

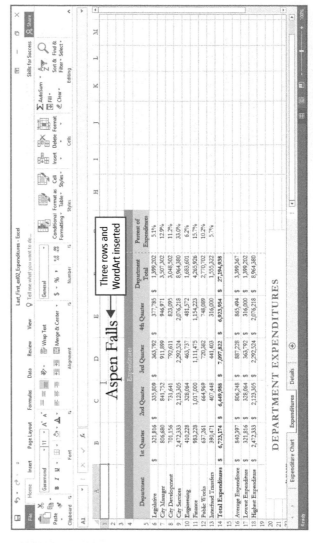

Excel 2016, Windows 10, Microsoft Corporation

SKILL 10: Preview and Print Multiple Worksheets

▶ Before you print an Excel worksheet, you can use Page Layout view to preview and adjust the printed document.

1. Verify that *Expenditures* is the active worksheet. Scroll down, and then click the column chart to select the chart. Click the **File tab**, and then click **Print**. Compare your screen.

   When an embedded chart is selected, only the chart will print.

2. Click the **Back button** ⊕. Click cell **A19** to deselect the chart.

3. Click the **View tab**, and then in the **Workbook Views group**, click the **Page Layout button**. On the left side of the status bar, notice that *Page: 1 of 2* displays, informing you that the data and the column chart would print on two pages.

4. Click the **Page Layout tab**, and then in the **Scale to Fit group**, click the **Width arrow**. Click **1 page**. Click the **File tab**, and then click **Print**. Compare your screen.

   1 of 1 displays at the bottom of the screen, indicating that the WordArt, the data, and the column chart will all print on one page.

5. Click the **Back button** ⊕. On the status bar, click the **Normal button** ▦ and then press Ctrl + Home to make cell **A1** the active cell.

■ **Continue to the next page to complete the skill**

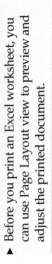

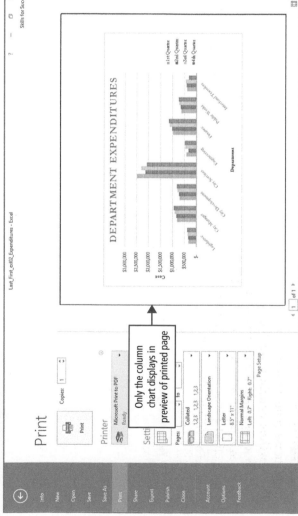

Only the column chart displays in preview of printed page

Excel 2016, Windows 10, Microsoft Corporation

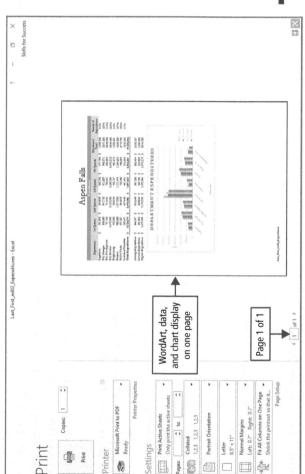

WordArt, data, and chart display on one page

Page 1 of 1

Excel 2016, Windows 10, Microsoft Corporation

6. Click the **Review tab**, and then in the **Proofing group**, click the **Spelling** button. Check the spelling of the worksheet. Click **Ignore All** for Interfund suggestion. When the message *Spell check complete. You're good to go!* displays, click **OK**.

7. **Save** the file.

8. Click the **File tab**, and then click **Print**. Under **Settings**, click the first button. Compare your screen.

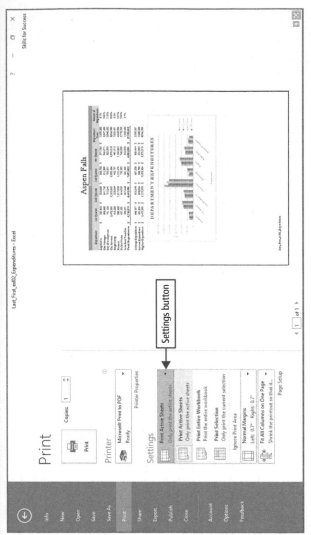

Settings button

Last_First_exl02_Expenditures - Excel

Excel 2016, Windows 10, Microsoft Corporation

9. On the displayed list, click **Print Entire Workbook**. Notice at the bottom of the screen that *1 of 3* displays and the chart sheet with the pie chart is the first page. Compare your screen.

10. At the bottom of the screen, click the **Next Page button** to preview the worksheet containing your **WordArt**, the data, and the column chart. **Save** the workbook. Submit the file as directed by your instructor. Otherwise, click the **Back** button.

11. If instructed, print the formulas. Display the worksheet formulas, AutoFit the column widths, and then print the formulas.

12. **Close** Excel. Submit the file as directed by your instructor.

➤ **DONE!** You have completed **Skill, and your file is complete!**

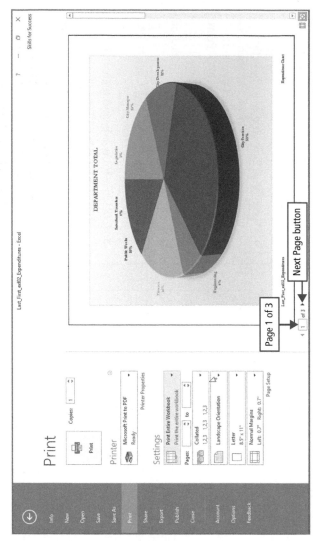

Page 1 of 3

Next Page button

Last_First_exl02_Expenditures - Excel

Excel 2016, Windows 10, Microsoft Corporation

More Skills 11

Validate Workbooks for Accessibility

To complete this project, you will need the following file:

- exl02_MS11Fares

You will save your file as:

- Last_First_exl02_MS11Fares

▶ *Accessibility*—technologies that adapt the display for nonvisual users.

▶ *Accessibility Checker*—finds potential accessibility issues and creates a report.

▶ *Alternative (Alt) text*—text used in documents and web pages to provide a text description of an object.

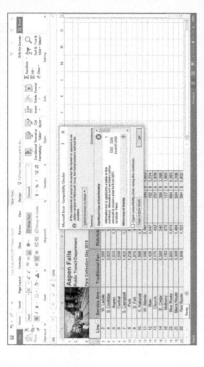

Excel 2016, Windows 10, Microsoft Corporation

1. **Start** Excel 2016. Open the student data file **exl02_MS11Fares**. Save the file in your chapter folder with the name Last_First_exl02_MS11Fares

2. On the **File tab**, click **Check for Issues**, and then click **Check Accessibility**. `MOS Obj`

3. In the **Accessibility Checker** pane, under **Errors** click **Picture 1 (Fares)**. Under **Additional Information**, read **Why Fix and How To Fix**.

4. Right-click the image in cell **A1:B3**. Click **Format Picture**, and then in the **Format Picture** pane, click **Size & Properties**. Click **Alt Text**, and then in the **Title** box type Transit Picture Close the **Format Picture** pane. Notice the error no longer displays in the **Accessibility Checker** pane. `MOS Obj`

5. In the **Accessibility Checker** pane, under **Warnings**, click **C1:F1 (Fares)**, and then read **Why Fix and How To Fix**. Click cell **C1**, and then on the **Home tab**, click the **Merge & Center** button. Repeat this technique to unmerge the remaining cells to remove the warnings.

6. Click cell **A4**. On the **Design tab**, in the **Properties group**, click in the **Table Name** box. Replace the text with TableFares and then press Enter.

   Defining table names can assist in the navigation of a worksheet for people with disabilities.

7. Right-click the table. In the short-cut menu click **Table**, and then click **Alternative Text**. In the **Alternative Text** dialog box, with the insertion point in the **Title** box, type Fares Table In the **Description** box type The table provides fare collection information for line, service area, traditional fares, and ticket prices. and then click **OK**. Notice there are no accessibility issues found in the **Inspection Results**. Close the **Accessibility Checker** pane.

8. On the **File tab**, click **Check for Issues**, and then click **Check Compatibility**. Compare your screen. In the **Summary** box it is explained that Alternative text has been applied to a table. Click **OK**. `MOS Obj`

9. **Save** the file, and then **Close** Excel. Submit the file as directed by your instructor.

- **You have completed More Skills 11**

More Skills 12

Change Chart Types

To complete this project, you will need the following file:

- exl02_MS12Specials

You will save your files as:

- Last_First_exl02_MS12Specials

▸ *Chart type* is a specific design of how data is displayed or compared in a chart.

▸ In a *bar chart*, the categories are displayed on the vertical axis, and the values are displayed on the horizontal axis. A bar chart illustrates comparisons among individual items.

▸ In a column chart, the values are displayed on the vertical axis, and the categories are displayed on the horizontal axis.

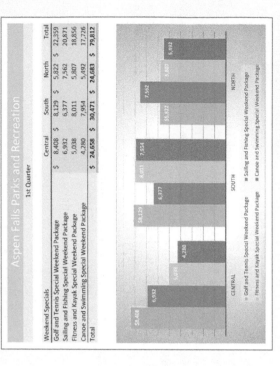

Excel 2016, Windows 10, Microsoft Corporation

1. Start Excel 2016. Open the student data file **exl02_MS12Specials**, and then save the file in your chapter folder as Last_First_exl02_MS12Specials

2. Add the file name in the worksheet's left footer, and then return to Normal view.

3. Select the range **A4:D8**. Click the **Insert tab**, and then in the **Charts group,** **MOS** **Obj** click the **Recommended Charts** button. In the **Insert Chart** dialog box, verify that the **Clustered Bar** thumbnail is selected, and then click **OK**.

   Recall that each of the cells bordered in blue is referred to as a data point—a value that originates in a worksheet cell.

   Related data points form a data series; for example, there is a data series for *Central*, a data series for *South*, and a data series for *North*.

4. On the **Design tab**, in the **Type group**, click the **Change Chart Type** button. In the **Change Chart Type** dialog box, on the **All Charts tab**, click **Line** to preview the data in a line chart.

5. In the left pane of the **Change Chart Type** dialog box, click **Column**, and then under **Clustered Column**, click the second thumbnail, and then click **OK** to change the chart type.

6. Move the chart so that the upper left corner is inside the upper left **MOS** **Obj** corner of cell **A12**. Use the lower right sizing handle to resize the chart so that the chart covers the range **A12:E27**.

7. At the top right corner of the chart, click the **Chart Elements** button, and then clear the **Chart Title** check box.

8. At the top right corner of the chart, click the **Chart Styles** button. Scroll down, and then click the fourth thumbnail—**Style 4**. At the top of the **Chart Styles** gallery, click **Color**, and then click the fourth color in the **Colorful** section—**Color 4**. **MOS** **Obj**

9. Click cell **A10** to deselect the chart. Click the **File tab**, and then click **Print** to preview the printed page.

10. **Save** the file, and then click **Close** Excel. Submit the file as directed by your instructor.

■ **You have completed More Skills 12**

More Skills 13

Copy Excel Data to Word Documents

To complete this project, you will need the following files:

- exl02_MS13House (Excel)
- exl02_MS13HouseIncome (Word)

You will save your files as:

- Last_First_exl02_MS13House (Excel)
- Last_First_exl02_MS13HouseIncome (Word)

▶ Each Microsoft Office application is designed for different purposes. Copying data from one application to another enables you to use the strengths of each application without having to retype the data.

MEMORANDUM

TO:	Richard Mack, Assistant City Manager
FROM:	Cyril Shore, Planning Council Director
DATE:	November 25, 2018
RE:	Aspen Falls Annual Household Income

Aspen Falls' mid-point (or median) household income was $56,332, about 17 percent higher than the United States and 11 percent higher than California as a whole. The average (or mean) household income for Aspen Falls was $63,965 or 21 percent higher than the nation and 15 percent higher than California as a whole. It is expected that Aspen Falls' income figures would be higher, reflecting a higher concentration of well-educated individuals. Following is the data and chart that reflect these numbers.

Location	Median	Mean
U.S.	$49,785	$54,763
California	$50,876	$55,963
Aspen Falls	$56,332	$61,965

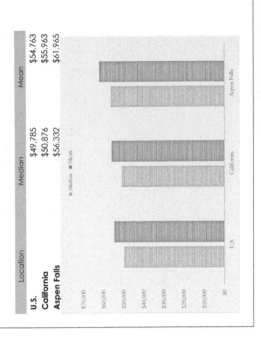

Excel 2016, Windows 10, Microsoft Corporation

1. **Start Excel 2016.** Open the student data file **exl02_MS13House,** and then save the file in your chapter folder as Last_First_exl02_MS13House

2. **Start Word 2016.** Open the student data file **exl02_MS13HouseIncome,** and then save the file in your chapter folder as Last_First_exl02_MS13HouseIncome

3. In the Word document, click the **Insert tab.** In the **Header & Footer group,** click the **Footer** button, and then click **Edit Footer.** On the **Header & Footer Tools Design tab,** in the **Insert group,** click the **Quick Parts** button, and then click **Field.** In the **Field** dialog box, under **Field names,** scroll down and then click **File Name.** Click the **OK** button. In the **Close group,** click the **Close Header and Footer button.**

4. At the bottom of the screen, on the taskbar, click the **Microsoft Excel** icon to display the Excel window. Select the range **A3:C6,** and then on the **Home tab,** in the **Clipboard group,** click the **Copy** button 🖹.

5. On the taskbar, click the **Microsoft Word** window. Press Ctrl + End to move to the end of the document. On the **Home tab,** in the **Clipboard group,** click the **Paste** button.

6. At the bottom of the screen, on the taskbar, click the **Microsoft Excel** icon to open the Excel window, and then press Esc to cancel the copy command.

7. Click the border of the chart to select the entire chart, and then on the Home tab, in the **Clipboard group,** click the **Copy** button 🖹.

8. Display the **Microsoft Word** window. Verify the insertion point is at the end of the document. On the **Home tab,** in the **Clipboard group,** click the **Paste** button.

9. Click the **File tab,** and then click **Print.** Compare your screen.

10. **Save** the file, and then **Close** ✕ Word and Excel. Submit the files as directed by your instructor.

■ **You have completed More Skills 13**

More Skills 14

Create Line Charts

To complete this project, you will need the following file:

- exl02_MS14Growth

You will save your file as:

- Last_First_exl02_MS14Growth

▶ A *line chart*, allows you to compare more than one set of values, each group of values is connected by a different line.

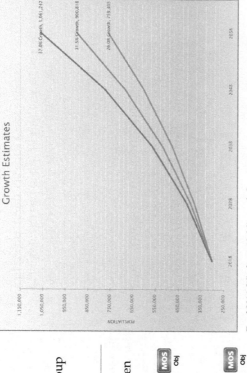

Growth Estimates

Excel 2016, Windows 10, Microsoft Corporation

1. Start Excel 2016. Open the student data file **exl02_MS14Growth**, and then save the file in your chapter folder as Last_First_exl02_MS14Growth

2. Select the range **A4:F7**. Click the **Insert tab**, and then in the **Charts group**, click the **Recommended Charts** button. In the **Insert Chart** dialog box, click the **All Charts tab**. Click **Line**, and then click the fourth chart—**Line with Markers**. Click **OK**. **MOS** **Obj**

3. On the **Design tab**, in the **Location group**, click the **Move Chart** button. In the displayed **Move Chart** dialog box, select the **New sheet** option button, replace the text with Growth Chart and then click **OK**. **MOS** **Obj**

4. On the **Design tab**, in the **Chart Layouts group**, click the **Quick Layout** button, and then click **Layout 6**. At the top right corner of the chart, click the **Chart Styles button**, and then click **Style 8**. Click the **Chart Styles button** to close the gallery. **MOS** **Obj**

   The years display at the bottom of the chart, and the population growth is represented by the lines in the chart.

5. Click the **Format tab**. In the **Current Selection group**, click the **Chart Elements arrow**, and then click **Vertical (Value) Axis**. In the **Current Selection group**, click the **Format Selection** button to open the Format Axis pane.

6. In the **Format Axis pane**, under **Axis Options**, in the **Minimum** box, replace the number with 250000 Press [Enter], and then watch the chart as the vertical axis minimum changes from 0 to 250,000. **MOS** **Obj**

7. In the **Format Axis pane**, scroll down and click **Tick Marks**. Scroll down and click the **Major type arrow**.

8. In the **Tick Marks** list, click **Cross** to display marks on the vertical axis.

9. In the **Format Axis pane**, click the **Axis Options arrow**, and then click **Chart Area** to display the Format Chart Area pane. Click the **Fill & Line button**, and then click **Fill**. Select the **Gradient fill** option button. **Close** the Format Chart Area pane.

10. At the top of the chart, click the **Chart Title**, type Growth Estimates and then press [Enter].

11. At the left side of the chart, click the vertical **Axis Title**, type Population and then press [Enter]. Compare your screen.

12. **Save** the file, and then **Close** Excel. Submit the file as directed by your instructor. **MOS** **Obj**

■ **You have completed More Skills 14**

The following table summarizes the **SKILLS AND PROCEDURES** covered in this chapter.

Skills Number	Task	Step	Icon	Keyboard Shortcut
1	Wrap text	Home tab → Alignment group → Wrap Text		
1	Middle align text	Home tab → Alignment group → Middle Align		
1	Center text	Home tab → Alignment group → Center		
1	Increase indent	Home tab → Alignment group → Increase Indent		
2	Insert the SUM function	Quick Analysis button → Totals → SUM		
2	Create an absolute cell reference	Select cell reference → Type $		F4
3	Apply the Percent style	Home tab → Number group → Percent Style	%	
3	Increase the number of display decimals	Home tab → Number group → Increase Decimal		
4	Calculate an average	Home tab → Editing group → AutoSum arrow → Average		
5	Calculate a minimum	Home tab → Editing group → AutoSum arrow → Min		
5	Calculate a maximum	Home tab → Editing group → AutoSum arrow → Max		
6	Insert a chart using Quick Analysis	Quick Analysis button → Charts → select chart		
7	Apply a chart style	Chart Style → Style		
7	Apply a chart layout	Design tab → Chart Layouts group → Quick Layout → Layout		
8	Insert a recommended chart	Insert tab → Charts group → Recommended Charts→ select desired chart		
8	Move a chart to its own worksheet	Design tab → Locations group → Move Chart → New sheet		
8	Change the chart type	Design tab → Type group → Change Chart Type → Type		
8	Change chart data labels	Design tab → Locations group → Move Chart → New sheet		
9	Insert WordArt	Insert tab → Text group → WordArt		
10	Adjust scale page width	Page Layout tab → Scale to Fit group → Width arrow → Page		
10	Print an entire workbook	File tab → Print → Settings → Print Entire Workbook		
MS 11	Check accessibility	File tab → Check for Issues → Check Accessibility		
MS 11	Insert Alt Text picture	Format picture → Size & Properties → Alt Text		
MS 11	Insert Alt Text table	Table → Alternative Text		
MS 11	Check compatibility	File tab → Check for Issues → Check Compatibility		
MS 13	Copy Excel data to documents	Home tab → Clipboard Group → Copy		
MS 14	Create line charts	Insert tab → Chart Group → Line Chart		

Project Summary Chart

Project	Project Type	Project Location
Skills Review	Review	In Book & MIL
Skills Assessment 1	Review	In Book & MIL
Skills Assessment 2	Review	Book
My Skills	Problem Solving	Book
Visual Skills Check	Problem Solving	Book
Skills Challenge 1	Critical Thinking	Book
Skills Challenge 2	Critical Thinking	Book
More Skills Assessment	Review	In Book & MIL
Collaborating with Google	Critical Thinking	Book

MOS Objectives Covered

Insert and deleting columns and rows

Insert references (relative, mixed, absolute, across worksheets)

Print individual worksheets

Perform calculations by using the MIN and MAX functions

Set print scaling

Perform calculations by using the AVERAGE function

Check accessibility

Create a new chart

Inspect a workbook for compatibility issues

Use Quick Analysis

Modify cell alignment and indentation

Resize charts

Wrap text within cells

Add and modify chart elements

Apply number formats

Apply chart layouts and styles

Apply cell styles

Move charts to a chart sheet

Name tables

Add alternative text to objects for accessibility

Key Terms

BizSkills Video

1. What are the best ways to network online?

2. What are some of the biggest pitfalls in using social media to communicate a personal brand?

Online Help Skills

1. Start Excel 2016, and then in the upper right corner of the start page, click the Help button [?].

2. In the Excel Help window Search help box, type Keyboard shortcuts and then press [Enter].

3. In the search result list, click Keyboard shortcuts in Excel. Maximize the Help window, and then compare your screen.

Excel 2016, Windows 10, Microsoft Corporation

4. Read the article to answer the following question: How can you use Key Tips to access the Ribbon?

Matching

Match each term in the second column with its correct definition in the first column by writing the letter of the term on the blank line in front of the correct definition.

_____ **1.** A command with which you can display text on multiple lines within a cell.

_____ **2.** A cell reference that refers to a cell by its fixed position in a worksheet and does not change when the formula is copied.

_____ **3.** Rules that specify the way numbers should display.

_____ **4.** The default format applied to numbers.

_____ **5.** The value(s) that determine(s) how a function should be used.

_____ **6.** A graphical representation of data in a worksheet that shows comparisons, patterns, and trends.

_____ **7.** A chart line that contains words as labels.

_____ **8.** A chart line that contains numeric data.

_____ **9.** The function that adds a group of values and then divides the result by the number of values in the group.

_____ **10.** The Excel feature that outlines all of the cells referenced in a formula.

A Absolute cell reference

B Argument

C AVERAGE function

D Category axis

E Chart

F General format

G Number format

H Range finder

I Text wrap

J Value axis

Multiple Choice

Choose the correct answer.

1. Automatically changing the column width to accommodate the longest column entry.
    - **A.** Drag and drop
    - **B.** AutoFit
    - **C.** Auto adjust

2. A green triangle that indicates a possible error in a formula.
    - **A.** Error indicator
    - **B.** Message
    - **C.** Dialog Box Launcher

3. A chart type useful for illustrating comparisons among related numbers.
    - **A.** Pie chart
    - **B.** Area chart
    - **C.** Column chart

4. A chart placed on a worksheet with the source data.
    - **A.** Chart sheet
    - **B.** Column chart
    - **C.** Embedded chart

5. The related data points in a chart.
    - **A.** Column
    - **B.** Data series
    - **C.** Chart point

6. The box that identifies the patterns or colors assigned to the data series.
    - **A.** Legend
    - **B.** Dialog box
    - **C.** Message box

7. A predesigned combination of chart elements.
    - **A.** 3-D chart
    - **B.** Chart layout
    - **C.** Chart

8. A prebuilt chart format that applies an overall visual look to a chart.
    - **A.** Data marker
    - **B.** Chart finder
    - **C.** Chart style

9. The chart type that best displays the relationship of parts to a whole.
    - **A.** Pie chart
    - **B.** Area chart
    - **C.** Column chart

10. A worksheet that contains only a chart.
    - **A.** Worksheet
    - **B.** Chart area
    - **C.** Chart sheet

Topics for Discussion

1. Search current newspapers and magazines for examples of charts. Which charts catch your eye, and why? Do the charts appeal to you because of their color or format? Is something intriguing revealed to you in the chart that you have never considered before? What are some formatting changes that you think make a chart interesting and valuable to a reader?

2. Do you think 3-D pie charts distort the data in a way that is misleading? Why or why not?

Skills Review

To complete this project, you will need the following file:

- exl02_SRRevenue

You will save your file as:

- Last_First_exl02_SRRevenue

1. **Start Excel 2016**, and open the file **exl02_SRRevenue. Save** the file in your chapter folder as Last_First_exl02_SRRevenue Add the file name in the worksheet's left footer and the sheet name in the right footer. Return to **Normal** view.

2. In the column heading area, point to the right boundary of column **A**, and then double-click to AutoFit the column width. Click the column **B** heading, and then drag right to select columns **B:F**. Click the right boundary of column B, and then drag to the right until the ScreenTip indicates *Width:13:00 (96 pixels)*.

3. Select the range **A1:F1**. On the **Home tab**, in the **Alignment group**, click the **Wrap Text, Middle Align**, and **Center** buttons.

4. Select the range **B2:E13**. Click the **Quick Analysis** button, click **Totals**, and then click the first option—**SUM**.

5. Select the nonadjacent ranges **B2:E2** and **B14:E14**. In the **Number group**, click the **Decrease Decimal** button two times. Select the range **B3:E13**. In the **Number group**, click the **Decrease Decimal** button two times. Select the range **B14:E14**. In the **Styles group**, click the **Cell Styles** button, and then click **Total**.

6. In cell F2, type =E2/E14 and then on the formula bar, click the **Enter** button. With cell F2 as the active cell, in the **Number group**, click the **Percent Style** button, and then click the **Increase Decimal** button once. In the **Alignment group**, click the **Center** button. AutoFill the formula in cell F2 down through cell F13. Click cell **A15**, and then compare your screen.

7. Click cell **B16**. Type =Av and then in the **Formula AutoComplete** list, double-click **AVERAGE**. For the function argument, select the range **B2:B13**, and then press Enter Using the same function argument range, in cell **B17**, enter the MAX function. Select the range **B16:B17**, and then AutoFill the formulas to the right through column **D**. Compare your screen.

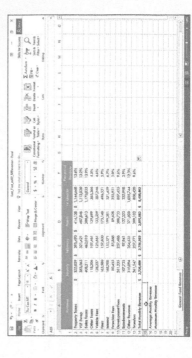

Excel 2016, Windows 10, Microsoft Corporation

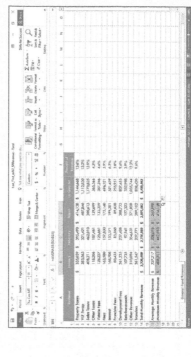

Excel 2016, Windows 10, Microsoft Corporation

◼ **Continue to the next page to complete this Skills Review**

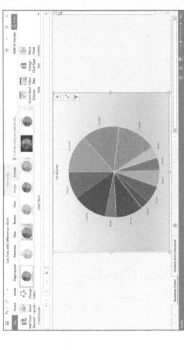

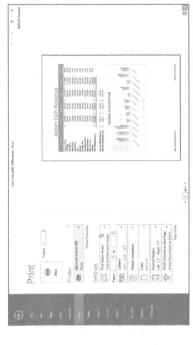

Excel 2016, Windows 10, Microsoft Corporation

Excel 2016, Windows 10, Microsoft Corporation

8. Select the range **A1:D13**. Click the **Quick Analysis** button, click **Charts**, and then click the **Clustered Column** thumbnail. Move and resize the chart to display in approximately the range **A19:F35**. At the top right corner of the chart, click the **Chart Styles** button, and then click the **Style 9** thumbnail. Select **Chart Title**, type General Fund Revenue and then press Enter.

9. Select the nonadjacent ranges **A1:A13** and **E1:E13**. Click the **Insert tab**, and then in the **Charts** group, click the **Recommended Charts** button. On the **All Charts** tab, click **Pie**, and then click **OK**.

10. On the **Design tab**, in the **Location group**, click the **Move Chart** button. In the **Move Chart** dialog box, select the **New sheet** option button, type the sheet name Revenue Chart and then click **OK**.

11. On the **Design tab**, in the **Chart Layouts group**, click the **Quick Layout button**, and then click **Layout 1**.

12. Click the **Chart Elements** button, click the **Data Labels arrow**, and then click **More Options**. In the **Format Data Labels** pane, under **Label Position**, click **Outside End**.

13. Click the **Label Options arrow**, and then click **Chart Area**. In the **Format Chart Area** pane, click the **Fill & Line** button, and then click **Fill**. Select the **Gradient fill** option button, and then **Close** the Format Chart Area pane. Compare your screen.

14. Click the **Insert tab**, and then in the **Text group**, click the **Header & Footer** button. In the **Page Setup** dialog box, click the **Custom Footer** button. Insert the **File Name** in the left section, and then insert the **Sheet Name** in the right section. Click **OK** twice.

15. Click the **General Fund Revenue worksheet tab**. Select the range **A1:A3**. On the **Home tab**, in the **Cells group**, click the **Insert arrow**, and then click **Insert Sheet Rows**. Click the **Insert tab**. In the **Text group**, click the **Insert WordArt** button, and then in the first row, click the second thumbnail—**Fill - Blue, Accent 1, Shadow**. Immediately type Aspen Falls Revenue Select the text in the WordArt. On the Mini toolbar, change the **Font Size** to **36**. Point to the bottom border of the WordArt, and then move the WordArt to center approximately within the range **A1:E3**.

16. Click cell **A1**. Click the **Page Layout tab**. In the **Scale to Fit group**, click the **Width arrow**, and then click the **1 page** button.

17. Click the **File tab**, and then click **Print**. Compare your screen.

18. **Save** the file, and then **Close** Excel. Submit the file as directed by your instructor.

DONE! You have completed this Skills Review

Skills Assessment 1

To complete this project, you will need the following file:

- exl02_SA1Debt

You will save your file as:

- Last_First_exl02_SA1Debt

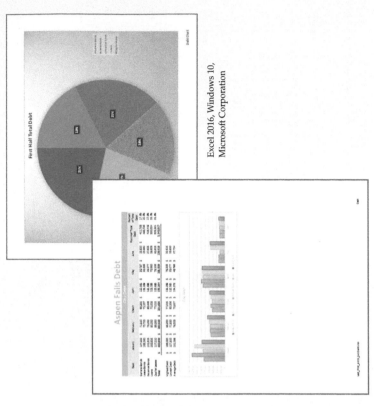

Excel 2016, Windows 10,
Microsoft Corporation

1. Start **Excel 2016**, and open the file **exl02_SA1Debt. Save** the workbook in your chapter folder as Last_First_exl02_SA1Debt Add the file name in the worksheet's left footer and the sheet name in the right footer. Return to **Normal** view.

2. Select the range **A2:I2**, and then apply the alignment **Wrap Text** and **Middle Align**.

3. Select the column headings **B:I**, and then AutoFit the column widths.

4. In the range **B8:H8**, insert the column totals, and then apply the **Total** cell style.

5. Select the nonadjacent ranges **B3:H3** and **B8:H8**, and then display no decimals. Select the range **B4:H7**, and then display no decimals.

6. In cell **I3**, calculate the *Percent of Total Debt*. In the formula, use an absolute cell reference when referring to cell **H8**. AutoFill the formula down through cell **I7**, and then format the results as percentages with one decimal place.

7. In the range **B10:G10**, insert a function to calculate the highest monthly debt. In the range **B11:G11**, insert a function to calculate the lowest monthly debt. In the range **B12:G12**, insert a function to calculate the average monthly debt.

8. Insert a **Pie** chart based on the nonadjacent ranges **A2:A7** and **H2:H7**. Move the pie chart to a chart sheet with the sheet name Debt Chart

9. For the pie chart, apply **Layout 6**, and then apply the **Chart Style 3**. Change the data label **Font Size to 12**, and then position to **Center**. Add the file name in the chart sheet's left footer and the sheet name in the right footer.

10. On the **Debt** worksheet, insert a **Clustered Column** chart based on the range **A2:G7**. Move the chart below the data, and then resize the chart to approximately the range **A14:I28**. Apply the chart **Style 5**. Change the chart title to City Debt

11. Insert three sheet rows at the top of the worksheet. Insert **WordArt**, using the style **Fill - Gold, Accent 4, Soft Bevel**. Change the WordArt text to Aspen Falls Debt and then change the **Font Size** to **36**. Move the WordArt to the top of the worksheet, centering it above the data.

12. Adjust the **Scale to Fit** to fit the WordArt, data, and column chart on one page.

13. Revise the Print Settings to **Print Entire Workbook**, and then compare your screen.

14. **Save** the file, and then **Close** Excel. Submit the file as directed by your instructor.

▶ **DONE! You have completed Skills Assessment 1**

Skills Assessment 2

To complete this project, you will need the following file:

■ exl02_SA2Cost

You will save your file as:

■ Last_First_exl02_SA2Cost

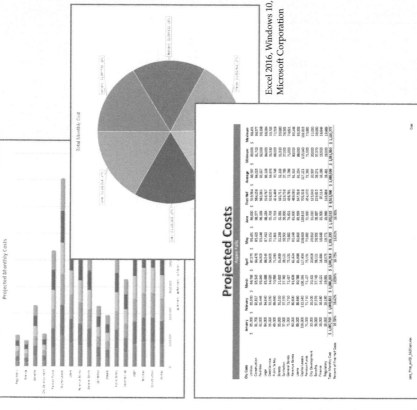

Excel 2016, Windows 10, Microsoft Corporation

1. Start **Excel 2016**, and then open the file **exl02_SA2Cost. Save the** workbook in your chapter folder as Last_First_exl02_SA2Cost Add the file name in the worksheet's left footer and the sheet name in the right footer. Return to **Normal** view.

2. For column **A**, AutoFit the column width. For columns **B:K**, change the column width to **11.00 (82 pixels)**.

3. In the range **B3:K3**, apply the **Center** alignment. In the range **A4:A20**, apply the **Increase Indent** alignment.

4. In the range **I4:I20**, insert a function to calculate the average monthly cost. In the range **J4:J20**, insert a function to calculate the minimum monthly cost. In the range **K4:K20**, insert a function to calculate the maximum monthly cost.

5. In row **21**, insert totals for columns **B:K**, and then apply the **Total** cell style. Format **B4:K4** and **B21:K21** with Currency, no decimals. Format **B5:K20** with Comma, no decimals.

6. In cell **B22**, calculate the *Percent of First Half Costs*. In the formula, use an absolute cell reference when referring to cell **H21**. Format the result as a percentage and display two decimals. AutoFill the formula to the right through column **G**.

7. Insert a **Stacked Bar** chart based on the range **A3:G20**. Move the stacked bar chart to a chart sheet named Projected Costs Apply the chart **Style 11**. Change the chart title to Projected Monthly Costs Add the file name in the chart sheet's left footer and the sheet name in the right footer.

8. Click the **Cost worksheet tab**. Insert a **Pie** chart based on the nonadjacent ranges **A3:G3** and **A21:G21**. Move the pie chart to a chart sheet named Total Monthly Costs Apply the chart **Layout 1**. Change the data label position to **Data Callout**, and then change the data label **Font Size** to **12**.

9. On the **Cost** worksheet, insert four blank lines at the top of the worksheet. Insert a WordArt with the **Fill - Black, Text 1, Outline - Background 1, Hard Shadow - Background 1** style. In the WordArt, type the text Projected Costs and then change the **Font Size** to **44**. Move the WordArt to the top of the worksheet, centering it above the data.

10. Scale the **Cost** worksheet to print on **1 page.**

11. **Print Preview** the workbook, and then compare your screen.

12. **Save** the file, and then **Close** Excel. Submit the file as directed by your instructor.

 DONE! You have completed Skills Assessment 2

My Skills

1. Start Excel 2016, and then open the file exl02_MYPersonalBudget. Save the file in your chapter folder as Last_First_exl02_MYPersonalBudget Add the file name in the worksheet's left footer, and then return to Normal view.

2. Change the alignments of the row 3 labels, and then indent the column A expense labels. In the range B14:E14, insert the column totals.

3. In the range B15:D15, insert a function to calculate the average monthly expense. In the range B16:D16, insert a function to calculate the maximum monthly expense.

4. In cell F4, calculate the *Expense as a Percent of Total*. In the formula, use an absolute cell reference when referring to the total. Format the results as percentages with one decimal, and then AutoFill the formula down through cell F13.

5. Apply the Total cell style where appropriate.

6. Insert a Pie chart based on the nonadjacent ranges A3:A13 and E3:E13.

7. Move the pie chart to an appropriate location below your data, and then resize the chart.

8. Format the pie chart with any of the chart options of your choice including layout, style, or color.

9. At the top of the worksheet, insert three blank rows. Insert a WordArt using your first and last names as the WordArt text. Move the WordArt above the data, and then resize to fit in the blank rows.

10. Adjust the scaling to fit the data and the pie chart on one page when printed. Print Preview the workbook, and then compare your screen.

11. Save the file, and then Close Excel. Submit the file as directed by your instructor.

DONE! You have completed My Skills

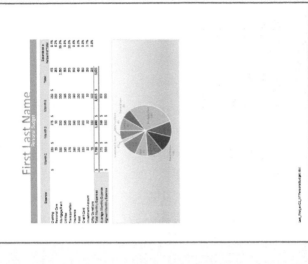

Excel 2016, Windows 10, Microsoft Corporation

Visual Skills Check

To complete this project, you will need the following file:

- exl02_ VSNetAssets

You will save your file as:

- Last_First_exl02_VSNetAssets

Start Excel **2016**, and then open the student data file **exl02_VSNetAssets.** **Save** the file in your chapter folder as Last_First_exl02_VSNetAssets Create the worksheet. Calculate the *Percent of Total Net Assets* using an absolute cell reference. In rows **13:15**, insert the statistical functions that correspond with the row labels. Format the values and text as shown. Create the pie chart, and then move and resize the chart as shown in the figure. The chart uses the **Layout 4** chart layout, and **Color 8**, with data label font size **12** and **Bold**. Insert the file name in the worksheet's left footer. **Save** the file, and then **Close** Excel. Submit the file as directed by your instructor.

✔ **DONE! You have completed Visual Skills Check**

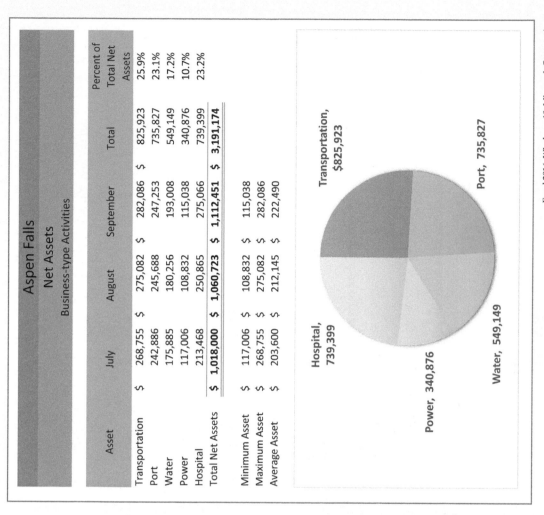

Aspen Falls
Net Assets
Business-type Activities

Asset	July	August	September	Total	Percent of Total Net Assets
Transportation	$ 268,755	$ 275,082	$ 282,086	$ 825,923	25.9%
Port	242,886	245,688	247,253	735,827	23.1%
Water	175,885	180,256	193,008	549,149	17.2%
Power	117,006	108,832	115,038	340,876	10.7%
Hospital	213,468	250,865	275,066	739,399	23.2%
Total Net Assets	$ 1,018,000	$ 1,060,723	$ 1,112,451	$ 3,191,174	
Minimum Asset	$ 117,006	$ 108,832	$ 115,038		
Maximum Asset	$ 268,755	$ 275,082	$ 282,086		
Average Asset	$ 203,600	$ 212,145	$ 222,490		

Transportation, $825,923

Port, 735,827

Hospital, 739,399

Water, 549,149

Power, 340,876

Skills Challenge 1

To complete this project, you will need the following file:

- exl02_SC1Budget

You will save your file as:

- Last_First_exl02_SC1Budget

Start Excel 2016. Open the file **exl02_SC1Budget,** and then save the file in your chapter folder as Last_First_exl02_SC1Budget During the fourth quarter of this year, the Accounting Department developed a summary of the proposed Aspen Falls budget. Correct the errors in the statistical functions—you may want to display the formulas. Use an absolute cell reference when correcting the percentage. Correct the number formats, and format the

labels appropriately. Modify the WordArt and the column chart. Verify that the WordArt, data, and column chart will print on one page. Add the file name in the worksheet's left footer. Save the file, and Close Excel. Submit the file as directed by your instructor.

 **DONE! You have completed Skills Challenge 1**

Skills Challenge 2

To complete this project, you will need the following file:

- exl02_SC2Classes

You will save your file as:

- Last_First_exl02_SC2Classes

Start Excel 2016, and then open the workbook **exl02_SC2Classes.** Save the file in your chapter folder as Last_First_exl02_SC2Classes Carter Horikoshi, the Art Center Supervisor, created a workbook to track how many students attended the Community Center classes last summer. He wants to determine if he should offer more classes this summer based on the number of students from last summer. He wants to know the total enrollment and the average enrollment for each month and for each class. He would like

to view a chart that summarizes the enrollment data. Using the skills you learned in this chapter, provide Mr. Horikoshi a workbook to assist him in his decision. Add the file name in the worksheet's left footer. Save the file and Close Excel. Submit the file as directed by your instructor.

 **DONE! You have completed Skills Challenge 2**

More Skills Assessment

To complete this project, you will need the following files:

- exl02_MSARecycling (Excel)
- exl02_MSARecycling (Word)

You will save your files as:

- Last_First_exl02_MSARecycling (Excel)
- Last_First_exl02_MSARecycling (Word)
- Last_First_exl02_MSARecycling (JPG)

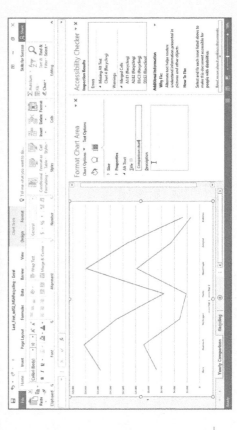

Excel 2016, Windows 10, Microsoft Corporation

1. Start Excel 2016. Open the workbook exl02_MSARecycling, and then save the file in your chapter folder as Last_First_exl02_MSARecycling

2. Select the **Clustered Bar Chart**. Use the **Chart Tools** to change the **Chart Type** to a **Clustered Column** chart. Apply **Chart Style 7** to the chart.

3. Start Word 2016. Open the student data file exl02_MSARecycling, and then save the file in your chapter folder as Last_First_exl02_MSARecycling

4. At the bottom of the screen, on the taskbar, click the **Microsoft Excel** icon to display the Excel window. Copy the *Recycling Revenue* chart.

5. Display the **Microsoft Word** window. Move to the end of the document, and then paste the chart from Excel. Resize the chart so that the right edge is at the right margin.

6. Select the chart, and apply **Alt Text** using the title Recycling Chart Close the Format Chart pane. **Save** the file, and then **Close** the Word document.

7. At the bottom of the screen, on the taskbar, click the **Microsoft Excel** icon to open the Excel window, and then deselect the copied cells.

8. Using data in the range **A5:C12**, create a **Stacked Line** chart. Move the Stacked Line chart to a chart sheet named Yearly Comparison and then clear the **Chart Title**. Click the **Recycling** sheet, and then **Save** the file.

9. Check Accessibility for the workbook. Format **Chart 1 (Yearly Comparison)** using Alt Text and apply Comparison Chart as the Title. Compare your screen.

10. Format **Chart 4 (Recycling)** using Alt Text and apply Recycling Revenue Chart as the Title.

11. Clear any warnings by unmerging cells as needed. Close all open panes.

12. **Save** the file, and then **Close** all open windows. Submit the files as directed by your instructor.

✓ **DONE! You have completed More Skills Assessment**

Collaborating with Google

To complete this project, you will need a Google account (refer to the Common Features chapter) and the following file:

- exl02_GPRentalRevenue

You will save your file as:

- Last_First_exl02_GPRentalRevenue

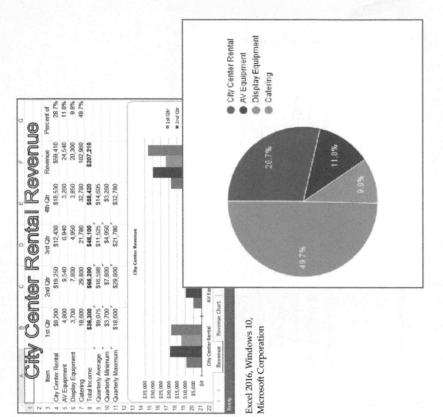

Excel 2016, Windows 10,
Microsoft Corporation

1. Log into your Google account, click **Google Apps** 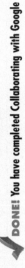, and then click **Drive** ◢. Create a new Google Sheet, and then replace the title with Rental Revenue

2. From the student data files, open **exl02_GPRentalRevenue**. Copy the range **A1:G9** from the *Revenue* worksheet, and then paste it in cell **A1** of the blank Google worksheet. Rename the sheet Revenue

3. Select the range **A1:G1**. Click **Center** ▤ align. Click **Format**, point to **Text wrapping**, and then click **Wrap**.

4. In cell **B7**, enter the **AVERAGE** function for the *1st Quarter*. Use AutoFill to copy the formula through **E7**.

5. In cell **B8**, enter the **MIN** function for the *1st Quarter*. Use AutoFill to copy the formula through **E8**.

6. In cell **B9**, enter the **MAX** function for the *1st Quarter*. Use AutoFill to copy the formula through **E9**.

7. In cell **G2**, calculate *Revenue as a Percent of Total Income* using absolute cell reference for **F6**. Format the result as a percentage with one decimal. AutoFill the formula down through **G5**.

8. Select rows 1 and 2. Click **Insert**, and then click **2 Rows above**. Click **Insert**, click **Drawing**, click **Actions**, and then click **WordArt**. Type City Center Rental Revenue press [Enter], and then click **Save & Close**. Move the WordArt to rows **1** and **2**. On the Insert tab, click Chart and resize.

9. Select the range **A3:E7**. Click **Insert**, and then click **Chart**. Verify the first thumbnail is selected, and then click **Insert**. Resize the chart to fit in cells **A13:G24**. Select the title, and then replace the current text with City Center Revenue

10. Select the nonadjacent ranges **A3:A7** and **F3:F7**. Click **Insert**, and then click **Chart**. Scroll down, select the **Pie Chart**, and then click

Insert. In the upper right corner of the chart, click the arrow, and then select **Move to own sheet . . .** Rename the sheet Revenue Chart Right click the chart title, and then click **Clear title**.

11. Click **File**, point to **Download as**, and then click **Microsoft Excel (.xlsx)**. Open the downloaded file, and then save the file in your chapter folder as Last_First_exl02_GPRentalRevenue Compare your screen.

12. Close all windows, and then submit your file as directed by your instructor.

✓ **DONE! You have completed Collaborating with Google**

chapter 6

The Internet and the World Wide Web

Chapter Objectives

1 Define the Internet, and explain how it works. (p. 209)

2 Describe methods for accessing the Internet. (p. 212)

3 Differentiate between the Internet and the World Wide Web and describe the elements that enable Web content to be displayed. (p. 215)

4 Describe several methods of finding information on the Web including the use of a URL, surfing, conducting searches, and sharing with other Web users through RSS feeds, blogs, wikis, and podcasts. (p. 222)

5 Identify features to look for when evaluating a Web site or its content. (p. 230)

6 List the most popular Internet services and explain what they do. (p. 233)

7 Describe the three types of e-commerce. (p. 239)

8 List the rules of netiquette. (p. 244)

9 List safe surfing procedures, and identify hazards of the Web. (p. 244)

205

It seems that being connected 24/7 has become a necessity in our world and that the Internet is no longer just for fun, but for work, social contact, education, and everyday information. You know how to use the Internet, but do you know how to use it effectively? How would you rate your search skills? How do you know whether the information from a Web source is reputable? Are you a potential victim of cybercrime? Is the site you are about to provide with your credit card number a secure site?

The Internet has created a shift in communication methods by providing a medium that allows interactivity. With the Internet, individuals can create information as well as consume it. Perhaps that is its real appeal, the ability to speak and be heard around the world, which is propelling its use to regions and populations isolated from media in the past.

The Internet offers many benefits and is ripe with pitfalls for those who don't understand it and the responsibilities that go along with Internet usage. This chapter is your guide to understanding the Internet and using it safely for personal, educational, and business purposes. Key concepts include those listed here:

- How the Internet works and how you connect to it
- The difference between the Web and Internet
- An overview of the different browsers
- The parts of a Web address
- Tools and strategies to streamline your Internet searches
- Key Internet services such as e-mail, chats, instant messaging, social networking, online discussions, and electronic mailing lists
- Different types of e-commerce
- Good online behavior and safe surfing techniques

Check out **f Facebook** for our latest updates

www.facebook.com

What Is the Internet and How Does It Work?

The **Internet**, also called the **Net**, is a global computer network made up of thousands of privately and publicly owned computers and networks that grew and interlinked, over time, into one giant network. In short, the Internet is a network of networks.

This idea of connecting computers of different designs and over distant locations started in the 1960s with the U.S. Department of Defense and project called ARPANET (Advanced Research Projects Agency Network). The purpose of the project was to create a form of secure communication for military and scientific purposes and to create a method for transferring such communications between computers. The outcome of the project was a network that consisted of four computers located at The University of California at Los Angeles, the University of California at Santa Barbara, the University of Utah, and Stanford Research Institute. In turn, each of these four nodes connected hundreds of other computers to the network. The Internet is the offspring of the ARPANET project. To learn more about the history of the Internet, go to **www.isoc.org/internet/history/brief. shtml**, a page posted by The Internet Society, an organization for professionals who are interested in supporting the technical development of the Internet.

Today, the Internet is composed of more than 750 million hosts. A **host** is a computer that has two-way access to other computers; it can receive requests and reply to those requests. These hosts are interconnected and geographically spread out over the world. Figure provides a simplified image of a single network that is set up to provide its users with access to the Internet and any of its hosts. A study done by the Internet Systems Consortium substantiates the astronomical growth of the Internet

by citing an increase of over 208 million hosts between 2008 and 2010.

The Internet has come a long way since its inception as a communication and file-exchange network for government agencies; scientific research; and, later, academic institutions. Today it has become a medium for discovering and exploring information, marketing products, shopping, taking classes, and socializing. Through a combination of surveys done by comScore, Inc., a global leader in measuring the digital world, the global Internet audience (defined as users ages 15 and older) as of December 2009, using home and work computers, was approaching 2 billion unique visitors. With these numbers constantly on the rise, the leap to three billion users is expected to come quickly.

But technology is not equally distributed, and Internet access and usage is no different. Countries or regions in which over 70 percent of the population has Internet access include the United States, Canada, Japan, United Kingdom, South Korea, and Spain. Countries in which less than 40 percent of the populate has Internet access include China, India, Brazil, Mexico, and the Philippines. The bar graph makes this inequity even more apparent.

Now that you know what the Internet is and a little about how it started, let's explore how it works and how it is used.

How the Internet Works

The unique feature about the Internet is that nobody owns it. It is best thought of as the granddaddy of networks in which

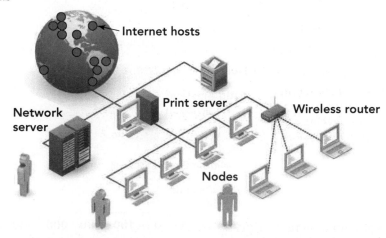

Both wired and wireless technologies are used to connect to the Internet.

every connected computer can exchange data with any other computer on the network. The term **cyberspace** is often used when talking about the Internet. It's an appropriate term because it captures the concept of the intangible, nonphysical territory that the Internet encompasses. The networks that make up the Internet are not maintained by one company or organization. Instead, the Internet is maintained by a conglomerate of volunteers across the world. Some governing bodies restrict control and/or provide equipment. But the majority of network servers and connectivity equipment are provided by universities, telecommunications companies, businesses, corporations, and services that sell Internet access. It really is amazing that it all works!

Architecture

The **Internet backbone**, the main high-speed routes through which data travels, are maintained by **network service providers (NSPs)** such as AT&T, NCI, Sprint, BBN, and UUNET. The equipment of these providers is linked at **network access points (NAPs)** so that data may, for example, begin its journey on a segment maintained by AT&T but cross over to a Sprint segment in order to reach its destination. Between your computer or business network and the Internet backbone are **routers**, specialized devices that connect networks, locate the best path of transmission, and ensure that your data reaches its destination. Visit **www.internet2.edu/about/** for information on a nonprofit consortium of universities, government agencies, and computer and telecommunication companies in over 50 countries that develop and deploy advanced networking applications and technologies.

Interoperability

The Internet does more than merely allow the free exchange of data among millions of computers; it provides the ability for computers to exchange data

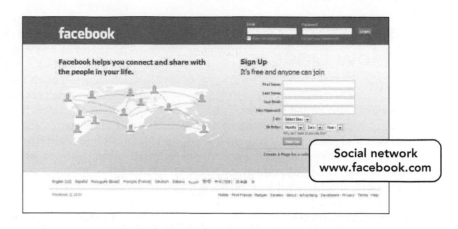

Social network
www.facebook.com

Entertainment
www.apple.com/itunes/store

The Internet, with applications in education, entertainment, marketing, and social networking, is the fastest and most universal form of mass media ever developed.

Source: www.internetworldstats.com/stats.htm

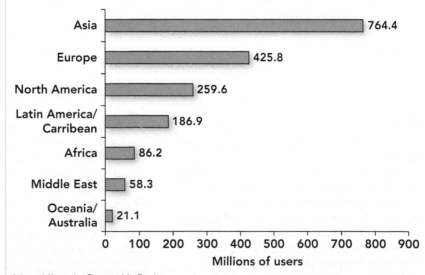

Region	Millions of users
Asia	764.4
Europe	425.8
North America	259.6
Latin America/Carribean	186.9
Africa	86.2
Middle East	58.3
Oceania/Australia	21.1

Internet Users by Geographic Region

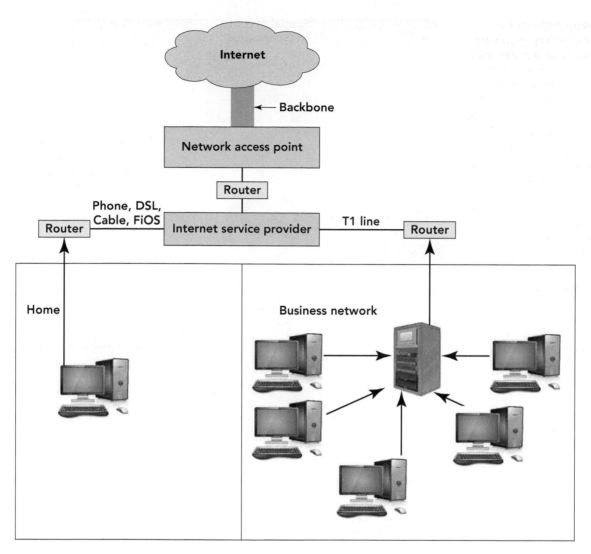

The Path Data Takes from Your Computer to the Internet

regardless of the brand, model, or operating system the computers are running. This feature is called **interoperability**. This remarkable characteristic of the Internet comes into play every time you use the network. When you access the Internet using a Mac, for example, you contact a variety of machines that may include other Macs, Windows PCs, UNIX machines, and even mainframe computers. You don't know what type of computer you're accessing and it doesn't make any difference.

The Internet's interoperability helps explain the network's popularity. No network could match the Internet's success if it forced people to use just one or two types of computers. The **TCP/IP (Transmission Control Protocol/ Internet Protocol)** suite of protocols, which supply the standard methods of

packaging and transmitting information on the Internet are responsible for enabling interoperability. When you obtain direct access to the Internet, usually through an Internet access provider, your computer is provided with a copy of the TCP/IP programs just as is every other computer that is connected to the Internet. The TCP/IP suite employs a two-layer communication design. The TCP layer, **Transmission Control Protocol**, manages the assembling of a message or file into smaller packets that are transmitted over the Internet and then received by a TCP layer on the destination computer that reassembles the packets into the original message. The lower layer, the **Internet Protocol (IP)**, handles the address part of each packet so that it gets to the right destination.

Now that you've learned about how the Internet works, the next section explores how you go about getting online.

Accessing the Internet: Going Online

When you access the Internet, it is referred to as *going online*. You usually do not connect directly to the Internet backbone. Instead, you usually connect to an Internet access provider that in turn connects you to the backbone via some type of wired or wireless connection.

Internet Access Providers

Internet access providers are companies or businesses that provide access to via Internet free, for a fixed monthly charge, or for an itemized per use fee.

**Special purpose
XO computer**

TCP/IP

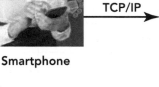

TCP/IP

TCP/IP

TCP/IP

Smartphone

Internet

Networked computers

Notebook

The TCP/IP suite of protocols ensures that any data traveling over the Internet is sent in the same format regardless of the type of computer, Internet access provider, or operating system being used.

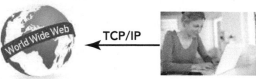

GREEN tech tips

It is easy to think of the Internet as just something out there, an intangible, having no effect on our physical world. In reality, 2009 estimates indicate that Internet data centers worldwide consumed 2 percent of global electricity production. Most of the energy was to power forced-air cooling systems in the data centers. One data center operator compared the heat emitted from a rack of servers in a data center to the amount of heat emitted by a 7-foot stack of toaster ovens. The energy to cool such centers undoubtedly did not come from green sources and cost $30 billion (U.S.).

Another way to cool the data centers is under development, with a working model named Aquasar expected to be completed in 2010. This new idea is to use water, not air, to cool the computing environment. Water cooled to 60–70°C

(158°F), cool enough to keep the processing chips below their maximum heat of 85°C (185°F), will be pumped through tiny channels in the computer systems of the data centers and will absorb heat from the metal along the way. The working model, developed by IBM Zurich and the Swiss Federal Institute of Technology Zurich (ETH), will be located on the ETH campus. In this prototype, the water used to absorb the heat from the computer systems will release that heat into the building and then recirculate to cool the computer system. It is estimated that this system will reduce the carbon footprint of the ETH campus by 85 percent and save up to 30 tons of carbon emissions a year. For more information, go to **www.youtube.com/watch?v=FbGyAXsLzIc** to view a video on this new cooling concept. ●

Some of the roles and responsibilities of an access provider are listed here:

- Providing and maintaining a connection to the Internet
- Supporting the hardware and software needed to service that connection
- Protecting their site and network from external threats such as viruses, hacker attacks, and other illegal activities
- Providing 24-hour customer service and technical support

Access providers fall into three categories: Internet service providers, online service providers, and wireless Internet service providers. Let's look at the features of each.

STUDENT VIDEO

An **Internet service provider (ISP)** is a company that traditionally provided access to the Internet and no additional services. Today these providers have added features to make them a one-stop source for Internet services. There are both local and national ISPs, each having varied services and pricing. If you are looking for an Internet service provider, you might want to start with "The List" (**www.thelist.com**). This is a buyer's guide to ISPs and can be searched by area or country.

An **online service provider (OSP)** is a for-profit firm that provides a proprietary network and offers special services that are available only to subscribers. Members may participate in instant messaging, chat rooms, and discussions, and take advantage of fee-based content, such as magazines and newspapers. When they began, online services provided a large amount of content that was accessible only by those who subscribed to that online service, whereas ISPs predominantly served to provide access to the Internet and generally provided little, if any, exclusive content of their own. The distinction between these two services has become less defined as OSPs today offer Internet access and ISPs offer more user services. Popular OSPs are MSN and AOL.

A **wireless Internet service provider** can be a local or national company that provides wireless Internet access to computers and other mobile devices, such as notebooks and smartphones. Some familiar providers are AT&T, T-Mobile, and Verizon Wireless. Requirements for a wireless connection include a portable device, an internal wireless adapter or a USB port for connecting an external adapter, and a wireless Internet access plan from a provider. Wireless connectivity for portable devices in your home or office is usually provided through a wireless router located in close proximity and connected to your provider. A **hot spot** is usually a public location like an airport, college campus, or coffee shop that provides Internet access for devices fitted with the wireless technology listed above. Some hot spots allow free access; others charge a nominal fee. When using a connection at a hotspot, always turn on your system's firewall and avoid accessing private information because transmissions at these locations are usually not encrypted and are susceptible to detection by others. For a list of free Internet access locations by state go to **www.wififreespot.com**.

To access the Internet backbone, access providers distribute software that runs on users' computers to enable the connection. Essentially, the provider acts

Links to news events, careers, and finance.

Access to e-mail and messenger require a sign-in.

Internet access providers, such as MSN, AT&T, and Comcast, provide Internet access and extra features to meet the needs of both individual and business subscribers.

as an access ramp to an expressway; in this case, the expressway is the Internet backbone. These various providers usually charge a monthly fee for Internet access, again like the fee you pay to use some expressways, but you can sometimes obtain free trial accounts for a certain number of days or hours.

Now that the difference between access providers has been covered, let's move on to the various types of physical connections that can be used to gain entry to the Internet.

Connection Options

In addition to obtaining an Internet account, you have to decide how you will access the Internet. Be aware that the speed of access advertised by an access provider is often a maximum. Few users actually find their usage reaching these advertised numbers. Your access choices typically include the following options:

- **Dial-up access.** If you are searching for an affordable connection solution and speed is not a high priority, then a dial-up provider will likely meet your needs. A dial-up connection does not require any special hardware; it uses your existing phone jack and dial-up modem configurations. The downside of this type of access

is the speed; it is the slowest of all Internet services. Many people use a dial-up connection as a backup for their existing broadband service.

- **Digital subscriber line (DSL).** A DSL connection offers faster access speeds than dial-up, while making use of ordinary phone lines with the addition of a special external modem. One drawback of DSL is that service doesn't extend more than a few miles from a telephone switching station or central office (CO). Although this distance is being extended, DSL service may be unavailable in some rural areas.

- **Cable access.** Many cable TV companies provide permanent online connections and offer high-speed Internet access, comparable to—and sometimes surpassing—DSL speeds. No phone line is needed, but a cable modem is required.

- **Satellite access.** If your geographical area has been overlooked by DSL and cable providers, go outside. If you have a clear view of the sky, then you can most likely get high-speed satellite Internet service! The connection to your high-speed satellite service is comprised of both indoor and outdoor equipment. Outside,

Types of Internet Access

Type	Price Range per Month	Speed of Access (receiving data)	Advantages	Disadvantages
Dial-up	$5 to $20	Slow: 56 kilobits per second (Kbps)	Availability Low user cost	Slow speed
DSL	$10 to $30	Average: 1.5 megabits per second (Mbps) Maximum: 7+ Mbps	Speed Reliability	Availability High user cost
Cable	$30 to $60	Average: 3 Mbps Maximum: 30+ Mbps	Speed Reliability	Availability High user cost
Satellite	$60 to $100	Average: 700 Kbps Maximum: 1.5 Mbps	Availability Speed	High user cost Reliability
Fiber-optic service	$40 to $140	Average: 15 Mbps Maximum: 50+ Mbps	Speed	Availability High user cost

there is an antenna and electronics to transmit and receive data, along with a connection to a small, unobtrusive dish. This equipment connects to an indoor receive unit (IRU) and indoor transmit unit (ITU) that connect to your computer through a simple USB connector. Satellite is more costly than cable or DSL, but if you live in a rural area, it might be a viable alternative to dial-up.

- **Fiber-optic service.** Fiber-optic lines running directly to the home provide users with an incredibly fast Internet connection, easily surpassing other methods. With more than 1.5 million customers (with a goal of 3 to 4 million by 2010) in at least 16 states, **fiber-optic service** is rapidly becoming a challenger to DSL and cable providers, especially in the suburbs. However, this service is still unavailable in many cities and rural areas and is usually offered by a limited number of providers. No modem is needed, but fiber-optic cable may have to be run to and within your home.

The Internet provides the infrastructure used to transport the ideas, queries, and information available on the World Wide Web to and from users.

If you don't need a constant, daily Internet connection, some businesses offer special leased lines for companies, educational institutions, and large organizations. Internet access is attained through the organization's network and is usually free to the users because the company or institution pays the bill.

Now that you understand the various ways to connect to the Internet, let's differentiate the Internet from its most popular entity, the World Wide Web.

The Internet and the Web: What's the Difference?

What's the difference between saying, "I'm on the Internet" versus "I'm on the Web"? Although many people talk as if the Internet and the Web were the same thing, they are not. Recall, the Internet is a network of hardware (computers, cables, and routers) through which any computer can directly access other computers and exchange data. The **World Wide Web** (or **Web** or **WWW**) is a portion of the Internet that contains billions of documents. So, the Internet is the physical connection of millions of networks, like an interstate, whereas the Web *uses* the Internet as its transport mechanism to distribute its collection of documents, called Web pages. The Web uses the Internet architecture in the same way cars and trucks use an interstate—to move goods and people.

Who owns or controls the Web? As with the Internet, no one owns the Web. Both involve thousands of publicly and privately owned computers and networks, all of which agree to follow certain standards and guidelines and share resources on the network. Standards and guidelines related to all aspects of the Web are published by the World Wide Web Consortium (W3C), an international organization based in Cambridge, Massachusetts. Visit **www.w3.org** to review the mission of the W3C, a list of its 332 members, and various Internet standards.

Besides the W3C, many other organizations contribute to the development of different aspects of the Internet and Web. Provides a list of some of the more established and recognized organizations and a brief description of their missions.

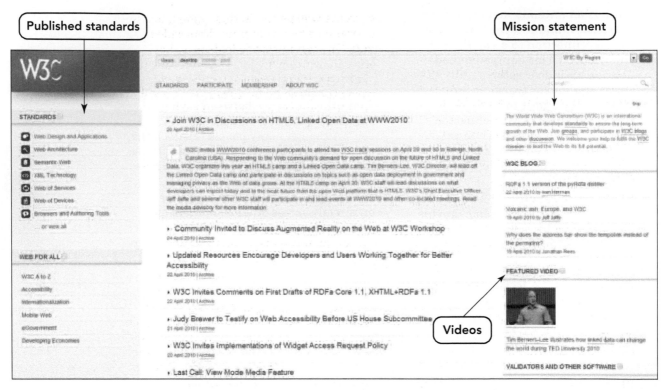

The W3C has members from all over the world that participate in the development of vendor-neutral standards for the Web.

Internet and Web Management Organizations

Name	Purpose
ICANN—Internet Corporation for Assigned Names and Numbers **www.icann.org**	Nonprofit, international organization responsible for coordinating the Internet's Domain Name System and assigning IP addresses.
IETF—Internet Engineering Task Force **www.ietf.org**	International community of information technology (IT) professionals, including network designers, operators, vendors, and researchers, responsible for developing Internet standards, best current practices, and informational documents.
ISOC—Internet Society **www.isoc.org**	Nonprofit, international association consisting of over 80 organizations and 28,000 individual members, formed to provide leadership in Internet-related standards, education, and policy for the benefit of people throughout the world.
IAB—Internet Architecture Board **www.iab.org**	Advisory body to the ISOC, this international committee of the IETF is comprised of 13 volunteers from the IT community who oversee the development of Internet architecture, protocols, procedures, and standards.
IRTF—Internet Research Task Force **www.irtf.org**	A task force of individual contributors from the research community working together in small, long-term research groups that report to the IAB and explore important topics related to the evolution of the Internet.
Network Solutions **www.networksolutions.com**	Organization responsible for managing the central domain name database.

Content on the Web

The documents of the Web, transported over the Internet, are called **Web pages**. Each page is a document or information resource created using the established standards and made viewable to a user through a program called a browser. The information on the page is in HTML or XHTML format and can include text, graphics, sound, animation, video, and hypertext links to other Web pages. A **Web browser** is a program on your computer that displays a Web document by interpreting the HTML or XHTML format, enabling you to view Web pages and activate the hyperlinks placed on a page. A **Web site** is a collection of related Web pages. A Web site typically contains a **home page** (also called an **index page**), which is a default page that's displayed automatically when you enter a site at its top level.

It's amazing to think that the Web's billions of documents are almost instantly accessible by means of the computer sitting on your desk. Tens of thousands of new Web pages appear every day. The Web has increased appeal due to its graphical richness, made possible by the integration of text and images.

In the following section, you'll learn how all of these pieces work together to make a Web page, starting with the concept of hypertext.

to create Web pages. In this system, text is surrounded by a pair of markers called *tags*. One tag starts the feature and another indicates where it is to stop. This pair of tags describes how the text located between them should be displayed. For example a line surrounded by h1 (level 1 heading) tags would be coded as:

```
<h1>Welcome to Computers Are Your
Future</h1>
```

and displayed by a browser as boldfaced, a larger font size, and left aligned.

XHTML combines the flexibility of HTML with the extensibility of **Extensible Markup Language (XML)**, a language designed to reduce the complexity of HTML. But what does this mean? Some HTML tags are only viewable in one browser or another. The only solutions that an HTML writer has are to avoid using those tags, use those tags and state that the page is meant for one browser or another, or write multiple pages and direct readers to the appropriate pages. With XHTML, however, if you need to define a tag for clarity across different browsers or create a new markup tag, you simply define the tag in an XHTML module and use it in your page as you would any other HTML tag. The browser interpreting the page reads the definition of the tag and presents it as defined. This feature makes a page truly compatible with all browsers.

The Hypertext Concept

Hypertext is a system in which objects (text, pictures, music, programs, and so on) can be creatively linked to each other. It works by means of **hyperlinks** (also called **links**), elements in an electronic document that act as the connector to another place in the same document or to an entirely different document. Typically, you click on the hyperlink to bring another object into view. Hyperlinks are an important ingredient of the World Wide Web.

This system of hypertext is created by a special code called **Hypertext Markup Language (HTML) or Extensible Hypertext Markup Language (XHTML)**. HTML is a language that uses a tag system of code

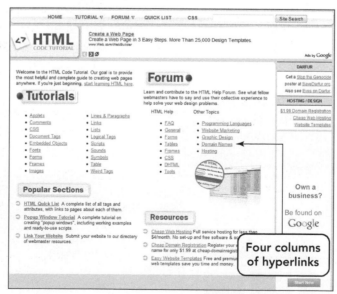

Hyperlinks, often displayed in blue characters and underlined, are perfect for tutorial Web sites. The user just clicks a hyperlink to view a Web page on a specific topic.

As stated earlier, the agency responsible for standardizing HTML and XHTML is the World Wide Web Consortium (W3C).

In addition to being a global hypertext system, the Web is a distributed hypermedia system. A **distributed hypermedia system** is a network-based content development system that uses multimedia resources, such as sound, video, and text, as a means of navigation or illustration. In this system, the responsibility for creating content is distributed among many people. The current generation of the Web, known as **Web 2.0**, takes this concept further by providing even more opportunities for individuals to collaborate, interact with one another, and create new content by using applications such as blogs, wikis, and podcasts. The more people who create content, the easier information creation and dissemination will become. For example, if you are researching the White House, you might link to **www.whitehouse.gov** for an overview of the current events taking place. From there you can click one of

several hyperlinks (links) that will take you to additional Web pages, like Photo and Videos, Briefing Room, and Issues, which zero in on the details of that topic. Notice in Figure that the arrows go in both directions. This is because the Web pages included in a Web site usually provide links to related pages, links that return you to the previous page, and almost always a link back to the home page. These crosslinks provide easy navigation and reduce backtracking.

The Web's distribution of content does have some drawbacks:

- Not all links work. There's no guarantee that the Web page's author will keep the page updated or active. The author can delete it or move it at any time without notice. For this reason, **dead links** (also called **broken links**), which are links to documents that have disappeared, are common on the Web.
- No individual or organization validates information posted on the Web. When

In hypertext documents, links can take you further into a site for more information or take you back to revisit a Web page you have already viewed.

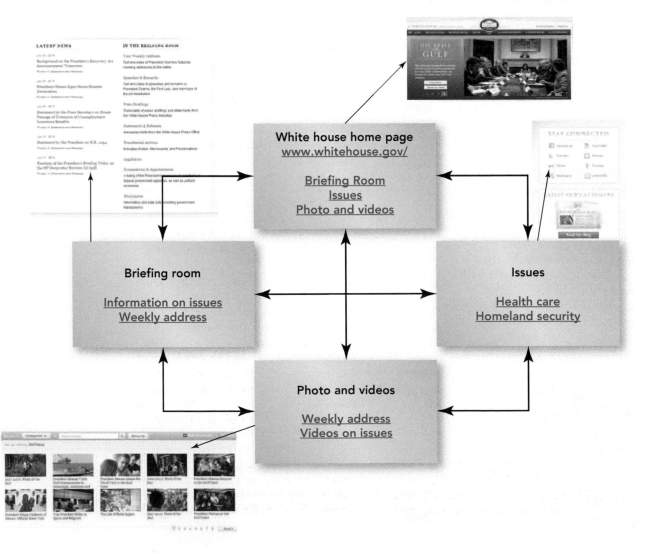

you create a hyperlink to a Web site you didn't create, investigate the credentials of the source and the accuracy of the content. This is critical to the integrity of your own Web site or Web page.

- Basic Web pages are not expensive to create or host. This has lead to the proliferation of Web content or information overload. This overload works both ways: The presenter can supply too much data, more than what is necessary to substantiate a point; and the researcher can get caught up in the search, becoming saturated with content and sidebars and losing focus.

Now that you understand hypertext and its use in providing a quick jump to Web content, let's discuss Web browsers and Web servers, items that enable us to view Web pages and make use of hyperlinks.

Viewing Content: Web Browsers

The first graphical Web browser, Mosaic, was released in 1993 and is credited with launching the Web on the road to popularity. Developed by the National Center for Supercomputing Applications at the University of Illinois, Mosaic was followed by two commercial products, Netscape Navigator and Microsoft Internet Explorer (IE). Initially, Netscape was extremely successful, but it eventually lost ground to Internet Explorer.

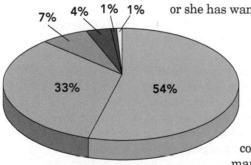

Source: http://gs.statcounter.com/

Although Internet Explorer still dominates the browser market, Firefox has captured a larger piece of the pie, and Google Chrome has made a good showing in its infancy.

The last version of Netscape was released in 2008. However, Mozilla Firefox, a new browser built using the Netscape model, began to challenge the popularity of Internet Explorer in 2004. As of April 2010, statistics showed IE with 54 percent of the market share and Firefox with 33 percent.

Google has recently joined the Internet browser competition full force with a very impressive entry, Chrome. Google Chrome takes a unique approach to browsing the Web by making complex features easy to use. In Google Chrome, every time you open a new tab, you'll see a visual sampling of your most visited sites, most used search engines, recently bookmarked pages, and closed tabs. You can drag tabs out of the browser to create new windows, gather multiple tabs into one window, or rearrange them. Every tab you use is run independently in the browser; so if one application crashes, it won't take anything else down. Even bookmarking is easy: Just click the star icon at the left edge of the address bar and you're done.

Another browser, Opera, originated as a research project in 1994. Within a year, it branched out into an independent company named Opera Software ASA. Today Opera is a high-quality product for navigating the Internet that is compatible with a wide range of operating systems.

Previously available exclusively for Mac users, Safari is now available for PCs as well. Safari provides the Mac look and feel in the Internet environment. It is lightweight, nonobtrusive, and enables tabbed browsing, spell checking for all fields, and snapback—a temporary marker that allows a user to return to a Web page even after he or she has wandered off the beaten path. Safari competes with the top browsers but lacks some features like parental and antiphishing controls. Displays the current market percentages for the top 5 browsers. Visit **http://internet-browser-review.toptenreviews.com/** for more detail on the individual features each browser offers.

All five browser programs are opened the same way and use similar features, such as tabbed browsing, navigation buttons, a search box, an address toolbar, and a status bar. When you first launch a browser, it may default to a preset home page from your ISP or the publisher of the browser software. You can either keep this as your home page, which will be displayed each time you start your browser, or you can change the browser's default home page, also referred to as customizing your browser. You can find the default home page settings in Internet Explorer under the Tools, Internet Options menu.

It is the browser that interprets and displays the content of a Web page and makes hyperlinks active. In short, browsers are meant to work with Web pages. Sometimes you need to upgrade your browser to the latest version so that you can fully enjoy the features of a Web site.

New Web page creation software is being developed all the time, and eventually older browsers don't have the capability of displaying the newest features or animations. Browsers use **plug-ins**, which are additional software programs, located on the user's computer, that extend the ability of the browser, usually to enable multimedia features. If a Web site requires a plug-in to function or be viewed properly, a pop-up message will appear in newer browsers, indicating which plug-in is needed, with an option to install the plug-in or cancel the installation. There are many kinds of plug-ins, but most Web surfers are probably familiar with one or more of those listed here:

- Acrobat Reader—allows pdf files to be read, navigated, and printed within a browser window.
- Adobe Flash Player—provides the interface to view Flash scripts, which create animation and sound and are embedded with a Web page, through a browser window.
- Adobe Shockwave Player—is used for interactive games, multimedia, graphics, and streaming audio and video.
- Apple QuickTime—enables movies, animation, music, and virtual reality worlds to be viewed within a browser window.
- Real Player—is used for streaming audio, video, movies, and live video broadcasts.
- Windows Media Player—enables MP3 and WAV files, movies, live audio, and live video broadcasts.

Another feature that browsers share is the ability to cache, or store, Web page files and graphics on a computer's hard drive. When you browse a Web page for the first time, the page is actually stored on your hard drive in a storage space referred to as **browser**

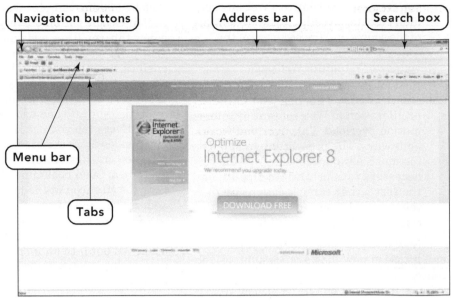

The major browsers have similar features.

cache. If the user attempts to retrieve the page again, the browser does not head back out on the Internet, but instead retrieves the page from the browser's cache. This eliminates excessive roundtrips to the server, brings the page up more quickly on the user's system, and greatly reduces Internet traffic. However, if you are visiting a news provider's Web site that is constantly updating current stories, browser cache might not seem like such a good idea. You really don't want to view old news. This problem has been solved by including HTTP directives, called freshness indicators, at the beginning of Web pages, images, and included scripts, that specify how long the page or item is considered fresh. If you retrieve the page within the allotted time, the page is retrieved from the browser's cache; otherwise the roundtrip is made back to the originating server and a new page is returned to the user. Because a browser's cache is not

FIGURE 6.15 You can change your default home page in your browser.

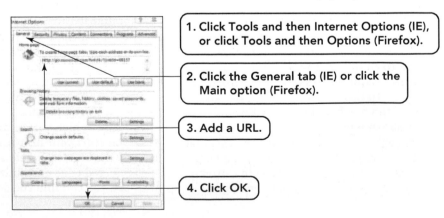

1. Click Tools and then Internet Options (IE), or click Tools and then Options (Firefox).

2. Click the General tab (IE) or click the Main option (Firefox).

3. Add a URL.

4. Click OK.

Internet Explorer

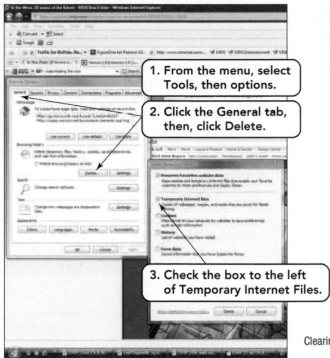

1. From the menu, select Tools, then options.

2. Click the General tab, then, click Delete.

3. Check the box to the left of Temporary Internet Files.

Firefox

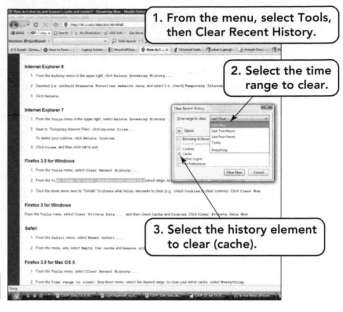

1. From the menu, select Tools, then Clear Recent History.

2. Select the time range to clear.

3. Select the history element to clear (cache).

Clearing cache on a shared system can provide a small measure of privacy.

deleted when a user logs off or a system is shut down, it is a good idea to clear the cache after every browser session, especially on shared systems. Figure provides the steps to clear the cache in the Internet Explorer and Firefox browsers.

Storing Content: Web Servers

Web sites and their associated images and scripts are housed on **Web servers**, a computer running special software that enables it to respond to requests for information or accept inputted information.

FAST FORWARD ▶▶

Video-on-demand (VOD), being delivered wirelessly over the Internet, is creating network slowdowns and congestion. There was a 63 percent increase in VOD users in the fourth quarter of 2009. Due to the increased demand for this service, its large swings in bandwidth, and excessive demands on a server, VOD can affect the performance of not only the video customer but also network applications. To accommodate this form of transmission, wireless networks need higher frequencies and wider bandwidth. Electrical engineers from the University of California, San Diego (UCSD), are working on developing technologies for the network of the future. The key to creating higher frequencies and wider bandwidth is advances in silicon-based circuits that operate at millimeter and microwave frequencies. Research at the university is focused on advanced radio-frequency CMOS chips, planar antennas, and system-level design that will increase data transfer 10 to 100 times, yet maintain the same energy consumption. Lawrence Larson, who leads the Radio Frequency Integrated Circuit (RFIC) group, captures the potential of the new technology by comparing the current connection and transport ability between your smartphone and tower to a straw. He claims that this technology under development will be the equivalent of replacing the straw with a fire hose. This analogy provides a good visual for the projected increased bandwidths and speed that research promises.

Millions of Web servers are located all over the world. When you click a hyperlink on a Web page, you either request information from a server (a list of sweatshirts available in size medium) or ask the server to accept your information (your order for three size medium sweatshirts in blue). Your browser sends a message to a Web server, asking the server to retrieve or accept the information. The server either sends the requested information or a confirmation that the sent information was received back to the initiating browser through the Internet. If the file isn't found, the server sends an error message.

Finding Information on the Web

With the millions of Web pages that make up the World Wide Web, how do you locate

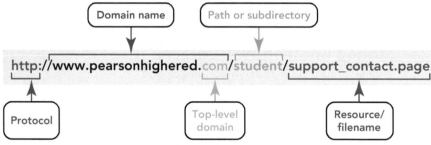

A complete URL has four parts: protocol, domain name, path, and resource/filename. This is the URL for the Pearson student support and contact page.

the ones that contain the information you want? Moving around the Web can feel like walking though a room with no lights; you're not sure where you are going and hope to bump into something you recognize. Although this method might lead you to the information you are looking for, there are more efficient and less frustrating methods to locate content on the Web. Let's look at of few of these techniques.

Web Addresses

To locate a resource on the Web, you have to know how to find the Web server on which it resides. Every host, computer, server, device, and application that communicates over the Internet is assigned an **Internet Protocol address (IP address)**, a numerical identification and logical address that is assigned to devices participating in a computer network. The IP address consists of four groups of numbers, separated by periods. The value in each group ranges from

0 to 255. As an example, 64.12.245.203 is the IP address for the AOL Web site.

IP addresses are either static or dynamic. A static IP address never changes. It's the type used by most major Web sites. A dynamic IP address is automatically assigned to a computer when you log on to a network. Internet service providers (ISPs) are assigned dynamic IP addresses that they, in turn, dispense to their customers. Although this numeric system works well for computers, it doesn't work as well for people. You could type the numeric address into your browser, but most of us find that it's much easier to use a URL. A **URL (Uniform Resource Locator)** is a string of characters that precisely identifies an Internet resource's type and location. It is much easier to access the AOL Web site by typing the URL, **www.aol.com**, than it is to remember 64.12.245.203.

At times, keying in a URL can seem tedious. A complete URL actually has four distinct parts: protocol, domain name, path, and resource/filename. Each component provides a piece of data needed to locate the site.

Protocol The first part of a complete URL specifies the **Hypertext Transfer Protocol (HTTP)**, the Internet standard that supports the exchange of information on the Web. The protocol name is followed by a colon and two forward slash marks (*//*). You can generally omit the http:// protocol designation when you're typing the URL of a Web page, because the browser assumes that you are browsing an unsecured hypertext Web page. For example, you can access **http://www. pearsonhighered.com/cayf** by typing **www.pearsonhighered.com /cayf**. Most browsers can also access information using other protocols such as FTP (File Transfer Protocol), used to transfer files from one computer on the Internet to another; POP (Post Office Protocol), used to receive e-mail; and HTTPS (Hypertext Transfer Protocol Secure), used when the content being transferred requires encryption and a secure identification of the server (as is required for financial transactions).

Domain Name The second part of a complete URL specifies the Web site's **domain name**, which correlates to the Web server's IP address. The domain name has two parts: a host name and a top-level domain name. Some domain names also include a prefix, the most common of which is "www." The **host name** is usually the name of the group or institution hosting the site. The **top-level domain (TLD) name** is the extension (such as .com or .edu) following the host name and indicates the type of group or institution to which the site belongs. This two-part identifier is referred to as the **Domain Name System (DNS)**. It links domain names with their corresponding numerical IP addresses, functioning like a phone book for the Internet. The Domain Name System enables users to type an address that includes letters as well as numbers, for example *pearsonhighered.com* instead of 165.193.140.24, its IP numerical address. Through a process called **domain name registration**, individuals and organizations register a *unique* domain name with a service organization, such as InterNIC, and are assigned a *unique* Internet address (IP address) that will be associated with that domain name. You can use your favorite search engine to search for domain name registrars to find other sites that provide this service.

Domain names can tell you a great deal about where a computer is located. For Web sites hosted in the United States, top-level domain names (the *last* part of the domain name) indicate the type of organization to which the Web site belongs. Outside the United States, the top-level domain indicates the name of the country from which the Web site is published or of which the owner is a citizen, such as .ca (Canada), .uk (United Kingdom), and .jp (Japan). For more information on domain names visit the Internet Corporation for Assigned Names and Numbers (ICANN) at **www.icann.org**.

Path The third part of a complete URL specifies the location of the document on the server. It contains the document's location on the computer, including the names of subfolders (if any). In the example in Figure, the path to the student contact page on the Web server at **www.pearsonhighered. com** is "student."

Resource/Filename The last part of a complete URL gives the file name of the resource you're accessing. A resource is a file, such as an HTML file, a sound file, a video file, or a graphics file. The resource's extension (the part of the file name after the period) indicates the type of resource it is. For example, HTML documents have the .html or .htm extension.

Many URLs don't include a resource name because they reference the server's default home page. If no resource name is specified, the browser looks for a file named *default* or *index*—a default page that's displayed automatically when you enter the site at its top level. If it finds such a file, it loads it automatically. For example, **www.microsoft.com/windows** displays the default Microsoft Windows home page. Other URLs omit both the path name and the resource name. These URLs reference the Web site's home page. For example, although entering **www.microsoft.com** into a browser's address bar displays Microsoft's home page, its actual URL is **http://www.microsoft. com/en/us/default.aspx**.

Surfing the Web

Once you've subscribed and connected to an Internet service provider and downloaded and opened a browser, you are ready to surf the Web. To access a Web page, you can do any of the following, as illustrated in Figure:

- **Type a URL in the Address bar.** You don't need to type http://. Watch for spelling errors, and don't insert spaces.

- **Click a tab in the browser window.** Both major browsers, IE and Firefox, offer **tabbed browsing**, which enables a user to have several Web pages open at once and switch quickly between them. You can customize your home page by adding tabs for sites that you frequently access. The tabs are not visible in Figure because the History list is extended.

- **Click a hyperlink.** Hyperlinks are usually underlined, but sometimes they're embedded in graphics or highlighted in other ways, such as with shading or colors. Most browsers indicate the presence of a hyperlink by changing the on-screen pointer to a hand shape when it is over a hyperlink.

Common Top-Level Domain Names

Top-Level Domain Name	Used By
.biz	Businesses
.com	Commercial sites
.edu	Educational institutions
.gov	Government agencies
.info	Information
.mil	Military
.name	Individuals
.net	Network organizations (such as ISPs)
.org	Nonprofit organizations

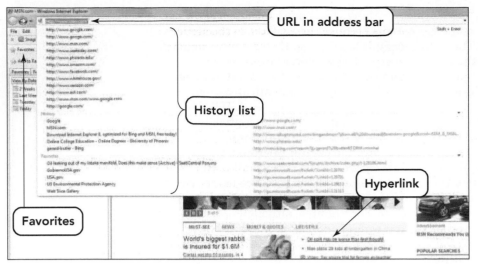

There are many ways to access a typical Web page.

- **Use the History list.** The **History list** is a list of previously visited Web pages. It is accessed in Internet Explorer by clicking the arrow to the right of the address bar and in Firefox by selecting the History option on the menu bar. Both browsers then display a drop-down list from which the user can select a Web page.

- **Make use of the Favorites or Bookmarks feature.** This feature, called Favorites in IE and Bookmarks in Firefox, is located on the menu bar. When selected, you can mark a Web page that you visit frequently. To return to that page later, simply click the Favorite or Bookmarks option and select the Web page name from the drop-down list. Favorites can be grouped into categories.

Uploading and Downloading After you have browsed the Web and accessed various Web pages, you may want to try downloading or uploading data. With **downloading**, a document or file is transferred from another computer to your computer, as in downloading music from iTunes. Your computer is the destination; the other computer is the source. With **uploading**, you transfer files from your computer to another computer, as you do when you upload a video you created to Youtube. In uploading, your computer is the source and the other computer is the destination. Most students download and upload files when using a Web-based course management system, such as Blackboard or Angel. These teaching systems allow an instructor and student to interact in classes delivered entirely online or to complement a face-to-face teaching situation. Students download course notes or application files to their own computers. When a student completes an assignment, he or she uploads the completed assignment to a drop box for the instructor to grade.

No matter how familiar you are with the source, you should exercise caution when downloading files of unknown origin from the Web. If you download software from a site that doesn't inspect files using up-to-date antivirus software, you could infect your computer with a virus. Most Internet users believe that it's safe to download software from Web sites maintained by software companies or files created with popular software. However, be aware that some viruses are spread in the data files of popular programs, such as Microsoft Word or Excel. Be sure to use an antivirus program to check any software or data files that you download. Now that you understand the basics of the Internet and Web, let's examine how to conduct research on the Web.

Sharing Information

Sometimes the best way to get information online is from an individual or agency that is also online and communicating or contributing through an online feed, conversation, or Web posting.

Really Simple Syndication One of the current ways to keep abreast of updates on news, weather, and sports in our fast-moving and informative world is through the use of **Really Simple Syndication (RSS)**. Once a user sets up a connection to a Web site that has an RSS feed, he or she will receive constant updates over the Internet from that site without any further involvement. The URL or Web page that allows its up-to-date information to be published on another Web site is said to have an RSS feed or is referred to as being *syndicated*.

So how does RSS work? A Web page that displays constantly changing data maintains a list of RSS feeds. Individuals interested in getting updated information from locations on the list can, through an RSS file, select sources from the list and receive the updated information on their own Web page. There are hundreds of Web sites that provide RSS feeds, for example, the *New York Times*, the BBC, Reuters, and many blogs. If your site will be updating several feeds, you can use an RSS aggregator. An **aggregator** is a program that remembers your subscription list, checks each site on a regular basis, alerts you if new information has been published, and organizes the results for you. Many RSS aggregators are available through your browser. Some are even integrated into your e-mail, and others are stand-alone applications.

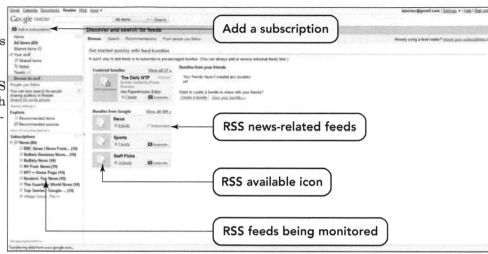

Google Reader is a free aggregator that can be set up by going to www.google.com/reader/view/.

Wikis Want to share information fast through the Web, for either personal or professional reasons? A wiki, a blog, or a podcast might be just what you need. A **wiki** (short for *wiki-wiki*, the Hawaiian word for "fast") is a simple Web page on which any visitor can post text or images, read previous posts, change posted information, and track earlier changes. No elaborate coding needed—just click to post, click to refresh the page, and you're done. If a visitor changes what you've posted and you don't like the change, just click to revert to an earlier version. Information referenced from a wiki should be verified through another source because wiki entries can be made by anyone and the content is not always verified. Next time you're online, surf over to **www. wikimusicguide.com**, an open-content music guide. Fans can create new pages, share information about their favorite songs or artists, and edit the entries others have created.

Wikis can be public or restricted to specific members. In addition to their use in the entertainment industry, this information-sharing option is being used by business and educational institutions to reduce e-mail and increase collaboration.

Blogs Another way to share information online is via a **blog** (short for Weblog). A blog is the Internet equivalent of a journal or diary. Bloggers post their thoughts and opinions, along with photos or links to interesting Web sites, for the entire world to see. Over 1 million blogs are posted on the Web. Some are meant for family and friends; some offer running commentary on politics and other timely topics; and others are written by employees about their jobs, interview hints, and various other subjects. Many Microsoft blogs

have loyal followings because of their insightful observations and technical know-how. If you are interested in finding out about the Microsoft interview process check out **http://microsoftjobsblog.com/blog/**. Here blogs are posted from individuals that have been interviewed and include everything from sample categories of questions to advice on how to dress. Visit **www.blogsearchengine.com** to search for blogs by subject and for FAQs about blogging. If you are interested in creating a blog, **www.blogger.com/start** is a great place to get started.

Podcasts If you'd rather get your information in an audio or video format, podcasts may be just what you need! Despite the name, and its link to music, **podcasts** have evolved from containing just sound

Blogs like this one from individuals who have gone through the Microsoft job interview process can provide valuable hints and advice.

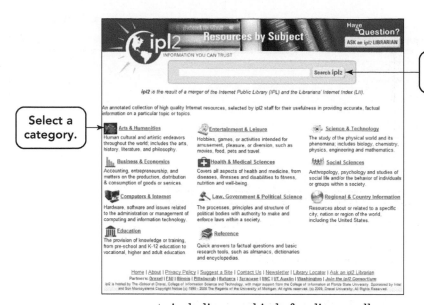

Use the search tool.

Subject guides can help you find the information you seek quickly.

Using Hyperlinks to Surf the Web

Although browsing or surfing the Web is easy and fun, it falls short as a means of information research. When you are looking for specific and reliable data, you need to employ more targeted methods.

Using hyperlinks on a reliable Web page could be a start. The URL of the link might provide you with some of the desired data. In general, starting this way usually has the user clicking link after link, searching for information that they never find.

to including any kind of audio as well as images and video. Podcasts files are released periodically by means of Web syndication, a delivery method that makes use of **podcatchers** (applications such as Apple Inc.'s iTunes or Nullsoft's Winamp) that can automatically identify and retrieve new files in a given series and make them available through a centrally maintained Web site.

You can listen to podcasts on your computer or on an MP3 player. You can go to sites that provide podcasts or sign up for one using an RSS feed. Imagine taking a physics class at Massachusetts Institute of Technology or catching the radio interview with your favorite musician that you missed last week. Podcasts can make it happen. Check the Podcast Directory at **http://podcast.com** and hear what's new!

Through the simplicity of wikis, blogs, and podcasts, the Web has been expanded into a means of interactive communication.

Some Web sites offer a **subject guide**, a list of subject-related categories such as business, news, or trends that, when selected, displays a page of more related links. These guides don't try to include every Web page on the World Wide Web, but they offer a selection of high-quality pages that represent some of the more useful Web pages in a given category. If you're just beginning your search for information, a subject guide is an excellent place to start.

A **portal** is a Web page that acts as a gateway to a lot of diverse sources and presents those sources in an organized way. It enables a user to locate fast-breaking news, local weather, stock quotes, sports scores, and e-mail with the click of a mouse. Portal sites usually use indexes and lists of links to provide a jumping-off point for your search. Sites such as MSNBC, AOL, iGoogle, and Yahoo! are examples of portals.

Portals usually make use of RSS to provide the viewer with the most update news and sporting events.

Access to e-mail is provided.

Appearance may be customized.

Favorite categories can be edited.

A side effect of your search method is the clickstream you leave in your wake. A **clickstream** is the trail of Web links you have followed to get to a particular site. Internet merchants are quite interested in analyzing clickstream activity so that they can do a better job of targeting advertisements and tailoring Web pages to potential customers.

If you can't find the information you're looking for using any of the methods above, try using a search engine. You've no doubt heard of Google, Yahoo!, Bing, and Ask. Although these and other Web search tools are far from perfect, knowing how to use them effectively (and knowing their limitations) can greatly increase your chances of finding the information you want.

Search engine returns can be extensive and broad in scope. A user has to be familiar with techniques that can be used to zero in on specific search content. Let's look at these techniques and strategies in more detail.

Using Search Engines

Using search engines is more complex than using the other methods of locating information on the Web. **Search engines** make use of databases of the Web pages they've indexed. To add pages to their databases, search engines make use of computer programs, referred to as **spiders**, to roam the World Wide Web via the Internet, visit sites and databases, and keep the search engine's database of Web pages up to date. Also known as *crawlers, knowledge bots,* or *knowbots,* they obtain new pages, update known pages, and delete obsolete ones. Most large search

Source: www.seoconsultants.com/search-engines/

Google gets approximately 76 billion searches a month of the 113 billion searches completed on all search engines.

engines operate several spiders all the time. Even so, the Web is so enormous that it can take six months to cover the content, resulting in a certain degree of "outdatedness." This outdatedness results in **link rot**, hyperlinks that no longer work and Web pages that have been removed or restructured. Such links can make a Web search frustrating and tedious.

Internet users seem to have their favorite search engine; however, Google is definitely at the top of the list. Displays April 2010 statistics on the four core search engines. As the chart illustrates, Google use far exceeded any of the others, with Yahoo! a distant second.

Feel like you're stuck in a rut? Not all search engines use the same strategy to locate Web content. Try using a different search engine. Visit sites like Mahalo (**www.mahalo.com**), Dogpile (**www. dogpile.com**), Find-Sounds (**www. findsounds.com**), SurfWax (**www. surfwax.com**), or BlogPulse (**www. blogpulse.com**) and see what you find !

To use a search engine, type one or more words that describe the subject

Search Engine Comparisons

Web Search Engine	Strategy Used to Obtain Results
Mahalo	Serves as a human-powered search engine and knowledge-sharing service.
Dogpile	Accumulates search results from leading search engines to present the best results in one easy-to-find place
FindSounds	Focuses on locating sound effects and musical instrument samples
SurfWax	Makes use of a patent pending spiraling matrix design to search, sort, and extract information in a simple natural interface
BlogPulse	Uses machine learning and natural language to provide a search engine that focuses on blogs

you're looking for into the search text box and click *Search* (or press *Enter*). Generally, it's a good idea to type several words (four or five) rather than just one or two. If you use only one or two words, the Web search will produce far more results than you can use.

Why do search engines sometimes produce unsatisfactory results? The problem lies in the ambiguity of the English language. Suppose you're searching for information on the Great Wall of China. You'll find some information on the ancient Chinese defensive installation, but you may also get the menu of the Great Wall of China, a Chinese restaurant; information on the Great Wall hotel in Beijing; and the lyrics of "Great Wall of China," a song by Billy Joel.

Specialized Search Engines Full Web search engines generally don't index specialized information such as names and addresses, job advertisements, quotations, or newspaper articles. To find such information, you need to use **specialized search engines**. Examples of such specialized search engines include Indeed, a database of more than 1 million jobs, and Infoplease, which contains the full text of an encyclopedia and an almanac.

You can save the results of your searches—the Web pages you visit by following the results links of a search engine—to your hard drive by using your browser's File, Save As menu sequence.

If you don't want or need the entire Web page, you can right-click the various elements of the page and choose from a variety of options (Save Target As, Save Picture As, Print Target, Print Picture, E-mail Picture). You can also use your mouse and cursor to highlight and then copy text on a Web page for pasting into a word-processing file or other document. The benefit of saving a Web page offline, to your own storage device, is that you can view that page later without connecting to the Internet. This is easily accomplished by opening your browser and then choosing the File, Open menu sequence. Simply browse through your folders and files to locate the Web page file and then open it.

Some Web sites have their own site search engines. You will often find this feature on the site's home page. It is usually a clearly marked box into which you type the keywords you are looking for. Some home pages will have a Search icon or button that will take you to the site's search page.

For the socially conscious Web searcher, there are search sites that will make donations to your favorite charity. Check out **www.goodsearch.com** and begin to donate to the charity of your choice.

Search Basics

By learning a few search techniques, you can greatly increase the accuracy of your Web searches. **Search operators**, which are symbols or words used for advanced searches, can be helpful. Most search engines include a link for advanced searches or provide search tips to explain which search operators you can use. Although specific methods may vary, some or all of the following techniques will work with most search engines.

Wildcards Many search engines enable you to use wildcards. **Wildcards** are symbols such as * and ? that take the place of zero or more characters in the position in which they are used. The use of wildcards, also called **truncation symbols**, to search for various word endings and spellings simultaneously is a technique called **truncation**.

Wildcards help you improve the accuracy of your searches and are

Search an entire site or specific resource.

Tabs act as reference tools.

Read current news and topics.

Specialized search engines, like Infoplease, provide access to selected reference tools and resources.

useful if you are unsure of the exact spelling of a word. Wildcards may be handled differently, depending upon the search engine used. So the search term *bank** might return *bank, banks, banking, bankruptcy, bank account,* and so forth.

Phrase Searches Another way to improve the accuracy of your searches is through **phrase searching**, which is generally performed by typing a phrase within quotation marks. This tells the search engine to retrieve only those documents that contain the exact phrase (rather than some or all of the words anywhere in the document).

Inclusion and Exclusion Operators

With many search engines, you can improve search performance by specifying an **inclusion operator**, which is generally a plus (+) sign. This operator states that you only want a page retrieved if it contains the specified word. By listing several key terms with this search operator, you can zero in on pages that only contain one or more of the essential terms. If the list of retrieved documents contains many items that you don't want, you can use the **exclusion operator**, which is generally a minus (−) sign. You can exclude the undesired term by prefacing it with the exclusion operator.

GREEN tech tips

Environmental concerns generate a lot of interest. Now there's even a "green" search engine—Green Maven (**www. greenmaven.com**). Use it to find environmentally conscious Web sites and news.

You can also find a variety of ecologically and socially conscious search engines that donate to various causes based on the searches people run. Two such engines are Ecosearch (**www.ecosearch.org**) powered by Google and GoodSearch (**www. goodsearch.com**) powered by Yahoo. There are, however, plenty of other such sites. Use them as you would your normal search engine, and you'll get great results. Don't just click to donate. Without attempting a legitimate search, you'll jeopardize the relationships that enable such sites to fund their initiatives. ●

Boolean Searches

Some search engines enable you to perform Boolean searches. **Boolean searches** use logical operators (AND, OR, and NOT) to link the words you're

Improving Your Search Results with Search Operators

Operator/Symbol	Example	Result
Inclusion/Plus sign (+)	CD+Radiohead	Web pages that contain all search terms listed, in any order. In this case, pages would include *both* the word **CD** *and* the word **RADIOHEAD**.
Exclusion/Minus sign (−)	CD+Radiohead − eBay	Web pages that contain all included search terms listed, but not the excluded term. In this case, pages would include *both* the word **CD** *and* the word **RADIOHEAD** but *not* the word **EBAY**.
Wildcards (*)	CD*	Web pages that include variations of the search term or additional words. For example, pages could include the terms **CD**, **CDs**, **CD Ripping**, **CD Files**, etc.
Quotation Marks (" ")	"Radiohead Just Push Play CD"	Web pages that contain the exact phrase in the order listed.

Terms	Examples	Result
AND	CD **AND** Radiohead	Returns the same result as using the plus sign (+)
OR	CD **OR** Radiohead	Web pages that include either or both of the search terms listed, usually providing a large number of hits. For this example, results would include *either* the word **CD** *or* the word **RADIOHEAD** or *both*.
NOT	CD **AND** Radiohead **NOT** eBay	Returns the same results as using the minus sign (−)
Parenthesis ( )	(CD **OR** MP3 **OR** Record) **AND** Radiohead	Search terms in parenthesis are located first, using the search operator provided. In this case, results would include pages that included any combination of **CD**, **MP3**, or **RECORD** *and* the word **RADIOHEAD**

searching for above. By using Boolean operators, you can gain more precise control over your searches. Let's look at a few examples.

The AND, OR, and NOT Operators

When used to link two search words, the AND operator tells the search engine to return only those documents that contain both words (just as the plus sign does). You can use the AND operator to narrow your search so that it retrieves fewer documents.

If your search retrieves too few documents, try the OR operator. This may be helpful when a topic has several common synonyms, such as car, auto, automobile, and vehicle. Using the OR operator usually retrieves a larger quantity of documents.

To exclude unwanted documents, use the NOT operator. This operator tells the search engine to omit any documents containing the word preceded by NOT (just as the minus sign does).

Using Parentheses Many search engines that support Boolean operators allow you to use parentheses, a process called **nesting**. When you nest an expression, the search engine evaluates the expression from left to right and searches for the content within the parentheses first. Such expressions enable you to conduct a search

with unmatched accuracy. To learn more about search engines, their specialized capabilities, and specific examples go to **www.internettutorials.net/**.

Using Information from the Web

After you've found information on the Web, you'll need to evaluate it critically. Anyone can publish information on the Web; many Web pages are not subject to the fact-checking standards of newspapers or magazines, let alone the peer-review process that safeguards the quality of scholarly and scientific publications. Although you can find excellent and reliable information on the Web, you can also find pages that are biased or blatantly incorrect.

Critically Evaluating Web Pages

As you're evaluating a Web page for possible use or reference, read with a critical eye and consider the issues raised here:

- Who is the *author* of this page? Is the author affiliated with a recognized institution, such as a university or a well-known company? Is there any evidence that the author is qualified and possesses credentials with respect to this topic?

- Does the author *reference* his or her sources? If so, do they appear to be from recognized and respected publications?

- Who is the Web page *affiliated* with? Who pays for this page? The association between the page server, sponsor, and author should be above board. The hosting organization should not be able to exert influence over the information on the site.

- Is the language *objective* and dispassionate, or is it strident and argumentative? Is it written in a form and level that suits the target population?

- What is the *purpose* of this page? Is the author trying to sell something or promote a biased idea? Who would profit if this page's information were accepted as true? Does the site include links to external information, or does it reference only itself?

- Does the information appear to be *accurate*? Is the page free of sweeping generalizations or other signs of shoddy thinking? Do you see many misspellings or grammatical errors that would indicate a poor educational background?

- Is this page *current*? The information should be up to date.

In the next section, you will explore the practical applications of Web research to both the work and school environments.

Using the Web for Schoolwork

Finding information on the Web can help you as a consumer. But how can it help you as a student? The following sections provide some helpful hints.

Authoritative Online Sources Many respected magazines and journals have established Web sites where you can search back issues, giving you the best of both worlds—the power and convenience of the Internet, plus material that is more reliable than the average Web page.

Locating Material in Published Works
Remember that the Web is only one of several sources you can and should use

for research. Many high-level research tools can be found in your institution's library. Additionally, librarians are trained research professionals who are there to assist you. As institutions have begun to offer distance-learning courses, student access to library materials has become a critical issue. To meet the needs of distance-learning students, many college libraries now provide online access to their services. You can almost certainly access and search your library's inventory of books and can often order them online. The library's search engine will allow you to search books (and sometimes articles) by author, title, or key term. Your library may also provide access to valuable search tools such as EBSCOhost, LexisNexis, and other professional databases. Sometimes you can access these online materials from off campus as well as on campus. Materials may be accessible only to faculty and students, or they may also be available to the general public. Check your library's home page to find out what Internet services are available.

ETHICS

The Internet and Web have produced an environment that makes accessing information from the comfort of your home or favorite coffee shop effortless. Locating the information is simple—and so is borrowing it and embedding it into your own work. By simply using copy and paste or right-clicking and selecting the *Save Image As* option, information, pictures, and data found on Web pages can be lifted from their source and inserted into another document or Web page under development. Copyright violations and infringements often occur with material that is available online, especially when it is re-used without permission. Make sure you understand your rights and responsibilities. Visit the Electronic Frontier Foundation (**www.eff.org**), a civil liberties group that defends your rights in the digital world, or the U.S. Copyright Office (**www.copyright.gov**) for more information on the ethical use of material you find on the Internet.

Google Scholar uses the power of Google to search scholarly literature and provide high-quality results for academic research.

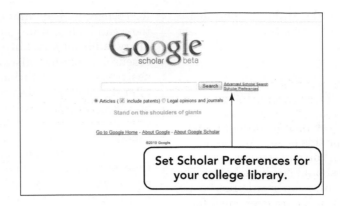

Set Scholar Preferences for your college library.

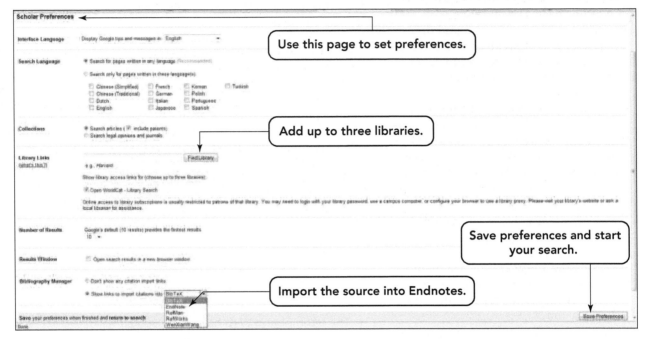

Use this page to set preferences.

Add up to three libraries.

Save preferences and start your search.

Import the source into Endnotes.

Also, visit Google Scholar (**http://scholar.google.com**) to search for scholarly literature from many academic disciplines. You can use the advanced search methods covered in this chapter and even personalize your searches to have Google Scholar indicate when materials are held by your local library. Google Scholar can help you locate peer-reviewed papers, theses, books, abstracts, and articles from academic publishers and professional sources.

Citing Online and Offline References
Including citations in your work is an important way to honor copyright and avoid accusations of plagiarism. Because citing Internet-based sources is not the same as citing traditional references, visit University of California Berkeley's General Guides site at **www.lib.berkeley.edu/**

Help/guides.html to learn how to properly cite online and electronic resources. You should know how to cite Web sites, e-mail messages, and online databases. When citing electronic resources, it is important to include the date the site was last accessed. Even more than the written and published sites, electronic sites are time sensitive.

Application developers like Microsoft have begun to include reference options within their current word processing programs. Such features prompt the user to input the necessary information into a template that the application then formats into the style the user selects, usually APA or MLA for college papers.

Now that you're familiar with how to evaluate information on the Web, let's look at some of the Internet's most useful services.

Exploring Internet Services

An **Internet service** is best understood as a set of standards (protocols) that define how two types of programs—a client, such as a Web browser that runs on the user's computer, and a server—can communicate with each other through the Internet. By using the service's protocols, the client requests information from a server program that is located on some other computer on the Internet.

At one time, some browsers, such as Netscape Navigator and the Mozilla Suite, were distributed as software suites that included client programs to handle e-mail, newsgroups, and chat services, as well as browsing. However, most current browsers, including Internet Explorer, Firefox, and Safari (for Macs), operate as stand-alone programs. Although it's still possible to obtain client software for some of these services, many of them are Web based and don't require any special software to use, but you may need to

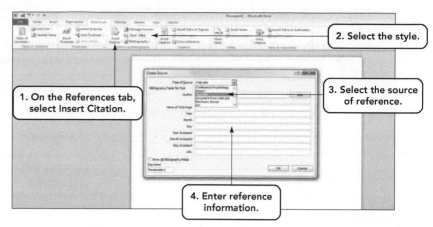

1. On the References tab, select Insert Citation.

2. Select the style.

3. Select the source of reference.

4. Enter reference information.

install an appropriate plug-in to ensure full functionality. Figure lists a selection of commonly used Internet services.

E-Mail: Staying in Touch

The most popular Internet service is e-mail. **E-mail** (short for **electronic mail**) is a software application that enables you to send and receive messages via networks. E-mail has become an indispensable tool for businesses and individuals due to its speed, convenience, and its ability to be saved and

Microsoft Word 2010 includes a References tab on the Ribbon where a user can add new citations, footnotes, endnotes, or bibliography references, with all of the appropriate formatting required by the selected style.

Commonly Used Internet Services

Service	Client	Web-Based	Comments
E-mail			
AOL Mail	X	X	Available with AOL Desktop installation or as Web-based service
Google Mail		X	
Microsoft Outlook	X		Part of the Microsoft Office suite
Instant Message			
AOL AIM	X	X	Available with AOL Desktop installation or as a Web-based service
Google Talk	X	X	Available for download or as Web-based service
Yahoo! Messenger		X	
Windows Live Messenger		X	Formerly MSN Messenger

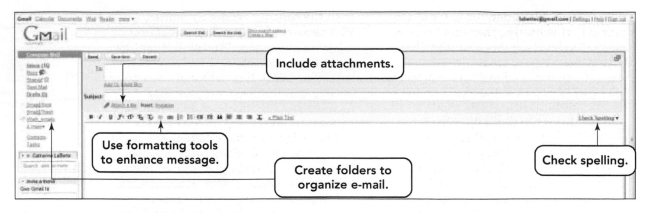

Include attachments.

Use formatting tools to enhance message.

Create folders to organize e-mail.

Check spelling.

E-mail can be saved and used to provide a record of past communications.

retrieved. However, for immediacy, text messaging is preferred. Both of these communications tools have become media of choice for interpersonal written communication, far outpacing the postal system.

When you receive an e-mail, you can reply to the message, forward it to someone else, store it for later action, or delete it. In addition to writing the text message, you can format the text, check spelling, organize your e-mail into folders, and include an e-mail attachment. An **e-mail attachment** can be any type of computer file—document, photo, audio, or video—that is included

with an e-mail message. If you receive an e-mail message containing an attachment, your e-mail program displays a distinctive icon, such as a paper clip, to notify you. E-mail usually arrives at the destination server in a few seconds. It is then stored on the server until the recipient logs on to the server and downloads the message.

To send an e-mail, you need to know the recipient's e-mail address. An **e-mail address** is a unique cyberspace identity for a particular recipient that follows the form myname@somedomain.com. The components of an e-mail address are the user

GREEN tech tips

The use of electronic communication methods can help us reduce the environmental effect of keeping in touch. Let's start with some facts:

- The average worker uses 10,000 sheets of copy paper a year. A large financial service company reported that they could save $700,000 a year if all copies were double-sided.

- The United States, which has less than 5 percent of the world's population, consumes 30 percent of the world's paper.

- Just under 50 percent of wood pulp goes to the production of paper. Reducing paper production would help reduce greenhouse gases. As an example, the greenhouse emission to create 40 reams of paper is equivalent to 1.5 acres of pine forest absorbing carbon for a year.

- It takes more than 1.5 cups of water to make one sheet of paper.

So in short, less is better. What can an average user do to help this environmental movement? Start by thinking before you print or copy. Ask yourself whether you really need a paper copy. If you do, how many do you need? Use the Print preview option of your application before printing. This eliminates printing a version with errors and having to reprint it. Change the setting on your printer to print double-sided by default (if it has that capability). Fit more on one page by changing margin and font size. And remember to recycle discarded paper.

These options may seem like small steps, but if individuals all over the world incorporate them into a daily practice, these small actions can spread and create a lasting environmental effect. •

name or other identifier, the name of the domain that is hosting the e-mail service, and the top-level domain that identifies the provider's type of institution. For instance, you can send mail to the president of the United States at the e-mail address president@whitehouse.gov. In this instance, the user name is "president," the domain is "whitehouse," and the top-level domain is ".gov" (for government). You can often tell quite a bit about someone just by seeing his or her e-mail address!

If you normally send e-mails to the same group of individuals frequently, you might consider creating a distribution list. A distribution list is a grouping of individuals in your contacts that you want to receive the same e-mails. Instead of listing each recipient individually in the "To" section of a new e-mail you select the precreated distribution list. Everyone in that list will receive the e-mail.

E-mail has many benefits:

- It is inexpensive, fast, and easy to access.
- It enables collaboration.
- It creates an electronic paper trail.
- It saves paper.

> "Attachments may **not** be delivered or they may be **blocked** by **e-mail system administrators** as potentially **unsafe**."

The benefits of e-mail are tempered by some potential problems that you should be aware of. Sometimes e-mail systems fail to properly send or receive mail.

Attachments may not be delivered or they may be blocked by e-mail system administrators as potentially unsafe. Messages can become corrupted and may not display properly. Sometimes, if you don't regularly check your mail, your Inbox may overflow, which causes messages received past the overflow point to be bounced out of the box and never delivered.

Perhaps the worst thing that can happen with e-mail is that you hastily send a message that you later wished you hadn't, or you use the Reply All or Forward feature to send inappropriate or irrelevant messages that can embarrass you or that inconvenience the receiver.

Spam: Can It Be Stopped?

Many e-mail users receive unsolicited e-mail advertising called **spam**. In fact, according to a report released in May 2009 from the security vendor Symantec, 90.4 percent of all e-mail (1 out of every 1.1 e-mails) is spam. This mail is sent by spammers, businesses or individuals that specialize in sending such mail. Spammers believe that they're doing only what direct-marketing mail firms do: sending legitimate advertising. But they don't acknowledge a crucial difference between unsolicited postal advertising and spam. With postal advertising, the advertiser pays for the postage. With spam, the recipient pays the postage in the form of lost time and productivity for individuals and businesses. A 2009 study estimated that the total cost of combined consumer and corporate spam in the United States was $108.8 billion annually. Some $92.2 billion of that cost comes from lost productivity and the balance from the cost of administering and purchasing preventative services and programs.

Most Internet users detest spam but feel helpless to prevent it. For businesses, spam is a costly nuisance. It's not unusual for a massive amount of spam messages to overwhelm mail servers, resulting in impaired service for legitimate, paying customers.

In most cases, little or nothing of worth is being peddled: pornographic Web sites, get-rich-quick scams, bogus stock deals, rip-off work-at-home schemes, health and diet scams, and merchandise of questionable quality. Some spam can contain **malware**, malicious software, that places a computer in the spammer's control. This type of software can wreak havoc on a user's system by deleting files and directory entries; it can also act as **spyware**, gathering data from a user's system without the user knowing it. This can include anything from the Web pages a user visits to personal information, such as credit card numbers.

Can you filter out spam? You can try. It's often possible to set up a spam or bulk mail folder in your e-mail account. Check your mail options for how to enable this service. A word of caution on using such filters: Sometimes filters can misroute messages. Check your trash and spam folders periodically to be sure

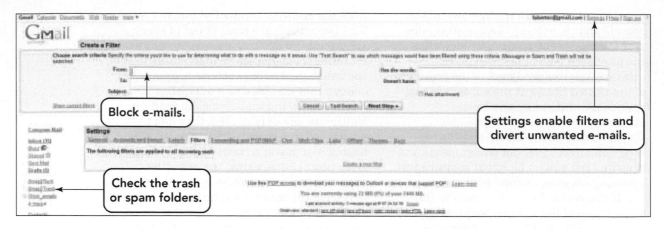

Block e-mails.

Settings enable filters and divert unwanted e-mails.

Check the trash or spam folders.

Check your e-mail account's mail settings to set spam filters.

important messages haven't been directed to the wrong folders.

Spam can originate from a new account, which is almost immediately closed down after the service provider receives hundreds of thousands of outraged complaints. The spammer just moves on to a new account. A more modern way to send spam is through a **botnet**, a set of computers infected with a malicious program that places the computers under the control of a **bot herder**. Vulnerable systems are ones without current security patches or antispam protection. Once infected, a machine becomes one of many zombies in a botnet and responds to commands given by the bot herder.

Some of the steps you can take to prevent spam include the following:

- Avoid posting your e-mail address in any public place.
- Don't open e-mail from a source that you do not recognize.
- Deactivate the preview option in your e-mail. The preview option automatically triggers the opening of the e-mail.
- Don't reply to spam or request to be removed from a spammer's mailing list.
- Modify your e-mail account to disable graphics.
- Get involved in reporting incidents of spam to help others and stop the source of the problem.
- Make sure that security patches on your system are current.

Increasingly, state and federal legislatures are attempting to pass laws against spam. Bills have been introduced in Congress, and the Senate's CAN-SPAM Act of 2003 is aimed at deceptive e-mails,

unsolicited pornography, and marketing. The Direct Marketing Association (DMA), an advocacy group for both online and offline direct marketers, counters that the appropriate solution is an opt-out system, in which spam recipients request that the sender of spam remove their names from the mailing list—but that's just what

ETHICS

With the widespread use of electronic communication, most offices today are equipped with Internet access. Many employers make new employees sign Internet usage clauses that limit the use of the company Internet connection to business-related tasks. How does the employer know whether an employee used the Internet to conduct personal business? One simple method is for the employer to check the browser's history feature. A second might be to review security cameras that have your monitor screen in the range of view. A third is by purchasing a program that allows eavesdropping on Internet use that can be used by a network administrator from a remote location to drop in on an Internet session of an employee.

By signing the Internet usage clause, the employee does agree to the company's policy of Internet use, but does that give the employer the right to use any methods of surveillance without notifying the employee? Some of these methods monitor more than Internet use. At what point are the rights of the individual violated for the good of the company?

e-mail users have been trained not to do because of fear that they'll receive even more spam. In addition, efforts to outlaw spam run afoul of free-speech guarantees under the U.S. Constitution's First Amendment, which applies to businesses as well as individuals. Furthermore, many spammers operate outside the United States, making effective legislation even more difficult. One solution under consideration is a congressional measure that would give ISPs the right to sue spammers for violating their spam policies.

Although it's no fun, most of us have learned to live with spam by following the simple rule: If you don't know who sent it—don't open it! For more information and tips on how to avoid spam, recent law enforcement actions against deceptive commercial e-mail and spammers, and a location to file a complaint, check out the Federal Trade Commission's spam site at **www.ftc.gov/spam**.

Instant Messaging: E-Mail Made Faster

What's faster than e-mail and more convenient than picking up the phone? Instant messaging (IM) systems alert you when a friend or business associate who also uses the IM system (a buddy or contact) is online (connected to the Internet). You can then contact this person and exchange messages and attachments, including multimedia files.

To use IM, you need to install instant messenger software from an instant messenger service, such as AOL's AIM or Microsoft's Windows Live Messenger, on your computer. You can use IM systems on any type of computer, including handhelds. Many IM services also give you access to information such as daily news, stock prices, sports scores, and the weather, and you can keep track of your appointments. There is no standard IM protocol, which means that you can send messages only to people who are using the same IM service that you are.

An increasing number of businesses and institutions are trying out IM services, with mixed results. On the one hand, IM is a novel and convenient way to communicate. On the other hand, voice communication is faster and richer. Other drawbacks to instant messaging include the misinterpretation of the tone of the message and the inability to save an IM for later retrieval, thus posing some legal issues for businesses and corporations.

Another threat to the use of IM is a phenomenon known as spimming. **Spimming** is spam that targets users of instant messaging. Spimming is to IM as spam is to e-mail. Be very careful about opening files or clicking on a link sent in an instant message by an unknown sender.

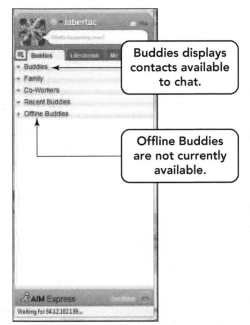

Buddies displays contacts available to chat.

Offline Buddies are not currently available.

Once a buddy is selected, the message window opens.

An IM to an offline buddy will be delivered when the person signs on.

Internet Relay Chat: Text Chatting in Real Time

Internet relay chat (IRC) is an Internet service that enables you to join chat groups, called **channels**, and participate in real-time, text-based conversations. Popular in the early days of the Internet, IRC has been replaced by tools like IM. Today it is mostly the province of specialized communities, such as gamers or programmers.

Instant messaging is a popular way for Internet users to exchange near real-time messages.

Social networking sites, like Ning.com, that allow users to create their own social network communities are becoming popular with political candidates and business entrepreneurs.

Social Networking: Helping People Connect

Social networking is a way to build expanding online communities. On a social networking site like Facebook or MySpace, you can create an online profile, invite friends and acquaintances to join your network, and invite their friends to join too. Some sites, like LinkedIn, are used by business professionals to expand their network of business contacts. Tired of Facebook or MySpace? Why not start your own social network? Ning (**www.ning.com**) is a site that encourages people to start their own social networking community. Artists, hobbyists, educators, athletes—the list continues to grow. Find a community to join or start your own!

Many privacy and security concerns surround the use and access of social networking sites. Statistics from a Pew Internet 2008 report support this concern, citing that 73 percent of American teens who participated in the survey indicated that they use social networking Web sites. This is a significant increase over statistics from 2007 and fuels the concern over security and the need to educate teens on the use and possible repercussion of postings placed on such sites. Once posted, pictures and content are easily shared and distributed to others, sometimes with detrimental effects. Users should give thought to the information they publicly display and consider the possible consequences. If you are searching for employment, make sure that your social networking site is not offensive. Employers are researching candidates' Facebook or MySpace sites to gain insight into a potential employee's personality and behavior.

Usenet: Joining Online Discussions

Usenet is a worldwide computer-based discussion system accessible through the Internet. It consists of thousands of topically named **newsgroups**, which are discussion groups devoted to a single topic. A newsgroup typically requires participants to use a program called a news reader. Each newsgroup contains articles that users have posted for all to see. Users can respond to specific articles by posting follow-up articles. Over time, a discussion thread develops as people reply to the replies. A **thread** is a series of articles that offer a continuing commentary on the same specific subject.

Usenet newsgroups are organized into the following main categories:

- **Standard newsgroups.** You're most likely to find rewarding, high-quality discussions in the standard newsgroups (also called world newsgroups). Figure lists the standard newsgroup subcategories.
- **Alt newsgroups.** The alt category is much more freewheeling. Anyone can create an alt newsgroup (which explains why so many of them have silly or offensive names).
- **Biz newsgroups.** These newsgroups are devoted to the commercial uses of the Internet.

The easiest way to access Usenet is through Google Groups (**http://groups. google.com**).

You can read and post messages, but be careful what you post on Usenet. When you post an article, you're publishing in the public domain. Sometimes articles are stored for long periods in Web-accessible archives.

A **message board** is similar to a newsgroup, but it is easier to use and does not require a newsreader. Many colleges and universities have switched to message boards for this reason.

Electronic Mailing Lists

Electronic mailing lists of e-mail addresses are similar in many ways to newsgroups and forums, but they automatically broadcast messages to all individuals on a mailing list. Because the messages are transmitted as e-mail, only individuals who are subscribers to the mailing list receive and view the messages. Some colleges and universities host electronic mailing lists. Eric Thomas developed the first electronic mailing list program, Listserv, in 1986 for BITNET. The most common freeware version of an electronic mailing list manager program is Majordomo.

VoIP

VoIP (Voice over Internet Protocol) allows a user to speak to others over a broadband Internet connection instead of traditional analog phone line. What do you need to use VoIP? This form of communication requires a broadband Internet connection, a VoIP service provider, and a normal telephone with a VoIP adapter or a computer with supporting software. Calls to others using the same service are usually free, whereas calls to those using other services can vary. Many businesses are using VoIP services, like Skype, to reduce their communication bills and operating expenses.

File Transfer Protocol: Transferring Files

File Transfer Protocol (FTP) is one way that files can be transferred over the Internet, and it is especially useful for transferring files that are too large to send by e-mail. Although you can use special FTP client software, such as WS_FTP Home, you can also transfer files to and from an FTP server simply by using your browser or Windows Explorer. FTP can transfer two types of files: ASCII (text files) and binary (program files, graphics, or documents saved in proprietary file formats).

In most cases, you need a user name and a password to access an FTP server. However, with **anonymous FTP**, files are publicly available for downloading. A word of warning: Due to the lack of security on an anonymous FTP site, do not use it to send sensitive information such as financial

Standard Newsgroup Subcategories

Subcategory Name	Description of Topics Covered
Comp	Everything related to computers and computer networks, including applications, compression, databases, multimedia, and programming
Misc	Subjects that do not fit in other standard newsgroup hierarchies, including activism, books, business, consumer issues, health, investing, jobs, and law
Sci	The sciences and social sciences, including anthropology, archaeology, chemistry, economics, math, physics, and statistics
Soc	Social issues, including adoption, college-related issues, feminism, human rights, and world cultures
Talk	Debate on controversial subjects, including abortion, atheism, euthanasia, gun control, and religion
News	Usenet itself, including announcements and materials for new users
Rec	All aspects of recreation, including aviation, backcountry sports, bicycles, boats, gardening, and scouting

account numbers and passwords. FTP sites are structured hierarchically—that is, they use a folder and file structure similar to that used on your own computer. Depending on how you access the site, downloadable files may appear as hyperlinks. Just click the link to download the file. If you access the site using Windows Explorer, you can use the same file management techniques you use to organize your own files.

FTP is also used to upload Web pages from your computer to the ISP or hosting service's Web server, making your Web site available to other Internet users.

E-Commerce

A large portion of Internet traffic and Web sites are associated with e-commerce. **Commerce** is the selling of goods or services with the expectation of making a reasonable profit. **E-commerce (electronic commerce)** is the use of networks or the Internet to carry out business of any type. Many **e-tailers** (Web-based retailers) hope that while you are surfing the Web, you will stop and make a purchase. Online merchants sell books, CDs, clothes, and just about anything else you might want to buy. If you've ever made a purchase online, you're one of millions engaging in e-commerce.

E-commerce supports many types of traditional business transactions, including buying, selling, renting, borrowing, and lending. E-commerce isn't new; companies have used networks to do business with suppliers for years. What is new is that, thanks to the Internet and inexpensive PCs, e-commerce has become accessible to anyone with an Internet connection and a Web browser.

The U.S. Census Bureau reported that total retail e-commerce sales for the fourth quarter of 2009 was $42.0 billion, an increase of 34.1 percent from the third quarter of 2009. For the fourth quarter of 2009, e-commerce sales accounted for 4.3 percent of total sales. There are three types of e-commerce: business-to-business (B2B), consumer-to-consumer (C2C), and business-to-consumer (B2C).

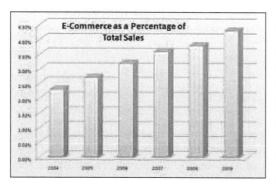

Statistics from the U.S. Census Bureau substantiate that e-commerce has been on the rise.

Business-to-Business E-Commerce (B2B)

When a business uses the Internet to provide another business with the materials, services, and/or supplies it needs to conduct its operations, they are engaging in **business-to-business (B2B) e-commerce**. Even though you might not personally engage in B2B, you'll probably recognize many of the industries and companies that do, for example, companies in the health care, aerospace and defense, real estate, automotive, and construction industries, and familiar computer and software companies such as Dell, IBM, and Microsoft.

In addition, many traditional and online retailers have special B2B units. For instance, the popular office supplies chain Staples has a B2B division that operates the Web site **www.staplesadvantage.com** for mid-size and Fortune 1000 companies. The Staples Contract division has experienced double-digit growth for the last seven years and launched the office supply industry's first online B2B catalog in 2007.

Unlike B2B, you may have engaged in the next type of e-commerce: consumer-to-consumer.

Consumer-to-Consumer E-Commerce (C2C)

The online exchange or trade of goods, services, or information between individual consumers is **consumer-to-consumer (C2C) e-commerce**. Often C2C e-commerce involves the use of an intermediate site, such as the popular online auction destination eBay. eBay has more than 89.5 million active users. The value of goods sold through eBay's online marketplaces, excluding autos, rose 24 percent in the fourth quarter of 2009 to $13.37 billion from $10.80 billion in the same quarter of 2008, with 58 percent of marketplace revenue from outside the U.S. Other C2C sites include craigslist and Amazon Marketplace.

Business-to-Consumer E-Commerce (B2C)

When a business uses the Internet to supply consumers with services, information, or products, they are engaging in **business-to-consumer (B2C) e-commerce**. B2C is essentially the same as shopping at a physical store—you have a need or want, and the online marketplace offers products and solutions. The primary difference is that

eBay is the most well-known C2C trading site. However, its competitors like Craig's List and Amazon Marketplace are also popular.

B2C e-commerce is not place or time specific, which means that you don't have to be in any particular place at any particular time to participate. This freedom of time and place enables you to shop whenever you wish and to choose from more products and services than could ever be assembled in any one physical location.

Online Shopping

The trend is for more Web users to purchase merchandise online. In addition, many more people use the Web to research purchases from brick-and-mortar stores.

Getting Good Deals Online Have you ever tried to comparison shop on the Web? After surfing at 10 different sites (or more!), it can be daunting to keep track of where you saw the best price on that new digital camera you want. You might want to turn to shopping portals such as PriceGrabber.com, Shopzilla, NexTag, and others. These sites help you conduct price and product comparisons. They also offer reviews on just about any product you can imagine. You can search and sort by brand, price range, or product rating. To save even more, you can also check sites that offer coupons and rebates, such as The Bargainist and eCoupons.

The Dot-Com Phenomenon

Much e-commerce occurs in the *dot-com world,* the universe of Web sites with the suffix *.com* appended to their names. This unique world has been in existence only since 1995. Before 1995, companies were not able to sell over the Internet. But in 1995, the government eliminated all taxpayer funding of the Internet and opened it up to commercial development. The period between 1995 and 2000 is referred to as the *dot-com boom.* As the dot-com crash of 2000 made painfully clear, not every online business is able to succeed.

Amazon.com is a dot-com company that has held its ground and become profitable. Amazon quickly discovered that books are a commodity well suited for online trade, but it didn't stop there. Its offerings have grown to include music, videos, groceries, tools, jewelry, and clothing. Amazon entices buyers to access, shop, and complete their sales online by offering professional and peer product reviews; author, artist, and subject matching; and book excerpts and music samples. Shoppers can choose from a variety of shipping options and track their purchases.

There are some drawbacks to B2C e-commerce. Buyers might miss speaking with a real sales clerk, being able to touch and feel the merchandise, and being able to take it home the same day, but many sellers are adopting creative solutions to these issues by offering online chats with live customer service representatives, various ways to view products, and a wide array of shipping options. One of the hallmarks of a successful online business is good customer service. Customers are reassured by sites that clearly post their contact information, offer pages of frequently asked questions, and respond quickly to customer inquiries.

Building Your Own Online Business

One of the tremendous advantages of B2C e-commerce is the low capital investment needed to start an online business. For less than $50, a person can open a Web storefront and start selling products online. In contrast, a brick-and-mortar business requires land, a building, utilities, display shelving, and salespeople. A Web-based storefront requires only an ISP, a Web site, and the ability to ship goods or services to customers.

The first thing you need to do when starting any business is to develop a business plan. You must decide what products to offer, determine your target market, and select how many items you plan to sell and at what price. Who will pay for shipping? Will there be service provided after the sale? Who are your competitors? What profit margin do you expect to achieve?

All businesses need to have a name, and an online business is no different, except that the online business's name is

Shopping comparison sites can help users locate items, compare prices, view consumer feedback, and buy products.

almost always the same as its Web site or domain name. So, after you've completed your business plan, you will need to shop for a domain name and a Web hosting service. Many Web hosting companies, such as 1&1 (**www.1and1.com**), offer domain name search and registration services as part of their package. You will most likely want a name with a .com extension. Try to pick a name that will be easy for your customers to remember.

You may also wish to employ an electronic shopping cart. This feature

Sites such as Bplans.com can help get your small business plan off to a good start.

is much like the physical shopping cart you'd use at a grocery store. It remembers your customer's order items and provides the results to the summary order page. Your Web site should project a professional image and be structured to meet your customers' needs to encourage their confidence in your product or service. Go to GoodPractices (**www.goodpractices.com**) for some Web site development guidelines.

You will also need to make arrangements for Web hosting, if you haven't already done so. Web hosting services provide server space, make your site available

to the public, and offer site management utilities such as preprogrammed shopping cart services. There are thousands of Web hosting companies. Many Web hosting services offer templates and other tools to make it simple to build a professional-looking site. Sites such as 1&1, GoDaddy, and Yahoo! offer a variety of pricing plans for personal and commercial sites. Expect to pay a start-up fee as well as a monthly amount that is usually based on a one-year contract.

You can ensure that your site gets listed with search engines by visiting each engine's Web site (**www.google.com**, **www.yahoo.com**, **www.msn.com**, and so on) and searching for "submitting my site." Provide the information requested, and then when someone searches for keywords that match your site, it will be one of the sites that are provided in the search results answer screen.

To operate a business, you need a way to receive payments. Just like in a traditional retail business, perhaps the best option may be to take credit cards. You should be aware that there are many costs involved with setting up and maintaining a credit card acceptance account—but the benefits may well outweigh the costs. Customers are comfortable using their credit cards online, and many feel more secure knowing that the credit card company is there in case of a dispute or fraudulent use.

One common method to accept credit cards is to use a PayPal merchant account. PayPal also acts as a secure intermediary, offering users the ability to make payments from their bank account, credit card, or PayPal account without revealing their personal financial

For online purchases, merchants prefer if customers use an electronic alternative like PayPal but customers may feel more secure using a credit card that provides dispute mediation and protection from fraud.

information to the seller. PayPal manages more than 40 million accounts worldwide. Transaction fees range from 2 to 3 percent, and there is a per-transaction fee of about 30 cents per transaction.

Other Areas of E-Commerce Growth

Making travel reservations is an area of e-commerce experiencing rapid growth. Sites such as Travelocity, Expedia, and CheapTickets enable leisure travelers to book flights, hotels, and car rentals online, as well as find the cheapest fares based on their trip parameters. Most travel sites provide e-tickets so that you can quickly check in at airport terminals by using small self-service kiosks.

Another rapidly growing online activity is banking. Access to your banking accounts enables you to use a Web browser to check account balances, balance your checkbook, transfer funds, and even pay bills online (Figure 6.43). In fact, 40 million Americans used online banking services by the end of 2005. The use of online banking is expected to grow by 55 percent by the end of 2011. By that time, some 76 percent of Americans (72 million households) will be using online banking services. Currently, banks that offer online banking gain a competitive advantage over those that do not because most customers now consider it a necessary and expected service, like ATMs. What else is in it for banks? Plenty. Online banking helps banks cut down on the expenses of maintaining bank branches and paying tellers and also allows them to provide advanced levels of electronic customer service.

The sale of stock through the Internet has only been possible since 1996; however, online stock trading now accounts for one out of every six stock trades, easily making it the fastest-growing application in B2C e-commerce. Offering secure connections through the customer's Web browser, online stock trading sites enable investors to buy and sell stocks online without the aid of a broker.

The attraction of online stock trading can be summed up in one word: cost. Fees paid to traditional, full-service brokerages can add up. But the most aggressive e-traders have cut the charges to $10 per

trade or less. E-traders, such as E*TRADE and Ameritrade, can offer such low prices because the trading is automatic—no human broker is involved.

Nonretail online services have spiked in activity in the last few years. These activities include dating services; credit reports; health and medical advice; news, weather, and sports information; real estate listings (for homes and apartments); and insurance products. These sites offer various levels of access and services for members and nonmembers. Some services, such as insurance quotes, up-to-the-minute news reports, and severe weather alerts, are free. You can also post dating profiles or receive diet and other health-related profiles as well as trial passes for sports subscriptions.

Sites such as Travelocity (www.travelocity.com) are popular because they help travelers find the cheapest fares and reservations available.

Online banking enables customers to access their accounts, balance checkbooks, and even pay bills online.

Rules of Netiquette

Along with the privilege of using the Internet comes the responsibility of using it correctly and not causing harm to others. Courtesy is as important in the online world as it is in reality.

Netiquette, short for Internet etiquette, is the code for acceptable behavior and manners while on the Internet. The basic rule is this: Talk to others the same way you would want them to talk to you. Some more specific, useful rules of netiquette for e-mail, chat rooms, instant messaging, and message boards include the following:

- Keep the message short.
- Avoid sarcasm or the use of phrases or words that could offend the reader.
- Read the message before sending or posting it, correcting spelling and grammar mistakes.
- Do not type in all capital letters as it means that you are yelling.
- Avoid sending a **flame**. Such messages express an opinion without holding back any emotion and are frequently seen as being confrontational and argumentative.

When you follow the rules of netiquette, you put your best foot forward and make a good impression. The other side of using the Internet is protecting yourself from those that are out to deceive or harm you. Let's look at some safe surfing suggestions to protect you from this dark side of technology.

Safe Surfing

Safe surfing seems to be a constant topic of discussion. Just as many hazards exist online as there are in the real world. The added online element is that individuals are difficult to recognize due to the anonymity the Internet provides.

Safe Surfing Guidelines

By taking some simple precautions you can make your Internet experience an enjoyable and safe activity.

- Never give out identifying information.
- Never respond to suggestive messages.
- Never open e-mail from an unknown source.
- Never allow a child to make arrangements for a face-to-face meeting alone, for any reason, without being accompanied by an adult.
- Remember individuals online may not be who they seem.
- Set reasonable rules and guidelines for computer use by children.
- Make using the computer a family activity.

Additional online hazards to avoid include malware; identity theft; threats to you and your family; and unscrupulous vendors.

Avoiding Malware

Malware refers to software programs designed and written to damage a computer system. Examples of malware events range from deleting files on a hard drive or removing directory information to gathering data from a user's system that can include Web sites the user visited and account numbers or passwords that were keyed in. It is unfortunate that there are individuals out there with malicious intent, but there are—and you must be prepared. You can keep your system free of malware by installing antivirus and antispyware utilities on your computer. These utility programs will seek and destroy the malware programs they find on your computer.

"More than **half a million** people find themselves **victims** of identity theft each year. . . . And, **nothing** is more **difficult** than restoring your credit after an **identity theft** has **destroyed** your credit rating."

Protecting Your Identity

More than half a million people find themselves victims of identity theft each year. Nothing is more frustrating than having to spend the time and energy to clean up the mess created by a loss of identification. And, nothing is more difficult than restoring your credit after an identity theft has destroyed your credit rating.

There are steps you can take to greatly reduce the risk of having your identity stolen or a portion of it pilfered. Try to avoid shoulder-surfers; these are individuals who stand close enough to see PIN numbers keyed in by users at ATMs and phone booths. When shopping with an e-merchant for the first time, look for the secure Web site features before entering any personal or credit card information. These features usually include one or several of the items in the following list:

- *https://* in the address of the site instead of the usual *http://*. The added "s" stands for "secure site" and means that the data is encrypted all the way from your computer to the computer that receives it. No other computer will be able to read your input as it passes along the Internet.
- A site seal provided by a security vendor, such as VeriSign, GeoTrust, or SSL.com
- A locked padlock symbol somewhere on the Web site that, when double-clicked, displays details of the site's security (make sure that the logo is not just an image and a fake)
- The logo from other site-security entities, such as Verified by Visa
- A message box that notifies you when you are leaving (or entering) a secure site

In addition to these visible identifiers, check out any feedback provided by previous purchasers or any comments by the Better Business Bureau. Shop only on Web sites that enable you to view their privacy policy. Make it a habit to print out privacy policies, warranties, price guarantees, and other important information. Most importantly, *never* include any financial account numbers or passwords in an e-mail or respond in any way to spam. And be sure to change the passwords on your accounts frequently.

Simply being watchful and careful with your personal information, completing transactions only on validated Web sites, and knowing the signs of a secure site will help you use the Web to its full potential safely.

Protecting Children in Cyberspace

With statistics supporting the use of social networks, chat rooms, and other forms of anonymous communication by minors, there have been some creative protective responses to insulate youth from cyberstalkers, cyberbullies, and other online predators. A couple in Fanwood, New Jersey, contacted CyberAngels (**www.cyberangels.org**), a volunteer organization of thousands of Internet users worldwide, after their computer-addicted 13-year-old daughter ran away from home. The group's purpose: to protect children in cyberspace.

CyberAngels was founded in 1995 by Curtis Sliwa, who also started the Guardian Angels (the volunteer organization whose members wear red berets as they patrol inner-city streets). Today, CyberAngels volunteers scour the Internet for online predators, cyberstalkers, and child pornographers, and they've been responsible for a number of arrests. Their Web site and newsletter provide many useful articles about practical safety measures to keep you and your loved ones safe and has brought their Children's Internet Safety Program to thousands of schoolchildren across the United States. So, what about the New Jersey couple? Their daughter is home and safe thanks to the CyberAngels, who successfully used their network to identify the child's online contact.

The Internet can be a dangerous place for young children and older ones too! **Cyberbullying** occurs when one individual targets another for some form of torment or abuse through digital tools. The term used to apply to children acting against other children. However, the recent suicide death of a teen in Missouri due to cyberbullying by a parent who masqueraded as another youth has shed light on the intensity of this problem. Online stalkers and sexual predators haunt social networking sites. **Cyberstalkers** use e-mail, instant messaging, chat rooms, pagers, cell phones, or other forms of information technology to make repeated, credible threats of violence against another individual or family

"**[Never]** include any **financial account numbers** or passwords in an **e-mail** or **respond** in any way to spam."

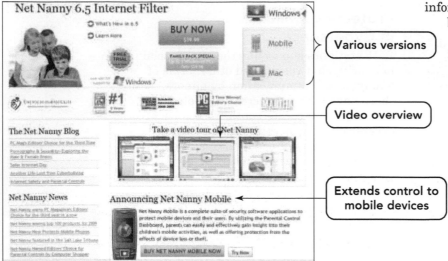

Various versions

Video overview

Extends control to mobile devices

Content-filtering software like Net Nanny are extending parental control from notebooks and desktop system to mobile devices.

member of an individual. To learn more about how to protect yourself or the children in your household, visit Stop Cyberbullying (**www.stopcyberbullying. org**), SocialSafety.org (**www. socialsafety.org**), and the Family Online Safety Institute (**http://fosi.org/icra/**).

Speaking with children about Internet safety practices, being aware of where and when they surf, and knowing who their cyberfriends are should be a top priority. Concerned parents can implement the parental controls that are provided by their ISPs or included in safety and security software. Web site blocking and content-filtering software and monitoring programs like Net Nanny (**www.netnanny.com**), and bsecure (**www.bsecure.com**) can add another level of security.

After covering the personal uses for the Internet and addressing its benefits and drawbacks, let's change the focus to the Internet user conducting business.

Avoiding E-Commerce Hazards

Although there are many benefits to engaging in e-commerce, it also entails risks. These risks include identity theft, personal information exposure, money loss, and being ripped off by unscrupulous charlatans. To protect yourself, carefully create user names and passwords, particularly at sites where you must pay for goods or services. It is also wise to avoid e-commerce with little-known companies, at least until you've taken the opportunity to check their legitimacy. Checking shopping portals or other review sites to locate feedback from other users or conducting an online search combining the company's name with keywords such as *problem*, *fraud*, or *scam* can help you be better informed.

Even though you are most likely protected from monetary losses by your credit card company, you should always be careful when giving out your credit card information—and do so only on secure sites. Never share credit card numbers, account numbers, user name, or password information with others, even if you receive an e-mail requesting that information from what seems to be a legitimate source.

Sometimes you will find that the seller is a person just like you—that the seller doesn't have the ability to take credit cards and that he or she has set up an account with an online transaction processing system such as PayPal. It is the seller who decides which vendor to use for the payment. For instance, if you see the PayPal logo on an eBay auction item site, it means that you can use PayPal as a payment option. In fact, sometimes this is the only option available. The PayPal Web site even offers a tool to help you manage your buying experience. The PayPal AuctionFinder searches eBay for items you've recently won and prefills your payment form with details taken straight from the item listing. With AuctionFinder, you can eliminate errors and pay for your items instantly. Always use extra care and caution whenever you conduct financial transactions on the Internet.

Use the Favorites Feature of the Internet Explorer (IE) Browser

The Favorites menu located on the menu bar in the IE browser window allows you to insert a Web page into the Favorites list, making it easier to access later by not having to retype the URL in the address bar. Once you make a page a Favorite, all you have to do is click the name and the Web page will display in the browser window.

In this section, we cover how to perform two actions with respect to managing your Favorites:

- Adding a Web page to the Favorites list
- Organizing your Favorite list into folders

To add a Web page to the Favorites list:

1. Enter the URL of the page you want to access in the browser's address bar.

   After the page appears, click *Favorites* on the menu bar.

2. From the drop-down menu that appears, select *Add to Favorites*.

3. In the Add a Favorite dialog box you can do these things:

   a. Name the page you are inserting into the Favorites list or use the default.

   b. Create a new folder and place the current page into that folder.

   c. Place the page into a folder that already exists by clicking the arrow to the right of the *Create in* option.

4. After selecting your option, click *Add*. The current page is now an entry in your Favorites list.

You can organize your Favorites list into folders while you are adding the page as described above or after pages have been placed in the Favorites list.

To organize your Favorites list after Web pages have been added:

1. Click *Favorites* on the menu bar.

2. Select the *Organize Favorites* option.

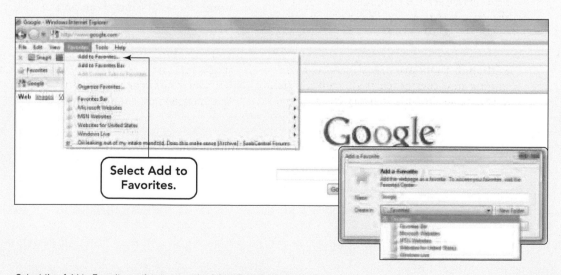

Select the *Add to Favorites* option to open the Add a Favorite dialog box.

3. In the Organize Favorites dialog box that appears, you have four choices: New Folder, Move, Rename, or Delete.

- Select *New Folder* to create and name a new folder.

- Highlight a Favorites entry and then select *Move*. A dialog box will open and ask you to select the location to which you want to move the entry.

- Select *Rename*, with an entry highlighted, and rename that entry in the top section of the dialog box.

- Select *Delete*, with an entry highlighted, to remove the entry from the Favorites list.

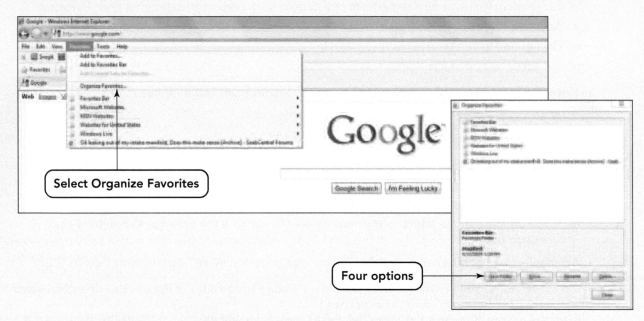

Your Favorites list can get very long. Adding folders will organize the list and make it easier to locate a site.

Chapter Summary

The Internet and the World Wide Web

- The Internet is the network of networks that, because of its interoperability, allows connected computers to exchange data regardless of model, brand, or operating system. Interoperability is made possible by the use of TCP/IP (Transmission Control Protocol/Internet Protocol) suite of protocols, the standard methods of packaging and transmitting information on the Internet.

- Users access the Internet by way of an Internet access provider. Access providers fall into three categories: Internet service provider (ISP), online service provider, and a wireless Internet service provider. A user connects to the access provider by way of a telephone modem, a digital service line (DSL), a cable modem, a satellite, or a fiber-optic cable.

- Whereas the Internet is a global computer network that connects millions of smaller networks, the World Wide Web is a global system of billions of hypertext documents, called Web pages. These documents use hyperlinks to connect to each other and the Internet as a transport mechanism. Web pages are displayed though a combination of elements, including hyperlinks to jump from one Web page to another, a browser to interpret the HTML tags and display the Web document, including enabling of hyperlinks, and a Web server that stores the Web pages and retrieves them when a request is made by a browser.

- Information on the Web can be located by entering the URL (Web address) in the address bar of the browser, general surfing, using searches with search operators to get more specific results, and using sites and technology that allow the sharing of information with other Web users, such as RSS feeds, blogs, and wikis. Search expressions can include search operators (+, −, *) or Boolean search terms (AND, OR, NOT) to narrow down the list of results.

- Features of a reliable Web source include an author with credentials, the affiliation of the Web site with the host, the objectivity of the material presented, the overall purpose of the site, and the accuracy and currency of the information.

- Popular Internet services include e-mail and instant messaging (IM) for sending messages, Internet relay chat (IRC) for text chatting, chat rooms, social networking sites for online communities, discussion groups, newsgroups, VoIP, message boards, and File Transfer Protocol (FTP) for file exchange, and e-commerce.

- There are three types of e-commerce, business-to-business (B2B), consumer-to-consumer (C2C), and business-to-consumer (B2C).

- When using the Web, be courteous and respect the rules of netiquette.

- Follow safe surfing guidelines, avoid malware, change your passwords frequently, never enter your account number unless you are on a secured site, watch the computer usage of your children, and install software to protect your children from cyberstalkers, cyberbullies, and undesirable Web sites. When conducting online business, be aware of security indicators on Web sites conducting e-commerce, and perform transactions only with secured sites.

Key Terms and Concepts

Identification

Label each item.

1. _____

2. _____

3. _____

4. _____

5. _____

6. _____

Matching

Match each key term in the left column with the most accurate definition in the right column.

_____ 1. hot spot

_____ 2. uploading

_____ 3. interoperability

_____ 4. portal

_____ 5. hyperlink

_____ 6. router

_____ 7. home page

_____ 8. clickstream

_____ 9. downloading

_____ 10. dead link

_____ 11. RSS

_____ 12. subject guide

_____ 13. browser

_____ 14. plug-in

_____ 15. link rot

a. Transferring a document or file from another computer to your computer

b. An element in an electronic document that acts as the connector to another place in the same document or to an entirely different document

c. The set of Web links that indicates the trail a user followed to reach a Web page

d. A method of providing constant information updates over the Internet without any user involvement

e. A public location, like an airport, college campus, or coffee shop, that provides Internet access for devices fitted with wireless technology

f. A list of subject-related categories that, when selected, displays a page of more related links

g. Additional software programs that extend the multimedia ability of a browser

h. Links to documents on the Web that have disappeared

i. Transferring a document or file from your computer to another computer

j. A program on the user's computer that interprets HTML or XHTML forms, enabling the user to view Web pages

k. A Web page that acts as a gateway to diverse sources presented in an organized way

l. Outdatedness due to the delay in accumulating data and updating a search engine's database

m. Specialized devices that connect networks, locate the best path of transmission, and ensure that your data reaches its destination

n. The default page that is automatically displayed when you enter a site at its top level

o. Describes the Internet's ability to work with computers and applications of different brands and models, through the use of a common protocol

Multiple Choice

Circle the correct choice for each of the following:

1. Which of the following is *not* a search operator?
   a. −
   b. +
   c. !
   d. *

2. Which of the following is an example of a valid IP address?
   a. 12.256.56.78
   b. 38.155.400.56
   c. 45.254.77.125
   d. 266.54.77.89

3. Which of the following is *not* a top-level domain name?
   a. .edu
   b. .car
   c. .net
   d. .gov

4. RSS feeds can be grouped together through the use of a(n) _____ program.
   a. browser
   b. aggregator
   c. syndication
   d. plug-in

5. Which Internet service is plagued by spam?
   a. Instant messaging
   b. E-mail
   c. VoIP
   d. Chat rooms

6. What does the appearance of a VeriSign logo on a Web site indicate?
   a. The site is a commercial site.
   b. The site has been recently updated.
   c. The site is hosted in the United States.
   d. The site is secure.

7. What term refers to the act of abusing or tormenting an individual through digital methods?
   a. Cyberbullying
   b. Cyberstalking
   c. E-tailing
   d. Flaming

8. Which is *not* a method of e-commerce?
   a. B2B
   b. C2C
   c. C2B
   d. B2C

9. What is the name of spam that targets users of instant messaging?
   a. Spimming
   b. Botnet
   c. Spyware
   d. Beacon

10. A(n) _____ is a Web page on which any visitor can post text or images, read previous posts, change earlier posts, and track changes.
    a. blog
    b. wiki
    c. newsgroup
    d. electronic mailing list

Fill-In

In the blanks provided, write the correct answer for each of the following.

1. _____ is a search technique that makes use of wildcards to locate words with various endings.

2. _____ is the next generation of the Web that provides increased opportunities for collaboration.

3. _____ is a unique numerical identifier for each computer or device connected to the Internet.

4. A(n) _____ is the equivalent of an Internet diary or journal.

5. A(n) _____ is a program that travels the Web and populates the database of a search engine.

6. _____ is unsolicited e-mail.

7. A(n) _____ provides individuals and businesses with access to the Internet via phone, DSL, cable, satellite, or fiber-optic lines, for a fee.

8. A(n) _____ is a series of articles that offer a continuing commentary on the same subject.

9. _____ is a worldwide computer-based discussion system accessible through the Internet.

10. E-bay is an example of a(n) _____ e-commerce site.

11. A(n) _____ is an angry or critical response to a violation of netiquette.

12. _____ is a type of spam that collects data from a user's system without his or her knowledge.

13. _____ is the online exchange or trade of goods, services, or information between two businesses.

14. A _____ is a method of sharing information over the Internet in audio, image, or video format.

15. A(n) _____ is a Web-based retailer.

Short Answer

1. Explain the difference between the Internet and the Web.

2. List the three types of access providers and give a brief description of each.

3. List three drawbacks of distributing content over the Web.

4. What is Real Simple Syndication (RSS)?

5. List the characteristics that help to evaluate the credibility of content on Web pages.

Teamwork

1. **Security Vendors** As a team, research at least three security certificate vendors. Provide a brief description of each and describe the logo that each is identified by. Then locate at least 10 Web sites that display one of the logos that you described. Present your vendor's descriptions, logos, and the 10 associated Web sites in a PowerPoint presentation. Remember to cite your references and include the full URL of your Web site examples.

2. **Evaluating Web content** Break into groups of two or three. Each group should locate a Web site with information on a topic being covered in class or another topic approved by the instructor. Evaluate the site based on the criteria listed in this chapter. Using your word processor, create a table to display your findings. List the criteria in column 1 and your evaluation in column 2. Using the reference feature of your word processor, create end notes and reference the Web sites used. Present your evaluations in a one- to two-page word processing document.

3. **Using a Search Engine** As a team, evaluate each of the search statements below and describe the result that each will achieve. Use **www.internettutorials.net** for help with symbols you might not understand. Then create the search string to meet the specified change. Take a screen capture of the results from each search. Complete the table that follows and turn in the completed table and the screen capture from each one of the five searches.

   To create a screen capture, first press *PrtScrn* on the keyboard while the search result is on the screen. Open the Word file you plan to submit for this question. Position the cursor in the location where you want the capture to appear, and from the contextual menu in the Word window select *Edit*, then select *Paste*. The PrintScrn image captured earlier will appear in the Word document. Then save and print the document.

4. **Web-Based Course Management Systems** Most colleges and universities use some sort of Web-based course management system to provide online classes or an additional resource for face-to-face classes. Evaluate the effectiveness of the course management system at your school by breaking into two groups. Have one group create a survey and distribute it to students that are using the system. Have the other group create a survey and distribute it to faculty that are using the system. The survey should contain 8 to 10 questions and focus on the type of materials that are posted on the system, the amount of time respondents use or access the system on a weekly basis, their opinion of the effectiveness of this media for learning, and the integrity of the learning that takes place in this environment. Distribute the survey to at least 10 students and 10 faculty members. As a team, collect and summarize the results. Present your summary and analysis of the data in a PowerPoint presentation.

5. **Digital Communication** As a team, create a survey to evaluate the digital communication preferences of students at your school. Include questions on the type of devices they use (smartphones, notebooks, desktops), the type of media they use (blogs, wikis, e-mail, text messaging, course management system), the amount they pay for the service (if they pay), the frequency of use, and some general questions like the gender and class level (freshman, sophomore, junior, or senior). Distribute the survey to at least 20 students on campus. Collect and analyze the responses. As a team, draw usage conclusions from the data collected. Use a PowerPoint presentation to present a summary of your results and the conclusions your team drew from the data.

Search String	Purpose	Change to Be Made	Search String with Change
Sports + Hockey		exclude the Sabres	
"Absence makes the heart grow fonder"		include Shakespeare	
logo sports		include baseball	
clothing + LLBean + women		remove women and add men	
Go Green + US		remove US and add clothing	

On the Web

1. **Blogging for Beginners** Go to **www.blogger. com/start** and create a blog that you will add content to daily for a week. The blog content is to be about your experience in using a blogging site, the features of the site that you like or don't like, and an evaluation of the whole experience. Invite some of your classmates to participate in the blog. Your blog will be your report, so make it detailed and professional. Provide your instructor with the blog address so he/she can follow the postings. Remember the blog and its content will be considered as your submitted assignment.

2. **Using an Aggregator** Use a search engine to locate free aggregators. Review a few aggregators and select one to use in this exercise. Aggregator sites usually have categories like news and sports that contain several Web sites having RSS feeds. Select a category and then view the individual subscriptions that are available. Use the *Add* option to subscribe to a feed, and include a few of your own preferred Web sites (ESPN, USA Today) with RSS feeds in the subscription list. When they appear, locate the manage subscription option and organize the ones you added by placing them into existing categories or by creating a new separate category. Delete a few of the ones that are in the category you chose. Check out some of the other features of the aggregator. There is usually an option to return to a home page, some way to track your reading trends, and even a way to share your reader with others. After using the program for a while, review your experience. In a one-page, double-spaced paper, describe the aggregator site you chose and explain why you chose that site. Also discuss how easy (or difficult) the site was to use, the amount of feeds you received, and whether or not you would use such a program. Include any other observations and bits of advice for another user. Remember to cite your references.

3. **Plug-ins: Are They Cool or Irritating** Go to **www.coolhomepages.com/** or **www.ebizmba. com/articles/best-flash-sites** to view Web sites that make use of Flash animation. Select and view three sites. Did you have to download a plug-in, or did you already have the necessary one on your system? Are the displayed graphics of high quality and does the animation enhance the site? How long was the load time? If the site had a Flash introduction, would you like the opportunity to skip the intro? Evaluate the three sites you viewed. Answer the previously listed questions and provide any other thoughts about your Flash experience in a one-page, double-spaced paper. Remember to cite the URL of each site.

4. **Internet Ethics** The one area of Internet use that seems to cause more controversy than others is downloading music. For some reason, the consensus is not as clear-cut on the legality of this behavior. Users compare downloading music to lending a CD to a friend. Producers and artists consider it theft. Using a search engine, identify at least two Web sites that facilitate music downloads. Review their policy, legal statements, and agreements. Who is liable if the sharing done on their site is found to be illegal? Are there any fees to subscribe to or use the site? In what country is the site being hosted? Attempt to locate statistics on the number of music downloads and the loss of revenue to the music and related industries related to downloading music files. In a PowerPoint presentation, review your findings for these and other related issues that you come across in your research. Suggest any viable solutions that you see as a compromise to this ongoing controversy. Remember to cite your references.

5. **Create Your Own Avatar** With all of the methods of animation that appear on the Internet, let's try one that is relatively new, an avatar. These talking images can be embedded within e-mails, Facebook pages, blogs, and Web sites. Using a search engine, locate a reputable Web site that allows you to create and publish you own avatar for free **www.voki.com** is just one suggestion). Some sites offer avatars of comic book characters, television personalities, and individuals from history. Locate a site and create and customize your avatar. Most sites allow you to choose an image and then change the features of that image. Once you have your avatar's appearance completed, you will need to add the words that you want the avatar to say. This can be done by recording the words yourself with a microphone, typing them into a text box, or uploading an audio file. If you are not using your own voice, you can select the voice to speak your content. Make the content of your recording focus on your experience with this method of communication. When your avatar is complete, publish it and send an e-mail to your instructor that includes the avatar.

Spotlight

Cloud Computing

Are you tired of storing your data on external hard drives, flash drives, and DVDs? Do you check these portable devices before you leave for school or work to make sure that they contain the information you need for the day? Are you frustrated with renaming versions of a file so that you know which file on which storage device is the most recent? Do you travel and need your files to be accessible from any location at any time of the day? If you answered yes to any of these questions, then cloud computing may be the solution you have been waiting for.

A few years ago cloud computing was a new buzzword and IT concept that was surrounded by confusion and uncertainty. Most individuals weren't sure exactly what cloud computing was. They didn't understand how it was going to affect IT departments, the academic environment, the business world, and enterprise planning for future technology resources. Today, *cloud computing* is a common term in IT circles, and articles about it, containing both positive and negative content, appear daily on RSS news feeds. It seems that it has gone from a buzzword to a reality while we were sleeping. No longer can it be ignored by individuals who use technology for work, education, or even entertainment. Cloud computing is here, and such companies as salesforce.com and Workday are trying to persuade the world that it is here to stay. This spotlight clarifies what cloud computing is, focusing on its essential characteristics, service categories, and deployment models, and pointing out both its positive and negative features. We'll also look at statistics that support cloud computing's predicted continuing growth.

What Is Cloud Computing?

The cloud has been a familiar image or symbol for the Internet for sometime; however, connecting it with the word *computing* has caused some confusion and created a blurry image. **Cloud computing**, according to the Computer Security Division of the National Institute of Standards and Technology, "is a model for enabling convenient, on-demand network access to a shared pool of configurable computing resources that can be rapidly provisioned and released with minimal management effort or service provider interaction. This cloud model promotes availability and is composed of five general characteristics: on-demand self-service, broad network access, resource pooling, rapid elasticity, and measured service".

That is quite a comprehensive definition. Let's start to break it down by first examining each of the listed general characteristics.

- **On-demand self-service.** The customer or subscriber, without the need to contact or interact with a human from the cloud provider (self-service), can increase or decrease computing requirements as needed (on-demand). Computing requirements can include such necessities as server use, network storage, and software applications.

- **Broad network access.** This is the most significant component of cloud computing. The services offered by a provider must be accessible over a network, from any location, and on any standardized platform, including mobile phones and PDAs. This means that the hardware and software that you use to perform tasks on your local computer are actually on someone else's system, the provider's. You access them through a network—for a fee. The Internet, the only network that provides this scope of capability, is the core of cloud computing and is associated with the cloud image that is a part of every cloud computing illustration.

The main component of cloud computing is the Internet, the broad network that acts as a delivery vehicle used to transport services from a provider to a subscriber.

- **Resource pooling.** This characteristic refers to the provider's ability to pool services to accommodate their use by multiple subscribers at the same time. These resources are assigned when a subscriber signs on and are dynamically reassigned as demands by other subscribers occur. The subscriber (user or client) is unaware of the location of the resources he or she is using or any reassignment taking place. In cloud computing, the user gets the programs and hardware support that he or she needs, and the provider (cloud owner) gets paid. In a cloud computing environment, the burden of work is on the cloud provider to maintain, upgrade, and administer the hosts (servers) that constitute their cloud.

- **Rapid elasticity.** This term refers to the ability of a subscriber to increase computing resources in spike or peak times without having to worry about overloading a system or having to purchase additional hardware for a minimal amount of high-performance need. The size and capacity of a cloud provider allow the subscriber to scale up or down as needed and pay for only the time and amount of services used.

- **Measured service.** The cloud provider must meter usage to use this information for billing, but more importantly, to analyze usage and respond appropriately. Predictions for changes and upgrades for a cloud provider are developed primarily from the data obtained from its usage meters. If it intends to keep subscribers, it must expand, reallocate, and change in a manner that meets its subscribers' needs.

In general, hosting computers (servers) and subscribers (clients) are the main components of cloud computing—just as they are in a traditional client/server network. So what distinguishes cloud computing from a traditional client/server network? There are three major differences:

- In cloud computing, the delivery of the services from the provider to a subscriber must be over the Internet.
- The services provided over the cloud by a provider are scalable; they can be increased or decreased as the needs of an individual subscriber or company

change. Services are typically offered and billed by the minute or hour.

- The services provided are managed completely by the cloud provider, the owner or manager of the host. The client or subscriber of the service does not have to worry about having a specific computer or operating system, or a certain processor or amount of RAM, and does not need to purchase software upgrades or download service patches. The subscribed services are not on the individual's computer or system. They are on the provider's hosts and are maintained by that provider and simply accessed by the subscriber.

Now that the main characteristics of cloud computing have been covered, let's investigate the three primary categories into which all cloud computing can be divided.

Cloud Computing Service Categories

The features offered by a cloud computing provider to a subscriber can be divided into three categories or models, depending on whether the services are hardware based, software based, or allow for application and interface development. The three main models of cloud computing services are: Infrastructure-as-a-Service (IaaS), Platform-as-a-Service (PaaS), and Software-as-a-Service (SaaS). Lets examine the focus of each.

INFRASTRUCTURE-AS-A-SERVICE (IAAS)

The category of cloud services that refers to the outsourcing of hardware, the equipment used to sustain the operations of a company or enterprise, is **Infrastructure-as-a-Service (IaaS)**. Because IaaS encompasses storage devices, actual servers, and network components it is also referred to as **Hardware-as-a-Service (HaaS)**. Providers of IaaS, such as Cloud.com, VMware, and Citrix, offer subscribers an offsite virtual datacenter as part of their information technology (IT) environment. This movement of the IT infrastructure from in-house to off premises aligns itself with the view that owning and operating a datacenter is no longer cost-effective.

Through the use of virtualization and grids, IaaS is able to provide the hardware structure and scalability needed for both small business and enterprise functions. In **virtualization**, the application and infrastructure are independent. This means that one physical machine can run several virtual machines. A **virtual machine** is not an actual physical machine, but a software-created segment of a hard drive that contains its own operating system and applications, which makes it behave as a separate physical machine in the eyes of the user. For a brief, humorous (yet informative) video on virtualization and cloud computing in plain English, go to **www.youtube.com/watch?v=XdBd14rjcs0&feature=player_embedded#!**

A **grid** is a combination of several computers or virtual machines that are connected over a network to make them appear and function as one single computer. The use of both virtualization and grids has made it possible for Infrastructure- as-a-Service to provide virtual datacenters and enable companies to eliminate the high cost of equipment and personnel to manage such a facility; focus more on their core business objectives; pay for only the equipment they use; and as a result, reduce the overall cost of doing business. The main factors driving enterprises to use Infrastructure-as-a-Service are as follows:

- Reduced budgeted outlay for equipment and its continual upgrade and maintenance
- Fast time to market with programs and ideas because the equipment needed to run them can be added to the cloud subscription
- The reassignment of IT personnel from a focus on learning and administering new equipment, because that is now done by the provider of the service, to more business-related tasks
- The replacement of unknown costs associated with running an in-house datacenter with known, pre-determined operating costs provided through set subscription rates based on the services used over a period of time

PLATFORM-AS-A-SERVICE (PAAS)

The category of cloud services that permits subscribers to have remote access to application development, interface development, database development, storage, and testing is **Platform-as-a-Service**. This is the feature that enables the creation and testing of subscriber-developed programs and interfaces, using a cloud provider's hardware and development environment. For the subscriber, this is a huge savings because the equipment

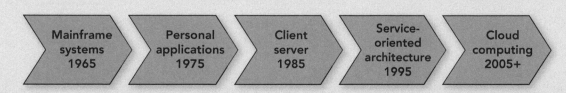

The development of IT infrastructure over time.

Mainframe systems 1965 → Personal applications 1975 → Client server 1985 → Service-oriented architecture 1995 → Cloud computing 2005+

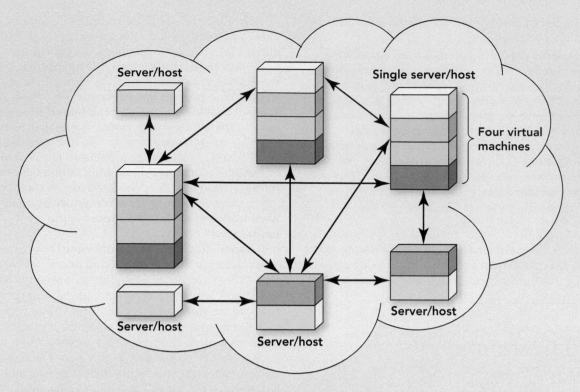

Virtualization and computer grids enable a cloud provider to create a network of widely dispersed computers and make it appear to run as a traditional centralized datacenter.

and software do not have to be purchased to test a possible application or interface and the fear of crashing a system during testing is alleviated by using the provider's secure test environment. Platform-as-a-Service providers include Google App Engine, Force.com, and Oracle SaaS.

SOFTWARE-AS-A-SERVICE (SAAS)

The most widely used and widely known form of cloud computing is **Software-as-a-Service (SaaS)**. The SaaS model of cloud computing enables software to be deployed from a cloud provider, delivered over the Internet, and accessed by a subscriber through a browser. Statistics from a recent survey of SaaS users by Datamation and THINKstrategies indicate that approximately 85 percent of subscribers are satisfied with the service, 80 percent would renew their subscriptions, and 61 percent would expand services. The primary reasons to subscribe to SaaS include these:

- Limited risk
- Rapid deployment
- Fewer upfront costs, such as the expense of purchasing a server
- Increased reliability as seen in reduced downtime caused by service disruptions
- Standardized backup procedures

- Lower total cost of ownership (TCO) through reduced hardware costs, software purchases, license agreements, and personnel to run and administer the systems

There are two major categories of SaaS: consumer services and business services. **Consumer-oriented services**, like those supplied by Google Apps and Google Docs, are offered to the public either on a subscription basis or, if supported by advertisement, for no cost. **Business services** are sold to enterprise and business organizations of all sizes, usually on a subscription basis. This category of SaaS services

Google Docs offers SaaS with a limited amount of storage to individual users, free of charge.

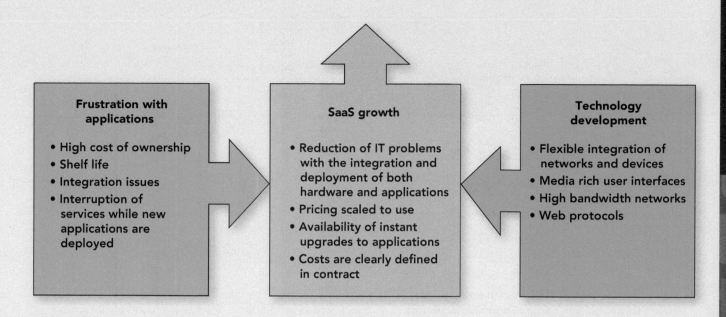

Key Factors in the High Success Rate of Software-as-a-Service

focuses on facilitating business practices, for example financial services and customer relationship management (CRM). Two of the main incentives for the success of Software-as-a-Service are the user's frustration with his or her installed applications and the maturity of technology that enables the sharing of an application by multiple users over a reliable, flexible, high-bandwidth network. Figure provides a more detailed list of factors behind the success of SaaS. Providers of Software-as-a-Service include Salesforce, Oracle on demand, and Google Apps.

The categories of cloud computing help to departmentalize cloud services, but how these services are deployed adds to their security and accessibility. Let's take a closer look at the main models of cloud deployment.

Cloud Deployment Methods

The way cloud services are accessed, owned, used, and physically located determines the deployment of the cloud service. There are three basic types of deployment models:

- **Private cloud.** A **private cloud** is operated for a single organization and its authorized users. The infrastructure can exist on-site or off-site and is controlled by either the organization or a contracted third party. A **community cloud** is an extension of a private cloud in which organizations with similar missions share the infrastructure to reduce cost. This variation of the private cloud disperses cost while providing a high level of

Features of Cloud Deployment Methods

Cloud Deployment	Managed by	Infrastructure Ownership	Infrastructure Location	Accessible by
Private cloud	Organization	Organization or third party	On premises or off premises	Trusted users
Public cloud	Third-party provider	Third-party provider	Off premises	Untrusted users
Hybrid cloud	Both the organization and third-party provider	Both the organization and third-party provider	Both on premises and off premises	Both trusted and untrusted users

Modified from **www.rationalsurvivability.com/blog/?p=743**

The type of cloud deployment chosen by an enterprise may be directly related to security issues.

conformity and security by allowing access only to trusted users. Google's Gov Cloud is an example of a community cloud.

- **Public cloud.** Available to the general public, large organizations, or a group of organizations, the **public cloud** offers the most risk because it is accessed by users that have not been authenticated or established as trusted. Its infrastructure is owned and operated by a cloud provider and is located off site.
- **Hybrid cloud.** The **hybrid cloud** deployment method is a combination of two or more clouds (private, community, or public) that are unique but are connected by common, standard technology that enables the sharing of applications and data. Its infrastructure can be located both on-site and off the premises, and it can be managed by both the organization and a cloud provider. Users can be trusted and untrusted.

A big difference between cloud deployment models is the concern over security. A careful needs assessment and examination of security requirements are key to making the right choices for cloud computing.

A private network operates in what can be viewed as its own private disconnected cloud. The only users are those authorized and approved by the organization that owns and manages the cloud. The entire private cloud, its services, and users are behind a firewall, a security device that is actually a combination of software and hardware that stops data from exiting a network or private cloud and filters data attempting to enter a network from the Internet or public cloud. While logged into a private network and accessing its resources, the right to use the Internet or public network may be denied.

A public cloud is the least secure deployment method because its infrastructure and resources are subscribed to from a cloud provider that operates

outside of the firewall. The provider of public cloud services is responsible for the security of the data and resources that it stores and provides to subscribers. This loss of control over security is a concern of some and a relief for other public cloud users.

A hybrid cloud is a combination of both types of deployment. In a hybrid cloud model, a portion of the cloud is private and behind the firewall, whereas another portion is public and outside of the firewall. Hybrids can be used to ease the transition from a private cloud to a public cloud or to secure portions of enterprise data in the private segment while still enabling access to the wide scope of services offered by public segment.

Any attempt to implement cloud computing will include a hard look at both the pros and cons of such a decision. Let's examine that area next.

Pros and Cons of Cloud Computing

Remember that technology is always changing, so the pros and cons of cloud computing will change with new developments. Additionally, something viewed as a negative feature by one enterprise or individual can be seen as an asset by another. A closer look at the current pros and cons of cloud computing might provide some insight into the features to consider if a move to the cloud is in your future.

THE PROS OF CLOUD COMPUTING

The cloud seems to present a delicate balance between benefits and risks. If subscribers are willing to manage some of the risks themselves and not rely completely on the provider, then the downside of cloud computing is less of a gamble. Let's first review the positive

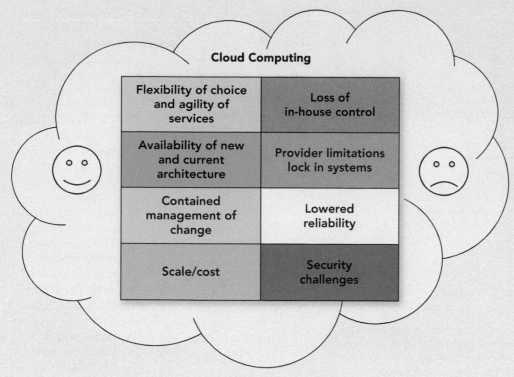

Cloud Computing

Flexibility of choice and agility of services	Loss of in-house control
Availability of new and current architecture	Provider limitations lock in systems
Contained management of change	Lowered reliability
Scale/cost	Security challenges

The Main Advantages (+) and Disadvantages (−) of Cloud Computing

providers to wrap an operating system and application in a self-contained segment of a hard drive, making it appear as if it were an independent stand-alone machine. Through the use of virtualization and a cloud operating system, hardware and associated technology can be maintained, redistributed, and redirected to accommodate a subscriber's request without major reconfiguration.

Choice and Agility

Without having to make costly commitments to hardware purchases and software licensing, cloud computing enables a subscriber to deploy solutions that best suit current needs and trends. It also allows flexibility to alter those solutions if the market or corporate financial situation changes. With this ability to amend solutions to match market demands comes the additional flexibility to choose among vendors. This freedom of choice is referred to as **interoperability**, the ability of a service from one provider to work with the services of another, without any subscriber interaction. What enables interoperability is **middleware**, a broad term for software that enables interoperability by assisting the passing of data among applications. Middleware provides a smooth and safe interface between network nodes and servers. The results are an improvement in overall performance and flexibility because a subscriber is not tied to one provider, an essential factor if a provider goes out of business or one of its datacenters goes down. Middleware is essential for scalability as well as interoperability in the cloud.

features of cloud computing in the light of today's technology.

Scale and Cost A big factor in transitioning to cloud computing for many organizations is the ability to meet increasing IT demands without having to absorb the high cost of equipment. This means that offerings can be expanded on a trial basis and analyzed to determine the business assets of such an implementation without accruing the "high cost of doing business." The organization or enterprise does not have to purchase equipment, license software, and hire personnel. If the innovation were not successful, the business's losses would be confined to the increase in the cloud subscription for the hardware, software, and management activities used for the period that the services were engaged. This is the beauty of cloud computing. Services can be scaled up or back depending on need. The only cost to the organization or enterprise is a change in their subscription rate that reflects the costs for only those services used.

Encapsulated Change Management The maintenance, upgrade, or even a total change to the infrastructure of an enterprise is no longer a huge concern because cloud providers make use of a cloud operating system and virtualization. A **cloud operating system**, like Windows Azure, is specially designed to run a cloud provider's datacenter and is delivered to subscribers over the Internet or other network. Recall that virtualization is used by cloud

Next-Generation Architectures The cloud enables innovation and creativity by allowing the testing and piloting of new database structures, languages, and framework through PaaS providers. Using this service provides a safe development environment, without the developer having to purchase expensive hardware and software or worrying that the deployment of the new application might interfere or crash their in-house system. Through cloud computing, innovation and foresight in IT areas are not a threat to the bottom line or current operations. Instead, they are viewed as futuristic and inventive.

Shifting from the positive to the negative, let's examine some of the shortcomings of cloud computing.

Lock-in Not all cloud providers offer interoperability or the agility of choice, so "buyer beware." If you foresee your needs changing or the need for a future application that one provider supplies and another does not, make sure that you are not locked in to your provider and can switch providers without losing your ability to access or read your data. Total interoperability within the cloud is one of the long-term goals of the "Open Cloud" movement.

Middleware is the reason that a change in provider, indicated by the dotted line, can appear seamless to a subscriber.

Reliability There is a possibility that the cloud provider will lose power, run into trouble, burn down, or simply go out of business. If any of these actions did occur and your provider did not have interoperable services, you might lose all of your data. If you believe that this could never happen, you are wrong. In mid-2009, within one week, there were power outages at several datacenters that host high-profile sites like the video site Daily motion, the credit card authorization service Authorize.net, and Microsoft's Bing Travel. Additionally, with the economy the way it is, it is not impossible that a cloud provider might have to go out of business for financial reasons. If this happens, how would you access your files? Once again "buyer beware." Read the subscription conditions carefully and look for the features that give you reliability, agility, and choice.

Lack of Control Some enterprise IT staff might be uncomfortable surrendering control over resources to someone else. Not only does cloud computing surrender control to a perfect stranger, but that stranger is someone somewhere in the cloud that in-house staff will probably never meet. Scheduled maintenance, upgrades, and backups are no longer done on the premises by employees but by the provider. Administrative tasks like adding users, deleting users, and altering access rights may be done either by the subscriber's IT staff or the provider. Letting go of the daily maintenance of your infrastructure can be a difficult concession to make to receive the benefits that the cloud offers.

Security There are hundreds, maybe thousands, of articles on the security, or lack of security, in the cloud. Many of the security concerns are centered on the data being stored on servers owned and controlled by the cloud provider not the subscriber. The main issues are over who actually owns the data, the secure storage of Social Security numbers and credit card numbers, and compliance with **Sarbanes-Oxley (SOX)**—an act administered by the Securities and Exchange Commission (SEC) that specifies the type of records that need to be stored and how long they must be kept, but leaves the method of storage up to the business.

This concern of ownership and security is heightened when a cloud provider, sometimes called the primary cloud, makes use of composite clouds. A **composite cloud** evolves when a primary cloud provider offers services that are distributed through another cloud provider. Such services can include storage, computing power, or application hosting. This nesting of cloud services can have serious reliability and security issues. In addition to ownership and compliance issues, there is also a loss of control over security when a service is deployed to a cloud provider.

With cloud computing **risk management**, the process of analyzing exposure to risk and determining how to best handle it within the tolerance level set by the enterprise, is transferred to the cloud provider. Chief security officers (CSOs) have the problem of defining the risk tolerance of the enterprise and then matching it with the risk tolerance of a cloud provider, a task that is not easily done. Choosing a private or hybrid cloud deployment is often based on security issues, with hybrid deployment often viewed as a transition or test of the services, including security, in the public cloud. An August 2009 survey of 200 information technology (IT) professionals reported that 43 percent felt that cloud computing was less secure than performing such services in house.

Another issue that CSOs have to deal with is that moving services to a cloud provider is often viewed by IT staff members as a threat to their positions. These individuals have the power to create havoc with corporate information and operations. In the same August 2009 report, 47 percent of the 200 IT professionals felt that a shift to cloud services was perceived as a prelude to a reduction in IT personnel. This is supported by the IBM claim that a business could see up to a 50 percent reduction in IT labor costs as the result of a shift to cloud computing.

So, in the end, it usually comes to some type of compromise between cost and risk management. For those shopping for a cloud provider, I guess the best advice is to realize that not all cloud providers are created equal. Conducting due diligence is essential when transferring services to the cloud. As the old saying goes, "All that glitters is not gold." For all of the positive arguments supporting cloud computing, those that oppose the technology can list an equal number of negative arguments. However, projections seem to indicate that even with its negative features, the future is in the cloud. A look at some of the current statistics and future projections might surprise you.

The Future of Cloud Computing

Every new and emerging technology sparks articles, arguments, and documentation from supporters and opponents. Cloud computing is no different. Statistics from an IDC report published in mid-2010 support the continued growth of cloud computing, despite the concerns over security. The report cited some interesting projections:

- In 2009, cloud services were centered in the western hemisphere, with the United States receiving 70.2 percent of the revenue. However, the report predicts that by 2014, that figure will decline to 51.4 percent, with Western Europe and the Asia/Pacific regions making up the difference.
- Worldwide revenue from public IT cloud computing was $16 billion in 2009. The report projects 2014 revenue to exceed $55.5 billion.
- Cloud computing is growing at a rate that is five times greater than any traditional IT product.
- Cloud applications (Software-as-a-Service) were the main service in 2009. The 2014 projection of revenue redistribution leans toward a decrease in the importance of this service (SaaS) and an increase in Infrastructure-as-a-Service (IaaS) and Platform-as-a-Service (PaaS).

Another survey completed in 2010 by the PEW Internet & American Life Project and Elon University's Imagining the Internet Center, using a nonrandom

sample of 895 Internet experts, supports the projection on migration to the cloud for applications and online storage.

Cloud computing is viewed as a means to test and distribute a new generation of killer apps, a method to penetrate global markets, and a means for smaller or medium-sized businesses to compete in the global market, because of decreased IT start-up costs.

As more and more organizations and individuals subscribed to cloud services, more and more providers appeared to compete for customers. This growth in providers led to the need for some guiding principles to provide a strategy for new cloud providers and realign those that already exist.

> "Conducting **due diligence** is **essential** when transferring **services** to **the cloud**."

GUIDELINES FOR THE GROWTH OF AN OPEN CLOUD

The current and predicted growth of cloud computing indicate that the number of cloud providers will also increase. In March 2009, the **Open Cloud Manifesto** was published. This document provided some guides and business practices for cloud providers in an attempt to guarantee subscribers the freedom of choice, flexibility, and openness they need in order to take full advantage of the benefits of cloud computing. Some of the key principles stressed include the following:

- Cloud providers must work together and collaborate to see that the vulnerabilities and assets of the cloud are addressed.
- A provider should not lock subscribers into its platform, thus removing their freedom of choice.
- Providers should reduce repetition of standards by using those in existence and create new ones that do not repeat or reinvent those that already exist.
- Any changes to the standards should be driven by subscribers, not the needs of the provider.

Since its publication, the manifesto has over 375 supporters and is still growing. You can view the complete document at **http://opencloudmanifesto.org/**

The Effect of Cloud Computing on the Enterprise

Cloud computing affects not only the workings of the information technology divisions of an enterprise but also the way the entire enterprise views and uses its cloud computing capability. Some of the effects that will result from shifting to the cloud for infrastructure, platform, and software include the following:

- IT costs will be more directly related to value. If the IT department can utilize the cloud to maximize capacity on demand and meet the fluctuating needs of its customers, the result of decreased computing costs will result in a decrease in the cost of goods sold—and thus an increase in overall market value of the enterprise.
- IT departments will be more agile. The ability of an enterprise to select or change providers as their needs change and the "open cloud" concept solidifies will make the corporate IT infrastructure more elastic, agile, and amenable to change.

- Creating and testing new innovations with a greatly reduced capital outlay will encourage businesses to promote creativity, resulting in more changes taking place in less time.
- The need to stay current with business and customer demands and requests is pushing the cloud toward real-time switching among cloud resources. Real-time switching is the seamless moving of cloud computing workloads between private clouds and public clouds to maximize the best value available at the time.

It appears that the sky is the limit and that the future is in the clouds!

Key Terms and Concepts

Multiple Choice

1. Which is *not* one of the three main categories of cloud computing services?
   a. Infrastructure-as-a-Service (IaaS)
   b. Platform-as-a-Service (PaaS)
   c. Communication-as-a-Service (CaaS)
   d. Software-as-a-Service (SaaS)

2. Which model of cloud computing services provides the servers, storage devices, and networks for a subscriber?
   a. Infrastructure-as-a-Service (IaaS)
   b. Platform-as-a-Service (PaaS)
   c. Communication-as-a-Service (CaaS)
   d. Software-as-a-Service (SaaS)

3. Which cloud deployment model is operated solely for a single organization and its authorized users?
   a. Community cloud   b. Hybrid cloud
   c. Public cloud   d. Private cloud

4. Which cloud characteristic refers to the ability of a subscriber to increase or decrease its computing requirements as needed without having to contact a human representative of the cloud provider?
   a. Rapid elasticity
   b. On-demand self service
   c. Broad network access
   d. Resource pooling

5. Which cloud deployment model is managed by a cloud provider, has an infrastructure that is off site, and is accessible to the general public?
   a. Community cloud
   b. Hybrid cloud
   c. Public cloud
   d. Private cloud

6. In which category of SaaS services does customer relationship management (CRM) software fall?
   a. Consumer services
   b. Communication services
   c. Infrastructure services
   d. Business services

7. Which statistic correctly represents cloud computing?
   a. In 2009, Western Europe received a majority of cloud computing revenue.
   b. Global cloud computing revenue for 2009 exceeded $16 million.
   c. Cloud computing growth is five times greater than any traditional IT product
   d. In 2009, the main cloud computing service was PaaS.

8. Which is considered the most widely used cloud computing service?
   a. Infrastructure-as-a-Service (IaaS)
   b. Platform-as-a-Service (PaaS)
   c. Communication-as-a-Service (CaaS)
   d. Software-as-a-Service (SaaS)

9. Interoperability is enabled by _____.
   a. a cloud operating system
   b. middleware
   c. a community cloud
   d. a composite cloud

10. Which refers to the practice of a primary cloud provider offering services that are distributed through another cloud provider?
    a. Hybrid cloud
    b. Composite cloud
    c. Virtualization
    d. Grid computing

Spotlight Exercises

1. View the video on cloud computing at **http://commoncraft.com/cloud-computing-video**. This is a very simple and easy to understand explanation of cloud computing. Using this video as a model, develop a simple PowerPoint presentation that explains how Software-as-a-Service can be beneficial for colleges and for students. Use a common cloud provider of SaaS, for example Google Docs, to make your presentation more specific and relative. Present the slide show to the class. Follow up the presentation with a discussion on how the cloud might be a viable option for your classmates as students or future employees.

2. Interview the chief information officer (CIO) at your school or the director of information technology (IT). Inquire about the possibility of the school moving to cloud computing. Ask if such considerations were included in the long-term plan and what the financial benefit for such a move would be to the school and the students. Come up with a few of your own questions to determine the direction that the administrators of your school are considering. Using a word processor, summarize your findings in a one-page, double-spaced report.

3. Create a free account in Google Docs, a Software-as-a-Service (SaaS) provider. Try the document, spreadsheet, and presentation applications for a few days. Transfer files from your portable storage device or hard disk drive to the cloud storage provided by Google Docs. Access the files in Google Docs' cloud storage from another location. See whether a file made in any of the applications on this site can be opened by any of the comparable Microsoft office applications. After a few days, using a word processor, summarize your experience in a one-page, double-spaced report.

4. A direct result of any new IT development is an abundance of new terms, acronyms, and organizations. Cloud computing is no different. Several cloud-related terms have surfaced: intercloud, cloud broker, and mashup. Additionally, several cloud-related organizations have emerged: Open Cloud Consortium, The Cloud Security Alliance, and The Global Inter-Cloud Technology Forum. Research each term and organization. For each term, provide a clear definition. Describe the mission of each organization. Compile your information into a one-page, double-spaced document. Remember to cite your sources.

5. This spotlight highlighted the three main categories of cloud services: IaaS, PaaS, and SaaS. Many providers provide additional services like MaaS, CaaS, and SaaS. In a PowerPoint presentation, using one or more slides for each service, define and provide details of at least five services not covered in this chapter. If possible, include the names of several cloud providers that offer each service. Remember to cite your references.

6. Using the Internet, locate five cloud providers. Using a table in a word processing document or a spreadsheet, list the five providers, their associated Web sites, and the services and resources that each offers.

Spotlight

Ethics

What's the difference between ethical and unethical behavior? Is it possible for an action to be unethical but still legal? You might not realize it, but in some way you probably face this question daily, especially when you use computers and, more specifically, the Internet. Have you downloaded any music recently, ripped any CDs lately, or copied music from a friend? Did you pay for that music? Have you watched a DVD movie or played a video game this weekend? Was the DVD or game a legally purchased copy? Perhaps you've posted a nasty comment about someone on a discussion board or sent an anonymous nasty e-mail that caused someone undo stress. These are some of the behaviors at school, home, or on the job to consider in the scope of ethical behavior.

Ethics is often described as knowing the difference between right and wrong, based on approved standards of social and professional behavior, and choosing to do what is right.
In other words, we *choose* to behave in an ethical way so we can live with our conscience. Ethics is not about whether we'll get caught but more about our ability to live with the decision we make.

This spotlight examines some of the most common issues in computer ethics, including ethical dilemmas, in which the difference between right and wrong is not so easy to discern. We look at ethical principles that can serve as guides for making decisions that might be difficult or in an unfamiliar area. Additionally, we consider the significance of a code of conduct. Ethical standards are provided to act as guides for computer users, professionals, and organizations. Finally we look at unethical behavior that is also illegal.

Ethical choices are often personal and are made with great consideration and thought by the individual making the choice. Hopefully, some of the insights in this chapter will help serve as a basic steering guide or reference points to alleviate some of the uncertainty surrounding making ethical decisions even when they are difficult.

Computer Ethics for Computer Users

It isn't always easy to determine the right thing to do. Even when you know what's right, it isn't always easy to act on it. Peer pressure is a tremendous force. Why should you be the one to do the right thing when you believe everyone else is getting away with using copied software and music files?

Computers cause new ethical dilemmas by pushing people into making decisions in unprecedented situations. **Computer ethics** is the use of basic ethical principles to help you make the right decisions in your daily computer use. Ethical principles help you think through your options.

Computers present new ethical dilemmas where individuals must choose among paths they are unfamiliar with.

ETHICAL PRINCIPLES

An **ethical principle** defines the standards that promote trust, fairness, good behavior, and kindness. These principles are used as justification for considering an act or a rule to be morally right or wrong. Over the centuries, philosophers have come up with many ethical principles. For many people, it's disconcerting to find that these principles sometimes conflict. An ethical principle is only a tool that you can use to think through a difficult situation. In the end, you must make your choice and live with the consequences.

The Belmont Report from the U.S. Department of Health, Education, and Welfare shows three of the most useful ethical principles:

- *An act is ethical if, were everyone to act the same way, society as a whole would benefit.*

- *An act is ethical if it treats people as an end in themselves rather than as a means to an end.*

- *An act is ethical if impartial observers would judge that it is fair to all parties concerned.*

If you still find yourself in an ethical dilemma related to computer use even after careful consideration of these ethical principles, talk to people you trust. They might be able to provide insight into the dilemma that you face, pointing out factors that you might have not considered, helping you to make the correct ethical decision. Make sure you have all the facts. Think through alternative courses of action based on the different principles. Would you be proud if your parents knew what you had done? What if your actions were mentioned in an article on the front page of your local newspaper? Can you live with your conscience? Remember, always strive to find a solution you can be proud of and live with.

FOLLOWING YOUR SCHOOL'S CODE OF CONDUCT

When you use a computer, one of the things you will have to determine is who owns the data, programs, and Internet access you enjoy. If you own your computer system and its software, the work you create is clearly yours, and you are solely responsible for it. However, when you use a computer at school or at work, it is possible that the work you create there might be considered the property of the school or business. In short, you have greater responsibility and less control over content ownership when you use somebody else's system than when you use your own.

Sometimes this question isn't just an ethical one but a legal one as well. How companies and schools enforce computer usage rules tends to vary. So where can you, the college computer user, find guidance when dealing with ethical and legal dilemmas? Your college or place of employment probably has its own code of conduct or **acceptable use policy** for computer users. You can usually find this policy on your organization's Web site (Figure 1B), in a college or employee handbook, or included in an employment contract that you have been asked to sign. You might call the help desk at your computing center and ask for the Web site address of the policy or request a physical copy of it. Read the policy carefully and follow the rules.

Common to most acceptable-use policies are such guidelines as these:

- **Respect yourself.** If you obtain an account and password to use the campus computer system, don't give your password to others. They could do something that gets you in trouble. In addition, don't say or do anything on the Internet that could reflect

Many organizations and schools publish their computer and network use (or acceptable use) policy on their Web site.

poorly on you, even if you think no one will ever find out. Internet content has a way of resurfacing.

- **Respect others.** Obviously, you shouldn't use a computer to threaten or harass anyone. You should also avoid using more than your share of computing resources, such as disk space. If you publish a Web page on your college's computers, remember that your page's content affects the college's public image.

- **Respect academic integrity.** Always give credit for text you've copied from the Internet. Obtain permission before you copy pictures. Don't copy or distribute software unless the license specifically states you have permission to do so.

Classroom computer etiquette is increasingly becoming an academic issue. Within their course syllabi, instructors are providing clear guidelines for the use of computers and portable devices, such as cell phones, in a classroom. Such statements may look like the excerpt below and even tie improper use to a grade reduction.

Appropriate Classroom Laptop Use . . . Although having a laptop [or other portable device] in class opens up new learning possibilities for students, sometimes students utilize it in ways that are inappropriate. Please refrain from instant messaging, e-mailing, surfing the Internet, playing games, writing papers, doing homework, etc., during class time. Acceptable uses include taking notes, following along with the instructor on PowerPoint, with demonstrations, and other whole-class activities, as well as working on assigned in-class activities, projects, and discussions that require laptop use. It is easy for your laptop

[or portable device] to become a distraction to you and to those around you. Inappropriate uses will be noted and may affect your final grade.

TEN COMMANDMENTS FOR COMPUTER ETHICS

The Computer Ethics Institute of the Brookings Institution, located in Washington, DC, has developed the following "Ten Commandments for Computer Ethics" for computer users, programmers, and system designers. Many businesses, academic institutions, and organizations post or refer to these principles:

1. Thou shalt not use a computer to harm other people.
2. Thou shalt not interfere with other people's computer work.
3. Thou shalt not snoop around in other people's computer files.
4. Thou shalt not use a computer to steal.
5. Thou shalt not use a computer to bear false witness.
6. Thou shalt not copy or use proprietary software for which you have not paid.
7. Thou shalt not use other people's computer resources without authorization or proper compensation.
8. Thou shalt not appropriate other people's intellectual output.
9. Thou shalt think about the social consequences of the program you are writing or the system you are designing.
10. Thou shalt always use a computer in ways that ensure consideration and respect for your fellow humans.

NETIQUETTE

General principles such as the "Ten Commandments for Computer Ethics" are useful for overall guidance, but they don't provide specific help for the special situations you'll run into online—such as how to behave properly in chat rooms or while playing an online game. As a result, computer and Internet users have developed a lengthy series of specific behavior guidelines called **netiquette** for the various Internet services available

Netiquette refers to guidelines for behaving properly in online interactions.

(such as e-mail, mailing lists, social networking sites, discussion forums, and online role-playing games) that provide specific pointers on how to show respect for others—and for yourself—while you're online. A document posted by the Responsible Use of the Network Working Group (RUN) of the Internet Engineering Task Force at **www.dtcc.edu/cs/rfc1855.html** provides detailed netiquette guides for online activities that effect one-to-one and one-to-many communications.

A consolidation of rules from the site above and **www.albion.com/netiquette** as well as other Internet sources are categorized and summarized below.

- **Discussion forums.** Before posting to a discussion forum, review the forum and various topics to see what kinds of questions are welcomed and how to participate meaningfully. If the forum has a FAQ (frequently asked questions) document posted on the Web, be sure to read it before posting to the forum; your question may already have been answered in the FAQ. Post your message under the appropriate topic or start a new topic if necessary. Your post should be helpful or ask a legitimate question. Bear in mind that some people using the discussion forum may not speak English as their native language, so don't belittle people for spelling errors. Don't post inflammatory messages; never post in anger. If you agree with something, don't post a message that says "Me too"—you're just wasting everyone's time. Posting ads for your own business or soliciting answers to obvious homework questions is usually frowned on.

- **E-mail.** Check your e-mail daily and respond promptly to the messages you've been sent. Download or delete messages after you've read them so that you don't exceed your disk-usage quota. Remember that e-mail isn't private; you should never send a message that contains anything you wouldn't want others to read. Always speak of others professionally and courteously; e-mail is easily forwarded, and the person you're describing may eventually see the message. Check your computer frequently for viruses that can propagate via e-mail messages. Keep your messages short and to the point; focus on one subject per message. Don't type in all capital letters; this comes across as SHOUTING. Spell check your e-mail as you would any other written correspondence, especially in professional settings. Watch out for sarcasm and humor in e-mail; it often fails to come across as a joke. Requesting a return receipt may be an acceptable academic policy to verify the submission of an assignment, but in some situations it might be considered an invasion of privacy.

- **Instant messages (IM) and text messages.** IM and text messages are ideal for brief conversa-

tions; but complex or lengthy discussions may be better handled in person, by e-mail, or by phone. IM can be easily misinterpreted because tone is difficult to convey. Never share bad news or a major announcement in a text message or send an IM while you are angry or upset. Don't assume that everyone knows what IM acronyms such as BRB (be right back) and LOL (laughing out loud) mean. Be mindful that some smartphone plans still charge for text messages. Also, remember to set away messages and use other status messages wisely.

- **Chat rooms.** Only visit chat rooms that are appropriate for your age and follow the rules and regulations of the chat. If you are unsure of the protocols, contact the administrator or host of the chat room. Say hello when you enter the room, and take some time to review the conversation currently taking place before jumping in. Avoid entering personal information, and respect other chatters. Foul language may get you expelled or permanently banned from the room. Some rooms allow you to put a chatter on ignore status if you are being bothered by that person. This type of behavior should be immediately reported to the administrator or chat room host.

Netiquette is important in the classroom. According to an article published in *The Journal of Higher Education*, several colleges have offered guidelines and suggestions for curbing misuse of computers in class and have set netiquette standards, like turning off the computer's volume before class begins.

In addition to respectful use of Internet services, playing computer games is another area in which you might face ethical dilemmas.

COMPUTER GAMES: TOO MUCH VIOLENCE?

Computer gaming isn't universally admired, but statistics support that it is universally on the increase. Sixty-five percent of households in the United States have at least one member who plays video games. Seventeen billion hours have been logged on Xbox Live by some 20 million players; this is roughly two hours for every person on the planet. To further support this growth, recent statistics estimate online gaming revenue at $15 billion. How is this related to ethics? Approximately 94 percent of the video games fall into the fantasy category and include such titles as *Halo*, *World of Warcraft*, and *Call of Duty: Modern Warfare*. These games emphasize strategy development and team play, but they also emphasize violent behaviors. Parents and politicians are concerned that children who play these games may be learning aggressive behaviors that will prove dysfunctional in real life.

> "Remember that **e-mail** isn't private; you should **never** send a **message** that contains anything you wouldn't **want** others **to read**"

Fears concerning the impact of violent computer games were heightened by the Columbine High School tragedy in 1999, in which two Littleton, Colorado, teenagers opened fire on teachers and fellow students before committing suicide. Subsequently, investigators learned that the boys had been great fans of splatter games such as *Doom* and *Quake* and may have patterned their massacre after their gaming experiences. In 2009, there was a school shooting in Germany that left 15 dead. A neighbor and childhood friend of the shooter was quoted as saying, "He [the shooter] was fascinated by video games; he used to play a shooting game called *Tactical Ops* and he used to watch horror films like *Alien* and *Predator*."

Still, psychologists disagree on the effect of violent computer games. Some point out that they're little more than an extension of the World War II "combat" games children used to play on street corners before television—and the computer—came along. Others claim that violent video games provide an outlet for aggression that might otherwise materialize in homes and schools.

One thing is for certain: Computer games are becoming more violent. In the past few years, the video game industry has released a slew of new titles that offer a more streamlined gaming experience, particularly when a player is connected to the Internet in multiplayer mode—and of course, much more realistic portrayals of violent acts.

So who is responsible? Is it the software manufacturers who create the programs? Is it the consumers who purchase and use the programs? More importantly, is there anything you can do about it? Refer back to the "Ten Commandments for Computer Ethics," especially numbers 9 and 10. Think about the personality of the person you are purchasing a game for or inviting to play a game. If the content of the game seems to be inappropriate, select a different game or activity. With regard to minors, parents certainly have a responsibility over what their children do, but what about you—do you make "good" decisions when it comes to your own exposure to violence?

Now that you know about the ethical issues individuals face, let's take a look at how organizations deal with computer ethics.

Computer Ethics for Organizations

Every day, newspapers carry stories about people getting into trouble by using their computers to conduct personal business while they're at work. In many cases, the offenders use company computers to browse the Web, make personal travel plans, send personal e-mail on company time, or to commit crimes such as cyberstalking or distributing pornography. The use of a company computer for non-business-related tasks is generally prohibited. Such policies are typically included in the company's acceptable use policy.

However, those are rules set by the company to control individuals' behavior while at work. What ethical responsibilities do the companies themselves have to their employees, customers, and the general public? A business or organization needs to protect its data from loss, damage, error, and misuse. Each business entity needs to have business continuity and disaster recovery plans in place to prevent and respond to security breaches or other malfunctions that occur.

Protecting data from loss or change is often simply a matter of following proper backup procedures. **Backup procedures** involve making copies of data files to protect against data loss, change, or damage from natural or other disasters. Without backup procedures, an organization may place its customers' information at risk. Moreover, it is unethical not to keep regular

Some computer games are both engrossing and violent.

backups, because the loss of the company's data could negatively impact the stakeholders in the business. What would happen to a bank, for example, if it lost all of its data and didn't have any backups? As our dependency on information increases, our tolerance for lost data is decreasing. It is this dependency that has led to the use of **continuous backups**, programs that automatically create a backup when a change in a system or a data file occurs.

Data errors can and do occur. It is the ethical responsibility of any organization that deals with data to ensure that its data is as correct as possible. Data that hasn't been properly maintained can have serious effects on the individual or associated organization.

Data misuse occurs when an employee or company fails to keep data confidential. A breach of confidentiality occurs when an employee looks up data about a person in a database and uses that information for something other than what was intended. For example, U.S. government workers accessed the passport files for 2008 presidential candidates John McCain, Barack Obama, and Hillary Clinton, in addition to more than 100 celebrities. Such actions are grounds for termination.

Companies may punish employees for looking up customer data, but many of them think nothing of

A backup system can help protect a business's information assets and enable the business to continue to operate as usual. A computer tape library is one way to store backed-up files.

considered the most innovative and far reaching. According to the ACM general moral imperatives, a computing professional

1. Contributes to society and human well-being
2. Avoids harm to others
3. Is honest and trustworthy
4. Is fair and takes action not to discriminate on the basis of race, sex, religion, age, disability, or national origin
5. Honors property rights, including copyrights and patents
6. Gives proper credit when using the intellectual property of others
7. Respects the right of other individuals to privacy
8. Honors confidentiality.

selling it to third parties. A mail-order company, for example, can gain needed revenue by selling customer lists to firms marketing related products. Privacy advocates believe that it's unethical to divulge customer data without first asking the customer's permission. These advocates are working to pass tougher privacy laws so the matter would become a legal concern, not an ethical one.

As an employee, what can you do to stop companies from misusing data or to protect your customers' privacy? Often, there's no clear-cut solution. If you believe that the way a company is conducting business poses a danger to the public or appears to be illegal, you can report the company to regulatory agencies or the press, an action called whistle-blowing. But what if your whistle-blowing causes your company to shut down, putting not only you but also all of your coworkers out of work? As this example illustrates, codes of ethics don't solve every ethical problem, and innocent individuals may suffer as a result of an ethical action; however, ethical principles at least provide solid guidance for most situations.

Computer Ethics for Computer Professionals

No profession can stay in business for long without a rigorous (and enforced) code of professional ethics. That's why many different types of professionals subscribe to ethical **codes of conduct**. These codes are developed by professional associations, such as the Association for Computing Machinery (ACM).

THE ACM CODE OF CONDUCT

Of all the computing associations' codes of conduct, the one developed by the ACM (**www.acm.org**) is

Like other codes of conduct, the ACM code places public safety and well-being at the top of the list.

CODE OF CONDUCT FOR THE INSTITUTE FOR CERTIFICATION OF COMPUTING PROFESSIONALS

Other organizations also have codes of conduct or define elements of good practice for professionals. The Institute for Certification of Computing Professionals is one such organization. It prides itself on the establishment of professional standards for those who work with computers. According to the organization, the essential elements related to conduct that identify a professional activity are as follows:

- A high standard of skill and knowledge
- A confidential relationship with people served
- Public reliance upon the standards of conduct and established practice
- The observance of an ethical code

SAFETY FIRST

Computer professionals create products that affect many people and may even expose them to risk of personal injury or death. Increasingly, computers and computer programs figure prominently in safety-critical systems, including transportation monitoring (such as with air traffic control) and patient monitoring in hospitals.

Consider the following situation. An airplane pilot flying in poor visibility uses a computer, called an autopilot, to guide the plane. The air traffic control system also relies on computers. The plane crashes. The investigation discloses minor bugs in both computer programs. If the plane's computer had been dealing with a person in the tower rather than a computer or if the air

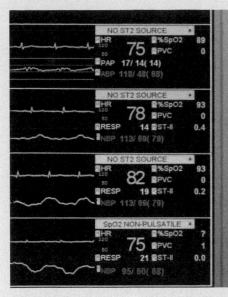

Patient monitoring in hospitals helps to create a safer environment, with audio warnings and information automatically transmitted to a central, monitoring station.

traffic control program had been interacting with a human pilot, the crash would not have occurred. Where does the liability lie for the loss of life and property?

Experienced programmers know that programs of any size have bugs. Most complex programs have so many possible combinations of conditions that it isn't feasible to test for every combination. In some cases, the tests would take years; in other cases, no one could think of all the possible conditions. Because bugs are inevitable and programmers can't predict all the different ways programs interact with their environment, most computer experts believe that it's wrong to single out programmers for blame.

Software companies are at fault if they fail to test and document their products. In addition, the organization that buys the software may share part of the blame if it fails to train personnel to use the system properly.

At the center of every computer code of ethics is the underlying intention of computer professionals to develop, maintain, upgrade, and evaluate programs and devices to preserve and protect human life and to avoid harm or injury. If the public is to trust computer professionals, those professionals must have the ethics needed to protect our safety and welfare—even if doing so means that the professional or the company he or she works for suffers financially.

Unlike the ethical dilemmas we've discussed up to now, right and wrong are more easily defined when it comes to matters of the law.

It's Not Just Unethical, It's Illegal Too

Some unethical actions are also illegal and have serious consequences. Let's start with something that gets many college students into serious trouble: plagiarism.

Imagine the following scenario. It's 4 AM, and you have a paper due for your 9 AM class. While searching for sources on the Internet, you find a Web site with an essay on your topic. What's wrong with downloading the text, reworking it a bit, and handing it in? Plenty.

The use of someone else's intellectual property (their ideas or written work) is called **plagiarism**. Plagiarism predates computers; in fact, it has been practiced for thousands of years. But, computers—and especially the Internet—make the temptation and ease of plagiarizing even greater. It's not only very easy to copy and paste from the Internet but some sites are actually set up specifically to sell college-level papers to the lazy or desperate. The sites selling the papers aren't guilty of plagiarism, but you are if you turn in the work as your own.

Plagiarism is a serious offense. How serious? At some colleges, even a first offense can get you thrown out of school. You might think it's rare for plagiarizers to be caught, but the truth is that college instructors are often able to detect plagiarism in students' papers without much effort. The tip-off can be a change in the sophistication of phraseology, writing that is a little too polished, or errors in spelling and grammar that are identical in two or more papers. Software programs such as Turnitin are available that can scan text and then compare it against a library of known phrases. If a paper has one or more recognizable phrases, it is marked for closer inspection. Furthermore, even if your actions are not discovered now, someone could find out later, and the evidence could void your degree and even damage your career.

The more well-known you are, the more you're at risk of your plagiarism being uncovered. Take noted historian and Pulitzer Prize–winning author Doris Kearns Goodwin, for example. In 2002, she was accused of plagiarizing part of her best-selling 1987 book, *The Fitzgeralds and the Kennedys*. Although she claimed her plagiarizing was inadvertent and due to inadequate research methods, she suffered a significant decline in credibility and even felt obligated to leave her position at the PBS news program *NewsHour with Jim Lehrer*. It took 15 years for Goodwin's plagiarism to come to light.

Plagiarism is both unethical and illegal: The unethical part is the dishonesty of passing someone else's work off as your own. The illegal part is taking the material without permission. Plagiarizing copyrighted material is called **copyright infringement**, and you can be sued and may have to pay damages in addition to compensating your victim for any financial losses due to your theft of the material. Trademarks, products, and patented processes are also protected. If you're tempted to copy anything from the Web, bear

Turnitin is one of the popular software packages used by professors at colleges and universities to identify instances of plagiarism.

in mind that the United States is a signatory to international copyright regulations, which specify that an original author does not need to include an explicit copyright notice to be protected under the law.

Does this mean you can't use the Internet source you found? No, you can use or refer to your source, but you must follow certain citation guidelines. In academic writing, you can make use of someone else's effort if you use your own words and give credit where credit is due. If you use a phrase or a few sentences from the source, use quotation marks. Attach a bibliography and list the source. For Internet sources, you should list the Web site's address (or Uniform Resource Locator [URL]), the date the article was published (if available), the date and time you accessed the site, the name of the article, and the author's name. You can usually find a link at the bottom of a Web site's home page that outlines the owner's copyright policy. If not, there is usually a "contact us" link that you can use to contact the owner. You cannot assume that it is legal to copy content from a Web site just because you cannot find a disclaimer. Starting with Microsoft Office 2007, adding citations to a research paper became even easier. One of the features of the software is a tool to help you organize and input the correct reference information in a variety of different referencing styles.

You'll often hear people use the term **fair use** to justify illegal copying. The fair use doctrine justifies *limited* uses of copyrighted material without payment to or permission from the copyright holder. This means that a *brief* selection from a copyrighted work may be excerpted for the purposes of commentary, parody, news reporting, research, and education. Such excerpts are short—generally, no more than 5 percent of the original work—and they shouldn't compromise the commercial value of the work. Of course, you must still cite the source. In general, the reproduction of an entire work is rarely justifiable by means of the fair use doctrine.

As a responsible computer user, you should be concerned not only about wrongly using someone else's words but also about the correctness of the content you create yourself. The written word carries a lot of power. Publishing words that are untrue about a business or individual could be crossing into dangerous, and illegal, territory.

LIBEL

The power of computers, with their ease of uploading, publishing, and reaching a huge group of viewers in seconds, has also caused an increase in cases of libel. In the United States, **libel** is the publication, in written or faxed form, of a false statement that injures someone's business or personal reputation. A plaintiff who sues for libel must prove that a false statement caused injury and demonstrate some type of resulting damage. This could include being shunned by friends and associates or the inability to obtain work because potential employers believed the false accusations. Some states allow a jury to assess damages based generally on harm to the person's reputation. It is in your best interest to ensure that any electronic publication statement you make about an individual or a corporation is truthful.

SOFTWARE PIRACY

Here's another common situation. You need to have Microsoft Office 2007 for your computer class. A friend gives you a copy that she got from her mom's office. You've just installed that copy on your computer. Have you done something wrong? Yes, of course you have! In fact, so has your friend. It is illegal for her to have a copy of the software from her mom's office in the first place.

Just like written works, most computer software (including computer games) is copyrighted, which means that you can't make copies for other people without infringing on the software's copyright. Such infringements are called **software piracy** and are a federal offense in the United States.

How serious is software piracy? The information technology industry loses billions of dollars a year because of piracy. If you're caught pirating software, you may be charged with a felony. If you're convicted of a felony, you could spend time in jail, lose the right to vote, and ruin your chances for a successful career.

When you purchase commercial software, you're really purchasing a **software license**, which generally grants you the right to make backups of the program disks and install the software. You need to read the license agreement to determine how many machines you can install the software on. You are not allowed to provide the program to others or modify the program's function. A blank sample of a software license can be

The Software & Information Industry Association (SIIA) is trying to raise consciousness about software piracy.

found at **www.lawsmart.com/documents/ software_license.shtml.** Note that this is a sample, and reading it is *not* a substitute for examining the software license for each program you purchase.

Free programs that users can copy or modify without restriction are called **public domain software**. However, don't assume that a program is public domain unless you see a note (often in the form of a Read Me text file) that explicitly identifies the file as being copyright free.

Unlike public domain software, you can't copy or modify **shareware** programs without permission from the owner. You can usually find the owner and licensing information by accessing the Help menu or by locating and reading a Read Me file that is usually placed in the same directory as the program. You may, however, freely copy trial or evaluation versions of shareware programs. When the evaluation period expires, you must pay a **registration fee** or delete the software from your computer.

Other programs qualify under the provisions of the Free Software Foundation's **General Public License (GPL)**, which specifies that anyone may freely copy, use, and modify the software, but no one can sell it for profit.

Organizations with many computers (including colleges) also have to be concerned about software piracy. A **site license** is a contract with the software publisher that allows an organization to use multiple copies of the software at a reduced price per unit. Taking copies outside the organization usually violates the contract. However, check the license agreement. Some organizations negotiate the agreement to allow employees to load the software on their home computers as well, as long as only one copy is in use at any one time and the programs are used for academic and noncommercial tasks.

Software manufacturers are working very hard to develop **copyright protection schemes** to thwart the illegal use of their programs. Increasingly, software is becoming **machine dependent**. This means that the program captures a machine ID during the installation process and writes that ID back to the software company's server during a mandatory online registration process. If you attempt to install the program on another machine, the code will be checked and the installation will terminate unless your license allows multiple installations. Microsoft checks your computer for a valid copy of its software before it will permit you to make updates, access templates, or download other add-ons.

How can you tell whether you're guilty of software piracy? All of the following actions are illegal:

- *Continuing to use a shareware program past the evaluation version's expiration date without paying the registration fee.*
- *Violating the terms of a software license, even if you've paid for the program. For example, if you have copies of the same program on your desktop and notebook computers but the license allows only one installation, you are in violation of the license.*
- *Making copies of site-licensed programs that you use at work or school and installing them on your home computer (unless expressly allowed through the license).*

- *Giving or selling copies of commercial software to others.*
- *Incorporating all or part of a GPL program in a commercial program that you offer for sale.*

Do you have pirated programs on your computer? The police aren't likely to storm into your home or dorm room and take you away kicking and screaming. Most software piracy prosecutions target individuals who are trying to distribute or sell infringing copies, or companies that have illegally made multiple copies for their employees. If you have any pirated software, you should remove those programs from your computer right away. In the future, consider whether your actions constitute software piracy before the software is installed on your computer. If you still don't see the need to delete pirated software from your computer, consider this: It's very, very wise to become accustomed to a zero-tolerance approach to pirated software. If you're caught with an infringing program at work, you could lose your job. A company can't risk retaining employees who expose the firm to prosecution. There are software auditing applications that a school or company can purchase to monitor software usage.

Some software sold on auction sites and installed on systems created by build-it-yourself computer vendors may be unlicensed (and therefore illegal) software. Ask for the product registration key and the original CDs or DVDs for any products purchased online or pre-installed on a system. A **product registration key** is a unique alphanumeric code specific to that particular copy of the program. It is necessary to enter this key after installation in order to validate its authenticity and activate the program. The key may be necessary later to download upgrades, patches, or templates.

The Business Software Alliance (BSA) helps combat software piracy by educating the public and businesses about the legal and safety issues regarding commercial software use. You can even fill out a confidential form on their Web site at **https://reporting.bsa.org/usa** to report incidences of piracy. By doing so, you could be eligible for a $1 million reward.

FILE SHARING: MUSIC, MOVIES, AND MORE

You may have heard that it's okay to download a copyrighted MP3 file as long as you keep it for no longer than 24 hours, but that's false. If you upload music copied from a CD you've paid for, you are violating the law. You can't justify spreading a band's copyrighted music around by saying it's "free advertising;" if the group wants advertising, they'll arrange it themselves. Moreover, don't fall into the trap of thinking that sharing MP3s is legal as long as you don't charge any money for them. Anytime you're taking royalties away from copyright holders, it's illegal.

Several years ago eschoolnews.com reported that more than 400 students were slated to be sued for allegedly using Internet2, a network of academic, business, government, and not-for-profit organizations, for music and movie piracy. The situation has not improved significantly. A 2008 survey found that the average digital music player contains 842 illegally copied songs. Although many people seem to believe that illegal file sharing is okay because so many others are doing it, the entertainment industry is fighting back. Ohio State University recently led the nation in music piracy—its students received more than 2,300 warning letters about pirated music in just one school year. A report by the Institution for Policy Innovation (IPI) indicates that not only is the copyright holder of the pirated digital product injured, but so are all citizens and taxpayers. As a result of global and U.S. piracy, the report states:

- The U.S. economy losses $12.5 billion annually.
- Approximately 71,000 jobs are lost in the United States in both the recording industry and related fields.
- U.S. workers lose $2.7 billion in annual earnings.
- U.S. federal, state, and local governments lose $422 million in annual tax revenue.

More recently, a 2009 report estimated 9 million pirated e-book copies were downloaded, representing nearly $3 billion in lost revenue. However, in April 2010, the U.S. Government Accountability Office issued a report on the economic effects of counterfeit and pirated goods. This statement concluded that after reviewing data from both government and outside sources, it was "difficult, if not impossible, to quantify economy-wide impacts." The reason for this statement is cited as being the inability to accurately detect and account for pirated activity due to the illegal and undetectable nature of piracy itself, and that prior statistics assumed that the obtaining of a pirated copy implied

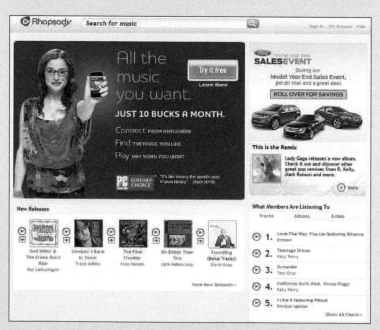

Sites such as Rhapsody offer fans the opportunity to play music, not download it, by connecting to their Web site for a price of $10 a month.

the loss of sale of a legitimate copy, again an assumption that is unsubstantiated. Statistics can always be argued and slanted to support one's favored opinion. However, any illegal or counterfeit copy of any product is a source of lost income in any economy. The size of the loss can be debated—but not the loss itself.

Students can face fines or even jail time for copyright infringement, but schools may also be penalized. Some colleges are taking steps to reduce their liability, such as limiting bandwidth and providing students with free, legal download service.

Key Terms and Concepts

Multiple Choice

1. Which action is *not* behavior that illustrates academic integrity?
   a. Citing the reference to a source of information that you copied from the Internet or a printed source
   b. Sharing licensed software without permission
   c. Obtaining permission before using an image obtained from the Internet or other source
   d. Using only your allotted share of computer resources

2. In which Internet interaction should the participant check the frequently asked questions document (FAQ) prior to posting his or her own question?
   a. E-mail   b. Chat room
   c. Discussion forum   d. Instant messaging

3. _____ is/are basic ethical principles or guidelines that can be used to help you make the right decisions in your daily computer use.
   a. Computer ethics   b. Netiquette
   c. Code of conduct   d. Acceptable use policy

4. What term refers to the act of using someone else's intellectual property as if it were your own?
   a. Acceptable use policy
   b. Piracy
   c. Libel
   d. Plagiarism

5. What defines the standards that promote trust, fairness, good behavior, and kindness, and is used as justification for considering an act or a rule to be morally right or wrong?
   a. Code of conduct
   b. Acceptable use policy
   c. Netiquette
   d. Ethical principle

6. Which is a true statement about ethics?
   a. Ethics is concerned about getting caught.
   b. Some unethical actions are legal.
   c. Ethical actions are evaluated by the consequences they produce, not their innate value of right or wrong.
   d. Peer pressure is not a factor in ethical behavior.

7. What is the term for publishing of a false statement that injures someone's business or personal reputation?
   a. Piracy
   b. Libel
   c. Plagiarism
   d. Whistle-blowing

8. Which action is considered illegal?
   a. Uploading music from a CD that you paid for
   b. Downloading a copyrighted MP3 file and listening to it for only 24 hours, then deleting it
   c. Sharing MP3s with others as long as you do not charge a fee for the music
   d. All of the above

9. What is the lengthy series of specific behavior guidelines developed for computer and Internet users in general?
   a. Netiquette
   b. "Ten Commandments for Computer Ethics"
   c. Code of conduct
   d. Acceptable use policy

10. The use of no more than 5 percent of a copyrighted document, without payment or permission, is called _____.
    a. Piracy
    b. Copyright infringement
    c. Fair use
    d. Plagiarism

Spotlight Exercises

1. Obtain the acceptable use policy provided by your school. Have you ever seen this policy without actively searching for it? If so, where did you see it for the first time? In a one-page, double-spaced report created in a word processing program, summarize the policy. Cite the statements that you think are the most aggressive and those that you believe are overkill or unnecessary. Overall, do you feel that the statement is being upheld by the student body, or is there a need for more enforcement?

2. Go to **www.ibackup.com** and view the demonstration located on the home page. In a PowerPoint presentation of at least five slides, provide a brief description of the various backup services that this site offers. Identify the services that are suitable for your home system and which ones might be suitable for the servers at your school. From what you discovered about this online company, would you make use of this service? Provide justification for your decision.

3. The disagreement between online auctions and software companies over who is responsible for the sale of pirated software is a constant debate. Using the Internet and your favorite browser, locate at least three policy statements regarding liability from online auction or other Web sites that sell software. Do these statements state who is responsible for the sale of a pirated product? Is any advice given to help the buyer determine whether a product is authentic? Do these statements indicate that you can obtain a refund or offer to act as an arbitrator between you and the seller if the product you receive cannot be authenticated? Present your statements of liability and answer to the questions above in a one-page, double-spaced report created in a word processing program.

4. Create a survey consisting of descriptions of several scenarios that could occur in an academic situation that requires the involved individual to make an ethical decision. For example, a student leaves the computer lab and forgets to logoff: If you were the next individual to sit at that computer, what action would you perform? Present at least five scenarios in your survey and administer it to 25 students at your school. Summarize the survey results and determine whether in these five situations the surveyed individuals responded more often in an ethical or an unethical manner. In a three- to five-minute presentation, describe your scenarios to the class and summarize the survey results.

5. With technology becoming more portable, popular, and embedded into social settings, computer ethics becomes even more important. Develop a list of five additional commandments for computer ethics that can be applied specifically to portable computing devices. Present your five commandments and the reasons for your choices in a one-page, double-spaced report created with a word processing program.

6. You downloaded the beta version of a software program over three months ago. The beta was good for a 90-day period that has now expired. You continue to get e-mails stating that your trial period has expired for this product and that you can purchase the final release version by going to a specified Web site. You ignore the e-mails and continue to use the expired beta version. Now every time you try to open the program, you are presented with several pop-ups warning you that you are using an expired and unauthenticated copy. You also notice that it is taking longer to load the program and that after 10 minutes of use the program automatically closes. Analyze the ethical issue of using an expired copy of a program. Do you feel it is right to continue using the program when the trial period has expired? Would you be more inclined to purchase the program if the trial program self-destructed on the expiration date instead of slowly deteriorating? Is it ethical for the manufacturer to slowly undermine your work with this gradual product degeneration? Present your opinions on the ethical issues concerning software offered for trial periods in a one-page, double-spaced report created in a word processing program.

7

Securing Your System: Protecting Your Digital Data and Devices

Threats to Your Digital Assets

Learning Outcome You will be able to describe hackers, viruses, and other online annoyances and the threats they pose to your digital security.

Identity Theft and Hackers 279

Objective Describe how identity theft is committed and the types of scams identity thieves perpetrate.

Objective List and describe the different types of hackers.

Objective Describe the various tools hackers use and the types of attacks they might launch against computers.

Computer Viruses 284

Objective Explain what a computer virus is, why they are a threat to your security, how a computing device catches a virus, and the symptoms it may display.

Objective List the different categories of computer viruses, and describe their behaviors.

Online Annoyances and Social Engineering 286

Objective Explain what malware is, and list the common types of malware.

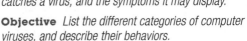

Objective Define spam, and describe strategies to combat it.

Objective Explain what cookies are and whether they pose a security threat.

Objective Describe social engineering techniques, and explain strategies to avoid falling prey to them.

Protecting Your Digital Property

Learning Outcome Describe various ways to protect your digital property and data from theft and corruption.

Restricting Access to Your Digital Assets 295

Objective Explain what a firewall is and how a firewall protects your computer from hackers.

Objective Explain how to protect your computer from virus infection.

Objective Describe how passwords and biometric characteristics can be used for user authentication on computer systems.

Objective Describe ways to surf the web anonymously.

Keeping Your Data Safe 306

Objective Describe the types of information you should never share online.

Objective List the various types of backups you can perform on your computing devices, and explain the various places you can store backup files.

Protecting Your Physical Computing Assets 311

Objective Explain the negative effects environment and power surges can have on computing devices.

Objective Describe the major concerns when a device is stolen and strategies for solving the problems.

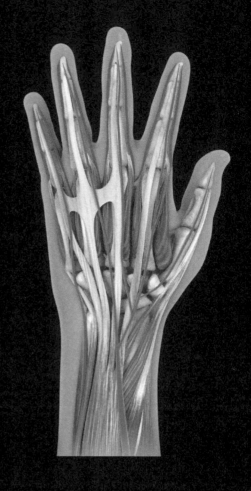

HOW COOL IS THIS?

Biometrics authentication for bank customers has gotten a major upgrade. Banks now use scanners that utilize **finger vein authentication technology**. The scanners read the unique vein patterns inside your finger to **verify your identity**. How does this improve upon fingerprint scans? Fingerprint scanning technology has flaws—impressions of your fingerprints can be left on scanner surfaces and can be duplicated to fool security devices. However, because your veins are inside your body, **they don't leave residue on scanners**. Perhaps your bank will offer this more secure technology soon! *(Nerthuz/Fotolia)*

Threats to Your Digital Assets

Learning Outcome **You will be able to describe hackers, viruses, and other online annoyances and the threats they pose to your digital security.**

The media is full of stories about malicious computer programs damaging computers, criminals stealing people's identities online, and attacks on corporate websites bringing major corporations to a standstill. These are examples of *cybercrime*—any criminal action perpetrated primarily through the use of a computer. *Cybercriminals* are individuals who use computers, networks, and the Internet to perpetrate crime. Anyone with a computer and the wherewithal to arm himself or herself with the appropriate knowledge can be a cybercriminal. In this part of the chapter, we'll discuss the most serious types of cybercrime you need to worry about as well as some online annoyances to avoid.

 identity theft and
HACKERS

Every year, the Internet Crime Complaint Center (IC3)—a partnership between the FBI and the National White Collar Crime Center—receives hundreds of thousands of complaints related to Internet crime. Four common categories of complaints the IC3 receives. Government impersonation scams involve people pretending to represent official organizations, such as the FBI, the IRS, or Homeland Security,

to defraud. Nonauction/non-delivery scams involve running auctions (or sales) of merchandise that does not really exist, wherein the perpetrators just collect funds and disappear without delivering the promised goods. Advance fee fraud involves convincing individuals to send money as a "good faith" gesture to enable them to receive larger payments in return. The scammers then disappear with the advance fees. Identity

Common Types of Cybercrimes Reported to the IC3

- **FBI-Related Scams**
- **Identity Theft**
- **Nonauction/ Non-Delivery of Merchandise**
- **Advance Fee Fraud**

theft involves the stealing of someone's personal information for financial gain. Although these complaints relate to some type of fraud, other complaints received involve equally serious matters such as computer intrusions (hacking), extortion, and blackmail. In this section, we'll look at both identity theft and hacking in more detail.

Identity Theft

Objective *Describe how identity theft is committed and the types of scams identity thieves perpetrate.*

What is the most financially damaging cybercrime plaguing individuals? Theft of personal data such as bank account numbers and credit/debit card numbers is of most concern to individuals because this information is usually used for fraudulent purposes. As noted above, **identity theft** occurs when a thief steals personal information such as your name, address, Social Security number, birth date, bank account number, and credit card information and runs up debts in your name. Many victims of identity theft spend months, or even years, trying to repair their credit and eliminate fraudulent debts.

What types of scams do identity thieves perpetrate? The nefarious acts cover a wide range:

- Counterfeiting your existing credit and debit cards
- Requesting changes of address on your bank and credit card statements, which makes detecting fraudulent charges take longer
- Opening new credit cards and bank accounts in your name and then writing bad checks and not paying off the credit card balances (ruining your credit rating in the process)
- Obtaining medical services under your name, potentially causing you to later lose coverage if the thief's treatment exceeds the limits of your policy's covered services
- Buying a home with a mortgage in your name, then reselling the house and absconding with the money (leaving you with the debt)

Many people believe that the only way your identity can be stolen is by a computer. However, the Federal Trade Commission (**ftc.gov**) has identified other methods thieves use to obtain others' personal information:

- Stealing purses and wallets, in which people often keep personal information such as their ATM PIN codes
- Stealing mail or looking through trash for bank statements and credit card bills
- Posing as bank or credit card company representatives and tricking people into revealing sensitive information over the phone
- Installing skimming devices on ATM machines that record information, such as account numbers and passcodes

Although foolproof protection methods don't exist, there are precautions that will help you minimize your risk, which we'll discuss later in this chapter.

With all the news coverage about identity theft and other cybercrimes, aren't people being more cautious? Although most people are aware of spam, a survey by the Messaging, Malware and Mobile Anti-Abuse Working Group (M3AAWG) found that half of e-mail users in North America and Europe have opened spam, some of which are designed to trick you into divulging sensitive information. The M3AAWG also discovered that 46% of people who opened spam did so intentionally—out of idle curiosity, to follow links to unsubscribe to unwanted e-mails (which only brings more spam), or because they are interested in the product being offered.

Hacking

Objective *List and describe the different types of hackers.*

What exactly defines a hacker? Although there's a great deal of disagreement as to what a hacker actually is, especially among hackers themselves, a **hacker** is most commonly defined as anyone who unlawfully breaks into a computer system—either an individual computer or a network.

Are there different kinds of hackers? Some hackers are offended by being labeled as criminals and therefore attempt to classify different types of hackers as follows:

- **White-hat hackers** (or **ethical hackers**) break in to systems for nonmalicious reasons, such as to test system security vulnerabilities or to expose undisclosed weaknesses.

Hacking humor. Hackers are a real problem in many instances, but don't let your fears overwhelm you! (© *Andy Singer www.andysinger.com*)

They believe in making security vulnerabilities known either to the company that owns the system or software or to the general public, often to embarrass a company into fixing a problem.

- **Black-hat hackers** break into systems to destroy information or for illegal gain. The terms *white hat* and *black hat* are references to old Western movies in which the heroes wore white hats and the outlaws wore black hats.

- **Grey-hat hackers** are a bit of a cross between black and white—they often illegally break into systems merely to flaunt their expertise to the administrator of the system they penetrated or to attempt to sell their services in repairing security breaches.

Regardless of the hackers' opinions, the laws in the United States and in many other countries consider *any* unauthorized access to computer systems a crime.

Hacking Tools and Attack Types

Objective *Describe the various tools hackers use and the types of attacks they might launch against computers.*

Could a hacker steal my debit card or bank account number? Hackers often try to break in to computers or websites that contain credit card information. If you perform financial transactions online, such as banking or buying goods and services, you probably do so using a credit or debit card. Credit card and bank account information can thus reside on your hard drive or an online business's hard drive and may be detectable by a hacker.

Aside from your home computer, you have personal data stored on various websites. For example, many sites require that you provide a login ID and password to gain access. Even if this data isn't stored on your computer, a hacker may be able to capture it when you're online by using a *packet analyzer (sniffer)* or a *keylogger* (a program that captures all keystrokes made on a computer).

What's a packet analyzer? Data travels through the Internet in small pieces called *packets*. The packets are identified with an IP address, in part to help identify the computer to which they are being sent. Once the packets reach their destination, they're reassembled into cohesive messages. A **packet analyzer (sniffer)** is a program deployed by hackers that looks at (or sniffs) each packet as it travels on the Internet—not just those addressed to a particular computer, but all packets coming across a particular network. For example, a hacker might sit in a coffee shop and run a packet sniffer to capture sensitive data

(such as debit/credit card numbers) from patrons using the coffee shop's free wireless network. Wireless networks such as these can be particularly vulnerable to this type of exploitation if encryption of data isn't enabled when the networks are set up.)

What do hackers do with the information they "sniff"? Once a hacker has your debit/credit card information, he or she can use it to purchase items illegally or can sell the number to someone who will. If a hacker steals the login ID and password to an account where you have your bank card information stored (such as eBay or Amazon), he or she can also use your account to buy items and have them shipped to him- or herself instead of to you. If hackers can gather enough information in conjunction with your credit card information, they may be able to commit identity theft.

Although this sounds scary, you can easily protect yourself from packet sniffing by installing a firewall (which we discuss later in this chapter) and using data encryption on a wireless network.

Trojan Horses and Rootkits

Besides stealing information, what other problems can hackers cause if they break into my computer? Hackers often use individuals' computers as a staging area for mischief. To commit widespread computer attacks, for example, hackers need to control many computers at the same time. To this end, hackers often use Trojan horses to install other programs on computers. A **Trojan horse** is a program that appears to be something useful or desirable, like a game or a screen saver, but while it runs it does something malicious in the background without your knowledge.

What damage can Trojan horses do? Often, the malicious activity perpetrated by a Trojan horse program is the installation of a backdoor program or a rootkit. **Backdoor programs** and **rootkits** are programs (or sets of programs) that allow hackers to gain access to your computer and take almost complete control of it without your knowledge. Using a backdoor program, hackers can access and delete all the files on your computer, send e-mail, run programs, and do just about anything else you can do with your computer. A computer that a hacker controls in this manner is referred to as a **zombie**. Zombies are often used to launch *denial-of-service attacks* on other computers.

Denial-of-Service Attacks

What are denial-of-service attacks? In a **denial-of-service (DoS) attack**, legitimate users are denied access to a computer system because a hacker

The term *Trojan horse* derives from Greek mythology and refers to the wooden horse that the Greeks used to sneak into the city of Troy and conquer it. Therefore, computer programs that contain a hidden, and usually dreadful, "surprise" are referred to as Trojan horses. *(Ralf Kraft/Fotolia)*

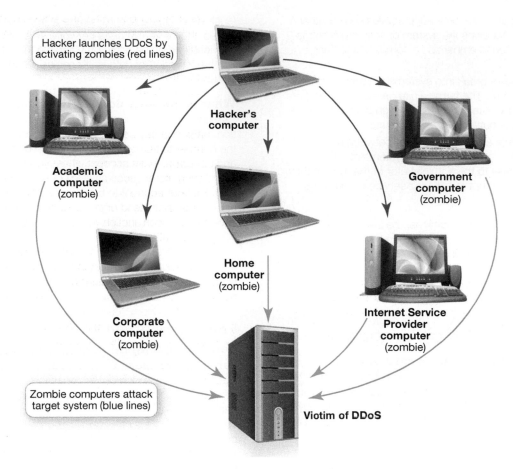

Zombie computers are used to facilitate a DDoS attack. *(Vovan/Shutterstock, Nicholas Monu/E+/Getty)*

is repeatedly making requests of that computer system through a computer he or she has taken over as a zombie. A computer system can handle only a certain number of requests for information at one time. When it is flooded with requests in a DoS attack, it shuts down and refuses to answer any requests for information, even if the requests are from a legitimate user. Thus, the computer is so busy responding to the bogus requests for information that authorized users can't gain access.

Couldn't a DoS attack be traced back to the computer that launched it? Launching a DoS attack on a computer system from a single computer is easy to trace. Therefore, most savvy hackers use a **distributed denial-of-service (DDoS) attack**, which launches DoS attacks from more than one zombie (sometimes thousands of zombies) at the same time.

A DDoS attack works. A hacker creates many zombies and coordinates them so that they begin sending bogus requests to the same computer at the same time. Administrators of the victim computer often have a great deal of difficulty stopping the attack because it comes from so many computers. Often, the attacks are coordinated automatically by botnets. A **botnet** is a large group of software programs

(called *robots* or *bots*) that runs autonomously on zombie computers. Some botnets have been known to span millions of computers.

Because many commercial websites receive revenue from users, either directly (such as via subscriptions to online games) or indirectly (such as when web surfers click on advertisements), DDoS attacks can be financially distressing for the owners of the affected websites.

How Hackers Gain Computer Access

How exactly does a hacker gain access to a computer? Hackers can gain access to computers directly or indirectly. Direct access involves sitting down at a computer and installing hacking software. It's unlikely that such an attack would occur in your home, but it's always a wise precaution to set up your computer so that it requires a password for a user to gain access.

Indirect access involves subtler methods. Many professional hackers use exploit kits. **Exploit kits** are software programs that run on servers and search for vulnerabilities of computers that visit the server. Exploit kits look for security holes in browsers and operating systems that haven't yet been patched by the users. When they detect a vulnerability,

YOUR COMPUTER

FTP
(port 21)

E-mail
(port 25)

HTTP (port 80)

DNS
(port 53)

Telnet
(port 23)

WEBSITE REQUEST

Open logical ports are an invitation to hackers.

they can deliver spyware, bots, backdoor programs, or other malicious software to your computer. Fortunately, most exploit kits take advantage of known vulnerabilities, so if your antivirus software and operating system is up to date, you should be secure. We'll discuss both of these topics later in the chapter.

Hackers also can access a computer indirectly through its Internet connection. Many people forget that their Internet connection is a two-way street. Not only can you access the Internet, but people on the Internet can access your computer.

Think of your computer as a house. Common sense tells you to lock your home's doors and windows to deter theft when you aren't there. Hooking your computer up to the Internet without protection is like leaving the front door to your house wide open. Your computer obviously doesn't have doors and windows like a house, but it does have logical ports.

What are logical ports? Logical ports are virtual—that is, not physical—communications gateways or paths that allow a computer to organize requests for information, such as web page downloads or e-mail routing, from other networks or computers. Unlike physical ports, such as USB ports, you can't see or touch a logical port; it's part of a computer's internal organization.

Logical ports are numbered and assigned to specific services. For instance, logical port 80 is designated for hypertext transfer protocol (HTTP), the main communications protocol for the web. Thus, all requests for information from your browser to the web flow through logical port 80. Open logical ports, like open windows in a home, invite intruders. Unless you take precautions to restrict access to your logical ports, other people on the Internet may be able to access your computer through them. Fortunately, you can thwart most hacking problems by installing a firewall, which we discuss later in the chapter. ■

BITS&BYTES

Are Your Photos Helping Criminals Target You?

All cell phones today contain GPS chips. The cameras in phones often use information gathered from the GPS chips to encode information onto photos in the form of geotags. A **geotag** is a piece of data attached to a photo that indicates your latitude and longitude when you took the photo. Geotagging is useful for applications that can take advantage of this information, but problems arise when you share geotagged photos on the web.

If you post a lot of photos, cybercriminals and cyberstalkers can use the information from the geotags on your photos to figure out the patterns of your movements. They may be able to ascertain when you're at work or that you're currently on vacation,

which leads them to determine prime times for burglarizing your home. Some sites such as Facebook and Twitter have measures in place to limit the amount of geotagged information that can be seen in photos in order to prevent their users from unwittingly revealing personal information. However, many photo-sharing sites don't have such protections in place.

The safest thing to do is not tag your photos with geotags in the first place. It's usually easy to disable location tracking on your smartphone in the settings. So stop geotagging your photos, and make it tougher for the cybercriminals to figure out your movements. For photos that already have geotags, you can remove them using software such as BatchPurifier LITE or Pixelgarde.

computer
VIRUSES

Creating and disseminating computer viruses is one of the most widespread types of cybercrimes. Some viruses cause only minor annoyances, whereas others cause destruction or theft of data. Many viruses are designed to gather sensitive information such as credit card numbers.

Virus Basics

Objective *Explain what a computer virus is, why they are a threat to your security, how a computing device catches a virus, and the symptoms it might display.*

What is a computer virus? A computer **virus** is a computer program that attaches itself to another computer program (known as the *host* program) and attempts to spread to other computers when files are exchanged.

Why are viruses such a threat to my security? Computer viruses are threatening because they are engineered to evade detection. Viruses normally attempt to hide within the code of a host program to avoid detection. And viruses are not just limited to computers. Smartphones, tablet computers, and other devices can be infected with viruses. Viruses such as SpyEye Mobile Banking are used to trick users into downloading an infected file to their phones, which then steals their online banking information.

I have an Apple computer, so I don't need to worry about viruses, do I? This is a popular misconception! Everyone, even Apple users, needs to worry about viruses. As the OS X and iOS operating systems have gained market share, the number of virus attacks against Apple operating systems is on the rise.

What do computer viruses do? A computer virus's main purpose is to replicate itself and copy its code into as many other host files as possible. This gives the virus a greater chance of being copied to another computer system so that it can spread its infection. However, computer viruses require human interaction to spread. Although there might be a virus in a file on your computer, a virus normally can't infect your computer until the infected file is opened or executed.

Although virus replication can slow down networks, it's not usually the main threat. The majority of viruses have secondary objectives or side effects, ranging from displaying annoying messages on the computer screen to destroying files or the contents of entire hard drives.

How does my computer catch a virus? If your computer is exposed to a file infected with a virus, the virus will try to copy itself and infect a file on your computer.

Downloading infected audio and video files from peer-to-peer file-sharing sites is a major source of virus infections. Shared flash drives are also a common source of virus infection, as is e-mail. Just opening an e-mail message usually won't infect your computer with a virus, although some new viruses are launched when viewed in the preview pane of your e-mail software. Downloading and running (executing) a file that's attached to the e-mail are common ways that your computer becomes infected. Thus, be extremely wary of e-mail attachments, especially if you don't know the sender. which computer viruses are often passed from one computer to the next:

1. An individual writes a virus program, attaches it to a music file, and posts the file to a file-sharing site.
2. Unsuspecting Bill downloads the "music file" and infects his computer when he listens to the song.
3. Bill sends his cousin Fred an e-mail with the infected "music file" and contaminates Fred's tablet.
4. Fred syncs his phone with his tablet and infects his phone when he plays the music file.
5. Fred e-mails the file from his phone to Susan, one of his colleagues at work. Everyone who copies files from Susan's infected work computer, or whose computer is networked to Susan's computer, risks spreading the virus.

How can I tell if my computer is infected with a virus? Sometimes it can be difficult to definitively tell whether your computer is infected with a virus. However, if your computer displays any of the following symptoms, it may be infected with a virus:

1. Existing program icons or files suddenly disappear. Viruses often delete specific file types or programs.
2. You start your browser and it takes you to an unusual home page (i.e., one you didn't set) or it has new toolbars.
3. Odd messages, pop-ups, or images are displayed on the screen, or strange music or sounds play.
4. Data files become corrupt. (However, note that files can become corrupt for reasons other than a virus infection.)
5. Programs stop working properly, which could be caused by either a corrupted file or a virus.
6. Your system shuts down unexpectedly, slows down, or takes a long time to boot up.

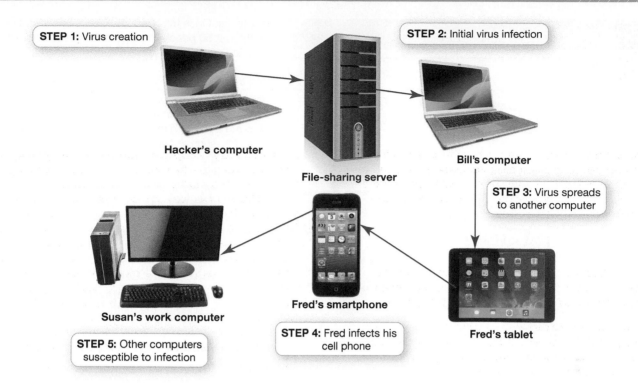

STEP 1: Virus creation

Hacker's computer

File-sharing server

STEP 2: Initial virus infection

Bill's computer

STEP 3: Virus spreads to another computer

Susan's work computer

STEP 5: Other computers susceptible to infection

Fred's smartphone

STEP 4: Fred infects his cell phone

Fred's tablet

Computer viruses are passed from one unsuspecting user to the next. *(Vovan/Shutterstock, Juffin/DigitalVision Vectors/Getty Images, Denis Rozhnovsky/Alamy, Ian Dagnall/Alamy, Stanca Sanda/Alamy)*

Types of Viruses

Objective *List the different categories of computer viruses, and describe their behaviors.*

What types of viruses exist? Although thousands of computer viruses and variants exist, they can be grouped into six broad categories based on their behavior and method of transmission.

Boot-Sector Viruses

What are boot-sector viruses? A **boot-sector virus** replicates itself onto a hard drive's master boot record. The **master boot record** is a program that executes whenever a computer boots up, ensuring that the virus will be loaded into memory immediately, even before some virus protection programs can load. Boot-sector viruses are often transmitted by a flash drive left in a USB port. When the computer boots up with the flash drive connected, the computer tries to launch a master boot record from the flash drive, which is usually the trigger for the virus to infect the hard drive.

Logic Bombs and Time Bombs

What are logic bombs and time bombs? A **logic bomb** is a virus that is triggered when certain logical conditions are met, such as opening a file or starting a program a certain number of times. A **time bomb** is a virus that is triggered by the passage of time or on a certain date. For example, the Michelangelo virus was a famous time bomb that was set to trigger every year on March 6, Michelangelo's birthday. The effects of logic bombs and time bombs range from the display of annoying messages on the screen to the reformatting of the hard drive, which causes complete data loss.

Worms

What is a worm? Although often called a virus, a **worm** is subtly different. Viruses require human interaction to spread, whereas worms take advantage of file transport methods, such as e-mail or network connections, to spread on their own. A virus infects a host file and waits until that file is executed to replicate and infect a computer system. A worm, however, works independently of host file execution and is much more active in spreading itself. Recently developed worms, like The Moon, even attack peripheral devices such as routers. Worms can generate a lot of data traffic when trying to spread, which can slow down the Internet.

Script and Macro Viruses

What are script and macro viruses? Some viruses are hidden on websites in the form of scripts. A **script** is a series of commands—actually, a miniprogram—that is executed without your knowledge. Scripts are often used to perform useful, legitimate functions on websites, such as collecting name and address information from customers. However, some scripts are malicious. For example, you might click a link to display a video on a website, which causes a script to run that infects your computer with a virus.

A **macro virus** is a virus that attaches itself to a document that uses macros. A *macro* is a short series of commands that usually automates repetitive tasks. However, macro languages are now so sophisticated that viruses can be written with them. In 1999, the Melissa virus became the first major macro virus to cause problems worldwide.

Major Categories of Viruses

Boot-sector Viruses
Execute when a computer boots up

Logic Bombs/Time Bombs
Execute when certain conditions or dates are reached

Worms
Spread on their own with no human interaction needed

Script and Macro Viruses
Series of commands with malicious intent

E-mail Viruses
Spread as attachments to e-mail, often using address books

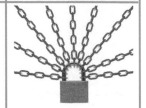

Encryption Viruses
Hold files "hostage" by encrypting them; ask for ransom to unlock them

(Tribalium81/Fotolia, Oleksandr Delyk/Fotolia, DedMazay/Fotolia, Theo Malings/Fotolia, Beboy/Fotolia, Lukas Gojda/Fotolia)

E-Mail Viruses

What is an e-mail virus? In addition to being a macro virus, the Melissa virus was the first practical example of an e-mail virus. **E-mail viruses** use the address book in the victim's e-mail system to distribute the virus. In the case of the Melissa virus, anyone opening an infected document triggered the virus, which infected other documents on the victim's computer. Once triggered, the Melissa virus sent itself to the first 50 people in the e-mail address book on the infected computer.

Encryption Viruses

What are encryption viruses? When **encryption viruses** (also known as *ransomware*) infect your computer, they run a program that searches for common types of data files, such as Microsoft Word files, and compresses them using a complex encryption key that renders your files unusable. You then receive a message that asks you to send payment to an account if you want to receive the program to decrypt your files. The flaw with this type of virus, which keeps it from being widespread, is that law enforcement officials can trace the payments to an account and may possibly be able to catch the perpetrators.

Additional Virus Classifications

How else are viruses classified? Viruses can also be classified by the methods they take to avoid detection by antivirus software:

- A **polymorphic virus** changes its own code or periodically rewrites itself to avoid detection. Most polymorphic viruses infect a particular type of file such as .EXE files, for example.
- A **multipartite virus** is designed to infect multiple file types in an effort to fool the antivirus software that is looking for it.
- **Stealth viruses** temporarily erase their code from the files where they reside and then hide in the active memory of the computer. This helps them avoid detection if only the hard drive is being searched for viruses. Fortunately, current antivirus software scans memory as well as the hard drive. ■

 online annoyances and
SOCIAL ENGINEERING

Surfing the web, using social networks, and sending and receiving e-mail have become common parts of most of our lives. Unfortunately, the web has become fertile ground for people who want to advertise their products, track our browsing behaviors, or even con people into revealing personal information. In this section, we'll look at ways in which you can manage, if not avoid, these and other online headaches.

Malware: Adware and Spyware

Objective *Explain what malware is, and list the common types of malware.*

What is malware? Malware is software that has a malicious intent (hence the prefix *mal*). There are three primary forms of malware: adware, spyware, and viruses. Adware and spyware are not physically destructive like viruses and worms, which can destroy data. Known collectively as *grayware*, most malware are intrusive, annoying, or objectionable online programs that are downloaded to your computer when you install or use other online content such as a free program, game, or utility.

What is adware? Adware is software that displays sponsored advertisements in a section of your browser window or as a pop-up box. It's considered a legitimate, though sometimes annoying, means of generating revenue for those developers who do not charge for their software or information. Fortunately, because web browsers such as Firefox, Chrome, and Edge have built-in pop-up blockers, the occurrence of annoying pop-ups has been greatly reduced.

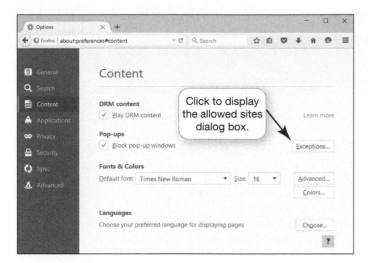
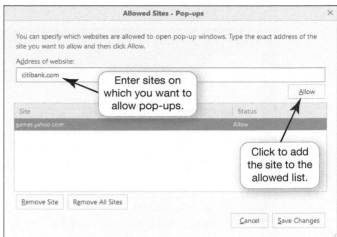

Firefox's Allowed Sites - Pop-ups dialog box lets you control which sites you'll allow to display pop-ups. *(Firefox logo® is a registered trademark of the Mozilla Foundation)*

>To display the pop-up blocker in Firefox, click the **Open Menu button**, *select* **Options**, *and then select the* **Content option**.

Some pop-ups, however, are legitimate and increase the functionality of the originating site. For example, your account balance may pop up on your bank's website. To control which sites to allow pop-ups on, you can access the pop-up blocker settings in your browser and add websites for which you allow pop-ups. Whenever a pop-up is blocked, the browser displays an information bar or plays a sound to alert you. If you feel the pop-up is legitimate, you can choose to accept it.

What is spyware? Spyware is an unwanted piggyback program that usually downloads with other software you install from the Internet and that runs in the background of your system. Without your knowledge, spyware transmits information about you, such as your Internet-surfing habits, to the owner of the program so that the information can be used for marketing purposes. Many spyware programs use tracking cookies (small text files stored on your computer) to collect information. One type of spyware program known as a **keystroke logger (key logger)** monitors keystrokes with the intent of stealing passwords, login IDs, or credit card information.

Can I prevent spyware from spying on me? Anti-spyware software detects unwanted programs and allows you to delete the offending software easily. Most Internet security suites now include anti-spyware software. You can also obtain stand-alone anti-spyware software and run it on your computer to delete unwanted spyware. Because so many variants of spyware exist, your Internet security software may not detect all types that attempt to install themselves on your computer. Therefore, it's a good idea to install one or two additional stand-alone anti-spyware programs on your computer.

Because new spyware is created all the time, you should update and run your anti-spyware software regularly. Windows comes with a program called Windows Defender, which scans your system for spyware and other potentially unwanted software. Malwarebytes Anti-Malware, Ad-Aware, and Spybot–Search & Destroy (all available from **download.com**) are other anti-spyware programs that are easy to install and update. An example of Windows Defender in action.

Spam

Objective *Define spam, and describe strategies to combat it.*

How can I best avoid spam? Companies that send out **spam**—unwanted or junk e-mail—find your e-mail address either from a list they purchase or with software that looks for e-mail addresses on the Internet. Unsolicited instant messages are also a form of spam, called *spim*. If you've used your e-mail address to purchase anything online, open an online account, or participate in a social network such as Facebook, your e-mail address eventually will appear on one of the lists that spammers get.

One way to avoid spam in your primary account is to create a free e-mail address that you use only when you fill out forms or buy items on the web. For example, both Outlook.com and Yahoo! let you set up free e-mail accounts. If your free e-mail account is saturated with spam, you can abandon that account with little inconvenience. It's much less convenient to abandon your primary e-mail address.

Another way to avoid spam is to filter it. A **spam filter** is an option you can select in your e-mail account that places known or suspected spam messages into a special folder (called "Spam" or "Junk Mail"). Most web-based e-mail services, such as Gmail and Yahoo!, offer spam filters. Microsoft Outlook also features a spam filter.

You can also buy third-party programs that provide some control over spam, including SPAMfighter, which you can download at download.com.

How do spam filters work? Spam filters and filtering software can catch as much as 95% of spam by checking incoming e-mail subject headers and senders' addresses against databases of known spam. Spam filters also check

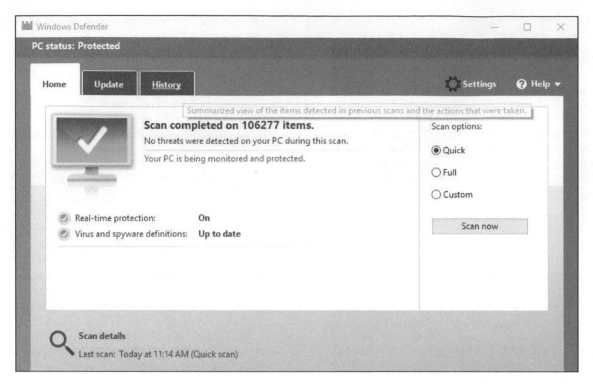

Routine scans of a computer by Windows Defender will detect and eliminate spyware and other unwanted types of software. *(Microsoft Windows Defender, Microsoft Corporation)*

your e-mail for frequently used spam patterns and keywords, such as "for free" and "over 21." Spam filters aren't perfect, and you should check the spam folder before deleting its contents because legitimate e-mail might end up there by mistake. Most programs let you reclassify e-mails that have been misidentified as spam.

How else can I prevent spam? Here are a few other ways you can prevent spam:

1. Before registering on a website, read its privacy policy to see how it uses your e-mail address. Don't give the site permission to pass on your e-mail address to third parties.

2. Don't reply to spam to remove yourself from the spam list. By replying, you're confirming that your e-mail address is active. Instead of stopping spam, you may receive more.

3. Subscribe to an e-mail forwarding service such as VersaForward (versaforward.com) or Sneakemail (sneakemail .com). These services screen your e-mail messages, forwarding only those messages you designate as being okay to accept.

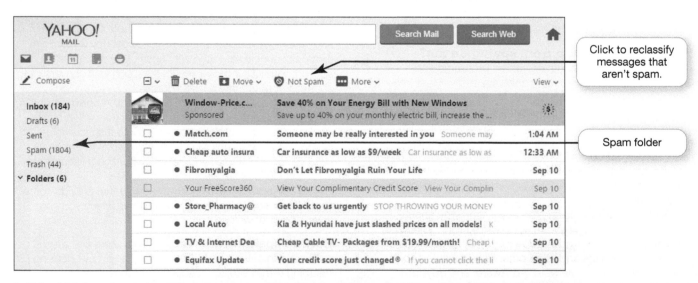

In Yahoo! Mail, messages identified as spam are directed into a folder called "Spam" for review and deletion. *(Reproduced with permission of Yahoo. ©2015 Yahoo. YAHOO! and the YAHOO! logo are registered trademarks of Yahoo.)*

Cookies

Objective *Explain what cookies are and whether they pose a security threat.*

What are cookies? Cookies are small text files that some websites automatically store on your hard drive when you visit them. When you log on to a website that uses cookies, a cookie file assigns an ID number to your computer. The unique ID is intended to make your return visit to a website more efficient and better geared to your interests. The next time you log on to that site, the site marks your visit and keeps track of it in its database.

What do websites do with cookie information? Cookies can provide websites with information about your browsing habits, such as the ads you've opened, the products you've looked at, and the time and duration of your visits. Companies use this information to determine the traffic flowing through their website and the effectiveness of their marketing strategy and placement on websites. By tracking such information, cookies enable companies to identify different users' preferences.

Can companies get my personal information when I visit their sites? Cookies do not go through your hard drive in search of personal information such as passwords or financial data. The only personal information a cookie obtains is the information you supply when you fill out forms online.

Do privacy risks exist with cookies? Some sites sell the personal information their cookies collect to web advertisers who are building huge databases of consumer preferences and habits, collecting personal and business information such as phone numbers, credit reports, and the like. The main concern is that advertisers will use this information indiscriminately, thus invading your privacy. And you may feel your privacy is being violated by cookies that monitor where you go on a website.

Should I delete cookies from my hard drive? Cookies pose no *security* threat because it is virtually impossible to hide a virus or malicious software program in a cookie. Because they take up little room on your hard drive, and offer you small conveniences on return visits to websites, there is no great reason to delete them. |Deleting your cookie files could actually cause you the inconvenience of reentering data you have already entered into website forms. However, if you're uncomfortable with the accessibility of your personal information, you can periodically delete cookies or

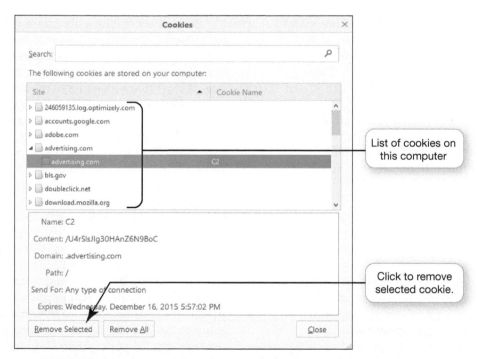

Tools are available, either through your browser (Firefox is shown here) or as separate programs, to distinguish between cookies you want to keep and cookies you don't want on your system. *(Firefox logo® is a registered trademark of the Mozilla Foundation)*
>*On the Firefox menu toolbar, click the* **Open Menu button**, *click* **Options**, *choose the* **Privacy option**, *choose* **Use custom settings for history**, *and then click the* **Show Cookies button** *to display the Cookies dialog box.*

ethics in IT

You're Being Watched ... But Are You Aware You're Being Watched?

Think you aren't being closely watched by your employer? Think again! A recent survey of employers by the American Management Association and the ePolicy Institute revealed that, of the employers surveyed:

- 73% monitored e-mail messages
- 66% monitored web surfing
- 48% monitored activities using video surveillance
- 45% monitored keystrokes and keyboard time
- 43% monitored computer files in some other fashion

As you can see, there is a high probability that you're being monitored while you work and when you access the Internet via your employer's Internet connection.

The two most frequently cited reasons for employee monitoring are to prevent theft and to measure productivity. Monitoring for theft isn't new—monitoring cameras have been around for years, and productivity monitoring has been used for assembly line workers for decades. However, the Internet has led to a new type of productivity drain of concern to employers. **Cyberloafing** (or *cyberslacking*) means using your computer for nonwork activities while you're being paid to do your job. Examples of cyberloafing activities include playing games and using social networks. Some employees even do multiple nonwork tasks at the same time, which is known as *multishirking*. Estimates of business productivity losses due to cyberloafing top $50 billion annually.

Do you have a right to privacy in the workplace? Laws such as the 1986 Electronic Communications Privacy Act (ECPA), which prohibits unauthorized monitoring of electronic communications, have been interpreted by the courts in favor of employers. The bottom line is that employers who pay for equipment and software have the *legal* right to monitor their usage.

George Orwell was right—Big Brother is watching you at work! It's legal for employers to monitor your computer usage. (Beatriz Gascon J/Shutterstock)

So, is it *ethical* for employers to monitor their employees? Certainly, it seems fair that employers ensure they're not the victims of theft and that they're getting a fair day's work from their employees, just as employees have an obligation to provide a fair effort for a fair wage. The ethical issue is whether employees are adequately informed of monitoring policies. Employers have an ethical responsibility (and a legal one as well, depending on the jurisdiction) not to place monitoring devices in sensitive locations such as bathrooms and dressing areas. However, in many states, the employer does not legally need to inform employees in advance that they're being monitored. Conscientious employers include monitoring disclosures in published employee policies to avoid confusion and conflict.

The bottom line? Because employers may have a legal right to monitor you in the workplace, operate under the assumption that everything you do on your work computer is subject to scrutiny and behave accordingly. Do your online shopping at home!

BITS&BYTES

I Received a Data Breach Letter ... Now What?

Data breaches are becoming more common, and companies that are the subject of data breaches now routinely notify customers of data breaches—usually by physical letter, but sometimes via e-mail. Here's what you should do if you receive such a letter:

1. Take it seriously. 22.5% of recipients of these letters become the victim of identity theft per a study by Javelin Strategy and Research.
2. Contact one of the three big credit bureaus (Equifax, Experian, and TransUnion) and have a fraud alert put on your credit report. This alerts people accessing your credit report that your identity information has been stolen and that the person who is applying for credit in your name might be an imposter.
3. For even better security, contact all three credit bureaus and have a credit freeze put on your credit reports. This prevents anyone (even you) from getting credit in your name. You can always unfreeze your accounts later if you need to apply for credit yourself.
4. Review your credit reports regularly. You are entitled to one free credit report per year from each of the three big agencies. Go to **annualcreditreport.com** and request a report from one of the agencies. Repeat the process every four months from a different agency. Review the reports for any suspicious activity.

---

configure your browser to block certain types of cookies. Software such as Powerful Cookies (available at **download .com**) also can help you monitor cookies.

Social Engineering

Objective *Describe social engineering techniques, and explain strategies to avoid falling prey to them.*

What is social engineering? Social engineering is any technique that uses social skills to generate human interaction that entices individuals to reveal sensitive information. Social engineering often doesn't involve the use of a computer or face-to-face interaction. For example, telephone scams are a common form of social engineering because it is often easier to manipulate someone when you don't have to look at them.

How does social engineering work? Most social engineering schemes use a pretext to lure their victims. **Pretexting** involves creating a scenario that sounds legitimate enough that someone will trust you. For example, you might receive a phone call during which the caller says he is from your bank and that someone tried to use your account without authorization. The caller then tells you he needs to confirm a few personal details such as your birth date, Social Security number, bank account number, and whatever other information he can get out of you. The information he obtains can then be used to empty your bank account or commit some other form of fraud. The most common form of pretexting in cyberspace is *phishing*.

Phishing and Pharming

How are phishing schemes conducted? Phishing (pronounced "fishing") lures Internet users to reveal personal information such as credit card numbers, Social Security numbers, or other sensitive information that could lead to identity theft. The scammers send e-mail messages that look like they're from a legitimate business such as an online bank. The e-mail usually states that the recipient needs to update or confirm his or her account information. When the recipient clicks on the provided link, he or she goes to a website. The site looks like a legitimate site but is really a fraudulent copy that the scammer has created. Once the e-mail recipient enters his or her personal information, the scammers capture it and can begin using it.

Is pharming a type of phishing scam? Pharming is much more insidious than phishing. Phishing requires a positive action by the person being scammed, such as going to a website mentioned in an e-mail and typing in personal information. **Pharming** occurs when malicious code is planted on your computer, either by viruses or by your visiting malicious websites, which then alters your browser's ability to find web addresses. Users are directed to bogus websites even when they enter the correct address of the real website. You end up at a fake website that looks legitimate but is expressly set up for the purpose of gathering information.

How can I avoid being caught by phishing and pharming scams? Follow these guidelines to avoid falling prey to such schemes:

- Never reply directly to any e-mail asking you for personal information.
- Don't click on a link in an e-mail to go to a website. Instead, type the website address in the browser.
- Check with the company asking for the information and only give the information if you're certain it's needed.
- Never give personal information over the Internet unless you know the site is secure. Look for the closed padlock, *https*, or a certification seal such as Norton Secured to help reassure you that the site is secure.
- Use phishing filters. The latest versions of Firefox, Chrome, and Edge have phishing filters built in, so each time you

Not sure whether you're on the Healthcare.gov website or a cleverly disguised phishing site? Norton Safe Web reassures you that all is well. *(U.S. Centers for Medicare & Medicaid Services, www. healthcare.gov)*

access a website, the phishing filter checks for the site's legitimacy and warns you of possible web forgeries.

- Use Internet security software on your computer that's constantly being updated.

Most Internet security packages can detect and prevent pharming attacks. The major Internet security packages—for example, McAfee and Norton—also offer phishing-protection tools. When you have the Norton Toolbar displayed in your browser, you're constantly informed about the legitimacy of the site you are visiting.

Scareware

What is scareware?
Scareware is a type of malware that downloads onto your computer and tries to convince you that your computer is infected with a virus or other type of malware. Pop-ups, banners, or other annoying types of messages will flash on your screen saying frightening things like, "Your computer is infected with a virus . . . immediate removal is required." You're then directed to a website where you can buy fake removal or antivirus tools that provide little or no value. Panda Security estimates that scareware scams

generate n excess of $34 million a month for cybercriminals. Some scareware even goes so far as to encrypt your files and then demand that you pay to have them unencrypted, which is essentially extortion.

Scareware is a social engineering technique because it uses people's fear of computer viruses to convince them to part with their money. Scareware is often designed to be extremely difficult to remove from your computer and to interfere with the operation of legitimate security software. Scareware is usually downloaded onto your computer from infected websites or Trojan horse files.

How do I protect myself against scareware? Most Internet security suites, antivirus, and anti-malware software packages now detect and prevent the installation of scareware. But make sure you never click on website banners or pop-up boxes that say "Your computer might be infected, click here to scan your files" because these are often the starting points for installing malicious scareware files on your computer.

> **Before moving on to Part 2:**
> 1. **Watch Replay Video 9.1 ↻.**
> 2. **Then check your understanding of what you've learned so far.**

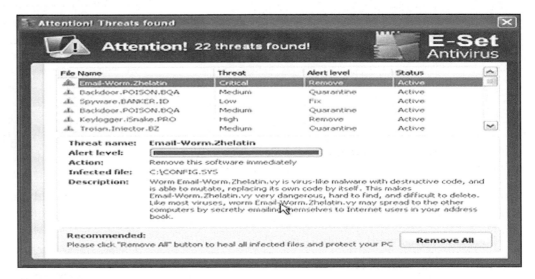

Preying on people's fears, scareware attempts to convince you that your computer is infected with a virus and you need to purchase a "solution." *(Reprinted courtesy of McAfee, Inc.)*

Most people have vast amounts of personal data residing in the databases of the various companies with which they conduct business. Amazon.com has your credit card and address information. Your bank has your Social Security number, birth date, and financial records. Your local supermarket probably has your e-mail address from when you joined its loyalty club to receive grocery discounts. All this data in various places puts you at risk when companies responsible for keeping your data confidential suffer a data breach.

A **data breach** occurs when sensitive or confidential information is copied, transmitted, or viewed by an individual who isn't authorized to handle the data. Data breaches can be intentional or unintentional. Intentional data breaches occur when hackers break into digital systems to steal sensitive data. Unintentional data breaches occur when companies controlling data inadvertently allow it to be seen by unauthorized parties, usually due to some breakdown in security procedures or precautions.

Unfortunately, data breaches appear to be quite common, as there always seems to be another one in the news. The Identity Theft Resource Center, a nonprofit organization that monitors data breaches, reported 5,541 data breaches for U.S. companies in the first eight months of 2015. At least 140.1 million records were exposed, although this data is not available for all the breaches. These breaches pose serious risks to the individuals whose data has been compromised, even if financial data is not involved. The data thieves now have the basis with which to launch targeted social engineering attacks even if they just have contact information, such as e-mail addresses.

With regular phishing techniques, cybercriminals just send out e-mails to a wide list of e-mail addresses, whether they have a relationship with the company or not. For example, a criminal might send out a general phishing e-mail claiming that a person's Citibank checking account had been breached. People who receive this e-mail that don't have any accounts at Citibank should immediately realize this is a phishing attack and ignore the instructions to divulge sensitive data.

But when cybercriminals obtain data on individuals that includes information about which companies those individuals have a relationship with, they can engage in much more targeted attacks known as **spear phishing**. Spear phishing e-mails are sent to people known to be customers of a company and have a much greater chance of successfully getting individuals to reveal sensitive data. If cybercriminals obtain a list of e-mail addresses of customers from Barclays Bank, for example, they can ensure that the spear phishing e-mails purport to come from Barclays and will include the customer's full name. This type of attack is much more likely to succeed in fooling people than just random e-mails sent out to thousands of people who might not have a relationship with the company mentioned in the phishing letter.

So how can you protect yourself after a data breach? You need to be extra suspicious of any e-mail correspondence from companies involved in the data breach. Companies usually never contact you by e-mail or phone asking you to reveal sensitive information or reactivate your online account by entering confidential information. Usually, these requests come via regular snail mail.

So, if you receive any e-mails or phone calls from companies you deal with purporting to have problems with your accounts, your best course of action is to delete the e-mail or hang up the phone. Then contact the company that supposedly has the problem by a phone number that you look up yourself either in legitimate correspondence from the company (say, the toll-free number on your credit card statement) or in the phone book. The representatives from your company can quickly tell if a real problem exists or if you were about to be the victim of a scam.

Not that kind of fishing! Spear phishing is a targeted type of social engineering. *(Ehrlif/Shutterstock)*

check your understanding // review & practice

For a quick review to see what you've learned so far, answer the following questions.

multiple choice

1. When a hacker steals personal information with the intent of impersonating another individual to commit fraud, it is known as

    a. impersonation theft.

    b. scareware theft.

    c. identity theft.

    d. malware theft.

2. An attack that renders a computer unable to respond to legitimate users because it is being bombarded with data requests is known as a _____ attack.

    a. stealth

    b. backdoor

    c. scareware

    d. denial-of-service

3. A series of commands that are executed without your knowledge is a typical attribute of a _____ virus.

    a. boot-sector

    b. script

    c. time bomb

    d. encryption

4. Software that pretends your computer is infected with a virus to entice you into spending money on a solution is known as

    a. scareware.

    b. spyware.

    c. adware.

    d. trackingware.

5. A technique that uses illegally obtained information about individuals to perform targeted attacks in the hopes of getting them to reveal sensitive information is known as

    a. spear phishing.

    b. pretexting.

    c. keystroke logging.

    d. logic bombing.

TECHBYTES WEEKLY

Stay current with TechBytes Weekly Newsletter.

Continue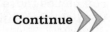

Protecting Your Digital Property

Learning Outcome **Describe various ways to protect your digital property and data from theft and corruption.**

Often, we can be our own worst enemies when using computing devices. If you're not careful, you might be taken in by thieves or scam artists who want to steal your digital and physical assets. As we'll discuss in this section, protecting yourself is key, and there are many relatively easy measures you can take to increase your level of security.

 restricting access to your
DIGITAL ASSETS

Keeping hackers and viruses at bay is often just a matter of keeping them out. You can achieve this by:

- Preventing hackers from accessing your computer (usually through your Internet connection)
- Using techniques to prevent virus infections from reaching your computer
- Protecting your digital information in such a way that it can't be accessed (by using passwords, for example)
- Hiding your activities from prying eyes

In this section, we explore strategies for protecting access to your digital assets and keeping your Internet-surfing activities from being seen by the wrong people.

Firewalls

Objective *Explain what a firewall is and how a firewall protects your computer from hackers.*

What is a firewall? A **firewall** is a software program or hardware device designed to protect computers from hackers. It's named after a housing construction feature that slows the spread of fires from house to house. A firewall specifically designed for home networks is called a **personal firewall**. By using a personal firewall, you can close open logical ports (communications pathways) to invaders and potentially make your computer invisible to other computers on the Internet.

Which is better, a software firewall or a hardware firewall? Both hardware and software firewalls will protect you from hackers. One type isn't better than the other. Although installing either a software or a hardware firewall on your home network is probably sufficient, you should consider installing both for maximum protection. This will provide you with additional safety, just as wearing multiple layers of clothing helps keep you warmer in the winter than a single layer.

Types of Firewalls

What software firewalls are there? Both Windows and OS X include reliable firewalls. The Windows Action Center is a good source of information about the security status of your computer. The status of your Windows Firewall is shown in the Windows Firewall dialog box. Security suites such as Norton Security, McAfee Internet Security, and Trend Micro Internet Security Suite also include firewall software. Although the firewalls that come with Windows and OS X will protect your computer, firewalls included in security suites often come with additional features such as monitoring systems that alert you if your computer is under attack.

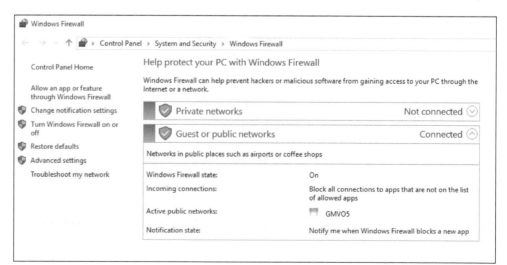

The Windows Firewall dialog box provides the status of your firewall. *(Windows 10, Microsoft Corporation)*

>*To view the Windows Firewall dialog box, access **Settings**, select **Network & Internet**, select **Wi-Fi**, and then click the **Windows Firewall link**.*

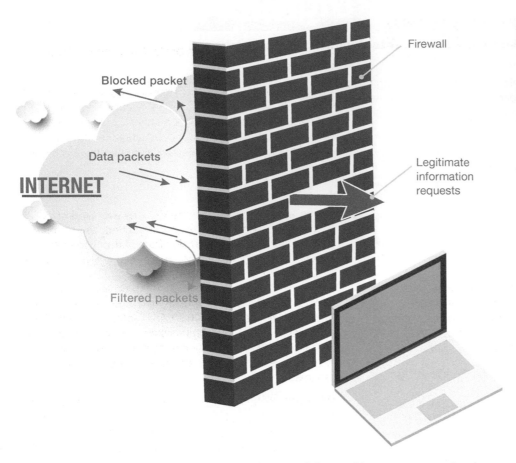

How do firewalls block access to your logical ports? As you'll recall, logical ports are virtual communications gateways or paths that allow a computer to organize requests for information from other networks or computers. Certain logical ports are very popular in hacker attacks. To block access to logical ports, firewalls examine data packets that your computer sends and receives. Data packets contain information such as the address of the sending and receiving computers and the logical port that the packet will use. Firewalls can be configured so that they filter out packets sent to specific logical ports in a process known as **packet filtering**. Firewalls are also often configured to ignore requests that originate from the Internet asking for access to certain ports. This process is referred to as **logical port blocking**. By using filtering and blocking, firewalls keep hackers from accessing your computer.

How do firewalls keep your network address secure?

Every computer connected to the Internet has a unique address called an *Internet Protocol address (IP address)*. Data is routed to the correct computer on the Internet based on the IP address. This is

Firewalls use filtering and blocking to keep out unwanted data and keep your network safe.

If you're using a security suite that includes a firewall, the suite should disable the firewall that came with your OS. Two firewalls running at the same time can conflict with each other and cause your computer to slow down or freeze up.

What are hardware firewalls? You can also buy and configure hardware firewall devices. Many routers sold for home networks include firewall protection. Just like software firewalls, the setup for hardware firewalls is designed for novices, and the default configuration on most routers keeps unused logical ports closed. Documentation accompanying routers can assist more-experienced users in adjusting the settings to allow access to specific ports if needed.

How Firewalls Work

How do firewalls protect you from hackers? Firewalls are designed to restrict access to a network and its computers. Firewalls protect you in two major ways:

1. By blocking access to logical ports
2. By keeping your computer's network address secure

similar to how a letter finds its way to your mailbox. You have a unique postal address for your home. If a hacker finds out the IP address of your computer, he or she can locate it on the Internet and try to break into it. This is similar to how a conventional thief might target your home after finding out you collect antique cars by using your street address to locate your house.

Your IP address for your home network is assigned to your router by your Internet service provider (ISP), but each device on your home network also has an IP address. Firewalls use a process called **network address translation (NAT)** to assign internal IP addresses on a network. The internal IP addresses are used only on the internal network and therefore can't be detected by hackers. For hackers to access your computer, they must know your computer's internal IP address. With a NAT–capable router/firewall installed on your network, hackers are unable to access the internal IP address assigned to your computer, so your computer is safe. You can use NAT in your home by purchasing a hardware firewall with NAT capabilities. Many routers sold for home use are also configured as firewalls, and many feature NAT.

Common Logical Ports

PORT NUMBER	PROTOCOL USING THE PORT
21	FTP (File Transfer Protocol) control
23	Telnet (unencrypted text communications)
25	SMTP (Simple Mail Transfer Protocol)
53	DNS (domain name system)
80	HTTP (Hypertext Transfer Protocol)
443	HTTPS (HTTP with Transport Layer Security [TLS] encryption)

Knowing Your Computer Is Secure

How can I tell if my firewall is protecting my computer? For peace of mind, you can visit websites that offer free services that test your computer's vulnerability. One popular site is Gibson Research Corporation (**grc.com**). The company's ShieldsUP and LeakTest programs are free and easy to run and can pinpoint security vulnerabilities in a system connected to the Internet. If you get a clean report from these programs, your system is probably not vulnerable to attack.

What if I don't get a clean report from the testing program? If the testing program detects potential vulnerabilities and you don't have a firewall, you should install one as soon as possible. If the firewall is already configured and common ports are identified as being vulnerable, consult your firewall documentation for instructions on how to close or restrict access to those ports.

Preventing Virus Infections

Objective *Explain how to protect your computer from virus infection.*

What is the best way to protect my devices from viruses? Earlier in the chapter, we discussed the various viruses that hackers may unleash on your system. There are two main ways to protect your computer from viruses: by installing antivirus software and by keeping your software up to date.

Antivirus Software

What antivirus software do I need? Antivirus software is specifically designed to detect viruses and protect your computer and files from harm. Symantec, Kaspersky, Trend Micro, and McAfee are among the companies that offer highly rated antivirus software packages. Antivirus protection is also included in comprehensive Internet security packages such as Norton Security, Trend Micro Internet Security, and McAfee Total Protection. These software packages also help protect you from threats other than computer viruses. For example, Windows 10 includes Windows Defender, which defends against malware as well as viruses.

How often do I need to run antivirus software? Although antivirus software is designed to detect suspicious activity on your computer at all times, you should run an active virus scan on your entire system at least once a week. By doing so, all files on your computer will be checked for undetected viruses.

Current antivirus programs run scans in the background when your CPU is not being heavily utilized. But you can also configure the software to run scans at times when you aren't using your system—for example, when you're asleep. (However, it's important to note that your computer has to be on and not in sleep mode for these virus scans to take place.) Alternatively, if you suspect a problem, you can launch a scan and have it run immediately.

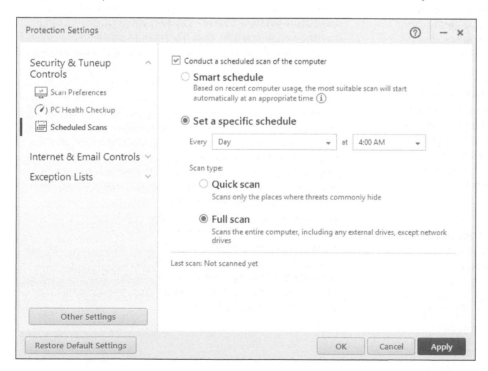

In Trend Micro Internet Security, you can set up virus scans to run automatically. This computer will be scanned every day at 4 a.m. *(Reprinted courtesy of Trend Micro Incorporated. All rights reserved.)*

How does antivirus software work? The main functions of antivirus software are as follows:

- *Detection*: Antivirus software looks for virus signatures in files. A **virus signature** is a portion of the virus code that's unique to a particular computer virus. Antivirus software scans files for these signatures when they're opened or executed and identifies infected files and the type of virus infecting them.

- *Stopping virus execution*: If the antivirus software detects a virus signature or suspicious activity, such as the launch of an unknown macro, it stops the execution of the file and virus and notifies you that it has detected a virus. It also places the virus in a secure area on your hard drive so that it won't spread to other files; this procedure is known as **quarantining**. Usually, the antivirus software then gives you the choice of deleting or repairing the infected file. Unfortunately, antivirus programs can't always fix infected files to make them usable again. You should keep backup copies of critical files so that you can restore them in case a virus damages them irreparably.

- *Prevention of future infection*: Most antivirus software will also attempt to prevent infection by inoculating key files on your computer. In **inoculation**, the antivirus software records key attributes about your computer files, such as file size and date created, and keeps these statistics in a safe place on your hard drive. When scanning for viruses, the antivirus software compares the attributes of the files with the attributes it previously recorded to help detect attempts by virus programs to modify your files.

Does antivirus software always stop viruses?
Antivirus software catches *known* viruses effectively. However, new viruses are written all the time. To combat unknown viruses, modern antivirus programs search for suspicious virus-like activities as well as virus signatures. To minimize your risk, you should keep your antivirus software up to date.

My new computer came with antivirus software installed, so shouldn't I already be protected?
Most new computers do come with antivirus software preinstalled. However, these are usually trial versions of the software that only provide updates to the software for a limited period of time, usually 90 or 180 days. After that, you have to buy a full version of the software to ensure you remain protected from new viruses. If you have Windows 10 and there is no third-party antivirus software installed, Windows Defender will be active by default so you should have some protection.

How do I make sure my antivirus software is up to date? Most antivirus programs have an automatic update feature that downloads updates for virus signature files every time you go online. Also, the antivirus software usually shows the status of your update subscription so that you can see how

Many protection packages, such as Trend Micro Internet Security, offer other types of security features besides basic malware protection. *(Reprinted courtesy of Trend Micro Incorporated. All rights reserved.)*

much time you have remaining until you need to buy another version of your software. Many Internet security packages offer bonus features such as cloud storage scanners and password managers to provide you with extra protection.

What should I do if I think my computer is infected with a virus? Boot up your computer using the antivirus installation disc. This should prevent most virus programs from loading and will allow you to run the antivirus software directly from your disk drive. (*Note*: If you download your antivirus software from the Internet, copy the files to a DVD in case you have problems in the future.) If the software does detect viruses, you may want to research them further to determine whether your antivirus software will eradicate them completely or whether you'll need to take additional manual steps to eliminate the viruses. Most antivirus company websites, such as the Symantec site (**symantec.com**), contain archives of information on viruses and provide step-by-step solutions for removing them.

How do I protect my phone from viruses? Because smartphones and other mobile devices run operating systems and contain files, they are susceptible to infection by viruses. Cybercriminals are now hiding viruses in legitimate-looking apps for download to mobile devices. Most antivirus software companies now offer antivirus software specifically designed for mobile devices. The Google Play store even offers very effective free products to protect your Android devices such as 360 Security and Avast! Mobile Security. In addition to providing protection from malware, these apps also provide other useful features such as the ability to wipe your phone's contents if it is lost or stolen.

Software Updates

Why does updating my operating system (OS) software help protect me from viruses? Many viruses exploit weaknesses in operating systems. Malicious websites can be set up to attack your computer by downloading harmful software onto your computer. According to research conducted by Google, this type of attack, known as a **drive-by download**, affects almost 1 in 1,000 web pages. To combat these threats, make sure your OS is up to date and contains the latest security patches.

Do OS updates only happen automatically? Prior to the release of Windows 10, you updated your Windows OS with an automatic update utility called Windows Update. You had the ability to decide when to download updates and when to install them. However, with Windows 10, you no longer have as many choices. Updates are now downloaded automatically whenever they are provided by Microsoft. You do have the choice to allow Windows to automatically schedule a restart of your computer to apply the updates or pick a more convenient

restart time manually. Mac OS X has a similar utility for gathering updates.

The Advanced Options screen for Windows Update provides a few other options. The most notable is the ability to receive updates for other Microsoft products (like MS Office). (Note that the ability to defer upgrades is not available on the Windows 10 Home edition—you must install updates as they are delivered by Microsoft).

Authentication: Passwords and Biometrics

Objective *Describe how passwords and biometric characteristics can be used for user authentication on computer systems.*

How can I best use passwords to protect my computer? You no doubt have many passwords you need to remember to access your digital life. However, creating strong passwords—ones that are difficult for hackers to guess—is an essential piece of security that people sometimes overlook. Password-cracking programs have become more sophisticated. In fact, some commonly available programs can test more than one million password combinations per second! Creating a secure password is therefore more important than ever.

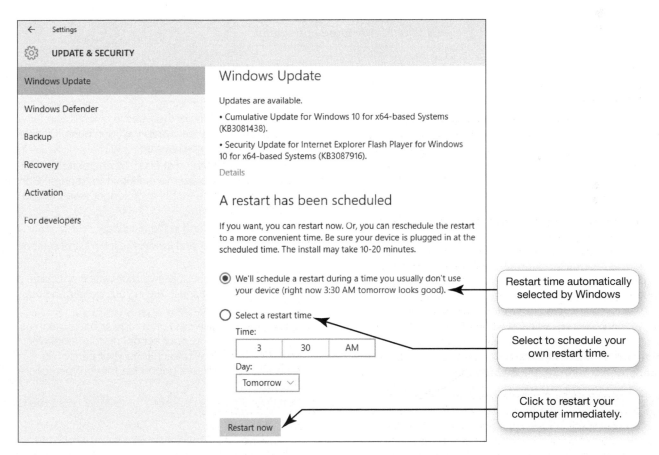

The Windows Update screen makes it easy for users to stay abreast of software updates and manage restarts. *(Windows 10, Microsoft Corporation)*

>*To access the Windows Update screen, from the Start menu, select **Settings**, select **Update & security**, then select **Windows Update**.*

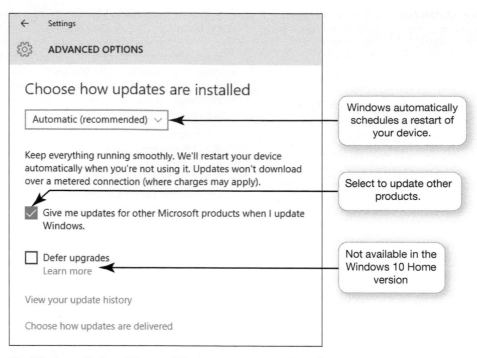

The Windows Update Advanced Options screen provides a few more user controlled update options. *(Windows 10, Microsoft Corporation)*
*>To access the Windows Update Advanced Options screen, scroll to the bottom of the Windows Update screen and click the **Advanced options link**.*

Many people use extremely weak passwords. The Imperva Application Defense Center, a computer-security research organization, conducted a review of 32 million passwords that were used at the website **rockyou.com**. More than 345,000 people were using "12345," "123456," or "123456789" as their password. And almost 62,000 people were using "password"! Passwords such as these are easy for hackers to crack.

Websites that need to be very secure, such as those for financial institutions, usually have strong defenses to prevent hackers from cracking passwords. But sites that need less security, such as casual gaming or social networking sites, might have less protection. Hackers attack poorly defended sites for passwords because many people use the same password for every site they use. So if a hacker can get your password from a poorly secured gaming site, they might be able to access your bank account with the same password.

Creating Strong Passwords

What constitutes a strong password? Strong passwords are difficult for someone to guess. Follow these guidelines to create strong passwords:

- Don't use easily deduced components related to your life, such as parts of your name, your pet's name, your street address, or the name of the website or institution for which you are creating the password (i.e., don't use "Citibank" for your online banking password).
- Use a password that is at least 14 characters long. Longer passwords are more difficult to deduce. Consider using a passphrase that is even longer (see the Bits & Bytes).
- Don't use words found in the dictionary.
- Use a mix of upper- and lowercase letters and symbols (such as # or %).
- Never tell anyone your password or write it down in a place where others might see it, like in your wallet or a sticky note on your computer screen!
- Change your passwords on a regular basis, such as monthly or quarterly. Your school or your employer probably requires you to change your password regularly. This is also a good idea for your personal passwords.
- Don't use the same password for every account you have.

Strong and Weak Password Candidates

PASSWORD	RATING	GOOD POINTS	BAD POINTS
Joysmith1022	Poor	• Contains upper- and lowercase letters • Contains letters and numbers	• Less than 14 characters • Contains name and birth date
test44drive6car	Mediocre	• 15 characters in length	• Contains three words found in the dictionary • Numbers repeated consecutively
8$RanT%5ydTTtt&	Better	• Good length • Contains upper- and lowercase letters • Contains symbols	• Upper- and lowercase letters repeated consecutively • Still contains one dictionary word (rant)
7R3m3mB3R$5%y38	Best	• All good points from above • Dictionary word (remember) has 3s instead of Es	• None

BITS&BYTES

CAPTCHA: Keeping Websites Safe from Bots

Automated programs called *bots* (or web robots) are used to make tasks easier on the Internet. For example, search engines use bots to search and index web pages. Unfortunately, bots can also be used for malicious or illegal purposes because they can perform some computing tasks faster than humans. For example, bots can be used on ticket-ordering sites to buy large blocks of high-demand concert tickets. They are also often used to post spam in the comment sections of blogs. Fortunately, website owners can deploy CAPTCHA software to prevent such bot activities.

CAPTCHA (Completely Automated Public Turing Test to Tell Computers and Humans Apart) programs used to generate distorted text and require that it be typed into a box. Newer programs, like Google's reCAPTCHA, monitor users' website behavior to determine if you are a human or a bot. reCAPTCHA merely asks you to click a check box and if it displays a green check, you have passed the bot test. If the app isn't sure if you are a human, it may ask you to type in some distorted text just like older versions of the program did. If you want to try integrating a CAPTCHA program into your website (to protect your e-mail address), go to **google.com/recaptcha**, which offers free CAPTCHA tools to help you protect your data.

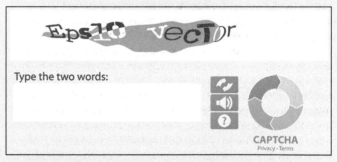

CAPTCHA programs like reCAPTCHA monitor a user's website behavior and can often determine if a user is human just by having the user check a box. If a green check mark appears, you are human! If the app isn't sure if you're a bot, you may be asked to enter some text. *(Metrue/Shutterstock)*

Drawing three gestures (a swipe and two circles) on this image (and repeating them once) sets your picture password options in Windows. *(Windows 10, Microsoft Corporation)*

If you have trouble thinking of secure passwords, there are many password generators available for free, such as the Strong Password Generator (**strongpasswordgenerator. com**).

How can I check the strength of my passwords?
You can use online password strength testers, such as the Password Meter (**passwordmeter.com**), to evaluate your passwords. The Password Meter provides guidelines for good passwords and shows you how integrating various elements, such as symbols, affects the strength score of your password.

How do I restrict access to my computer? Windows, OS X, and most other operating systems have built-in password (or passcode) protection for files as well as the entire desktop. After a certain period of idle time, your computer is automatically password locked, and your password (or PIN) must be entered to gain access to the computer. This provides excellent protection from casual snooping if you need to walk away from your computer for a period of time. If someone attempts to log on to your computer without your password, that person won't be able to gain access. It's an especially good idea to use passwords on laptop computers, smartphones, and tablets because this provides additional protection of your data if your device is lost or stolen.

Windows allows you to use picture passwords. You select a picture and then draw three gestures on it—either straight lines, circles, or taps. This picture then works as an additional method for accessing your computer. You just unlock your computer by repeating the gestures. But if you forget your gestures, you can always access your computer via the conventional password.

Managing Your Passwords

How can I remember all of my complex passwords? Good security practices suggest that you have

different passwords for all the different websites that you access and that you change your passwords frequently. The problem with well-constructed passwords is that they can be hard to remember. Fortunately, password-management tools are now available. They take the worry out of forgetting passwords because the password-management software does the remembering for you.

Where can I obtain password-management software? Most current Internet security suites and web browsers make it easy to keep track of passwords by providing password-management tools. For example, Microsoft Edge will remember passwords for you. When you go to a website that requires a login, Microsoft Edge will display a dialog box prompting you to have Microsoft Edge remember the password for the site. Then, when you return to the site and type in your user name, Microsoft Edge will fill in the password information for you using a process known as *auto complete*. However, there are some passwords that you shouldn't have your browser remember, such as your online banking password. So be selective when using this feature.

Biometric Authentication Devices

Besides passwords, how else can I restrict the use of my computer? A **biometric authentication device** is a device that reads a unique personal characteristic such as a fingerprint or the iris pattern in your eye and converts its pattern to a digital code. When you use the device, your pattern is read and compared to the one stored on the computer. Only users having an exact fingerprint or iris pattern match are allowed to access the computer.

Because no two people have the same biometric characteristics (fingerprints and iris patterns are unique), these devices provide a high level of security. They also eliminate the human error that can occur in password protection. You might forget your password, but you won't forget to bring your fingerprints

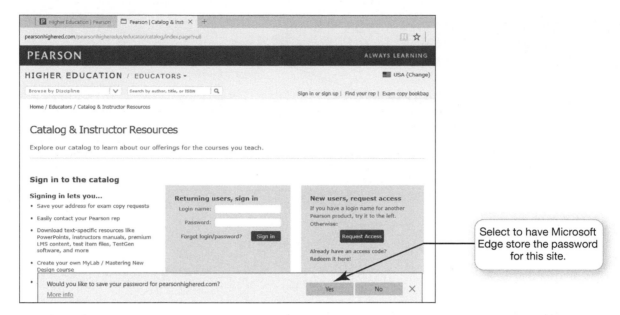

The password dialog box in Microsoft Edge displays whenever you type in a password for a website for which Microsoft Edge hasn't yet stored the password. *(Screenshot of Pearson Higher Education website, Pearson Education, Inc.)*

when you're working on your computer! Some smartphones, such as the iPhone, now include fingerprint readers. But since Touch ID (the Apple software for fingerprint identification) has already been hacked, you might be safer using a regular password. Other biometric devices, including voice authentication and facial recognition systems, are now widely offered in laptops, tablets, and smartphones (such as the Samsung Galaxy phones).

Face recognition software is now available on laptops. You might forget your password, but you won't forget to bring your face! *(Jochen Tack/Alamy)*

Anonymous Web Surfing: Hiding from Prying Eyes

Objective *Describe ways to surf the web anonymously.*

Should I be concerned about surfing the Internet on shared, public, or work computers? If you use shared computers in public places such as libraries, coffee shops, or student unions, you never know what nefarious tools have been installed by hackers on a public computer. When you browse the Internet, traces of your activity are left behind on that computer, often as temporary files. A wily hacker can glean sensitive information long after you've finished your surfing session. In addition, many employers routinely review the Internet browsing history of employees to ensure workers are spending their time on the Internet productively.

What tools can I use to keep my browsing activities private when surfing the Internet? The current versions of Mozilla Firefox, Microsoft Edge, and Google Chrome include privacy tools (called Private Browsing, InPrivate, and Incognito, respectively) that help you surf the web anonymously. When you choose to surf anonymously, all three browsers open special versions of their browser windows that are enhanced for privacy. When surfing in these windows, records of websites you visit and files you download don't appear in the web browser's history files. Furthermore, any temporary files generated in that browsing session are deleted when you exit the special window.

Are there any other tools I could use to protect my privacy? Portable privacy devices, such as the Ironkey Personal Flash Drives (**ironkey.com**), provide an even higher level of surfing privacy. Simply plug the device into an available

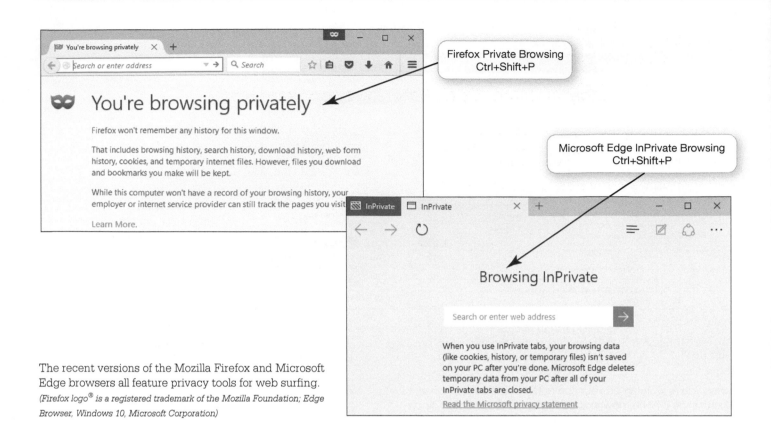

The recent versions of the Mozilla Firefox and Microsoft Edge browsers all feature privacy tools for web surfing. *(Firefox logo® is a registered trademark of the Mozilla Foundation; Edge Browser, Windows 10, Microsoft Corporation)*

USB port on the machine on which you'll be working. All sensitive Internet files, such as cookies, passwords, Internet history, and browser caches, will be stored on the privacy device, not on the computer you're using. Privacy devices such as these often come preloaded with software designed to shield your IP address from prying eyes, making it difficult (if not impossible) for hackers to tell where you're surfing on the Internet. These privacy devices also have password-management tools that store all of your login information and encrypt it so it will be safe if your privacy device falls into someone else's hands.

Is there anything else I can do to keep my data safe on shared computers? Another free practical solution is to take the Linux OS with you on a flash drive and avoid using the public or work computer's OS. The interfaces of many Linux distros look almost exactly like Windows and are easy to use. There are several advantages to using a Linux-based OS on a public or work computer:

- Your risk of picking up viruses and other malicious programs is significantly reduced because booting a computer from a flash drive completely eliminates any interaction with the computer's OS. This, in turn, significantly reduces the chance that your flash drive will become infected by any malware running on the computer.
- Virus and hacking attacks against Linux are far less likely than attacks against Windows. Because Windows has about 90% of the OS market, people who write malware tend to target Windows systems.

- When you run software from your own storage medium, such as a flash drive, you avoid reading and writing to the hard disk of the computer. This significantly enhances your privacy because you don't leave traces of your activity behind.

Pendrivelinux (**pendrivelinux.com**) is an excellent resource that offers many different versions of Linux for download and includes step-by-step instructions on how to install them on your flash drive. If you're a Mac user, the Elementary OS Luna distro of Linux provides a close approximation of OS X, so you can feel right at home.

How can I protect sensitive data transmissions if I have to use a public wireless network? Virtual private networks (VPNs) are secure networks that are established using the public Internet infrastructure. Using specialized software, servers and data transmission protocols, VPNs are used to send information on the public Internet in a such a manner that the data is as secure as sending it on a private network. VPNs used to be only used by businesses. But with public concerns about information security on the rise, many VPN software providers (such as Private Internet Access and Nord VPN) are marketing affordable solutions to individuals. So if you routinely transmit sensitive information, you should consider a personal VPN solution.

Make sure to use some (or all) of these methods to keep your activities from prying eyes and to restrict access to your digital information. ■

BITS&BYTES

Multi-Factor Authentication: Don't Rely Solely on Passwords!

Computer system security depends on authentication—proving the user is who they say they are. There are three independent authentication factors:

- Knowledge factor: Something the user knows (password, PIN)
- Possession factor: Something the user has (ATM card, mobile phone)
- Inherence factor: Something only the user is (biometric characteristics, such as fingerprints)

Multi-factor authentication requires two of the three above factors be demonstrated before authorization is granted. At the bank's ATM machine, you present an ATM card (something you have) and then use a PIN code (something you know) to access your account.

For online access, multi-factor authentication often relies on the use of mobile phones. For instance, when you register a Google account, you supply your mobile phone number. If you then want to make changes to your account, you supply the password (something you know). The second step of authentication is Google sending an SMS message with a unique code to your mobile phone. Retrieving the code and entering it online proves you have the phone (something the user has) and serves as the second authentication step.

Multi-factor authentication is much safer than single-factor authentication. So make use of it when it is offered to you to enhance your account security.

Multi-Factor Authentication

Possession factor:
Something the user has
(ATM card, mobile phone)

Knowledge factor:
Something the user knows
(password, PIN)

Inherence factor:
Something only the user is
(biometric characteristics, such as fingerprints)

Strong Authentication:
Two of the three factors

(LoloStock/Fotolia, Jamie/Fotolia, Jamdesign/Fotolia)

keeping your
DATA SAFE

People are often too trusting or just plain careless when it comes to protecting private information about themselves or their digital data. In this section, we discuss ways to keep your data safe from damage, either accidental or intentional.

Protecting Your Personal Information

Objective *Describe the types of information you should never share online.*

If a complete stranger walked up to you on the street and asked you for your address and phone number, would you give it to him or her? Of course you wouldn't! But many people are much less careful when it comes to sharing sensitive information online. And often people inadvertently share information that they really only intended to share with their friends. With cybercrimes like identify theft rampant, you need to take steps to protect your personal information.

What information should I never share on websites? A good rule of thumb is to reveal as little information as possible, especially if the information would be available to everyone. Gives you some good guidelines.

Your Social Security number, phone number, date of birth, and street address are four key pieces of information that identity thieves need to steal an identity. This information should never be shared in a public area on any website.

How can I tell who can see my information on a social network? Social networking sites like Facebook make privacy settings available in your profile settings. If you've never changed your default privacy settings in Facebook, you're probably sharing information more widely than you should.

How can I protect my information on Facebook? To begin, you need to change your privacy settings in your profile from some of the default options. In general, it's a bad idea to make personal information available to the public, although this is a default setting for some items in Facebook. It's a good idea to set most of the options in your profile's Basic Information section to Friends or to Only Me because, presumably, these are personal details you should wish to share only with friends.

In the Contact Information section, restricting this information only to friends or to yourself is imperative. You don't want scammers contacting you via e-mail or snail mail and trying to trick you into revealing sensitive information.

Backing Up Your Data

Objective *List the various types of backups you can perform on your computing devices, and explain the various places you can store backup files.*

How might I damage the data on my computer? The data on your computer faces three major threats:

1. Unauthorized access
2. Tampering
3. Destruction

Internet Information-Sharing Precautions

Information Identity Thieves Crave

STOP

- Social Security Number
- Full Date of Birth
- Phone Number
- Street Address

Never make this information visible on websites!

Other Sensitive Information

CAUTION

- Full Legal Name
- E-mail Address
- Zip Code
- Gender
- School or Workplace

Only reveal this information to people you know—don't make it visible to everyone!

(Mograph/Fotolia, Kevin Largent/Fotolia)

BITS&BYTES

Social Networking: Looking Beyond Facebook

Are the posts you see on Facebook too general for your liking? Do you wish you could participate in a social networking community with more people who share your specific interests or passions? Facebook is the largest social networking site, but it isn't the only option out there. Many social networking sites exist that cater to specific types of users or interests.

Are you a graduate student that needs to monitor progress in a specific field of research? Try **Academia.edu**, which is a site specifically designed to promote the sharing of research papers in the academic community. If cooking is your passion, start your own food blog on **cucumbertown.com** and gain followers who like your recipes. People who love clubbing can meet at **dontstayin.com** and find out about events at clubs in a specific area. Trying to learn English as a second language? **Englishbaby.com** is a community of ESL students and teachers dedicated to helping members learn conversational English and slang. Free English lessons are posted every day! The Experience Project (**experienceproject.com**) encourages members to post personal experiences and form groups based on people with similar experiences or interests.

So no matter where your interests lie, there is probably a social network that caters to you. If you can't find one that suits you, then use **ning.com** and create your own specialized social network!

As noted earlier, a hacker can gain access to your computer and steal or alter your data. However, a more likely scenario is that you'll lose your data unintentionally. You may accidentally delete files. You may drop your laptop on the ground, causing the hard drive to break and resulting in complete data loss. A virus from an e-mail attachment you opened may destroy your original file. Your house may catch fire and destroy your computer. Because many of these possibilities are beyond your control, you should have a strategy for backing up your files. **Backups** are copies of files that you can use to replace the originals if they're lost or damaged.

What types of files do I need to back up? Two types of files need backups:

1. **Program files** include files used to install software, usually found on DVDs or downloaded from the Internet. As long as you have the DVDs in a safe place, you shouldn't need to back up these program files. If you've downloaded a program file from the Internet, however, you should make a copy of the program installation files on a removable storage device as a backup.

2. **Data files** include files you've created or purchased, such as research papers, spreadsheets, music and photo files, contact lists, address books, e-mail archives, and your Favorites list from your browser.

What types of backups can I perform? There are two main options for backing up files:

1. An **incremental backup** (or **partial backup**) involves backing up only files that have changed or have been created since the last backup was performed. Using backup software that has an option for incremental

An Effective Backup Strategy

Files to Back Up

- **Program files:** Installation files for productivity software (i.e., Microsoft Office)
- **Data files:** Files you create (term papers, spreadsheets, etc.)

Types of Backups

- **Incremental (partial):** Only backs up files that have changed
- **Image (system):** Snapshot of your entire computer, including system software

Where to Store Backup Files

- Online (in the cloud)
- External hard drives
- Network-attached storage devices or home servers

backups will save time because backing up files that haven't changed is redundant.

2. An **image backup** (or **system backup**) means that all system, application, and data files are backed up, not just the files that changed. Although incremental backups are more efficient, an image backup ensures you capture

changes to application files, such as automatic software updates, that an incremental backup might not capture. The idea of imaging is to make an exact copy of the setup of your computer so that in the event of a total hard drive failure you could copy the image to a new hard drive and have your computer configured exactly the way it was before the crash.

Where should I store my backups? To be truly secure, backups must be stored away from where your computer is located and should be stored in at least two different places. You wouldn't want a fire or a flood destroying the backups along with the original data. You have three main choices for where to back up your files:

1. *Online (in the cloud)*: The beauty of online storage is that you don't need to be at your home computer or lug around your external hard drive to access your data. More importantly, because the information is stored online, it's in a secure, remote location, so data is much less vulnerable to the disasters that could harm data stored in your computer or external hard drive. Free storage options include Microsoft OneDrive (**onedrive.com**) and ADrive (**adrive.com**). However, image backups probably won't fit within the storage limits offered by

free providers. For a fee, companies such as Carbonite (**carbonite.com**) and IBackup (**ibackup.com**) provide larger storage capacity.

2. *External hard drives*: External hard drives, or even large-capacity flash drives, are popular backup options that are usually connected to a single computer. Although convenient and inexpensive, using external hard drives for backups still presents the dilemma of keeping the hard drive in a safe location. Also, external hard drives can fail, possibly leading to loss of your backed-up data. Therefore, using an external hard drive for backups is best done in conjunction with an online backup strategy for added safety.

3. *Network-attached storage (NAS) devices and home servers*: NAS devices are essentially large hard drives connected to a network of computers instead of one computer, and they can be used to back up multiple computers simultaneously. Home servers also act as high-capacity NAS devices for automatically backing up data and sharing files.

How often should I back up my data files? You should back up your data files every time you make changes to them, which can be difficult to remember to do. Fortunately, most backup software can be configured to do backups

A Comparison of Typical Data Backup Locations

BACKUP LOCATION	PROS	CONS
Online (in the Cloud) 	• Files stored at a secure, remote location • Files/backups accessible anywhere through a browser	• Most free storage sites don't provide enough space for image backups
External Hard Drive 	• Inexpensive, one-time cost • Fast backups with USB 3.0 devices connected directly to your computer	• Could be destroyed in one event (fire/flood) with your computer • Can be stolen • Slightly more difficult to back up multiple computers with one device
Network-Attached Storage (NAS) Device and Home Server	• Makes backups much easier for multiple computing devices	• More expensive than a stand-alone external hard drive • Could be destroyed in one event (fire/flood) with your computer • Can be stolen

(Mipan/Fotolia, Prapass Wannapinij/Fotolia, Darkdesigns/Fotolia)

automatically so you don't forget to perform them. For example, with the Windows File History utility, you can have Windows automatically save your data files from your libraries, desktop, contacts, and favorites to an external hard drive or NAS device. The default setting for File History saves files you changed every hour to the backup location you specify. File History even keeps previous versions of the file on the backup drive so you can revert to a previous version of the file if you need to do so.

To set up File History, you first need to connect an external hard drive to your computer or a NAS device (or home server) to your network. You can then access File History through the Control Panel (in the System and Security group) and set it up. Once configured, your data files will be backed up as often as you indicate. You can also restore files that you've backed up from the File History utility.

How often should I create an image backup?
Because your program and OS files don't change as often as your data files, you can perform image backups on a less frequent basis. You might consider scheduling an image backup of your entire system on a weekly basis, but you should definitely perform one after installing new software.

How do I perform an image backup?
Windows includes the System Image Backup utility, which provides a quick and easy way to perform image backups. You can access this utility from the System Image Backup link on the File History screen, which launches the Backup and Restore (Windows 7) screen. Before starting this utility, make sure your external hard drive or NAS device is connected to your computer or network and is powered on. To set it up, follow these steps:

1. Click the Create a system image link. Select the location (drive) for your backup files and click Next to proceed.

2. On the second screen, you can select the drives/partitions from your computer to be backed up. Notice that all the drives/partitions that are required for Windows to run are preselected for you. Windows will back up all data files and system files on all selected drives/partitions. Click Next to proceed.

3. On the third screen, click Start backup to start your system image.

After the system image backup runs for the first time, you will see the results of the last backup and the date of the next scheduled backup on the Backup and Restore (Windows 7) screen. If the scheduled backup time is not convenient for you, click the Change settings link to select an alternative time.

From the Backup and Restore screen, you can also create a system repair disc. A system repair disc contains files that can be used to boot your computer in case of a serious Windows error.

What about backing up Apple computers?
For OS X users, backups are very easy to configure. The Time Machine feature in OS X detects when an external hard drive is connected to the computer or a NAS device is connected to your network. You're then asked if you want this to be your backup drive. If you answer yes, all of your files (including OS files) are automatically backed up to the external drive or NAS device.

Should I back up my files that are stored on my school's network?
Most likely, if you're allowed to store files on your school's network, these files are backed up

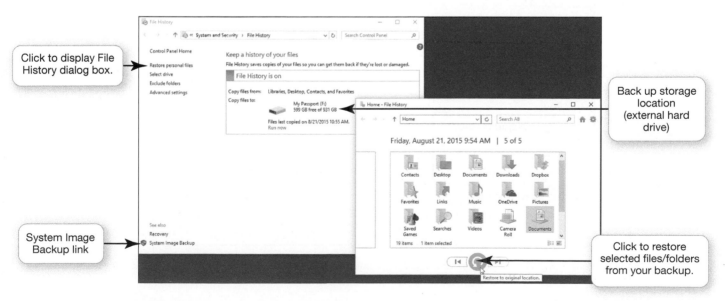

You can use the Windows File History utility to back up files and restore files from a previous backup. *(Windows 10, Microsoft Corporation)* >*Right-click* **Start**, *select* **Control Panel**, *select* **System and Security**, *and then click the* **File History link**.

regularly. You should check with your school's network administrators to determine how often they're backed up and how you would request that files be restored from the backup if they're damaged or deleted. But don't rely on these network backups to bail you out if your data files are lost or damaged. It may take days for the network administrators to restore your files. It's better to keep backups of your data files yourself, especially homework and project files, so that you can immediately restore them. ■

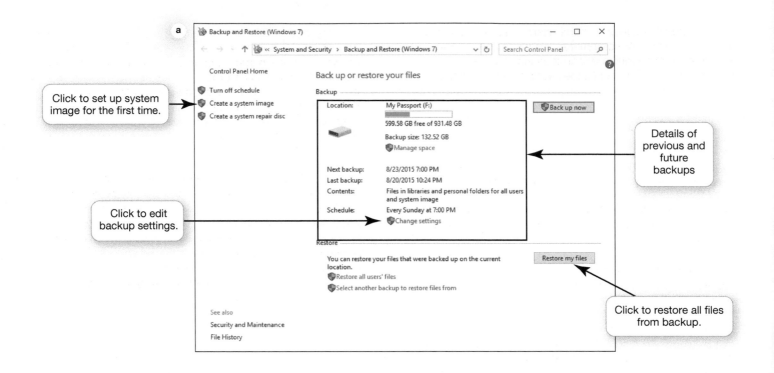

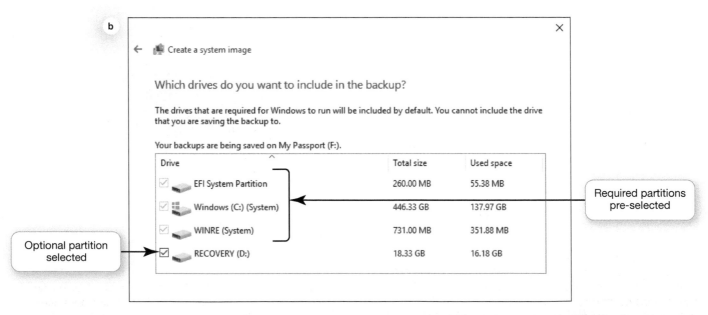

(a) The Backup and Restore utility allows you to perform an image backup and restore from one. (b) Select partitions to be included in the system image backup. *(Windows 10, Microsoft Corporation)*

protecting your physical
COMPUTING ASSETS

Your computer, tablet, and phone aren't useful to you if they're damaged. Therefore, it's essential to select and ensure a safe environment for these devices. This includes protecting them from environmental factors, power surges, power outages, and theft.

Environmental Factors and Power Surges

Objective *Explain the negative effects environment and power surges can have on computing devices.*

Why is the environment critical to the operation of my computer equipment? Computers are delicate devices and can be damaged by the adverse effects of abuse or a poor environment. Sudden movements, such as a fall, can damage your computing device's internal components. You should make sure that your computer sits on a flat, level surface, and if it's a laptop or a tablet, you should carry it in a protective case.

Electronic components don't like excessive heat or excessive cold. Don't leave computing devices and phones in a car during especially hot or cold weather because components can be damaged by extreme temperatures. Unfortunately, computers generate a lot of heat, which is why they have fans to cool their internal components. Chill mats that contain cooling fans and sit underneath laptop computers are useful accessories for dissipating heat. Make sure that you place your desktop computer where the fan's intake vents, usually found on the rear of the system unit, are unblocked so air can flow inside.

Naturally, a fan drawing air into a computer also draws in dust and other particles, which can wreak havoc on your system. Therefore, keep the room in which your computer is located as clean as possible. Finally, because food crumbs and liquid can damage keyboards and other computer components, consume food and beverages away from your computer.

What is a power surge? Power surges occur when electrical current is supplied in excess of normal voltage. Old or faulty wiring, downed power lines, malfunctions at electric company substations, and lightning strikes can all cause power surges. A **surge protector** is a device that protects your computer against power surges.

Note that you should replace your surge protectors every two to three years. Also, after a major surge, the surge protector will no longer function and must be replaced. And it's wise to buy a surge protector that includes indicator lights, which illuminate when the surge protector is no longer functioning properly. Don't be fooled by old surge protectors—although they can still function as multiple-outlet power strips, they deliver power to your equipment without protecting it.

Besides my computer, what other devices need to be connected to a surge protector? All electronic devices in the home that have solid-state components, such as TVs, stereos, printers, and smartphones (when charging), should be connected to a surge protector. However, it can be inconvenient to use individual surge protectors on everything. A more practical method is to install a **whole-house surge protector**. Whole-house surge protectors function

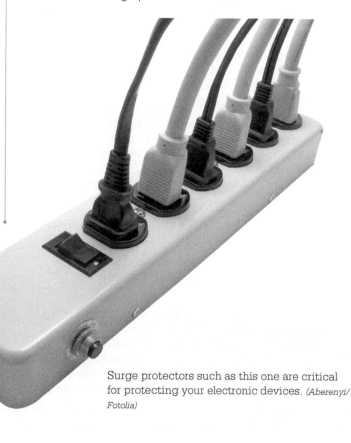

Surge protectors such as this one are critical for protecting your electronic devices. *(Aberenyi/ Fotolia)*

Surge protector

A whole-house surge protector is usually installed at the breaker panel or near the electric meter.

like other surge protectors, but they protect *all* electrical devices in the house. Typically, you'll need an electrician to install a whole-house surge protector, which will cost $300 to $500 (installed).

Is my equipment 100% safe when plugged into a surge protector? Lightning strikes can generate such high voltages that they can overwhelm a surge protector. As tedious as it sounds, unplugging electronic devices during an electrical storm is the only way to achieve absolute protection.

Preventing and Handling Theft

Objective *Describe the major concerns when a device is stolen and strategies for solving the problems.*

What do I need to worry about if my computing device is stolen? Although theft of computer equipment is not classified as a cybercrime (it is considered larceny), the theft of tablets, smartphones, notebook computers, and other portable computing devices is on the rise. The resale value for used electronic equipment is high, and the equipment can

be easily sold online. And because they're portable, laptops, tablets, and phones are easy targets for thieves. You have four main security concerns with mobile devices:

1. Keeping them from being stolen
2. Keeping data secure in case they are stolen
3. Finding a device if it is stolen
4. Remotely recovering and wiping data off a stolen device

Keep Them Safe: Alarms

What type of alarm can I install on my mobile device? Motion alarm software is a good, inexpensive theft deterrent. Free software such as LAlarm (**lalarm.com**) is effective for laptops. Apps such as Motion Alarm and Alarmomatic help secure your iPad or iPhone. Alarm software either detects motion, like your device being picked up, or sounds near your device and then sets off an ear-piercing alarm until you enter the disable code. Thieves normally don't like it when attention is drawn to their activities, so alarms can be a very effective theft deterrent.

Keeping Mobile Device Data Secure

How can I secure the data on my mobile devices? Encrypting the data on your mobile device can make it extremely difficult, if not impossible, for thieves to obtain sensitive data from your stolen equipment. *Encryption* involves transforming your data using an algorithm that can only be unlocked by a secure code (or key). Encrypted data is impossible to read unless it's decrypted, which requires a secure password, hopefully known only to you.

Safe is an app that provides 256-bit encryption, which is very hard to crack, for data and images on your iPhone and iPad. If your password is not entered, no one can access the data and images on your iPhone or iPad. Mobile Strong-Box is a similar app for Android devices. SensiGuard and SafeHouse are available for laptop computers to provide encryption for files or even entire hard drives.

Software Alerts and Data Wipes

How can my computer help me recover it when it is stolen? You've probably heard of LoJack, the theft-tracking device used in cars. Similar systems now exist for computers. Tracking software such as Absolut LoJack (**lojack.absolute.com/en**), PC PhoneHome, and Mac PhoneHome (**brigadoonsoftware.com**) enables your computer to alert authorities to the computer's location if it is stolen. A similar tracking app for Android and iOS devices is iHound.

To enable your mobile device to help with its own recovery, you install the tracking software on your device. The software contacts a server at the software manufacturer's website each time the device connects to the Internet. If your device is stolen, you notify the software manufacturer. The software manufacturer instructs your device to transmit tracking information, such as an IP address, WiFi hotspot, or cell tower location, that will assist authorities in locating and retrieving the mobile device.

What if the thieves find the tracking software and delete it? The files and directories holding the software aren't visible to thieves looking for such software, so they probably won't know the software is there. Furthermore, the tracking software is written in such a way that even if the thieves tried to reformat the hard drive, it would detect the reformat and hide the software code in a safe place in memory or on the hard drive. This works because some sectors of a hard drive are not rewritten during most reformatting. That way, the tracking software can reinstall itself after the reformatting is complete.

What if my device can't be recovered by the authorities? In the event that your laptop can't be recovered, software packages are available that provide for remote recovery and deletion of files. Absolute LoJack has these features and allows you to lock your device to keep the thieves from accessing it or to remotely wipe its contents by deleting all your data from your laptop.

For all iOS devices, Apple offers the Find My iPhone service, which is now part of iCloud. Enabling this service on your device provides you with numerous tools that can assist you in recovering and protecting your mobile devices. Did you forget where you left your iPad? Just sign in with your Apple ID at the iCloud website to see a map showing the location of your iPad. You can send a message to your device, remotely password lock the device, or wipe all data from the device to completely protect your privacy. For Android devices, Where is My Droid? offers similar features, such as texting your device and having it reply with its location. You can even capture images with the front and rear cameras to see what your device is looking at (such as the thief)!

How can I ensure that I've covered all aspects of protecting my digital devices? Provides a guide to ensure you haven't missed critical aspects of security. If you've addressed all of these issues, you can feel reasonably confident that your data and devices are secure. ■

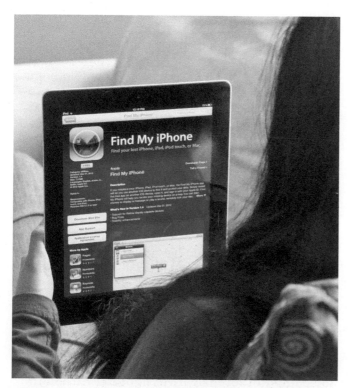

The Find My iPhone app can really help if your iOS device goes astray. You can play a sound to help you find it (if it's misplaced where you are), display a message on the device (Lost Mode), or erase all data on the device. *(LearningStockImages/Alamy)*

Computer Security Checklist

Firewall

- Do all your computers and tablets have firewall software installed and activated before connecting to the Internet?
- Is your router also able to function as a hardware firewall?
- Have you tested your firewall security by using the free software available at grc.com?

Virus and Spyware Protection

- Is antivirus and anti-spyware software installed on all your devices?
- Is the antivirus and anti-spyware software configured to update itself automatically and regularly?
- Is the software set to scan your device on a regular basis (at least weekly) for viruses and spyware?

Software Updates

- Have you configured your operating systems (Windows, OS X, iOS) to install new software patches and updates automatically?
- Is other software installed on your device, such as Microsoft Office or productivity apps, configured for automatic updates?
- Is the web browser you're using the latest version?

Protecting Your Devices

- Are all computing devices protected from electrical surges?
- Do your mobile devices have alarms or tracking software installed on them?

Before moving on to the Chapter Review:

1. Watch Replay Video 9.2 ↺.
2. Then check your understanding of what you've learned so far.

DIG DEEPER

Computer Forensics: How It Works

On law enforcement TV shows, you often see computer technicians working on suspects' computers to assist detectives in solving crimes. It may look simple, but the science of computer forensics is a complex, step-by-step process that ensures evidence is collected within the confines of the law.

Forensic means that something is suitable for use in a court of law. There are many branches of forensic science. For example, forensic pathologists provide evidence about the nature and manner of death in court cases involving deceased individuals. **Computer forensics** involves identifying, extracting, preserving, and documenting computer evidence. Computer forensics is performed by individuals known as *computer forensic scientists*, who rely primarily on specialized software to collect their evidence.

Phase 1: Obtaining and Securing Computer Devices

The first step in a computer forensics investigation is to seize the computer equipment that law enforcement officials believe contains pertinent evidence. Police are required to obtain a warrant to search an individual's home or place of business. Warrants must be very specific by spelling out exactly where detectives can search for evidence and exactly what type of evidence they're seeking. If a warrant indicates that the police may search an individual's home for his laptop computer, they can't then confiscate a tablet computer they notice in his car. It is important to specify in the warrant all types of storage devices where potential evidence might be stored, such as external hard drives, flash drives, and servers.

Once permission to collect the computers and devices containing possible evidence has been obtained, law enforcement officials must exercise great care when collecting the equipment. They need to ensure that no unauthorized persons are able to access or alter the computers or storage devices. The police must make sure the data and equipment are safe; if the equipment is connected to the Internet, the connection must be severed without data loss or damage. It's also important for law enforcement officials to understand that they may not want to power off equipment because potential evidence contained in RAM may be lost. After the devices are collected and secured, the computer forensic scientists take over the next phase of the investigation.

Phase 2: Cataloging and Analyzing the Data

It's critical to preserve the data exactly as it was found, or attorneys may argue that the computer evidence was subject to tampering or altering. Because just opening a file can alter it, the first task is to make a copy of all computer systems and storage devices collected. The investigators then work from the copies to ensure that the original data always remains preserved exactly as it was when it was collected.

After obtaining a copy to work from, forensics professionals attempt to find every file on the system, including deleted files. Files on a computer aren't actually deleted, even if you empty the Recycle Bin, until the section of the hard disk they're stored on is overwritten with new data. Therefore, using special forensic software tools such as SIFT, EnCase, and FTK, the forensic scientists catalog all files found on the system or storage medium and recover as much information from deleted files as they can. Forensic software like FTK can readily detect hidden files and perform procedures to crack encrypted files or access protected files and reveal their contents.

The most important part of the process is documenting every step. Forensic scientists must clearly log every procedure performed because they may be required to provide proof in court that their investigations did not alter or damage information contained on the systems they examined. Detailed reports should list all files found, how the files were laid out on the system, which files were protected or encrypted, and the contents of each file. Finally, computer forensic professionals are often called on to present testimony in court during a trial.

Criminals are getting more sophisticated and are now employing anti-forensics techniques to foil computer forensic investigators. Although techniques for hiding or encrypting data are popular, the most insidious anti-forensics techniques

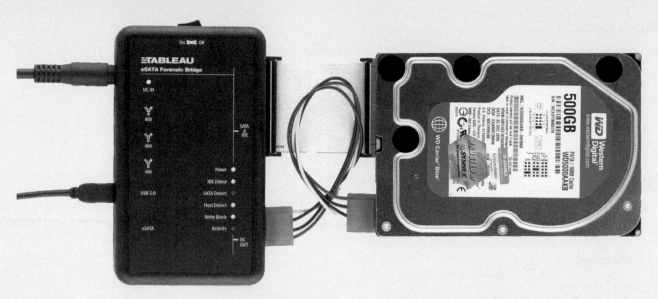

Portable computer forensic devices make it easy to copy storage devices at crime scenes. *(Lance Mueller/Alamy)*

are programs designed to erase data if unauthorized persons (i.e., not the criminal) access a computer system or if the system detects forensics software in use. When computer forensic investigators detect these countermeasures, they must often use creative methods and

custom-designed software programs to retrieve and preserve the data.

Computer forensics is an invaluable tool to law enforcement in many criminal investigations, but only if the correct procedures are followed and the appropriate documentation is prepared.

check your understanding // review & practice

For a quick review to see what you've learned so far, answer the following questions.

multiple choice

1. Firewalls work by closing _____ in your computer.
    a. logical ports
    b. software gaps
    c. logical doors
    d. backdoors

2. _____ involve using a physical attribute such as a fingerprint for authentication.
    a. Backdoors
    b. Rootkits
    c. Biometrics
    d. Trojan horses

3. A backup of only the files on your computing device that have been created (or changed) since the last backup is known as a(n)
    a. total backup.
    b. incremental backup.
    c. image backup.
    d. global backup.

4. Antivirus software looks for _____ to detect viruses in files.
    a. virus artifacts
    b. virus signatures
    c. virus bots
    d. virus VPNs

5. Updating your operating software on a regular basis helps prevent system corruption from _____, which are malicious websites downloading harmful software to your computer.
    a. CAPTCHA
    b. pharming
    c. phishing
    d. drive-by-downloads

Continue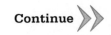

summary //

Major Threats to Your Digital Assets

Learning Outcome You will be able to describe hackers, viruses, and other online annoyances and the threats they pose to your digital security.

Identity Theft and Hackers

Objective *Describe how identity theft is committed and the types of scams identity thieves perpetrate.*

- Identity theft occurs when a thief steals personal information about you and runs up debts in your name. Identify thieves can obtain information by stealing mail, searching through trash, or tricking people into revealing information over the phone or via e-mail. Identity thieves counterfeit existing credit cards, opening new credit card and bank accounts, change your address on financial statements, obtain medical services, and buy homes with a mortgage in the victim's name.

Objective *List and describe the different types of hackers.*

- White-hat hackers break into systems for nonmalicious reasons such as testing security to expose weaknesses. Black-hat hackers break into systems to destroy information or for illegal gain. Grey-hat hackers often break into systems just for the thrill or to demonstrate their prowess.

Objective *Describe the various tools hackers use and the types of attacks they might launch against computers.*

- Packet analyzers (sniffers) are programs used to intercept and read data packets and they travel across a network. Trojan horses are programs that appear to be something else but are really a tool for hackers to access your computer. Backdoor programs and rootkits are tools used by hackers to gain access to and take total control of a computer system. Denial-of-service attacks overwhelm computer systems with so many requests for data that legitimate users can't access the system.

Computer Viruses

Objective *Explain what a computer virus is, why they are a threat to your security, and how a computing device catches a virus, and the symptoms it might display.*

- A computer virus is a computer program that attaches itself to another computer program and attempts to spread to other computers when files are exchanged. Computer viruses can display annoying messages, destroy your information, corrupt your files, or gather information about you. Computers catch viruses when exposed to infected files. This can occur from downloading infected files, downloading and running infected e-mail attachments, or sharing flash drives that contain infected files. Symptoms of virus infection include: (1) files or app icons disappear, (2) browser is reset to an unusual home page, (3) odd messages, pop-ups, or images are displayed, (4) data files become corrupt, and (5) Programs stop working properly

Objective *List the different categories of computer viruses, and describe their behaviors.*

- Boot-sector viruses copy themselves onto the master boot record of a computer and execute when the computer is started. Logic bombs and time bombs are viruses triggered by the completion of certain events or by the passage of time. Worms can spread on their own without human intervention, unlike conventional viruses. Macro viruses lurk in documents that use macros (short series of commands that automate repetitive tasks). E-mail viruses access the address book of a victim to spread to the victim's contacts. Encryption viruses render files unusable by compressing them with complex encryption keys. Polymorphic viruses periodically rewrite themselves to avoid detection. Stealth viruses temporarily erase their code and hide in the active memory of the computer.

Online Annoyances and Social Engineering

Objective *Explain what malware is, and list the common types of malware*

- Malware is software that has a malicious intent. Adware is software that displays sponsored advertisements in a section of your browser window or as a pop-up box. Spyware collects information about you, without your knowledge, and transmit it to the owner of the program.

Objective *Define spam, and describe strategies to combat it.*

- Spam is unwanted or junk e-mail. Spim is unsolicited instant messages, which is also a form of spam. Spam filters in e-mail systems forward junk mail to their own folder. Never reply to spam or click on unsubscribe links as this usually just generates more spam.

Objective *Explain what cookies are and whether they pose a security threat.*

- Cookies are small text files that some websites automatically store on your hard drive when you visit them. Cookies are usually used to keep track of users and personalize their browsing experience. Cookies do not pose a security threat although some individuals view them as privacy violations.

Objective *Describe social engineering techniques, and explain strategies to avoid falling prey to them*

- Social engineering is any technique that uses social skills to generate human interaction that entices individuals to reveal sensitive information. Phishing lures people into revealing personal information via bogus e-mails that appear to be from legitimate sources and direct people to scammer's websites. Pharming occurs when malicious code is planted on your computer, either by viruses or by your visiting malicious websites, which then alters your browser's ability to find web addresses. Scareware attempts to convince you that your computer is infected with a virus and then tries to sell you a "solution." Most Internet security software packages have scareware, phishing and pharming protection built-in.

Protecting Your Digital Property

Learning Outcome **Describe various ways to protect your digital property and data from theft and corruption.**

Restricting Access to Your Digital Assets

Objective *Explain what a firewall is and how a firewall protects your computer from hackers.*

- A FIREWALL is a software program or hardware device designed to protect computers from hackers. Firewalls block access to your computer's logical ports and help keep your computer's network address secure. Firewalls use PACKET FILTERING to identify packets sent to specific logical ports and discard them. Firewalls use network address translation to assign internal IP addresses on networks. The internal IP addresses are much more difficult for hackers to detect.

Objective *Explain how to protect your computer from virus infection.*

- ANTIVIRUS SOFTWARE is specifically designed to detect viruses and protect your computer and files from harm. Antivirus software detects viruses by looking for VIRUS SIGNATURES: code that specifically identifies a virus. Antivirus software stops viruses from executing and quarantines INfected files in a secure area on the hard drive. Virus software must be constantly updated to remain effective.

Objective *Describe how passwords and biometric characteristics can be used for user authentication on computer systems.*

- Secure passwords contain a mixture of upper- and lowercase letters, numbers, and symbols and are at least 14 characters long. Passwords should not contain words that are in the dictionary or easy-to-guess personal information. Utilities built into web browsers and Internet security software can be used to manage your passwords.

- A biometric authentication device is a device that reads a unique personal characteristic to identify an authorized user. Fingerprint readers, iris scanners and facial recognition software are common examples of biometric security devices.

Objective *Describe ways to surf the web anonymously.*

- Privacy tools built into web browsers help your surf anonymously by not recording your actions in the history files. USB devices containing privacy tools are available that prevent the computer you are using from storing any information about you on the computer. Virtual private networks (VPNs) are secure networks that can be used to send information securely across the public Internet.

Keeping Your Data Safe

Objective *Describe the types of information you should never share online.*

- Reveal as little information as possible about yourself. Your Social Security number, phone number, date of birth, and street address are four key pieces of information that identity thieves need to steal an identity.

Objective *List the various types of backups you can perform on your computing devices, and explain the various places you can store backup files.*

- An INCREMENTAL BACKUP involves backing up only files that have changed or have been created since the last backup was performed. An IMAGE BACKUP (or SYSTEM BACKUP) means that all system, application, and data files are backed up, not just the files that changed. You can store backups online (in the cloud), on external hard drives, or on network-attached storage (NAS) devices.

Protecting Your Physical Computing Assets

Objective *Explain the negative effects environment and power surges can have on computing devices.*

- Computing devices should be kept in clean environments free from dust and other particulates and should not be exposed to extreme temperatures (either hot or cold). You should protect all electronic devices from power surges by hooking them up through surge protectors, which will protect them from most electrical surges that could damage the devices.

Objective *Describe the major concerns when a device is stolen and strategies for solving the problems.*

- The four main security concerns regarding computing devices are (1) keeping them from being stolen, (2) keeping data secure in case they are stolen, (3) finding a device if it is stolen, and (4) remotely recovering and wiping data off a stolen device.

- Software is available for installation on devices that will (1) set off an alarm if the device is moved, (2) help recover the device, if stolen, by reporting the computer's whereabouts when it is connected to the Internet, and (3) allow you to lock or wipe the contents of the device remotely.

key terms //

chapter quiz // assessment

For a quick review to see what you've learned, answer the following questions. Submit the quiz as requested by your instructor.

multiple choice

1. Which of the following is NOT a major type of cybercrime reported to the IC3?

   a. Government impersonation scams

   b. identity theft

   c. malware fraud

   d. advance fee fraud

2. Viruses that load from USB drives left connected to computers when computers are turned on are known as

   a. boot-sector viruses.

   b. script viruses.

   c. polymorphic viruses.

   d. encryption viruses.

3. Software designed to close logical ports in your computer is known as a(n)

   a. firewall.

   b. packet filter.

   c. anti-malware blocker.

   d. network address translator.

4. Which is NOT a tool hackers use to gain access to and take control of your computer?

   a. Trojan horse

   b. backdoor programs

   c. rootkits

   d. phishing software

5. A computer that a hacker has gained control of in order to launch DoS attacks is known as a _____ computer.

   a. rootkit

   b. compromised

   c. zombie

   d. breached

6. A backup of all the files on your computer, which essentially creates a "snapshot" of what your computer looks like at that point in time, is known as a(n)

   a. total backup.

   b. incremental backup.

   c. image backup.

   d. modification backup.

true/false

_____ **1.** Password strength is solely determined by the length of the password.

_____ **2.** One of the best and simplest ways to keep hackers out of your computer is to use a firewall.

_____ **3.** Sending e-mails to lure people into revealing personal information is a technique known as phishing.

_____ **4.** Encrypting data is not an appropriate measure for protecting mobile devices such as smartphones.

critical thinking

1. Protecting Your Data from Data Breaches

You most likely have provided personal information to many websites and companies. What information have you provided to companies that you wish you had never disclosed? What types of information have companies asked you to provide that you believe was unnecessary? List specific companies and examples of the extraneous information.

2. Phishing

Have you or anyone you know ever been a victim of a phishing scam? What sorts of scams have you heard about? Research and discuss at least three types of common scams.

team time //

Protecting a Network

Problem

Along with easy access to the web comes the danger of theft of digital assets.

Task

A school alumnus is in charge of the county government computer department. The network contains computers running Windows 10, Windows 8, Windows 7, and OS X. He asked your instructor for help in ensuring that his computers and network are protected from viruses, malware, and hackers. He is hoping that there may be free software available that can protect his employees' computers.

Process

1. Break the class into three teams. Each team will be responsible for investigating one of the following issues:

    a. **Antivirus software:** Research alternatives that protect computers from viruses. Find three alternatives and support your recommendations with reviews that evaluate free packages.

    b. **Anti-malware software:** Research three free malware alternatives and determine whether the software can be updated automatically. You may want to recommend that the county purchase software to ensure that a minimum of employee intervention is needed to keep it up to date.

    c. **Firewalls:** Determine if the firewall software provided with Windows 10, Windows 8, Windows 7, and OS X is reliable. If it is, prepare documentation (for all three OSs) for county employees to determine if their firewalls are properly configured. If additional firewall software is needed, research free firewall software and locate three options that can be deployed by the county.

    d. Present your findings to the class and provide your instructor with a report suitable for eventual presentation to the manager of the county office network.

Conclusion

With the proliferation of viruses and malware, it is essential to protect computers and networks. Free alternatives might work, but you should research the best protection solution for your situation.

Content Control: Censorship to Protect Children

In this exercise, you'll research and then role-play a complicated ethical situation. The role you play might or might not match your own personal beliefs; in either case, your research and use of logic will enable you to represent the view assigned. An arbitrator will watch and comment on both sides of the arguments, and together, the team will agree on an ethical solution.

Problem

Many parents use web-filtering software (content-control software) to protect their children from objectionable Internet content. In 2000, the U.S. federal government began requiring libraries to use content-control software as a condition to receiving federal funds under the provisions of the Children's Internet Protection Act (CIPA). Some states, such as Virginia, have passed laws requiring libraries to install filtering software even if they did not receive federal funds. Upon installation of the software, it's up to the library administrators to decide what content is restricted. Therefore, content restriction can vary widely from library to library.

Research Areas to Consider

- U.S. Supreme Court case *United States v. American Library Association* (2003)
- Content-control software and First Amendment rights
- Violation of children's free speech rights
- Children's Internet Protection Act (CIPA)

Process

1. Divide the class into teams. Research the areas above and devise a scenario in which someone has complained about innocuous content that was blocked.

2. Team members should write a summary that provides background information for their character—for example, library patron, library administrator, or arbitrator—and that details their character's behaviors to set the stage for the role-playing event. Then, team members should create an outline to use during the role-playing event.

3. Team members should present their case to the class or submit a PowerPoint presentation for review by the class, along with the summary and resolution they developed.

Conclusion

As technology becomes ever more prevalent and integrated into our lives, more and more ethical dilemmas will present themselves. Being able to understand and evaluate both sides of the argument, while responding in a personally or socially ethical manner, will be an important skill.

Computer Security

You have been asked to prepare a report on computer security using Word 2016. You have written the majority of the report, but you have to make some final modifications and refinements such as adding the results of some research of good antivirus software, adding a cover page, and generating a table of contents.

You will use the following skills as you complete this activity:

- Create and Modify Tables
- Insert Tab Stops
- Add Watermark
- Insert Cover Page

- Create and Update Table of Contents
- Add Footnote
- Use Find and Replace

Instructions:

1. Open *TIA_Ch9_Start* and save as **TIA_Ch9_LastFirst**.
2. Find all instances of *e-mail* and replace with **e-mail**.
   a. Hint: Click **Replace** in the Editing group on the Home tab, type **e-mail** in the Find what box, and type **e-mail** in the Replace with box. Click **Replace All**.
3. Find the first instance of malware. Place the cursor after the word *malware* (before the period) and insert the footnote: **Malware is defined as software that is intended to gain access to, or damage or disable, computer systems for the purposes of theft or fraud.** Close the Navigation pane.
   a. Hint: Use Find in the Editing group on the Home tab to locate malware.
   b. Hint: Click **Insert Footnote** in the Footnotes group on the References tab to insert a footnote.
4. In the section, *Types of Viruses*, highlight the six lines of text that outline the categories of computer viruses and variants. Add a Right Align Tab Stop at 1½" and a Left Align Tab Stop at 2".
   a. Hint: To set tab stop, display ruler, select tab stop style from Select tab box to the left of the ruler, click at the desired position on the ruler.
5. Place cursor at the end of the paragraph in the Antivirus Software section. Press **Enter**, then insert a **3×4 Table**. Type **Product Name, Description/Review**, and **Cost** in the top three cells. Adjust the width of the Description/Review column to **3.5"** and the width of the Cost column to **1"**.
   a. Hint: Click **Table** in the Tables group on the Insert tab, and drag to select the desired grid.
6. Add a row at the top of the table, **Merge Cells**, type **Antivirus Software Reviews**, and **Align Center** the contents. Format the table with **Grid Table 4—Accent 1 style**.
   a. Hint: Click **Insert** above in the Rows & Columns group on the Table Tools Layout tab.
7. Open a browser, and go to **www.pcmag.com/reviews/antivirus**. Research four antivirus software programs and place the software name, review, and cost of the software in the respective columns in the table.
   a. Hint: Press **tab** at the end of the third row to add an additional line to the table to accommodate a fourth review.
8. Press **Ctrl+Home**, then insert the **Banded Cover Page**. Ensure *Computer Security* displays as the title and *your name* displays as the Author. Delete the Company and Address placeholders.
9. Insert **Page Numbers** at the bottom of the page using the **Plain Number 3 format**. Ensure Different First Page is checked. Close Header and Footer.
10. On the page 2 of the document, insert a **Page Break** before the report title, Computer Security.
11. Place the cursor at the top of the new blank page, and insert a **Table of Contents** using the Contents format.
    a. Hint: Click **Table of Contents** in the Table of Contents group on the References tab.
12. Press **Ctrl+End**, scroll up and change the heading style of *Firewalls* to **Heading 2**, change the heading style of *Software Firewalls* and *Hardware Firewalls* to **Heading 3**.
13. Update the Table of Contents to reflect the changes in headings, ensure you update the entire table.
    a. Hint: Click anywhere in the Table of Contents, and click **Update Table**, and then click **Update entire table**.
14. Add a **Draft 1 Watermark** to the report.
    a. Hint: Click **Watermark** in the Page Backgroup group on the Design tab.
15. Save the document and submit based on your instructor's directions.

Index